Economic Analysis of Law in European Legal Scholarship

Volume 20

The purpose of the book series "Economic Analysis of Law in European Legal Scholarship" is to publish high quality volumes in the growing field of law and economics research in Europe, from a comprehensive theoretical and practical vantage point. In particular, the series will place great emphasis on foundational and theoretical aspects of economic analysis of law and on interdisciplinary approaches in European Legal Scholarship. Following Nobel laureate Ronald Coase's famous essay "The Problem of Social Cost" (1960) fifty years ago law and economics has become the lingua franca of American jurisprudence. In recent decades, law and economics has also gained widespread popularity in Europe and its influence on Legal Scholarship is growing significantly.

Therefore, the economic analysis of law in European Legal Scholarship academic book series illustrates how law and economics is developing in Europe and what opportunities and problems – both in general and in specific legal fields – are associated with this approach within the legal traditions of European countries. Rather than further exploring economic analysis as such, the main focus of this series lies on the implementation of economic methods in legislation and legal adjudication from a European perspective. It takes into account the particular challenges the European legal systems face. Volumes will address law and economics research in Europe from a critical and comparative viewpoint. The studies in this series are strong and bold narratives of the development of economic analysis of law in European Legal Scholarship. Some are suitable for a very broad readership.

Contributions in this series primarily come from scholars in Europe. The purpose is to provide the next generation of European lawyers with the models and skills needed to understand and improve the economic analysis of law in their own legal field. The series includes monographs focusing on specific topics as well as collections of essays covering specific themes.

Adrianus Johannes van Heusden

The Law and Economics of Personalization

Taking Marketing Seriously

Springer

Adrianus Johannes van Heusden
Voorhout, The Netherlands

ISSN 2512-1294 ISSN 2512-1308 (electronic)
Economic Analysis of Law in European Legal Scholarship
ISBN 978-3-032-01467-2 ISBN 978-3-032-01468-9 (eBook)
https://doi.org/10.1007/978-3-032-01468-9

This Springer imprint is published by the registered company Springer Nature Switzerland AG
The registered company address is: Gewerbestrasse 11, 6330 Cham, Switzerland

To my father,
Aad van Heusden Sr.,
whose unwavering spirit and timeless
wisdom continue to guide me,
shaping every step I take.

Acknowledgments

This book reflects the culmination of years of research and collaboration, enriched by the contributions and support of many exceptional individuals.

I would like to express my deepest gratitude to Prof. Klaus Mathis and the University of Lucerne. Klaus, your support has been pivotal in shaping my academic path. Through the research visit you facilitated, as well as the numerous conferences and colloquia you invited me to, you offered me invaluable opportunities to engage with leading scholars and refine my ideas. The University of Lucerne provided an intellectually stimulating environment that profoundly influenced my thinking, and I am proud to consider it my second academic home. Your commitment to fostering scholarly dialogue and your encouragement throughout my journey have left an enduring impact.

To Prof. Michael Faure, your mentorship has been a guiding force in my academic career. Michael, your ability to challenge, inspire, and motivate has helped me push the boundaries of my research. I will always treasure the insights gained during our stimulating discussions and moments like our memorable seminar in Beijing. Your unwavering dedication and expertise have been instrumental in the creation of this book. To Prof. Franziska Weber, your consistent encouragement has been invaluable. Your intellectual contributions and ability to challenge my perspectives have pushed me to reach greater heights. To Prof. Ann-Sophie Vandenberghe, I owe sincere thanks for your faith in my potential and for helping shape the foundation of this project. Your thoughtful guidance and encouragement during the early stages of my research were crucial in setting this journey on the right course.

Finally, I dedicate this book to my parents, Cecilia van Heusden-Perez Arciniegas and Aad van Heusden Sr. To my beloved mother, your unwavering support, wisdom, and encouragement have been my greatest source of strength. Your belief in me, even in the most challenging moments, has carried me through. Everything I have achieved, including this book, is a testament to your love and sacrifices. To my father, though you are no longer with us, your lessons and values remain deeply ingrained in my heart. You taught me the importance of perseverance, integrity, and ambition, and your words continue to inspire me every day: “Self-confidence is the foundation for a good performance." This book is part of my promise to honor your legacy and carry the Van Heusden name with pride.

To all of you, thank you for making this journey possible.

Adrianus Johannes van Heusden

Competing Interests The author has no competing interests to declare that are relevant to the content of this manuscript.

Disclaimer

This book is based on the author's dissertation submitted for fulfilment of the requirements for the degree of PhD in Law & Economics at Erasmus University Rotterdam, in collaboration with the University of Bologna and the University of Hamburg, which was successfully defended in public on 13 March 2025.

The information and views set out in this book reflect those of the author and do not necessarily reflect the official opinion of the European Institutions. In particular, the matters addressed in this book dealing with the work of the European Union solely reflect the personal views of the author.

Contents

About the Author

Adrianus Johannes (Aad) van Heusden is a lawyer-economist whose passion for law and economics runs like a red thread through his academic career. He holds two bachelor's degrees in Law and Economics from Erasmus University Rotterdam, as well as three master's degrees: an M.Sc. in Economics and Business (cum laude), an LL.M. in Commercial Law, both from Erasmus University Rotterdam, and a European Master in Law and Economics (EMLE, cum laude) from the Universities of Haifa, Ghent, and Aix-Marseille. In 2020, he won the Best Thesis Award for his thesis "The Impact of Branding on Boilerplates: A Law and Economics Analysis of Standard-Form Contracting." He completed his Ph.D. on the interplay between AI-driven marketing and consumer policy, conducting an in-depth analysis of the practice of personalized marketing. He was awarded an Erasmus Trustfonds Scholarship for his research, which facilitated a research stay at the University of Lucerne, Switzerland. His areas of expertise include microeconomics, marketing, consumer law, and digital regulation, with a particular emphasis on the Digital Services Act (DSA). Currently, he works at the European Commission as the DSA Officer for the Netherlands. Aad is fluent in Dutch, Spanish, English, French, German, and Italian.

Abbreviations

ACM	The Netherlands Authority for Consumers and Markets
AI	Artificial Intelligence
AI Act	EU Artificial Intelligence Act
AVMS	Audiovisual Media Services Directive
BDA	Big Data Analytics
CBA	Cost–Benefit Analysis
CJEU	Court of Justice of the European Union
CRD	Consumer Rights Directive
DMA	Digital Markets Act
DSA	Digital Services Act
EC	European Commission
EDPB	European Data Protection Board
EU	European Union
GDPR	General Data Protection Regulation
MCAD	Directive on Misleading and Comparative Advertising
ML	Machine Learning
OBA	Online Behavioral Advertising
OECD	Organization for Economic Co-operation and Development
OFT	Office of Fair Trading (UK)
RCT	Rational Choice Theory
TFEU	Treaty on the Functioning of the European Union
UCPD	Unfair Commercial Practices Directive
UCTD	Unfair Contract Terms Directive
VLOP	Very Large Online Platform
VLOSE	Very Large Online Search Engine

List of Tables

Chapter 1
Introduction

Abstract This chapter introduces the shift from traditional to personalized marketing driven by advancements in artificial intelligence, machine learning, and big data analytics. While these technologies promise benefits such as tailored consumer experiences and improved engagement, they also raise critical concerns about consumer welfare, equity, and autonomy. By focusing on advertising, pricing, and contracting, the chapter outlines the regulatory challenges posed by hyper-personalization and sets the stage for an interdisciplinary law and economics analysis. The discussion emphasizes the need for a comprehensive framework to address the complex interplay between marketing innovation and consumer protection in the digital age.

1.1 Background

The buzz word is *personalization*.[1] The advent of *artificial intelligence* (AI), *machine learning* (ML), and *big data analytics* (BDA) has revolutionized digital marketing. The technological developments of the digital age have caused a radical shift from generalized to personalized marketing. AI-driven marketing has opened a wide array of possibilities for marketers to explore new ways of targeting marketing communications. Where traditional marketing is aimed at appealing to the masses, marketing in the digital age is all about addressing each consumer personally and interactively.[2] The main principle of personalized marketing is interacting

[1] Personalization is an umbrella term for which no unified definition exists in academic research, see Strycharz et al. (2019). In general, it refers to creating data-driven individualized interactions with the consumer. It encompasses phenomena such as individualization, segmentation, one-to-one marketing, targeting, and customization, see Vesanen and Raulas (2006). The concept of personalization is seen as being central to the discipline of marketing, see Chandra et al. (2022), p. 1530. In this study, personalization refers to personalized marketing communications, which include sales, promotions, and information provision (for example, personalized prices, advertisements, offers, and terms), cfr. Strycharz et al. (2019); Strycharz and Duivenvoorde (2021).

[2] Kotler and Armstrong (2016), p. 29.

A. J. van Heusden, *The Law and Economics of Personalization*, Economic Analysis of Law in European Legal Scholarship 20,
https://doi.org/10.1007/978-3-032-01468-9_1

with the consumer at the most individualized level possible.[3] Where the degree of personalization was limited in the past, the capacity of AI-driven marketing to collect vast amounts of data, employ sophisticated BDA to identify patterns and create individualized consumer profiles, and automate processes has enabled the approximation of perfect personalization.[4] This consists of tailoring marketing communications to individuals' characteristics, interests, and behaviors.[5]

Personalized marketing has transcended the confines of traditional marketing and brought the concept of consumer targeting to an unprecedented level.[6] Due to its benefits for both businesses and consumers, personalized marketing is embraced by marketers. It promises better matching of consumer needs and preferences, higher conversion rates, and more consumer engagement, making it an appealing marketing strategy.[7] The projected profitability of personalized marketing makes the practice particularly desirable for marketers.[8] Its importance and usage have, therefore, been continuously rising.[9]

At the same time, however, the tools that allow for more precise targeting of consumers also enable the identification of consumers' vulnerabilities, idiosyncratic circumstances, and unique characteristics.[10] It has become possible to predict psychological traits and emotional states and use this information to steer consumers' behavior and shape the environment in which they make choices.[11] A few real-life examples are provided by leaked documents, which demonstrate how advertisers could effectively target teenagers' psychological vulnerability (i.e., feeling insecure, stressed, and emotional) on Facebook through advanced profiling,[12] how Uber increased prices for consumers whose mobile devices were running low on battery when ordering the ride,[13] and how Cambridge Analytica's performed psychographic profiling (i.e., based on psychological variables[14]) to steer individuals into a certain political direction.[15] Accordingly, concerns are voiced that these developments in personalization pose a risk to consumers' autonomy, welfare, and fundamental rights.[16]

---

[3] Rathore (2020).

[4] Kotras (2020).

[5] Bol et al. (2018).

[6] Okorie et al. (2024).

[7] Liao and Yang (2021).

[8] Rathore (2020).

[9] Chandra et al. (2022).

[10] Strycharz and Duivenvoorde (2021).

[11] Burr et al. (2018); Burr and Cristianini (2019).

[12] Tiku (2017).

[13] Golson (2016).

[14] These include, *inter alia*, personality traits, values, attitudes, behavior, activity, interest, and opinions. See, for example, Wells (1975); Burkell and Regan (2019); Helberger et al. (2021).

[15] Gibney (2018).

[16] Calo (2014); Mik (2016); André et al. (2018); Susser et al. (2019); Spencer (2020).

The question arises whether the promises of personalized marketing will not be overridden by considerable perils that have the potential to harm consumers. It is argued that this *dark side* of personalized marketing is underexposed and deserves further attention in order to protect consumers against the potential negative consequences of *hyper-personalization* in the digital age.[17]

The dark side of personalization can be classified into three categories: the extraction of value, the exploitation of biases, and the shaping of preferences.[18] The common denominator is that big data technologies allow for *digital market manipulation*, which means exploiting consumer frailty at an individual level.[19] Consumers face various forms of personalized transactions in online markets.[20] Personalization comprises a multitude of marketing practices, yet in this study the focus lies on three specific personalization practices: personalized advertising, pricing, and contracting. Together, these encompass the three abovementioned areas of concern regarding personalized marketing.

Personalized advertising refers to the practice of targeting consumers with highly-individualized marketing communications.[21] The main benefit of personalized advertising marketers advocate is that consumer preferences can be precisely met.[22] However, this presumes that consumer preferences are solely an exogenous factor. This overlooks the endogenous aspect of preferences, namely that they can also be shaped.[23] Through personalized advertising, it is feasible to shape consumer preferences and steer consumption patterns. More specifically, consumer reality can be curated by filtering and framing the information they receive.[24] Consumers' preferences do not only arise from an individual thought process impacted by their personal beliefs, but also through an internal response to stimuli carefully designed by marketers, who look for profit optimization rather than consumer individuation.[25] In other words, marketers do not only use consumer preferences, but they also try to alter them. The fact that marketing efforts shape preferences is not novel since this has been a practice of all times. However, big data technologies facilitate individual targeting to such an extent that the power of preference shaping has increased to an unprecedented level.[26] Consequently, the degree to which algorithm-induced preferences reflect consumers' "true" preferences is debatable.[27]

[17] Trzaskowski (2021), p. 3.

[18] Wagner and Eidenmüller (2019). These categories will be further explained in Chap. 2.

[19] Calo (2014).

[20] Chandra et al. (2022).

[21] Discussed in Chap. 4.

[22] Vesanen (2007).

[23] Sunstein (1993); Porat (2021).

[24] Pariser (2011).

[25] Wagner and Eidenmüller (2019), p. 599.

[26] Grafanaki (2017).

[27] Wagner and Eidenmüller (2019), p. 602.

Based on state-of-the-art insights from behavioral marketing and advanced data analytics, marketers can exploit consumer biases systemically.[28] Through sophisticated AI-driven marketing strategies, consumers can be steered into strategically set rationality traps.[29] In other words, companies are analyzing consumer behavior to identify consumer vulnerability. As Calo (2014) describes it: "Emerging methods of big data present a new and vastly more efficient way to identify cognitive bias by attempting to pinpoint profitable anomalies."[30] The threat of BDA in terms of bias exploitation comes in two forms: the emergence of technological tools that facilitate systematic exploitation at an unprecedented scale and the possibility to exploit biases at an individual level through personalization.[31]

Personalized advertising is reinforced by algorithmically-determined personalized prices,[32] whereby it becomes possible to approximate the *reservation price* of consumers. That is to say, a price can be set that comes close, if not matches exactly, consumers' *maximum willingness to pay* (WTP). In this way, the *consumer surplus* that would have accrued to the consumer under a uniform price is transferred to the seller.[33] The theoretical scenario of first-degree price discrimination has become a reality, opening the way for maximal value extraction.[34]

The sophisticated use of algorithms for personalization does not stop at pricing and advertising. A wide array of profiling and targeting possibilities can be explored. To fully personalize the consumer experience and decision-making process, the transaction, including the contracting phase, can be individualized.[35] This effectively means that AI has opened the door for personalized contracting,[36] and in doing so, new concerns regarding information asymmetries and power imbalances in the merchant-consumer relationship are raised.[37] Personalized contracts complement the pricing and advertising elements of the marketing strategy and have a mutually reinforcing effect.

A key element for the personalized marketing strategies to work is the collection of copious amounts of data from consumers. The more data collected, the more accurate predictive analytics work.[38] Consent notices ensure that consumers' assent is acquired, allowing the seller to proceed with personalization tactics. To specify,

---

[28] Discussed in Chap. 3.

[29] Wagner and Eidenmüller (2019), p. 593.

[30] Calo (2014), p. 1010.

[31] Wagner and Eidenmüller (2019), p. 594.

[32] Esteves and Resende (2019).

[33] The notion of consumer surplus will be further explained in Sect. 2.2.2. In short, consumer surplus refers to the difference between the price a consumer would be willing to pay for a good and the (lower) effective price to be paid.

[34] First-degree price discrimination will be further analyzed in Chap. 4.

[35] Golobardes (2022).

[36] Discussed in Chap. 5.

[37] Ebrahim (2021).

[38] Leszczynska and Baltag (2024).

due to the *signing-without-reading problem,*[39] sellers are practically guaranteed that the necessary consent will be obtained. This is problematic since standard forms, including privacy notices, ensure that vast amounts of data can be collected, facilitating the implementation of personalized marketing strategies. Accordingly, the ability to personalize the *boilerplate* (also known as the standard form), that is already not being read in its standardized form, will have far-reaching implications for the consumer. For example, the boilerplate can be altered to positively impact business profits by adding non-salient charges, such as higher overdraft fees, in the fine print of contracts with clients that have a history of payment delays. This can lead to adverse financial effects for the consumer.[40]

Considering the various applications of personalized marketing, it is argued that consumer policy in the digital age lags behind the developments in online marketing.[41] The traditional apparatus of consumer protection is regarded to be overdue for change, and a discussion about the empowerment of consumers in the digital age is necessary.[42]

The threat of online manipulation is a growing reality, and contemporary ML offers the tools to influence emotions and modify the behavior of individuals.[43] More specifically, algorithms facilitate the automation of personalization and the development of testing strategies that find the most effective persuasion mechanism for a specific individual.[44] Every aspect of online marketing communications can be adjusted in real time and is continuously being improved.[45] The power of marketers to persuade consumers is drastically enhanced, whereas consumers' ability to withstand the influence is compromised, thereby blurring the line between persuasion and manipulation.[46] If personalized marketing ultimately leads to a situation in which individual biases and vulnerabilities can be exploited while the practice still falls through the cracks of the legal system through its sophistication, online manipulation in consumer markets will be lurking.[47]

Where traditional group-targeted marketing might have led to some *scattershot manipulation,*[48] that is, only a minority of consumers would be susceptible to bias or vulnerability, current personalized marketing is specifically tailored to each individual and their individual biases and vulnerabilities, thereby most effectively capitalizing on their susceptibility to manipulation. It is highly data-driven, adaptive to

[39] De Geest (2016).

[40] This example will be elaborated in Chap. 5.

[41] Ebrahim (2021), p. 873.

[42] Ebrahim (2021); Helberger et al. (2021); Golobardes (2022); Fassiaux (2023).

[43] Council of Europe (2019), p. 8.

[44] Esteller-Cucala et al. (2019).

[45] Kohavi and Thomke (2017).

[46] Strycharz and Duivenvoorde (2021), p. 2. The concepts of persuasion and manipulation will be further elaborated in Sect. 3.2.3.

[47] Helberger et al. (2021), p. 111.

[48] Spencer (2020).

consumers' responses in real-time (i.e., an ongoing process), non-transparent due to its complexity, and continuously improving.[49] This marks an essential difference between the well-known marketing practices known for decades and the potential for manipulation through personalized marketing in the digital age.[50]

Personalized marketing presents a new challenge to consumer protection in the digital age that has the potential to create new disparities and vulnerabilities in society.[51] The ability of EU consumer policy to deal with personalized marketing has received relatively scarce attention.[52] In particular, the impacts on areas other than privacy and data security, such as consumer welfare, distributive justice, consumers' fundamental rights, and the degree to which additional regulation is justified, merit further attention.[53]

1.2 Research Questions

Accordingly, this deliberation has led to the following four central and interrelated research questions:

1. *How is personalized marketing in the digital age different from traditional marketing from a consumer policy perspective?*
2. *To what extent does personalized marketing pose a threat to consumer welfare? Moreover, to what degree is it problematic in terms of equity and consumer autonomy?*
3. *To what extent is personalized marketing addressed under the current EU legal framework?*
4. *To what extent can consumer policy regarding personalized marketing be improved by virtue of legal reforms?*

A four-step framework unites these research questions. The first step is to analyze the practice of personalized marketing and determine to what extent it differs from the marketing types well-documented in existing literature. Second, the analysis of personalized marketing will help to determine to what degree there is an actual threat to consumer welfare and, more importantly, in what specific ways. The analysis starts with identifying the effects on consumer welfare (the main criterion)[54]; however, special attention will also be devoted to equity and consumer autonomy considerations to complement the analysis. This will provide a more comprehensive picture of the challenges that personalized marketing poses. Third, the extent to

[49] Zarsky (2019), p. 169.

[50] Calo (2014), p. 1014; Spencer (2020), pp. 992–993.

[51] Bol et al. (2018).

[52] Strycharz and Duivenvoorde (2021), p. 2.

[53] Helveston (2016), p. 859; Strycharz and Duivenvoorde (2021), p. 9.

[54] The focus on consumer welfare will be further explained in Sect. 1.4.

which the existing legal framework has already addressed the subject of study will be determined. This precludes reinventing of the wheel and enables the identification of potential gaps. The final step is to present policy proposals addressing the potentially identified gaps in the consumer policy framework.

Following the four-step framework in this study will allow for the identification of its added value to existing literature, the assessment of the promises and perils of personalized marketing, the evaluation of the applicable legal framework, and the presentation of policy proposals that aim to enhance consumer policy in the digital age.

1.3 Relevance

Personalized marketing is becoming increasingly important in consumer markets and its multidisciplinary nature has garnered attention from various domains such as business management, consumer research, computer science, psychology, and law, to name a few.[55] However, it has not been analyzed yet from a law and economics perspective.

From a scientific perspective, this study aims to contribute to the literature by providing the first interdisciplinary law and economics analysis of personalized marketing. In addition, the study differentiates itself by looking at three specific personalized marketing practices: pricing, advertising, and contracting. The goal is to give a comprehensive picture of each of the practices, the effects, the applicable legal framework, and potential improvements that can be made in terms of consumer policy.[56]

An interdisciplinary approach is encouraged because it will lead to a broader view of the policy questions at stake compared to research that relies upon a sole discipline. Incorporating and integrating insights from various disciplines will benefit the academic debate and the formulation of policy proposals. In the same way legal matters increasingly touch upon several branches of the law, a helicopter view is needed. It is argued that consumer policy issues in the digital age necessitate contributions from various disciplines.[57] Consequently, this study distinguishes itself from the literature on personalized marketing by taking a law and economics approach to address this particular consumer policy challenge.

Furthermore, this study adds to the law and economics analysis by devoting special attention to the concepts of equity and consumer autonomy, typically highlighted from a consumer law perspective. The efficiency-equity trade-off permeates

---

[55] Chandra et al. (2022), p. 1530.

[56] What is meant by consumer policy and what it encompasses will be further discussed in Sects. 2.2.2 and 2.4.4.

[57] Jabłonowska et al. (2018); Micklitz and Saumier (2018); Seizov et al. (2019).

numerous law and economics analyses[58] and the analysis of personalized marketing is characterized by it. Shedding light on fairness-based considerations will provide a more complete view of the issue at hand. Discussing this trade-off will pinpoint the problematic aspects of personalized marketing and function as a starting point for further scientific research and debate.

This study presents an amalgamation of various personalization techniques to provide an in-depth understanding of marketing personalization as a whole. In the existing literature, many studies focus on one particular personalized practice (e.g., personalized pricing). However, the interrelation with other marketing personalization techniques (such as the interplay between personalized advertising, pricing, and contracting) is underexposed. Moreover, studies that discuss personalized marketing as a general phenomenon lack a thorough analysis of the versatility of the practices, which is necessary to grasp the intricacies of personalized marketing. This study, however, takes a special position in the existing literature concerning personalized marketing, since it provides an extensive overview of the different practices, discusses them separately, and finds the common denominator before discussing the topic of regulation. This way, the insights of the study can be used in future research as a starting point for divergent discussions on how to regulate. The findings of the study can then be used to advise the regulation of one specific practice or personalized marketing as a whole.

From a societal perspective, this research is relevant because it analyzes a new phenomenon that has the potential to disrupt online consumer markets through its innovativeness and corresponding impact on consumers' position in the market.[59] The potential gains that can be obtained by businesses seem to create worries as to what extent it is achieved at the expense of consumers. Personalized marketing has the potential to target consumers more effectively and thereby open up the possibility of extracting more value from consumers. It is, therefore, relevant to see to what degree consumers' welfare is safeguarded by the current legal framework and to what degree improvements in consumer policy can or should be made.

Moreover, marketing has a substantial effect on the workings of consumer markets. Marketing can ameliorate information inefficiencies. However, it can also exacerbate information asymmetries. The ability of personalized marketing to capitalize on information asymmetries and consumer vulnerabilities in order to extract consumer surplus can have profound negative implications for consumer welfare. It has been demonstrated that marketing can contribute to wealth inequality due to its redistributive effects.[60] Therefore, the potential for consumer manipulation that can facilitate the decline of consumer welfare should be closely investigated.

Due to the prospective distortionary effects that can be caused by personalized marketing, it is, from a societal perspective, relevant to analyze the practice in-depth and determine to what extent further legislative action is needed.

[58] Mathis (2009).

[59] Galli (2020).

[60] De Geest (2018).

The research will be relevant to various key stakeholders, including policymakers, consumers, consumer organizations, marketers, businesses active in business-to-consumers (B2C) relationships, and legal practitioners. The advent of personalized marketing practices poses complex challenges to policymakers since the traditional legal apparatus of consumer policy seems to lag behind the developments in marketing. This also renders it difficult for consumer authorities to take legal action and safeguard consumer protection in the current market. A call to action is made to make consumer policy fit for the digital age.[61] This research aims to present guidelines to help develop adequate policies that contribute to this goal.

In contrast, personalized marketing can be highly valuable to marketers and businesses active in consumer markets. The practice is, therefore, generally welcomed by these parties and more regulation would impact its profitability. For this reason, the study's outcomes could be of interest to proponents of personalized marketing.

In the legal context, personalized marketing has been discussed amongst scholars and practitioners. However, there is still considerable uncertainty as to what degree legal action can be undertaken against operators of personalized marketing techniques. A thorough law and economic analysis of the practice and its applicable legal framework is missing.

Consequently, various parties are involved in the issue at stake, and in one way or another, they will be impacted by potential changes in consumer policy. The insights from this study will, thus, not only have academic but also societal relevance.

1.4 Methodology

This study will take an interdisciplinary law and economics approach to analyzing personalized marketing. Insights and perspectives from various economic and legal resources will be combined and translated into overall assessments of the personalized marketing practices and corresponding policy proposals. The law and economics analysis will draw insights from a multitude of perspectives, which include the traditional (neoclassical) approach complemented by information economics, the behavioral approach, and, within the latter, empirical research.

The economic analysis of consumer law is a particularly apt methodology for studying inefficiencies in consumer markets. In addition, the potential effects of regulatory intervention on consumer welfare can be investigated.[62] The use of economic theories and insights to analyze the efficiency of laws and predict how specific legal rules will affect human behavior can be highly valuable.[63] In law and economics applications, this also entails evaluating the effects of introducing legal

[61] European Commission (2020); European Commission (2023).

[62] Vickers (2004); Van den Bergh (2007).

[63] Faure and Visscher (2018), p. 1.

rules.[64] Two questions are then raised: What should be maximized (i.e., the *maximand*), and how should it be maximized (i.e., aggregation techniques)? The selection of the appropriate maximand is subject to debate and there is no unequivocal answer as to what specific goal should be set when defining social welfare for legal policy.[65]

In this study, the basic premise of the analysis will be the maximization of *total welfare* (i.e., *the principle of wealth maximization*).[66] This is the standard criterion in the economic analysis of law to determine if there is a market failure and if so, whether legal intervention is justified.[67] In essence, wealth maximization amounts to a traditional efficiency analysis, in which the effects on *producer* and *consumer surplus* are examined as a whole (i.e., *total surplus analysis*). However, if the economic analysis of personalized marketing cannot provide a clear-cut answer regarding the desirability of the practice in terms of efficiency (i.e., ambiguous total welfare effects), special attention will be devoted to the so-called *consumer welfare hypothesis*.[68] According to this hypothesis, maximizing consumer welfare rather than total welfare should be the primary goal in competition and consumer law.[69] The consumer welfare hypothesis approach is different from the mainstream approach followed in law and economics.[70] It should, however, not be seen as a replacement for the total welfare criterion, but rather as a concurrent criterion that in certain markets (i.e., markets regulated by consumer and competition law) can provide further guidance in deciding on the desirability of legal intervention. In particular, when there are inferential disagreements between the efficiency criteria.[71] Since the analysis of personalized marketing take place in a consumer policy context, it is argued in this study that the consumer welfare hypothesis can be a helpful tool to eliminate potential ambiguities and decide on the necessity of legal intervention.[72]

However, as has been extensively criticized in law and economics literature, the focus on welfare alone may negate the pursuit of other goals, such as the distribution of resources, justice, or fairness.[73] Such considerations are essential for policy discussions, especially in a consumer context.[74] For this reason, the analysis will be *broadened* by looking at equity and consumer autonomy concerns regarding per-

[64] Parisi (2013), p. 278.

[65] Parisi (2013), p. 278.

[66] Posner (1979).

[67] Veljanovski (1981), p. 7.

[68] Esposito (2022).

[69] Esposito (2022).

[70] Esposito (2023).

[71] Esposito (2023).

[72] Esposito (2022) demonstrates, by analyzing EU competition and consumer case law, that courts seem to rule in accordance with the consumer welfare hypothesis (i.e., focus on consumer welfare rather than total welfare).

[73] Mathis (2009).

[74] See Sect. 2.4.4 for a further elaboration of this argument.

sonalized marketing and the potential justification for legal intervention. Distributive justice and consumer autonomy will, therefore, be included as fundamental ingredients of social welfare. In this way, a more comprehensive assessment of the efficiency-equity trade-off that permeates the analysis can be provided.

The economic analysis of law will be both *positive* and *normative*. The positive analysis will focus on the workings of personalized marketing and its effects. In contrast, the normative part will investigate whether the consumer policy goals that ought to be pursued are achieved by the current legal framework and it will present policy proposals to improve the current state of affairs.

The study uses a systematic research method for assessing consumer policy issues from a law and economics perspective.[75] In essence, economic insights are used to examine personalized marketing, its corresponding implications, and its effects on consumers' position in the market. After that, the legal framework is evaluated, and, based on the gaps found, policy proposals that consider the efficiency-equity trade-off and that can be justified from both an economic and a legal perspective are presented.

Even though personalized marketing is the primary subject matter of this study, the analytical method can be used to assess other policy questions as well. This study endeavors to promulgate this analytical method in order to foster a stepwise approach to consumer policy challenges. Stepwise in this regard consists of the following steps: first of all, emphasis is placed on assessing the merits of the practice, followed by identifying the potential implications for consumers, after which the legal framework is examined to see where it is lacking. In the final step, potential policy proposals are presented that aim to the fill the potentially identified gaps. This framework aims to prevent premature jumps to regulation, which could result in adverse effects.[76]

1.5 Scope of the Research

The study deliberately opts for the law and economics approach. This means that inspiration is drawn from the rationales and evidence provided by the field of economics, with particular attention to findings in the marketing literature. However, more research areas are relevant to analyzing personalized marketing, such as computer science, information technology, and psychology.[77] An in-depth investigation of the technologies driving algorithmic marketing and corresponding discussions on the design of algorithms will fall outside the scope of the research. In this study, references to such sources will be made, but no extensive account of research fields apart from law and economics will be provided.

---

75 Cfr. Bar-Gill (2008).

76 Van den Bergh (2000).

77 Chandra et al. (2022), p. 1530.

The focus of the legal analysis mainly lies on the fields of law that relate to consumer policy. More specifically, consumer protection law (interchangeably marketing law), data protection law, and recent digital regulations (e.g., the *Digital Services Act* (DSA)[78]). Due to the versatility of personalized marketing, it is indispensable for the analysis to include findings from other legal fields such as competition law, law and technology, contract law, and human rights law. Due to the size of the relevant market actors and the data-driven nature of personalized marketing, the topic merits further analysis from competition law, platform liability, and tax law perspectives. However, an in-depth analysis from these perspectives falls outside the scope of the research. Where possible, references to relevant studies in fields outside the scope of consumer policy will be made.

The research is carried out in the European context to enable the drafting of general policy advice for both national legislators in European countries and European institutions. This means that the analyses will be conducted by looking at the common core of the EU *acquis* concerning consumer protection in the context of personalized marketing. Rather than looking at the specific legal systems of the Member States, the *Ius Commune* of EU consumer policy will be reviewed (some exceptions will be made for the sake of illustration).[79] In this way, it becomes possible to apply economic insights generally without the need to account for the specificities of the respective national legal systems. This will facilitate the incorporation of insights from the economic and legal debates occurring across and outside the EU. It does entail, however, that extensive reviews of doctrinal views that are dependent on the national legal system will fall outside the scope of this research. Doctrinal and jurisprudential insights that pertain to the EU *acquis* as a whole will naturally be taken into account. The general observations on personalized marketing made in this research can be used as a starting point for research that looks at the practice in a national context. Although the focus lies on the EU, the systematic approach followed in the study aims to make the insights transposable to jurisdictions outside the EU and encourage the international legal debate.

The research focuses on the substantive part of consumer policy. It looks at the rules that are currently in place and investigates whether they can be improved. This means that the study will look at the regulatory part of consumer policy rather than at the enforcement part. Even though enforcement is an essential part of consumer policy, it is outside the scope of the research to discuss this aspect in-depth. Occasionally, the discussion necessitates mentioning enforcement; however, references to other studies will be made for in-depth discussions. The justification for this limitation is that it allows the study to focus on the myriad of challenges that can be encountered in regulating personalized marketing. Also, analyzing the role

---

[78] Regulation (EU) 2022/2065 of the European Parliament and of the Council of 19 October 2022 on a Single Market For Digital Services and amending Directive 2000/31/EC (Digital Services Act). https://eur-lex.europa.eu/legal-content/EN/TXT/?uri=celex%3A32022R2065. Referred to as "DSA".

[79] Bussani and Mattei (1997).

of enforcement would sacrifice the ability to go into the details of personalized marketing and its corresponding regulatory issues.

The focus of this research is limited to business-to-consumer (B2C) contracts. Business-to-business (B2B) and consumer-to-consumer (C2C) contracts will fall outside its scope. In particular, in the B2B context, personalized marketing is also becoming a subject of debate.[80] However, the approach taken in this study is specifically focused on analyzing personalized marketing from a consumer policy perspective.

The scope of personalized marketing is of such proportions that it is unfeasible to review all possible applications. For this reason, the core of the research will be limited to investigating three prominent personalization techniques: personalized advertising, pricing, and contracting. The justification for this choice is threefold. First, it allows for a higher generalizability of the research findings because three impactful marketing strategies are chosen.[81] It is plausible to assume that if these three marketing strategies display certain characteristics and cause specific effects, similar trends will be found in the analysis of other personalized marketing strategies.[82]

Second, the chosen marketing strategies constitute the main parts of the consumer experience. That is to say, the advertisement grabs the consumer's attention and concomitantly a price is displayed, and when the consumer wants to conclude the sale, the contract becomes relevant.

Third, each marketing strategy is in a different developmental stage. Personalized advertising is already an established practice, and many examples can be found in practice. In this sense, it is a mature practice. Personalized pricing is becoming a more ubiquitous practice and is strongly being developed and applied. Finally, personalized contracting is in its launching phase, whereby the potential future applications and corresponding effects are not yet evident. Accordingly, looking at personalization in different stages will provide more insights into its development and the future-proofness of EU consumer policy.

No new empirical study will be conducted for the analysis of personalized marketing. However, scientific research that examines certain marketing practices empirically will be incorporated and translated into policy. Incorporating empirical findings into the research will increase the validity of the results by providing evidence for specific identified effects. Empirical evidence can provide further insights into the critical parts of personalized marketing that require substantiation. Relevant empirical evidence will be presented to substantiate the identified effects, especially in the economic analysis parts. Both qualitative and quantitative resources will be gathered and combined for the analysis. Since a substantial body of economic studies exists that scrutinizes the effects of the different aspects of personalized marketing, this research aims to be of added value by synthesizing these insights and

[80] See, for instance, De Jong et al. (2021); Moradi and Dass (2022); Hall (2023).

[81] Strycharz et al. (2019); Spencer (2020); Strycharz and Duivenvoorde (2021).

[82] Chandra et al. (2022).

translating them into policy rather than undertaking empirical studies that duplicate existing findings.

To answer this study's research questions, the research focuses on integrating the scientific insights of the existing literature and expounding them for the personalized marketing context. Hitherto, such an attempt has been lacking in existing literature, particularly from a law and economics perspective. The present study aims to fill that gap by clearly linking the insights from economic studies to consumer policy. Conducting further empirical studies will fall outside the scope of the study, yet future research that contributes to providing more insights into the research questions is highly encouraged.

It must be noted that the scope of applicable consumer policy will be limited to the main legislations. To illustrate, when discussion consumer protection law, the focus will lie on the *Unfair Commercial Practices Directive* (UCPD)[83] and the *Unfair Contract Terms Directive* (UCTD).[84] This means that an exhaustive account of all highly specific legislations, such as *the Directive on Financial Services Contracts Concluded at a Distance,*[85] the *Consumer Credit Directive II,*[86] and the *Regulation on Key Information Documents for Packaged Retail Investment and Insurance-based Investment Products,*[87] is beyond the scope of this research. Nevertheless, parts of the EU *acquis* that are particularly pertinent to personalized marketing will be reviewed, although longer descriptions of legislations or proposals fall outside the scope of this research.

In terms of updated legislation and novel literature, developments and publications after September 1, 2024, are not considered.

---

[83] Directive 2005/29/EC of the European Parliament and of the Council of 11 May 2005 concerning unfair business-to-consumer commercial practices in the internal market and amending Council Directive 84/450/EEC, Directives 97/7/EC, 98/27/EC and 2002/65/EC of the European Parliament and of the Council and Regulation (EC) No 2006/2004 of the European Parliament and of the Council ('Unfair Commercial Practices Directive'). https://eur-lex.europa.eu/legal-content/EN/TXT/?uri=celex%3A32005L0029. Referred to as the "UCPD".

[84] Council Directive 93/13/EEC of 5 April 1993 on unfair terms in consumer contracts. https://eur-lex.europa.eu/legal-content/EN/TXT/?uri=celex%3A31993L0013. Referred to as the "UCTD".

[85] Directive (EU) 2023/2673 of the European Parliament and of the Council of 22 November 2023 Amending Directive 2011/83/EU as Regards Financial Services Contracts Concluded at a Distance and Repealing Directive 2002/65/EC. https://eur-lex.europa.eu/legal-content/EN/ALL/?uri=CELEX%3A32023L2 673.

[86] Directive (EU) 2023/2225 of the European Parliament and of the Council of 18 October 2023 on Credit Agreements for Consumers and Repealing Directive 2008/48/EC. https://eur-lex.europa.eu/eli/dir/2023/2225/oj.

[87] Regulation (EU) No 1286/2014 of the European Parliament and of the Council of 26 November 2014 on key information documents for packaged retail and insurance-based investment products (PRIIPs). https://eur-lex.europa.eu/legal-content/EN/TXT/?uri=celex%3A32014R1286.

References

André Q, Carmon Z, Wertenbroch K, Crum A, Frank D, Goldstein W, Yang H (2018) Consumer choice and autonomy in the age of artificial intelligence and big data. Cust Needs Solut 5:28–37
Bar-Gill O (2008) The behavioral economics of consumer contracts. Minn Law Rev 92(3):749–802
Bol N, Dienlin T, Kruikemeier S, Sax M, Boerman SC, Strycharz J et al (2018) Understanding the effects of personalization as a privacy calculus: analyzing self-disclosure across health, news, and commerce contexts. J Comput-Mediat Commun 23(6):370–388
Burkell J, Regan PM (2019) Voter preferences, voter manipulation, voter analytics: policy options for less surveillance and more autonomy. Internet Policy Rev 8(4):1–24
Burr C, Cristianini N (2019) Can machines read our minds? Minds Mach 29:461–494
Burr C, Cristianini N, Ladyman J (2018) An analysis of the interaction between intelligent software agents and human users. Minds Mach 28(4):735–774
Bussani M, Mattei U (1997) The common core approach to European private law. Colum J Eur Law 3(3):339–356
Calo R (2014) Digital market manipulation. Geo Wash Law Rev 82(4):995–1051
Chandra S, Verma S, Lim WM, Kumar S, Donthu N (2022) Personalization in personalized marketing: Trends and ways forward. Psychol Mark 39(8):1529–1562
Council of Europe (2019) Declaration by the Committee of Ministers on the manipulative capabilities of algorithmic processes. Adopted by the Committee of Ministers on 13 February 2019 at the 1337th meeting of the Ministers' Deputies. Council of Europe. https://search.coe.int/cm/pages/result_details.aspx?ObjectId=090000168092dd4b
De Geest G (2016) Signing without reading. In: Marciano A, Ramello GB (eds) Encyclopedia of law and economics. Springer, Cham, pp 1–8
De Geest G (2018) Rents: how marketing causes inequality. Beccaria Books, Leuven
De Jong A, De Ruyter K, Keeling DI, Polyakova A, Ringberg T (2021) Key trends in business-to-business services marketing strategies: developing a practice-based research agenda. Ind Mark Manag 93:1–9
Ebrahim TY (2021) Algorithms in business, merchant-consumer interactions, & regulation. West Va Law Rev 123(3):873–906
Esposito F (2022) The consumer welfare hypothesis in law and economics: Towards a synthesis for the 21st century. Edward Elgar Publishing, Cheltenham
Esposito F (2023) What can the consumer welfare hypothesis do for you? At least three things… EU Law Live (Forthcoming). SSRN. https://ssrn.com/abstract=4512592
Esteller-Cucala M, Fernandez V, Villuendas D (2019) Experimentation pitfalls to avoid in A/B testing for online personalization. In: Proceedings of the 27th Conference on User Modeling, Adaptation and Personalization, pp 153–159
Esteves RB, Resende J (2019) Personalized pricing and advertising: who are the winners? Int J Ind Organ 63:239–282
European Commission (2020) A Europe fit for the digital age: New online rules for users. European Commission. https://commission.europa.eu/strategy-and-policy/priorities-2019-2024/europe-fit-digital-age
European Commission (2023) Digital fairness—Fitness check on EU consumer law. European Commission. https://ec.europa.eu/info/law/better-regulation/have-your-say/initiatives/13413-Digital-fairness-fitness-check-on-EU-consumer-law_en
Fassiaux S (2023) Preserving consumer autonomy through European Union regulation of artificial intelligence: a long-term approach. Eur J Risk Regul 14:710–730
Faure MG, Visscher LT (2018) Rechtseconomie en privaatrecht in de Lage Landen. In: Dirix E, Falconis J (eds) Interdisciplinariteit in het recht: Law and…-bewegingen in het privaatrecht. Intersentia, Antwerp, pp 15–39
Galli F (2020) AI and consumers manipulation: What is the role of EU fair marketing law? Catolica Law Rev 4(2):35–64

Gibney E (2018) The scant science behind Cambridge Analytica's controversial marketing techniques. Nature. https://www.nature.com/articles/d41586-018-03880-4
Golobardes MA (2022) Algorithmic personalization of consumer transactions and the limits of contract law. J Law Market Innov 1(1):17–43
Golson J (2016) Uber knows you'll probably pay surge pricing if your battery is about to die. The Verge. https://www.theverge.com/2016/5/20/11721890/uber-surge-pricing-low-battery
Grafanaki S (2017) Drowning in big data: abundance of choice, scarcity of attention and the personalization trap, case for regulation. Rich J Law Technol 24(1):1–66
Hall S (2023) B2B digital marketing strategy: how to use new frameworks and models to achieve growth. Kogan Page Publishers, London
Helberger N, Lynskey O, Micklitz HW, Rott P, Sax M, Strycharz J (2021) EU consumer protection 2.0: Structural asymmetries in digital consumer markets. Joint report from EUCP2.0 Project BEUC, pp 1–207
Helveston MN (2016) Consumer protection in the age of big data. Wash Univ Law Rev 93(4):859–918
Jabłonowska A, Kuziemski M, Nowak AM, Micklitz HW, Pałka P, Sartor G (2018) Consumer law and artificial intelligence: Challenges to the EU consumer law and policy stemming from the business' use of artificial intelligence. Final report of the ARTSY project. EUI Department of Law Research Paper (2018/11):1–79
Kohavi R, Thomke S (2017) The surprising power of online experiments. Harv Bus Rev 95(5):74–82
Kotler P, Armstrong G (2016) Principles of marketing, 16th edn. Pearson, London
Kotras B (2020) Mass personalization: Predictive marketing algorithms and the reshaping of consumer knowledge. Big Data Soc 7(2):1–14
Leszczynska M, Baltag D (2024) "Can I have it non-personalised?" An empirical investigation of consumer willingness to share data for personalized services and ads. J Consum Policy 47:345–372
Liao SH, Yang CA (2021) Big data analytics of social network marketing and personalized recommendations. Soc Netw Anal Min 11:1–19
Mathis K (2009) Efficiency instead of justice? Searching for the philosophical foundations of the economic analysis of law. Springer, Dordrecht
Micklitz HW, Saumier G (2018) Enforcement and effectiveness of consumer law. In: Micklitz HW, Saumier G (eds) Enforcement and effectiveness of consumer law. Springer, Cham, pp 3–45
Mik E (2016) The erosion of autonomy in online consumer transactions. Law Innov Technol 8(1):1–38
Moradi M, Dass M (2022) Applications of artificial intelligence in B2B marketing: challenges and future directions. Ind Mark Manag 107:300–314
Okorie GN, Egieya ZE, Ikwue U, Udeh CA, Adaga EM, DaraOjimba OD, Oriekhoe OI (2024) Leveraging big data for personalized marketing campaigns: a review. Int J Manage Entrep Res 6(1):216–242
Pariser E (2011) The filter bubble: what the Internet is hiding from you. Penguin UK, London
Parisi F (2013) The language of law and economics. Cambridge Books, Cambridge
Porat A (2021) Changing people's preferences by the state and the law. Theor Inq Law 22(2):215–246
Posner RA (1979) Utilitarianism, economics, and legal theory. J Legal Stud 8(1):103–140
Rathore B (2020) Personalization and profits: the impact of AI on targeted digital marketing. Int J Transcont Discov 7(1):1–14
Seizov O, Wulf AJ, Luzak J (2019) The transparent trap: a multidisciplinary perspective on the design of transparent online disclosures in the EU. J Consum Policy 42:149–173
Spencer SB (2020) The problem of online manipulation. Univ Ill Law Rev 2020(3):959–1006
Strycharz J, Duivenvoorde BB (2021) The exploitation of vulnerability through personalized marketing communication: are consumers protected? Internet Policy Rev 10(4):1–27

Strycharz J, van Noort G, Helberger N, Smit E (2019) Contrasting perspectives–practitioner's viewpoint on personalized marketing communication. Eur J Mark 53(4):635–660
Sunstein CR (1993) Endogenous preferences, environmental law. J Legal Stud 22(2):217–254
Susser D, Roessler B, Nissenbaum H (2019) Technology, autonomy, and manipulation. Internet Policy Rev 8(2):1–22
Tiku N (2017) Get ready for the next big privacy backlash against Facebook. Wired. https://www.wired.com/2017/05/welcome-next-phase-facebook-backlash/
Trzaskowski J (2021) Your privacy is important to us! Restoring human dignity in data-driven marketing. Ex Tuto, Copenhagen
Van den Bergh RJ (2000) Averechts recht. Intersentia, Antwerpen
Van den Bergh RJ (2007) Economische analyse van het consumentenrecht. In: Weterings WTC (ed) De economische analyse van het recht. Boom Juridische Uitgevers, Den Haag, pp 119–140
Veljanovski CG (1981) Wealth maximization, law and ethics—On the limits of economic efficiency. Int Rev Law Econ 1(1):5–28
Vesanen J (2007) What is personalization? A conceptual framework. Eur J Mark 41(5/6):409–418
Vesanen J, Raulas M (2006) Building bridges for personalization: a process model for marketing. J Interact Mark 20(1):5–20
Vickers J (2004) Economics for consumer policy. Proc Br Acad, pp 287–310
Wagner G, Eidenmüller H (2019) Down by algorithms: Siphoning rents, exploiting biases, and shaping preferences: Regulating the dark side of personalized transactions. Univ Chicago Law Rev 86(2):581–610
Wells WD (1975) Psychographics: a critical review. J Mark Res 12(2):196–213
Zarsky TZ (2019) Privacy and manipulation in the digital age. Theor Inq Law 20(1):157–188

Chapter 2
Consumer Law and Economics

Abstract Consumer protection laws play a pivotal role in regulating market dynamics. This chapter delves into the primary analytical approaches employed in law and economics to assess consumer policy. It first examines the traditional consumer law and economics framework, rooted in rational choice theory (RCT) and complemented by insights from information economics. It then explores the behavioral law and economics approach, which integrates findings from behavioral science and empirical research. After evaluating these frameworks and their application to consumer protection challenges, the chapter introduces the concept of personalized marketing in the digital age, presenting it as a novel issue demanding innovative economic analysis of consumer law.

2.1 Introduction

The law and economics paradigm applies economic theories and insights to analyze the efficiency of laws and predicts how certain legal rules will affect human behavior.[1] Under this paradigm, there exists a multiplicity of approaches, which together aim to accurately describe the complex reality of private law.[2] In this chapter, the two most prominent law and economics approaches to consumer law will be described and their merits will be discussed.[3] Thereafter, the chapter introduces a new challenge to the existing approaches in the form a *marketing-induced market failure.* The manifestation of this market failure will be introduced in the current chapter but will be further elaborated in Chaps. 3–5.

This chapter will first discuss the traditional law and economics perspective on consumer law, whereby the foundations of the economic analysis of consumer law will be considered. Thereafter, the traditional view on the desirability of regulation

[1] Faure and Visscher (2018), p. 15.

[2] De Geest (1994), pp. 456–468.

[3] Pomar and Golobardes (2018).

A. J. van Heusden, *The Law and Economics of Personalization*, Economic Analysis of Law in European Legal Scholarship 20,
https://doi.org/10.1007/978-3-032-01468-9_2

in consumer markets will be discussed. In other words, does the market work, or is intervention necessary? Next, the behavioral law and economics approach will be introduced and the corresponding empirical turn in consumer law and economics will be highlighted. After the review of the existing approaches, the stage will be set for a broadened law and economics approach to consumer law.

2.2 The Law and Economics of Consumer Law

The term *traditional consumer law and economics* is a reference to the distinction made by Van den Bergh and Heremans (1987) between "old" and "new" law and economics.[4] The *old law and economics* encompassed a stream of literature in which economists aimed at explaining the formal implications of legal rules that explicitly referred to economic activities, such as competition law, regulations of industrial and commercial processes, and tax law. *New law and economics*, in contrast, applies economic insights to fields of law that are not necessarily explicitly related to the domains of economic activity. Examples of this are contract law, tort- and liability law, family law, and procedural law.[5] In essence, the distinction highlights the development of applying economic analysis to new fields of law. In this chapter, the law and economics analysis is applied to new developments in the realm of consumer law. In this sense, it concerns new law and economics.

The label traditional law and economics is used to refer to the law and economics approach that is based on neoclassical economics complemented with insights from information economics.[6] To fully understand the law and economics of consumer law, it is essential to first consider the foundations of the traditional approach and review its most important aspects.

2.2.1 The Traditional Consumer Law and Economics Approach

The traditional law and economics paradigm is based on the *rational choice model* (RCM). A decision is rational when it fulfills three requirements,[7] namely: (1) out of the existing alternatives, individuals will choose the one that is best for them, based on their expectations of how the alternatives fare under their pre-existing preferences; (2) these expectations are based on the available information; (3) and the optimal amount of information is collected. A rational actor will thereby maximize its *expected utility*, which is determined by the multiplication of the probabili-

[4] Van den Bergh and Heremans (1987).

[5] Van den Bergh and Heremans (1987), pp. 145–147.

[6] Van Heusden (2023).

[7] Pacces and Visscher (2011).

ties of the potentially different outcomes and the corresponding utility that they generate in case of materialization. This maximization process occurs under various constraints, such as time, money, and cognitive resources.[8] Furthermore, the traditional law and economics approach believes in the functioning of the market, yet it does acknowledge that market failures occur. A market failure refers to a "situation in which an unregulated market is inefficient because prices fail to provide proper signals to consumers and producers", which means that aggregate welfare (consumer and producer surplus) is not maximized.[9] Law is seen as a reaction or remedy to market failures.[10]

Moreover, the traditional lawyer-economist looks at how the law incentivizes behavior among economic actors. Accordingly, the law is not seen as an end in itself but as a means to achieving a socially desirable outcome.[11] The concept of *efficiency* is thereby highly important since it will constitute the basis of the analysis. The concept of efficiency, however, has been the subject of many studies in the field of *welfare economics* and there are various definitions. A full elaboration on the concepts of efficiency falls outside of the scope of this chapter. The two most common definitions are *Pareto-efficiency* and *Kaldor-Hicks efficiency.* According to the *Pareto criterion*, a change is an improvement when it makes one person better off without making another person worse off.[12] An allocation of resources is *Pareto-efficient* or *Pareto-optimal* when no further *Pareto improvements* can be made. *Kaldor-Hicks efficiency* means "that state A is to be preferred to state B if those who gain from the move to A gain enough to compensate those who lose."[13] The compensation is hypothetical and the preferred alternative is chosen by comparing aggregate payoffs of the various alternatives and choosing the optimizing option (i.e., the biggest difference between gains and losses).[14] Two alternative criteria are the *Nash criterion of welfare*[15] and the *Rawlsian maximin principle*. Pursuant to the Nash criterion, the grand product of the utility of all members of society needs to be taken. Under the *Rawlsian maximin principle*, also known as the *difference principle,*[16] social policy should pursue the maximization of the minimum gain, which benefits the least-advantaged members of society.[17]

As can be seen, the definition varies and can lead to contradicting results, however, in the traditional law and economics literature, the goal of the efficiency

---

[8] Pacces and Visscher (2011).

[9] Pindyck and Rubinfeld (2013), p. 334.

[10] Faure and Visscher (2018), p. 15.

[11] Faure and Visscher (2018), p. 16.

[12] Cooter and Ulen (2016), p. 14.

[13] Parisi (2013), p. 162.

[14] Parisi (2013), p. 163.

[15] Nash Jr. (1950).

[16] Rawls (1971).

[17] Parisi (2013), p. 248.

analysis is to achieve *maximal total welfare* or reduce *total societal costs*.[18] Nevertheless, the traditional lawyer-economist does not argue that efficiency should be the only criterium that is being taken into account when it comes to policymaking. Alternative criteria such as reasonableness or fairness, in particular regarding distribution, can be pursued, yet the efficiency analysis will provide the policymaker with the price that has to be paid to pursue such values.[19]

In sum, the traditional law and economics paradigm is based on the *rationality assumption*, as it studies the role of the law as a means for changing the relative prices attached to alternative individual actions. Accordingly, a change in the legal structure will affect human behavior by altering the relative price structure and thereby the constraint of the optimization problem. The goal of *wealth maximization* can, therefore, be promoted or constrained by legal rules.[20]

2.2.2 Foundations of Consumer Law

The first question that comes to mind when talking about consumer law is how it should be defined. Nowadays, consumer law is pervasive in all aspects of everyday life, such as consumer credit, advertising, product safety, and e-commerce. Ramsay (2007) describes consumer law as "all laws and regulations affecting consumption and the structuring of consumer markets."[21] This means that it overlaps with various areas of law like competition law, intellectual property law, and data protection law. Howells and Wilhelmsson (2017) define consumer law as "referring to the class of norms which are specially designated to protect the consumer in his or her dealings with an enterprise."[22] They describe the aim of consumer law as:

> the consumer law norms purport to regulate or intervene in the market in order to put the consumer into a better position than he or she would be in without the regulation (and sometimes to place the consumer in the same position as he or she would have been in given a perfectly competitive market).[23]

Other scholars contend that consumer law aims to balance the power between producers and consumers. Bourgoignie (1992), for example, states that consumer law should, therefore, be regarded as a specific branch of law.[24] He defines consumer law as: "the body of norms, rules, structures, and tools, which are the juridical elaboration of different private or public, voluntary or mandatory initiatives, and

[18] Faure and Visscher (2018), p. 16.

[19] Faure and Visscher (2018), p. 27.

[20] Parisi (2004a), p. 262.

[21] Ramsay (2012), p. 1.

[22] Howells and Wilhelmsson (2017), p. 1.

[23] Howells and Wilhelmsson (2017), p. 2.

[24] Bourgoignie (1992), p. 304.

which contribute to the improvement of the legal protection of consumers in the economic market."[25]

These definitions all have three elements in common, namely (1) a body of rules or norms (2) that regulate private relationships in the market (3) to improve the position of the consumer vis-à-vis the seller. Accordingly, consumer law can be seen as an instrument of consumer policy that aims to promote the legitimate interests of consumers by improving their protection.

The emergence of the *European Union* (EU) has accelerated the growth of consumer law through its extensive European regulation.

Article 169 of the *Treaty on the Functioning of the European Union* (TFEU) states the aim of the EU clearly:

> in order to promote the interests of consumers and to ensure a high level of consumer protection, the Union shall contribute to protecting the health, safety, and economic interests of consumers, as well as to promoting their right to information, education and to organise themselves in order to safeguard their interests.[26]

In essence, *EU consumer policy* seeks to empower consumers, enhance their welfare, and protect them.[27] This means that consumer policy is not only a tool to protect consumers but also to promote their interests. In this way, it is of *legal assistance* to the consumer, which has been defined as "the various legal manifestations of economic and social policy intended to promote the interests of consumers within the economic system."[28] Consumer policy is aimed at aiding consumers "in perceiving, expressing, and pursuing the rights assigned to them in the socio-economic order."[29] Accordingly, it can be argued that consumer policy has a wide scope of application.

The concept of *the consumer* plays a central role in consumer law, yet no unified definition exists. There is a continuous debate as to how the concept of a consumer should be constructed and there are significant differences between its construction in legal doctrine and materialization in national laws.[30] In EU consumer law, different definitions are used in different contexts, which vary from country to country.

---

[25] Stuyck (2000), p. 369.

[26] Article 169 Treaty on the Functioning of the European Union. (1992). https://eur-lex.europa.eu/EN/legal-content/summary/treaty-on-the-functioning-of-the-european-union.html. Referred to as "TFEU".

[27] Document 52007DC0099. Communication from the Commission to the Council, the European Parliament and the European Economic and Social Committee - EU Consumer Policy strategy 2007–2013 - Empowering consumers, enhancing their welfare, effectively protecting them {SEC(2007) 321} {SEC(2007) 322} {SEC(2007) 323}. COM/2007/0099 final. https://eur-lex.europa.eu/legal-content/EN/TXT/?uri=celex%3A52007DC0099.

[28] Bourgoignie (1992), p. 305.

[29] Bourgoignie (1992), p. 305.

[30] Everson (2006).

The notion of the consumer has been defined in multiple consumer protection directives, but also in the *Brussels 1 Recast*[31] and *Rome 1*[32] regulations.

Overall, the notion of a consumer can be defined as "a natural person who is acting for the purposes which are outside his trade, business, and profession."[33] Nonetheless, within EU consumer law, broader concepts of the term consumer are used. One example can be found in the *Package Travel Directive,*[34] which defines a consumer as "a person who takes or agrees to take the package or any person on whose behalf the purchase of the package is made or to whom the package is transferred." Similar extensions can be found in the *Misleading and Comparative Advertising Directive* (MCAD)[35] and the *Product Liability Directive* (PLD).[36]

Furthermore, in consumer law, different types of consumers can be found. First, the *Court of Justice of the European Union* (CJEU) came to the notion of an *average consumer*, in its 1998 judgment *Gut Springenheide,*[37] The average consumer "is reasonably well informed and reasonably observant and circumspect." This definition has continued to be used as the standard in EU consumer law and was also adopted as the standard test for misleading and aggressive advertising and other forms of unfair commercial practices.[38]

---

[31] Regulation (EU) No 1215/2012 of the European Parliament and of the Council of 12 December 2012 on jurisdiction and the recognition and enforcement of judgments in civil and commercial matters. https://eur-lex.europa.eu/LexUriServ/LexUriServ.do?uri=OJ:L:2012:351:0001:0032:en:PDF.

[32] Regulation 593/2008. Regulation (EC) No 593/2008 of the European Parliament and of the Council of 17 June 2008 on the law applicable to contractual obligations (Rome I). https://eur-lex.europa.eu/LexUriServ/LexUriServ.do?uri=OJ:L:2008:177:0006:0016:en:PDF.

[33] Valant (2015).

[34] Directive (EU) 2015/2302 of the European Parliament and of the Council of 25 November 2015 on package travel and linked travel arrangements, amending Regulation (EC) No 2006/2004 and Directive 2011/83/EU of the European Parliament and of the Council and repealing Council Directive 90/314/EEC. https://eur-lex.europa.eu/legal-content/EN/TXT/?uri=CELEX%3A32015L2302.

[35] Council Directive 84/450/EEC of 10 September 1984 relating to the approximation of the laws, regulations and administrative provisions of the Member States concerning misleading advertising. https://eur-lex.europa.eu/legal-content/EN/TXT/?uri=CELEX%3A31984L0450.

[36] Council Directive 85/374/EEC of 25 July 1985 on the approximation of the laws, regulations and administrative provisions of the Member States concerning liability for defective products. https://eur-lex.europa.eu/legal-content/EN/TXT/?uri=celex%3A31985L0374.

[37] Case C-210/96, Gut Springenheide and Rudolf Tusky v. Oberkreisdirektor des Kreises Steinfurt, ECLI:EU:C:1998:369. The Court of Justice of the European Union. https://eur-lex.europa.eu/legal-content/EN/TXT/?uri=CELEX%3A61996CJ0210.

[38] First Council Directive 89/104/EEC of 21 December 1988 to approximate the laws of the Member States relating to trade marks. https://eur-lex.europa.eu/legal-content/en/TXT/?uri=CELEX%3A31989L0104; Directive 2000/13/EC of the European Parliament and of the Council of 20 March 2000 on the approximation of the laws of the Member States relating to the labelling, presentation and advertising of foodstuffs. https://eur-lex.europa.eu/legal-content/EN/ALL/?uri=celex%3A32000L0013; Directive 2005/29/EC of the European Parliament and of the Council of 11 May 2005 concerning unfair business-to-consumer commercial practices in the internal market and amending Council Directive 84/450/EEC, Directives 97/7/EC, 98/27/EC and 2002/65/EC of the European Parliament and of the Council and Regulation (EC) No 2006/2004 of the European Parliament and of the Council ('Unfair Commercial Practices Directive'). https://

Under the *Unfair Commercial Practices Directive* (UCPD), the definition was extended as follows: "a consumer who is reasonably well-informed and reasonably observant and circumspect, taking into account social, cultural and linguistic factors."[39] Using the average consumer benchmark, the CJEU can determine the threshold of consumer protection. Nonetheless, the concept could be regarded as being pluriform since the term "average consumer" is open to different interpretations in the national systems of the different Member States, considering the varying contexts of the respective national laws.[40] Accordingly, there is a certain extent of legal uncertainty surrounding the concept.

Moreover, EU law identifies another type of consumer, namely, the *vulnerable consumer*, which is defined as a: "clearly identifiable group of consumers who are particularly vulnerable to the practice or the underlying product because of their mental or physical infirmity, age or credulity."[41] This classification of vulnerability is mainly endogenous in the sense that this type of vulnerability is the result of causes (temporary or permanent) that are inherent to the consumer.[42] This notion of vulnerability is heavily criticized in the literature for being too narrow, which will be further discussed in Sect. 2.4.1. In any case, the differentiation[43] exists to offer a higher level of protection for certain groups of consumers.[44]

In practice, a consumer is perceived as an individual that purchases goods and services for personal use. One can speak of *consumer behavior* as "the acquisition, consumption, and disposal of products, services, time, and ideas by decision-making units."[45] In this sense, the decision-making unit refers to the individual, the consumer. Consumer behavior is of paramount importance for the growth of the economy, and it can, therefore, be seen as the essence of a developed society.[46] For this reason, the protection of consumers' interests becomes an essential goal for the legislator.

---

eur-lex.europa.eu/legal-content/EN/TXT/?uri=celex%3A32005L0029. Referred to as the "UCPD"; Directive 2006/114/EC of the European Parliament and of the Council of 12 December 2006 concerning misleading and comparative advertising (codified version). https://eur-lex.europa.eu/legal-content/EN/TXT/?uri=CELEX%3A32006L0114.

[39] Recital 18, UCPD. This recital codified case C-210/96.

[40] Mak (2011), p. 30.

[41] Article 5(3) UCPD.

[42] Waddington (2013).

[43] The UCPD also looks at commercial practices specifically targeted at a group of consumers, whereby the average member of that group is used as the benchmark. This is also called the *target group benchmark*.

[44] It should be noted that the concept of the vulnerable consumer is also discussed outside the construction of the average consumer, and it is argued that its scope should wider than that defined in the UCPD, see Šajn (2021).

[45] Jacoby and Morrin (2015).

[46] McNeal (2007), p. 20.

A key element of consumer interests that needs to be protected is *consumer welfare*.[47] This is where the legal analysis intersects with the economic analysis. Consumer welfare is defined as "consumer surplus, which is the part of total surplus that accrues to consumers."[48] To specify, consumer surplus is "the difference between the price a potential buyer would be willing to pay for a unit of goods and the (lower) effective price to be paid."[49] The other part is producer surplus, which refers to the surplus that accrues to the sellers. That is to say, producer surplus is "the difference between the minimum price that a potential seller will accept and the (higher) effective price achieved."[50] Consumer and producer surplus forms the total surplus, which is also called *aggregate economic welfare*.[51]

It must be noted, however, that the definition of consumer welfare is contested as being too narrow and that it should also include various qualitative criteria that are difficult to quantify and measure. To illustrate, it is contended that consumer welfare needs to be expressed in economic and non-economic terms, in which *social justice* is a component as well. Consumer welfare should aim to achieve social objectives, such as warranting the health and safety of consumers, which could be less efficient in economic terms but are of overriding interest.[52]

It could be argued that if consumers are well-protected and their interests are promoted by the law, consumer welfare will automatically improve as well. However, this overlooks the relevance of a well-functioning market in which effective competition serves the interest of consumers.[53] In addition, the adverse effects of regulation need to be taken into account since these could lead to losses in consumer surplus or *deadweight losses*.[54]

Thus, the functioning of the market is inextricably linked to consumer law. Intervening in the market might lead to adverse effects, yet not providing consumers with adequate protection might lead to the same or even worse outcomes. The extent to which intervention in the market is desirable is, therefore, dependent on the type of market failure in the market and the effects it has on consumer welfare.

---

[47] Document 52007DC0099. Communication from the Commission to the Council, the European Parliament and the European Economic and Social Committee - EU Consumer Policy strategy 2007–2013 - Empowering consumers, enhancing their welfare, effectively protecting them {SEC(2007) 321} {SEC(2007) 322} {SEC(2007) 323}. COM/2007/0099 final. https://eur-lex.europa.eu/legalcontent/EN/TXT/?uri=celex%3A52 007DC0099.

[48] Brodley (1987), p. 1033.

[49] Mathis (2009), p. 150.

[50] Mathis (2009), p. 150.

[51] Salop (2010), p. 336.

[52] Cseres (2006), pp. 129–130.

[53] Pelkmans (1984).

[54] Van den Bergh (2000); Parisi (2013), p. 75. Deadweight loss refers to the loss of economic surplus that occurs when the market equilibrium is not Pareto-optimal.

2.2.3 *Market Failures in Consumer Markets*

In consumer law and economics, there exist three main justifications for regulatory intervention in consumer markets, namely *information asymmetries*, *transaction costs*, and *unequal bargaining power*.[55]

The first market failure covers *information asymmetries*. Information asymmetry is defined as an imbalance of information between parties to a transaction, whereby one party has an informational advantage over the other party.[56] To achieve *allocative efficiency* (i.e., resources move to the highest valuing user[57]), the parties to an exchange must have full information about the existing alternatives, their contents, and the consequences of the transaction. This assumption of full information cannot be satisfied in consumer markets, which means that the theoretically possible allocative efficiency cannot be attained. The extent to which full information is lacking is dependent on the type of good in question.

In the case of a *search good*, the buyer can ascertain the qualities of the product before the purchase. For *experience goods*, the consumer can only obtain this knowledge after the purchase when the product is used.[58] *Credence goods* form the last category and are distinct from search and experience goods because credence qualities cannot be accurately evaluated even after using the product. The assessment of their value requires additional costly information.[59] To illustrate, concerning repair services, it is onerous for the consumer to assess the quality of the repair. If the consumer wants to be fully certain that the repair has been conducted accurately, an expert opinion needs to be requested, which is costly. Due to the associated costs, consumers accept a degree of uncertainty when it comes to the quality of the goods or services. Accordingly, significant informational deficits can occur when consumers want to buy goods or services with experience or credence good characteristics.[60]

As a result of the informational deficit, the first consequence is the emergence of *moral hazard*. Moral hazard refers to an ex-post information asymmetry. Under moral hazard, the problem lies with non-observable behavior or costly monitoring.[61] The term moral hazard has various definitions and applications in economics. It is relevant to, for example, principal-agent relationships, insurance contracts, and bailouts. To illustrate, the definition of moral hazard in insurance is as follows:

---

[55] It must be emphasized that the analysis focuses specifically on the role of unequal bargaining power and deliberately sets aside the discussion about *market power* as it is known in competition law and economics. To prevent confusion with the concept of market power in competition law, the term unequal bargaining power will be used.

[56] Cooter and Ulen (2016), p. 41.

[57] Parisi (2013), p. 8.

[58] Nelson (1970).

[59] Darby and Karni (1973), pp. 68–69.

[60] Rekaiti and Van den Bergh (2000), p. 379.

[61] Parisi (2013), p. 15.

"Moral hazard arises when the behavior of the insured person or entity changes after the purchase of insurance so that the probability of loss or the size of the loss increases."[62] In general, moral hazard refers to a situation, in which there is a conflict of interests whereby one party maximizes its utility to the detriment of the other party due to the lack of control or enforcement. It is particularly onerous for one of the parties to monitor the degree of care or effort of the other party. It is, therefore, also called the *hidden action problem*.[63] Consequently, the presence of information asymmetries prevents the market in the short-term from achieving allocative efficiency.

The second consequence of information asymmetries is that the consumer faces difficulties with discerning the quality attributes of the product or service. This can give rise to *adverse selection* in the market,[64] also called the *hidden information problem*.[65] Adverse selection has three elements; (1) there is a random variation in the quality of the product, (2) parties have different amounts of information regarding the actual quality of the good, and (3) sellers of the lower-quality good are willing to sell at a lower price than the sellers of the higher-quality good.[66] This means that the consumer will discount the varying levels of quality in the price and will be willing to pay a price that is based on the price of an average-quality good in the market.[67] Since consumers will not be willing to pay the price for which high-quality sellers offer the products, the highest-quality sellers will leave the market. The overall quality will decrease, and consumers will reassess their valuation of the average quality in the market. Through a process of *unraveling*, there will be a *race to the bottom*, which will in the long-term result in a market that only offers products of inferior quality. This is a welfare-decreasing outcome because transactions between the sellers of high-quality products and consumers that are willing to buy these goods do not take place as a result of a lack of trustworthy information.

In sum, moral hazard and adverse selection are consequences that arise due to information asymmetries, which are to the detriment of both consumers and sellers. Through adverse selection and moral hazard, information asymmetries lead to an overall decrease in consumer, but also total welfare, which can make a case for regulation.

Transaction costs are the second factor that can lead to market failure.[68] Transaction costs can be defined as all costs associated with economic exchanges. These costs include both "ex-ante bargaining costs associated with the negotiation and conclusion of the contract and the ex-post costs of monitoring and enforcing the

[62] Cooter and Ulen (2016), p. 48.

[63] Varian (2009), p. 725; Cooter and Ulen (2016), p. 41.

[64] Akerlof (1970).

[65] Varian (2009), p. 725.

[66] Parisi (2013), p. 4.

[67] Kim (1985).

[68] Williamson (1979). Williamson popularized the concept of transaction costs and emphasized transaction cost-based reasoning.

contracts."[69] Legal rules can significantly affect the size of the transaction costs. Therefore, it is of paramount importance to consider transaction costs in the analysis of legal regimes and the design of contract processes, governance mechanisms, and institutions.[70]

Inextricably related to the concept of transaction costs is the *Coase Theorem*.[71] The theorem holds that in the absence of transaction costs "regardless of the initial allocation of rights and the choice of remedies for their protection, the market and the free bargaining of the parties will lead to their efficient final allocation."[72] The legal system creates legal rights and entitlements, and these might initially not be assigned to the highest-valuing user. The parties will have incentives to engage in negotiation to transfer the entitlement to the highest-valuing user until there is no more positive surplus to be obtained from the exchange.[73] Ultimately, the good will end up with the highest-valuing user. This situation is attainable when *Coasian bargaining* occurs, which means that bargaining can take place without transaction costs. The legal implication of this is that "if one assumes rationality, no transaction costs, and no legal impediments to bargaining, all misallocations of resources would be fully cured in the market by bargains."[74]

Applying this rationale to consumer markets, one could argue that in the absence of transaction costs, government intervention through consumer protection policies would be dispensable in competitive markets (i.e., no monopolies are causing unequal bargaining positions). The consumer and the seller would be in the position to bargain for a deal that would be optimally beneficial to both of them. However, the assumption of no transaction costs does not hold in practice. Several different types of transaction costs that are related to consumer markets can be identified; *search and information costs*, *negotiation costs*, *contracting costs*, and *monitoring and enforcement costs*.[75] These transaction costs can impede welfare-enhancing transactions and, therefore, a *prima facie* justification of government intervention to remedy this market failure can be given.

Transaction costs have a two-sided impact. From the consumer perspective, transaction costs can impede the execution of an otherwise welfare-increasing transaction. If the consumer needs to spend additional funds, time, or effort to conclude a contract, this might inhibit a mutually beneficial exchange. When the transaction costs exceed the gains from the transaction, the consumer will not conclude the contract. To minimize transaction costs for the consumer, consumer policies

[69] Parisi (2013), p. 279.

[70] Parisi (2013), p. 279.

[71] Coase (1960).

[72] Parisi (2013), p. 47.

[73] Parisi (2013), p. 49.

[74] Calabresi (1968), p. 68.

[75] Luth (2010), p. 28.

could, for example, aim at the simplification of receiving and understanding information, which will improve consumer decision-making.[76]

The flip side of this course of action is that transaction costs are increased on the side of the seller. The seller will need to comply with the additional regulations, and this leads to additional costs. The transaction costs will then be passed on to the consumer, which renders the intervention ineffective.[77] Regulation can therefore have an adverse effect, whereby the main goal, i.e., minimizing overall transaction costs, is not achieved.

Accordingly, from an economic point of view, it is in the interest of both the consumer and the seller to minimize transaction costs. As Demsetz (1968) puts it: "exchange will tend to be conducted in ways that economize on the cost of transacting."[78] Increasing transacting costs would decrease overall welfare, and, therefore, parties are most likely to do business with a competitor when transaction costs can be lowered. In a consumer setting, this would mean that the consumer would seek an alternative when the current seller offers a deal that is associated with high transaction costs. Due to this competitive pressure, firms are induced to minimize transaction costs and strive for maximum efficiency.

However, practice shows otherwise. It can be highly profitable for firms to increase the transaction costs for consumers.[79] For example, in the case of mail-in rebates, the seller increases the transaction costs for consumers to obtain a rebate in comparison with directly offering the product at a reduced price. To specify, the consumer needs to fill out a form, find the necessary applicable information, and send it back to the seller or manufacturer. This creates an additional hurdle for consumers, which in many cases leads to the failure of obtaining the rebate. Accordingly, the seller can attract customers by offering a discount, but in the end, it will most likely only have to provide the discount to a fraction of the customers. In this sense, the inflation of transaction costs for the consumer is more profitable to the seller in comparison with lowering transaction costs by offering a direct discount at the beginning of the purchase.[80] Although overall welfare from the transaction is decreased, the seller can choose this strategy to maximize its gains from the transaction.[81] For this reason, consumer policy might be desirable to remedy this type of market failure.

The third market failure is that of *unequal bargaining power*.[82] This market failure immediately raises controversy between lawyers and economists. In legal literature regarding consumer protection, the justification of intervention is based on the

---

[76] Sovern (2006).

[77] Van den Bergh (2000).

[78] Demsetz (1968), p. 34.

[79] Sovern (2006).

[80] Sovern (2006) provides an extensive account of how inflating transaction costs can be beneficial for sellers.

[81] Sovern (2006), p. 1637.

[82] It needs to be recalled that this concept refers to the market failure of market power. For the sake of clarity, a different terminology is used that is specifically applicable to the consumer context.

unequal bargaining power of the consumer vis-à-vis the seller. Consumer protection policy is based on a set of rules that are aimed at protecting "weak" consumers from manipulations and abuses by sellers through the improvement of their bargaining position.[83] By increasing the bargaining power of the consumer, a level playing field is created in which consumers can withstand the economic power and advanced knowledge of the seller in the marketplace.[84]

From an economic perspective, the concept of unequal bargaining power might be seen as a market failure whereby the seller enjoys a temporary position of market power due to the particular circumstances created by the vending techniques employed by the seller.[85] Rather than being a bargaining power problem, it would concern a *situational monopoly*. This monopoly can be described as follows:

> Situational monopolies arise out of particular circumstances surrounding particular exchanges, where this transaction-specific market power is exploited opportunistically to extract *quid pro quos* ..., which, while socially positive, cannot in the normal competitive environment surrounding the type of transaction in question justify anything like the commitment extracted for them.[86]

The situational monopoly does not arise from the weaker bargaining position of the consumer but from a temporary informational advantage. The seller has a situational monopoly because it has convinced the consumer that it will be far more costly to seek out alternatives than concluding the contract at the moment it is offered.[87] Hence, there is a *monopoly rent* that sellers can earn by virtue of the particular selling procedures they employ.[88]

Due to unequal bargaining power, stronger parties can exploit their advantage and obtain the benefits of a contract without committing themselves to any future course of action.[89] This can be seen in the context of standard forms. Firms provide contracts to consumers (i.e., the terms and conditions), in which they almost completely limit their commitment to fully complying with the express and implied contract warranties.[90] To illustrate, in a sample of 54 software titles that ranked in the top one hundred bestselling software products, in 53 cases the licensors provided an *End User License Agreement* (EULA) on their website, in which an e-disclaimer erased the protection that was provided by the warranties on the website. Consumers, on the contrary, were contractually obliged to perform their obligations as described in the contract.[91]

---

[83] Rekaiti and Van den Bergh (2000), p. 371.

[84] Rekaiti and Van den Bergh (2000), p. 373.

[85] Rekaiti and Van den Bergh (2000), p. 387.

[86] Trebilcock (1997), p. 101.

[87] Rekaiti and Van den Bergh (2000), p. 378.

[88] Rekaiti and Van den Bergh (2000), p. 379.

[89] Bridgeman (2006).

[90] Hillman and Barakat (2008), p. 1.

[91] Hillman and Barakat (2008).

Nonetheless, mandating consumer protection that would fully balance the bargaining power between the consumer and the seller would substantially increase transaction costs and prices. For instance, a potential solution to empower consumers would be to put an outright ban on the use of standard forms. However, this would be detrimental to both the consumer and the seller. The benefits of standard-form contracts, such as minimizing contract drafting costs, reducing business expenses, and the efficient allocation of risks based on business experience, would disappear.[92] If for every contract, the terms need to be negotiated separately, transaction costs would increase substantially, more expenses would need to be incurred, and the profitability of the transaction for both the seller and the consumer would go down. Besides, the additional costs would likely be passed on to the consumer, which would harm consumer welfare. Accordingly, it is vital to distinguish between business practices that increase transaction costs unnecessarily (i.e., not leading to benefits for both parties) and those that are acceptable.[93] Based on this rationale, regulation could be assessed. Hence, from a law and economics perspective, the aim should be "to find the proper balance between the protections upon which a rational party with equal bargaining power would insist and those that she would gladly give up in exchange for savings in time and money."[94]

2.2.4 Traditional Devices of Consumer Law

Consumer law devices are aimed at protecting the consumer against the more advantaged position of the seller and promoting consumer interests in the market. To understand why the government, in certain cases, intervenes by virtue of consumer protection policies instead of having market forces generate an efficient solution, the concept of allocative efficiency needs to be recalled. Allocative efficiency is used to evaluate how alternative mechanisms allocate resources and entitlements efficiently. *Allocatively efficient* means that the resources move to the highest-valuing user.[95] This concept is problematic in consumer law since two assumptions need to hold, namely: (1) consumers act rationally by choosing courses of action in line with their preferences, thereby maximizing their utility, and (2) consumers must acquire all necessary information with respect to the alternatives among which they can choose and the effect that each option carries.[96] In practice, these assumptions do not seem to hold.[97] Accordingly, in certain cases, the market will be unable

---

[92] Kessler (1943), pp. 631–632; Rakoff (1983), p. 1230; Hillman and Rachlinski (2002), p. 438.

[93] Sovern (2006), p. 1701.

[94] Bridgeman (2006), p. 994.

[95] Parisi (2013), p. 8.

[96] Rekaiti and Van den Bergh (2000), p. 374.

[97] See, generally, Arrow (1982); Conlisk (1996).

to lead to an allocatively efficient outcome and market intervention can be *prima facie* justified.[98]

There is a multiplicity of devices to be found in consumer law, but in this section, the focus lies on the five devices that have been subject to significant scrutiny in the law and economics literature: mandated disclosure, cooling-off periods, mandatory legal warranties, default rules, and boilerplate regulation.

2.2.4.1 Mandated Disclosure

Article 169 TFEU emphasizes consumers' *right to information.* The reasoning behind this provision is that providing information will aid consumers in the decision-making process while maintaining their autonomy. Accordingly, the right to information is a legal instrument to remedy the market failure of information asymmetries. The practical implementation of the right to information can be seen in the regulations governing *mandated disclosure*. Mandated disclosure can be described as the requirements that prompt the discloser to provide disclosees with information to let them make better decisions, thereby preventing the discloser from abusing its superior position. The rationale is that consumers should be aided in their decision-making process. In other words, protecting the less sophisticated in their dealings with the more sophisticated.[99]

In principle, mandated disclosure can be seen as a limited intrusive device to remedy the market failure of information asymmetries. The options of the consumer are not restricted, as under a *mandatory prohibition*, but it is aimed at assisting the consumer in making better-informed choices.[100] In addition, the information requirements elucidate the implicit and vague information obligations that are stated under the general rules of contract law. The requirements mention explicitly which party carries the burden to provide the information that is relevant to the transaction.[101] This should make it clearer for the seller what information should be provided and for the consumer what can be expected from the seller.

Nonetheless, the effectiveness of mandated disclosure has been highly disputed in the law and economics literature. There is vast empirical evidence that demonstrates that mandated disclosure does not effectively enhance consumer awareness, understanding, or behavior.[102] The reasons why mandated disclosure fails to improve consumer knowledge can be attributed to the difficulty of successfully implementing the regulation by three actors: the lawmakers, the disclosers, and the disclosees. Lawmakers need to assess if regulation is necessary, if mandated disclosure is the

[98] Ogus (2004), p. 38. The justification will be further elaborated in Sect. 2.2.6.

[99] Ben-Shahar and Schneider (2014).

[100] Beales et al. (1981).

[101] Schaub (2017), p. 43.

[102] For an extensive elaboration on the inefficacy of mandated disclosure, see Ben-Shahar and Schneider (2014).

best form of regulation, what the proper scope of the mandate is, if the quantity of the disclosure will be answered (i.e., consumers' understanding and assimilation of information), and if the standard can be articulated effectively (i.e., method of disclosure).[103] Based on these objectives, it is evident that lawmakers face an exceedingly difficult task, whereby on different levels errors can occur.

Disclosers can encounter significant challenges when it comes to interpreting the mandate (i.e., handling vague standards), assembling the data which needs to be disclosed (i.e., costly data acquisition and provision), implementing the mandate, and accepting the contents of the mandate (i.e., are there valid reasons for the discloser to resist the mandate such as exceptional complexity or predicted ineffectiveness of the disclosure).[104]

The disclosees, which are the consumers, can have significant difficulties with acquiring, understanding, processing, remembering, and analyzing the disclosed information. When consumers are faced with a dense contract with too much information, consumers will refrain from reading,[105] since it will be too burdensome for consumers to take all the relevant information into account. In other words, the costs of assessing all relevant information will be higher than the potential benefits. One possible consequence is that it leads to a *crowding-out effect* of useful information. Due to the substantial amount of information that is disclosed, consumers' attention to relevant pieces of information is reduced.[106]

Mandated disclosure can also have anticompetitive effects. The costs of complying with the requirements of the regulation can be significantly higher for smaller and medium enterprises in comparison with large firms. The mandated disclosure requirement increases the fixed costs for the smaller enterprises to a level that could impede their entrance into the market or hinder their ability to compete with larger firms that can bear the costs of compliance more easily.[107]

Furthermore, mandated disclosure can undermine other consumer protection devices. To illustrate, if the seller discloses all information in accordance with the requirements of the regulation, it becomes practically unfeasible to invoke the *unconscionability* of a term. In the setting of standard-form contracts, unconscionability is normally invoked when a term was hidden in the contract. Hence, the reasonable expectations of the consumers could not be met. However, if the content of the term complies with the regulation, the hidden or surprising aspect of the term cannot hold anymore since everything has been disclosed.[108] In other words, without mandated disclosure, sellers have an incentive to hide terms, but once they are required to disclose, the adverse effect of the regulation is that sellers actually ben-

---

[103] Ben-Shahar and Schneider (2014) provide a comprehensive analysis of the different factors that impede successful use of mandated disclosures.

[104] Ben-Shahar and Schneider (2014).

[105] This refers to the information overload phenomenon, which will be further discussed in Sect. 2.3.2.

[106] Craswell (2006), p. 584.

[107] Easterbrook and Fischel (1984).

[108] Ben-Shahar and Schneider (2014).

efit, knowing that unconscionability claims related to surprising or hidden terms are no longer a viable option for consumers. Finally, mandated disclosure can lead to distributional effects which contribute to inequality. It has been found that especially the more educated and wealthier consumers profit the most from the disclosures, whereas the less educated and poorer consumers are worse off.[109]

All in all, the analysis of the mandated disclosure shows that this legal device is far from being effective in remedying the market failure of information asymmetries in consumer markets. In principle, it is a desirable method of intervention due to its non-intrusive character and respect for *consumer autonomy*.[110] Nevertheless, an exploration of the incentives, costs, and consequences of the regulation demonstrates that mandated disclosure is not the panacea for information asymmetries. This does not mean, however, that its use should be stopped or that it is a meritless instrument. Mandated disclosure can be effective to a certain point, but an excessive quantity can distort consumer decision-making without leading to an improvement in understanding.[111]

2.2.4.2 Cooling-off Periods

A cooling-off period can be defined as: "a specified period of time, within which the consumer has the right to withdraw from a concluded contract."[112] The rationale behind introducing a mandatory cooling-off period comes from the desire to promote the interests of the consumer vis-à-vis the economically more powerful and knowledgeable sellers in the marketplace.[113]

The right to withdrawal can economically be justified when the consumers most efficiently learn about the attributes of a product after inspecting the product at home, provided that it does not depreciate rapidly, or it depreciates in a way for which compensation can be measured and deducted.[114] This opportunity takes the circumstances of the consumer into account when making a purchase decision. In some cases, it can be difficult to ascertain the quality and working of a product without a reasonable amount of time to inspect and evaluate it.

Furthermore, consumers can be taken by surprise and conclude a contract that is against their interests. The cooling-off period provides consumers with a period of time to evaluate their decision and control for regretful decisions.[115] The economic justification for the use of cooling-off periods is that they improve the accuracy of the pricing mechanism in signaling the quality of the product on the market. More

---

[109] Mandell (1973); McNeil et al. (1979); Kinsey and McAlister (1981).

[110] The concept of consumer autonomy will be further elaborated in Sect. 2.4.4.

[111] Mitts (2014).

[112] Rekaiti and Van den Bergh (2000), p. 372.

[113] Rekaiti and Van den Bergh (2000), p. 373.

[114] Ben-Shahar and Posner (2011).

[115] Rekaiti and Van den Bergh (2000), p. 376.

specifically, because a divergence from the expectations of the consumer will lead to the return of a product, it is in the interest of the seller (i.e., to avoid return and/or administration costs) to let the price reflect the true quality of the product. The differences in quality will be signaled by the price and this eventually leads to the improvement of overall quality. As a consequence, adverse selection and quality deterioration are counteracted.[116]

Nevertheless, several disadvantages come with the provision of cooling-off periods that diminish the economic desirability of this mechanism. First, the cooling-off period can lead to substantial *cost accumulation.*

On the one hand, the costs attributable to the contract performance can make the transaction costs exceed the benefits. This can, for example, be caused by an external event, which makes performance after the cooling-off period more costly than at the moment of contract conclusion.

On the other hand, the cooling-off period can increase overall transaction costs. Specifically, if the cooling-off period is only granted to consumers, it introduces additional costs for sellers, who must account for the possibility that consumers may withdraw from the contract. For example, consumers may return products after initial use or change their minds about the transaction, creating logistical and administrative burdens for the seller. Moreover, cooling-off periods delay the finalization of transactions, increasing both uncertainty and costs. To compensate for these costs, the sellers will ask for higher prices and, thus, the costs of the protection will be passed on to the consumers.[117]

Second, there can be moral hazard on the part of consumers. A prominent example of this is the practice of *wardrobing*. Consumers purchase an item, use it, and send it back within the cooling-off period to get a refund. This creates substantial costs for the seller. Besides the shipment costs, the sellers make losses on the product since part of the value has been diminished by the use. In addition, it has been found that the mandatory provision of cooling-off periods decreases reciprocal behavior by consumers. The adoption of a statutory entitlement weakens the fairness considerations by consumers in the decision-making process. On the contrary, when cooling-off periods are offered voluntarily by the seller, the buyer reciprocates by not exploiting the seller.[118] The seller provides the consumer voluntarily with withdrawal rights to create mutual trust, thereby increasing the willingness to buy. Thus, when consumers receive this right voluntarily, they will feel compelled to act reciprocally. In the case of mandatory rights, there is a *crowding-out effect* that works in two ways. Sellers will not be able to offer voluntary withdrawal rights, which prevents them from attracting consumers with their services, and consumers will have a decreased willingness to act in a reciprocal (fair) way as soon as a monetary reward or a fine is introduced since the behavior is not motivated anymore by

[116] Van den Bergh (1997).

[117] Rekaiti and Van den Bergh (2000), p. 382.

[118] Borges and Irlenbusch (2007).

altruism but by legal incentives.[119] Hence, there will be more misuse of the mandatory granted cooling-off period.

A potential remedy to this problem could be the use of *rental payments*, whereby the consumer needs to pay an amount of money proportionate to the time the product was possessed and, possibly, used. In this way, the costs that are incurred by the seller are also taken into account.[120] Nonetheless, the effectiveness of returning costs in remedying the misuse of withdrawal rights is disputed. It is argued that return costs are seen as additional costs that are part of the transaction. Return costs only affect the fairness considerations of consumers when the fair choice is also welfare-optimizing for the consumers themselves.[121]

Third, cooling-off periods can lead to *adverse effects*. If the cooling-off period leads to substantial losses to sellers, it could be the case that certain sellers will leave the market, leading to decreased competition. In addition, if compliance with the regulation is too burdensome, sellers will try to circumvent it, which will detract from its effectiveness. An example of this could be found in the financial industry, in which banks would conclude the contract with the consumers but would only supply the loan after the cooling-off period had lapsed to prevent financial losses.[122]

All in all, the cooling-off period is being employed as a device to remedy irrational behavior, situational monopolies, and information asymmetries. Based on the economic analysis of the device, it has become possible to identify its shortcomings. There is a trade-off between providing the consumer with sufficient time to collect and process all relevant information and containing the increase in costs as a result of regulation.

2.2.4.3 Mandatory Legal Warranties

Legal warranties can be defined as "all legally enforceable claims (be they based directly on legal provisions or contractual clauses) by the buyer of a given good against the seller, in case the product reveals itself defective, faulty, or otherwise unsuitable for the agreed purpose."[123] The warranties establish a standard of quality that must not be violated. Thus, in case the product does not comply with the reasonable standard of quality that may be expected, the seller is obliged to rectify the problem by repair, replacement, or compensation.[124]

The difference between conventional and legal warranties is found in the party that gives them. Under conventional warranties, the parties to the contract

119 Smits (2011).

120 Stuart (1977), p. 163.

121 Borges and Irlenbusch (2007).

122 Rekaiti and Van den Bergh (2000), p. 384.

123 Pomar (2001), pp. 3–4.

124 Noll (2003).

incorporate the warranty, whereas legal warranties are mandated by law.[125] In economic literature, three functions of warranties have been identified; the *insurance function*, the *quality signaling function*, and the *risk reduction function*.[126]

The insurance function indicates the wish of the consumers to be insured against an unexpected and adverse eventuality. A warranty guarantees the buyer that the negative consequences of a product failure will be resolved by the seller by virtue of repair, replacement, or compensation.[127] In return for this warranty, the buyer pays a higher price, which can be implicit or explicit, that covers the increase in production costs for the seller. This trade-off is justified based on the assumption that the consumer is *risk averse*. If the consumer is risk averse and the seller is risk neutral, *optimal risk sharing*, from an economic point of view, would be obtained by offering complete coverage. If the seller is also risk averse, like the consumer, the optimal coverage for both parties would be partial, which means that each party bears part of the loss.[128]

The warranty also serves as an instrument to signal quality.[129] Consumers perceive warranties as a signal of quality that assures reliability.[130] If the seller offers a high-quality product, it will be more willing to provide a warranty on the product. The inverse holds for a seller of low-quality products since it would make a loss on the warranty. Accordingly, the consumer can distinguish between high-quality and low-quality products based on the offered warranty. This is a solution to the so-called *market of lemons* problem.[131]

Nonetheless, similar to the mandatory provision of cooling-off periods, mandatory legal warranties can lead to the loss of informational value. More specifically, the signaling function of the warranty is comprised due to the set standard. It becomes more difficult for consumers to distinguish which products are of higher or lower quality. Besides, the signaling ability of the seller is limited since offering the warranty voluntarily as a sign of product quality is substituted by the mandatory nature of the warranty.[132] It could be argued, however, that the mandatory character of the warranties does not prevent sellers from offering warranties that exceed the period set by the legal standard. In other words, if sellers are confident in the quality of their products and they want to signal this to the consumers, they could still offer a longer warranty period.

The incentive function of the warranty distinguishes itself from the two other functions because it is based on the assumption that the buyer and seller influence the rate of failure. The insurance and quality functions, in contrast, take the failure

---

[125] Noll (2003).

[126] Pomar (2001).

[127] Pomar (2001).

[128] Parisi (2004b).

[129] Pomar (2001), p. 5.

[130] Boulding and Kirmani (1993).

[131] Akerlof (1970).

[132] Noll (2003).

rate as a given. From the consumers' perspective, warranties could reduce their incentive to exercise *reasonable care* for the product. The negative consequences of the misuse of the product are shifted to the seller through the warranty. This could give rise to moral hazard or adverse selection problems. Moral hazard may happen because consumers exercise less care since their level of care cannot always be readily verified by the seller or a third party. Adverse selection would happen because the fixed warranty attracts more high-risk buyers than low-risk buyers. The former group knows that they will experience more product failures and, thus, the warranty is a benefit they want to obtain. Since no different prices can be charged to high- and low-risk buyers, *cross-subsidization* will take place.

From the sellers' perspective, the warranty can induce an investment in the quality of the product to prevent large losses from its obligations under the warranty. In the absence of warranties, it could be economically profitable to lower the production costs and offer a lower quality to be more competitive, yet the warranty counteracts this incentive by inducing the sellers to care for quality maintenance and product failure risk. In addition, more stringent or longer warranty standards might encourage producers to invest more in product durability and repairability.[133]

Consequently, a balance must be struck whereby optimal incentives are given to both parties. This can be achieved by incentivizing the seller to invest in risk reduction for aspects of the warranty in which the seller has a comparative advantage and incentivizing the buyer to exercise more care by excluding coverage on certain parts of the warranty. This would amount to the implementation of the so-called *investment theory of warranties*.[134] According to this theory, warranty terms will be allocated to the party that can avoid losses at the least cost, which in certain cases is the seller (e.g., preventive investment in quality) and in other cases the consumer (e.g., searching for products that best fit their intended use). Moreover, warranties will be limited by manufacturers to risks that virtually all consumers share, and for additional coverage, consumers can self-insure or seek alternative forms of insurance.

2.2.4.4 Default Rules

Due to the practical infeasibility of including all relevant contingencies into one contract, parties work with incomplete contracts, in which only the essential contingencies are explicitly addressed. This amounts to contracting according to the *theory of incomplete contracts*.[135]

A ramification of an incomplete contract is that gaps exist that need to be filled. From an ex-ante perspective, *default rules* can define the rights and obligations of each party in parts of the contract that are devoid of agreed-upon stipulations.

[133] Maitre-Ekern and Dalhammar (2016).

[134] Priest (1981).

[135] Hart and Moore (1988).

Default rules are defined as "rules determined by the legislator that the parties to a transaction are permitted to deviate from."[136]

Another term for default rules is *dispositive rules*, which are different from *cognate rules* that are unconditional and cannot be departed from. The default rules can be *tailored*, indicating what the parties to the contract would have wanted, or *untailored*, indicating what the majority of parties in such a contract setting would have wanted.[137]

The rationale behind the implementation of default rules is based on four reasons.[138] Principally, default rules work as gap fillers by providing a legal arrangement where an incomplete contract is lacking. Second, transaction cost minimization. Optimally designed default rules can reduce the drafting costs of a contract. Third, it enables the achievement of certain ends desired by the legislator, which can, for instance, be the adherence to a specific norm or the creation of legal rights. Lastly, default rules can also force the disclosure of information. If a party does not reveal relevant and valuable information to the other party, it can be penalized through a *penalty default rule*. This rule aims to lower transaction costs by incentivizing the disclosure of information. The reasoning is that "penalty defaults are purposefully set at what the parties would not want - in order to encourage the parties to reveal information to each other or third parties (especially the courts)."[139]

Two principles are guiding the optimization of default rules. First, the principle of *opt-out cost minimization*. This is based on a majoritarian rationale, which indicates that the rule should be followed by the majority of parties, which leads to substantial cost savings concerning opt-outs and the acquisition of information. Second, the *principle of expected-value maximization*. The rule should maximize overall value in comparison with other alternatives, conditional upon no opting-out by consumers. This leads to cost savings when the majority of the parties stick with the default option.[140]

The appropriate goal of default rules is dependent on the perspective of the legislator. From a purely legal perspective, default rules can be placed between the desires of maintaining parties' *contracting autonomy* and achieving a degree of *material justice*.[141] The classical economic view emphasizes the cost-saving nature of default rules. This stems from the incomplete contracts theory, which attributes a gap-filling function to default rules. To a certain extent, this view sides with the focus on parties' autonomy. Its main goal remains, however, the maximization of contractual efficiency. In consumer law, default rules are employed to encourage parties to achieve the desired outcome that is beneficial to both parties, while promoting the interests of the consumer. The behavior can be nudged toward a specific

[136] Becher and Bar-Gill (2012), p. 30.

[137] Ayres and Gertner (1989).

[138] Becher and Bar-Gill (2012), pp. 31–32.

[139] Ayres and Gertner (1989), p. 91.

[140] Bar-Gill and Ben-Shahar (2016), p. 141.

[141] Mathis and Burri (2016).

desired end, which can be the welfare of the parties or the promotion of social values.[142] The desired end can in turn be to remedy market failures such as transaction costs, information asymmetries, or unequal bargaining power. To further enhance consumer protection, the default rules in consumer contracts can be drafted one-sidedly to the benefit of the consumer, thereby promoting a pro-consumer interpretation of the default rules.[143]

Nonetheless, the effectiveness of default rules in a consumer contract is questionable since sellers can surreptitiously contract around them by means of their boilerplate. This can be done through disclosure templates in which in a cost-saving and non-salient manner the consumer can be led away from the default rules by stimulating them to choose the opt-out. The result is that "practically every consumer contract comes with boilerplate language disclaiming the default warranty."[144] In other words, the working of default rules can be hampered through ingeniously drafted boilerplates. The effectiveness of the default rules consumer law device is, therefore, closely related to boilerplate regulation.

2.2.4.5 Boilerplate Regulation

The boilerplate governs all aspects of the contract that have not been part of the *essentialia negotii* negotiations between the seller and the consumer. When it comes to the boilerplate, there is a considerable signing-without-reading problem.[145] This creates an incentive for sellers to insert one-sided terms to their benefit. Hence, to protect the consumer, consumer law provides substantive quality regulation when it comes to boilerplates. The law determines which terms of a contract can be seen as unfair or unconscionable and should be excluded from the contract.

There is a vast body of literature on the effectiveness of this consumer law device. An in-depth analysis of this device merits further discussion but falls outside the scope of this section. Therefore, a full account of boilerplate regulation, analyzed through a law and economics perspective, will be given in Chap. 5. Nonetheless, to briefly summarize the discussion, from an economic perspective, boilerplate regulation can be justified. There is an information asymmetry problem that leads to suboptimal outcomes. Consumers do not read the small print,[146] which allows the seller to insert one-sided terms instead of terms that are mutually beneficial (i.e., efficiency-maximizing). It is unlikely that consumers will be able to discipline the market, due to the aforementioned no-reading problem.[147] Accordingly, by virtue of contract

[142] Mathis and Burri (2016).

[143] Ben-Shahar and Bar-Gill (2013), p. 122.

[144] Ben-Shahar and Bar-Gill (2013), p. 123.

[145] De Geest (2016), p. 2.

[146] Further explained in Chap. 5.

[147] De Geest (2016).

clause regulation (e.g., the UCTD with Annex 1 indicating unfair terms[148]), certain terms can be classified as unfair, thereby making them inapplicable to the contract, which provides the consumer with an adequate level of protection against onerous one-sided terms.

2.2.5 *The Market Works: Market Solutions*

The devices of consumer law have been the topic of widespread controversy in the consumer law and economics literature. The effectiveness of the devices has been questioned and concerns were raised regarding the net benefits of additional regulation. The discussion of the devices from a law and economics perspective merits further attention, especially because the lion's share of traditional consumer law and economics articles propound that the market works and that it can generate efficiency in consumer markets. They argue that under conditions of perfect competition and market efficiency, the market can provide solutions to various consumer issues, whereas regulation will lead to adverse effects.[149]

To start with, it is argued that the private provision of information will automatically take place in the market since it will be beneficial for high-quality producers to signal their product quality. The higher-quality sellers do not want to be associated with the lower-quality sellers and in case the consumers are unable to discern product quality by means of the pricing mechanism, signaling will take place. This creates a *snowball effect* whereby sellers are induced to signal their quality through the voluntary disclosure of information. As a result, a process of *unraveling* takes place in which verifiable information, both favorable and unfavorable, is voluntarily disclosed by sellers.[150] By examining all disclosed information and looking at the sellers that do not disclose all information or remain silent, consumers can more easily form their opinions about the quality that is offered in the market. A corollary of this unraveling process is that if the government intervenes through mandated disclosure requirements, the *signaling function* of the voluntary function is impeded. If voluntary disclosure can take place while the costs of emitting information are low or negligible, mandated disclosure laws can work adversely.[151]

It must be noted, however, that unraveling is less likely to take place in markets in which product information is relatively difficult to understand. When the fraction of consumers that can understand the disclosed information is small, it is less probable that voluntary disclosure will occur.[152] In addition, due to competitive forces,

[148] Council Directive 93/13/EEC of 5 April 1993 on unfair terms in consumer contracts. https://eur-lex.europa.eu/legal-content/EN/TXT/?uri=celex%3A31993L0013. Referred to as the "UCTD".

[149] See, for example, Epstein (2008).

[150] Grossman (1981).

[151] Grossman (1981).

[152] Fishman and Hagerty (2003).

voluntary disclosure might be thwarted. Disclosing information can induce more intense competition among sellers of products with similar quality. The lower-quality sellers can profit from not disclosing information if part of the high-quality sellers do not disclose. The reason for this is that the threat of unraveling is not credible.[153]

Furthermore, tort and liability law demonstrate the importance of insurance in mitigating risks. To prevent the incurrence of significant losses, individuals insure themselves against the probability that certain risks materialize. Analogously, it could be argued that if consumers risk non-performance by sellers, they can insure themselves. This takes away the need for legal remedies under consumer law. Insurance companies could aggregate data from consumer claims and monitor which sellers are "good" and which are "bad". Consequently, consumers can be informed about the degree of quality in the market, and through blacklists, consumers know with whom they should not transact.[154]

The practice of insuring consumer transactions already takes place on a large scale in the area of e-commerce. An example of this is the "Trusted Shops" trust mark which provides consumers with a money-back guarantee process and a system of consumer reviews.[155] Both assurance and insurance can significantly increase consumers' willingness to buy, thereby making it a useful instrument to facilitate B2C transactions.[156]

Moreover, reputation works as a consumer protection device that is generated by the market itself. Reputational concerns can incentivize sellers to improve their product quality and customer service. Sellers' actions in the present influence their costs and benefits in the future. If the seller abuses consumers' trust in the present by not fulfilling the set expectations, the seller will incur losses in the future as a result of its established bad reputation. For this reason, sellers that want to survive in the market need to consider the long-term consequences of their present actions.[157] Hence, reputational incentives can induce the seller to ensure consumer satisfaction and prevent opportunistic behavior.[158]

Reliance on reputation can also be regarded as a rational act since it is a metric that indicates an individual's qualities. If individuals have a "good" reputation, it will be in their interest to act accordingly, whereas if they have a "bad" reputation they failed to act appropriately in the past and they should be encouraged to improve their status. The informational nature of reputation works as an imperfect substitute for knowledge about the quality of a certain product or service.[159] In this way,

---

[153] Board (2009).

[154] Ben-Shahar (2010).

[155] Loebbecke and Hornig (2001).

[156] Boo et al. (2007).

[157] Parisi (2013), p. 256.

[158] Bebchuk and Posner (2006).

[159] Shenkar and Yuchtman-Yaar (1997), p. 1365.

reputation operates as a warranty that can aid individuals in their decision-making process.[160]

The emergence of online ratings has emphasized the importance of reputation building. Although the ratings can predominantly be found online, their influence on brick-and-mortar stores (i.e., physical establishments) may not be underestimated.[161] Consumers take full advantage of the reputational information that is available on the Internet to form their beliefs about the sellers in the marketplace.[162] The use of consumer ratings has become one of the most valuable sources of information-sharing between consumers, sellers, and producers.[163] Therefore, it is debatable to what extent mandated disclosure requirements contribute to better decision-making. Rather than reading the extensive standard forms, consumers inspect the ratings of a seller to determine if they want to conclude a contract. Rating systems can to a large degree contribute to the solving of information asymmetries in the market and the development of these systems is an ongoing process.[164] To solve the lack of trustworthiness of certain rating systems, initiatives have started that consist of third-party certification systems that provide consumers with more reliable information about the reputation of a seller.[165]

Overall, the combination of reputation scores and ratings can form a credible threat for firms to improve their customer service and products. Although consumer law provides several legal remedies that enable the consumer to seek redress against a contract breach by the seller, their effectiveness is contestable. It is unlikely that the consumer will instigate proceedings against the seller for a breach of contract. In most cases, it concerns the sale of products or services of relatively modest value which is not proportional to the costs of a legal procedure. In addition, in the absence of class actions, collective action problems can prevent consumers from taking action as a group. Therefore, there is no significant threat of liability for sellers under contract law.[166]

Negative reputation scores, in contrast, can pose a credible threat to businesses. A negative rating can deter consumers from transacting with the seller in question, which can have significant financial effects on the firm in the long term. It is, therefore, in the best interest of the seller to prevent such a situation and resolve consumer complaints satisfactorily. The threat of a consumer harming the reputation of a company can be more credible than the threat of a consumer seeking legal redress.[167] It must be noted, however, that to work effectively, reputation scores need

[160] Heymann (2011), p. 1360.

[161] Li and Hitt (2010).

[162] Wan et al. (2018).

[163] Pee (2016).

[164] Clemons (2007).

[165] buySAFE is an example of such an initiative.

[166] Ben-Shahar (2010).

[167] Ben-Shahar (2010).

to be verified and warranted.[168] To illustrate, online review mechanisms can be unreliable, which causes consumers to make decisions based on incorrect information.[169] This can originate from four sources of unreliability: "lack of reviews, biased reviews, fake reviews, and platforms' presentation, processing, and ranking practices."[170] If inaccurate information is not remedied by the market, this could lead to the demise of the online review mechanism. This would be an inefficient outcome since the benefits that an online review mechanism offers, such as efficient information gathering, low-cost quality signaling, and reduced transaction costs (e.g., compared to third-party certification), would be lost.[171]

Accordingly, there is an incentive for the regulation of review mechanisms to safeguard accuracy and reliability. Through legislative protection, self-regulation, and consumer awareness, a review mechanism can play a significant role in the provision of useful and reliable consumer information.[172]

Closely related to reputation is the concept of *relational contracts*. Relational contracts are "informal agreements governed by unwritten codes of conduct and sustained by reputational concerns."[173] It is in the interest of long-term oriented sellers to preserve an enduring relationship. Hence, relationship building can in certain instances prevail over the enforcement of legal rights. The parties rely on informal consumer devices, rather than the formal devices provided by law.[174] This induces cooperation, which is beneficial to both parties, thereby removing the need for statutory regulation. Introducing mandatory regulation can take away the incentive for companies to voluntarily accommodate the needs of the consumer. To illustrate, in the case of standard-form contracts, companies can decide to not enforce a certain term of the boilerplate to provide the customer with a special service that preserves the mutual relationship.[175] If the specific duties of the sellers or the rights of the consumers are laid out in mandatory statutory law, the room for provision of customized services can be constricted. The reliance on informal devices is substituted by reliance on formal devices imposed by law.

Additionally, *consumer learning* is an endogenous process that spontaneously takes place in the market as a reaction to the various risks that consumers encounter in B2C transactions. Through self-education, consumers learn from the market and adapt themselves accordingly. In essence, a process of *maturation* occurs.[176] Consumers make errors in their decision-making process, but the negative feedback they get as a result of it creates a starting point for gradual improvements. Through

---

168 Busch (2016); Ranchordás (2018).

169 Narciso (2022), p. 351.

170 Narciso (2022), p. 352.

171 Narciso (2017), p. 16.

172 Narciso (2022), p. 365.

173 Parisi (2013), p. 252.

174 Cooter and Ulen (2016), pp. 299–305.

175 Bebchuk and Posner (2006).

176 Epstein (2006).

a process of trial and error, consumers learn what aspects should be considered in their dealings with sellers and which sellers should be avoided altogether. Consumer learning can in certain cases be the most effective form of protection.[177]

Lastly, it could be argued that the creation of consumer law devices derogates the need for *consumer-based innovations*. To specify, in case consumer protection is not provided by law, which deteriorates the position of the consumer vis-à-vis the seller, consumers are forced by the market to invent strategies that prevent them from incurring substantial losses. Consumers could, for example, renegotiate their transactions with the sellers to minimize the risk of losses.[178] In addition, initiatives could be launched that minimize the probability of incurring substantial losses due to non-performance. For example, third-party intermediaries could be established that oversee B2C transactions. As a result of the formal contractual duties that have been created by law, the likelihood that such market-based solutions become prominent consumer protection tools is reduced.

2.2.6 Welfare Effects of Regulatory Interventions

In cases of market failures in which the market is not able to correct itself, government intervention might increase social welfare by remedying the failure. The question that subsequently arises is: When is government intervention desirable? A basic rule of thumb could be that the benefits of the intervention should outweigh its costs. In practice, this simple rule of thumb has been proven to be onerous to comply with. The reason for this is that the government is not a fully efficient institution, that is to say, many resources are lost due to errors, lobbying, and bureaucracy.[179] Accordingly, the degree to which regulatory intervention increases social welfare is dependent on the extent to which the government can efficiently remedy market failures.

As mentioned before, in consumer markets, the three main market failures are information asymmetries, transaction costs, and unequal bargaining power.[180] Some argue that the government could remedy these market failures through consumer law. However, when it comes to regulation one must be cautious of not replacing a market failure with a *regulatory failure*.[181] Economic regulation requires an in-depth understanding of the functioning of the market. It can be difficult for the government to obtain the optimal amount of information for an accurate intervention. Moreover, the success of the implemented regulation also depends on many

[177] See Epstein (2008) for a discussion on consumer learning in credit markets.

[178] Ben-Shahar (2010).

[179] Ogus (2004).

[180] Of note is that the focus lies on the consumer aspect of market power and not on competition law considerations. Depending on the perspective taken, the unequal bargaining power can also be classified as a situational monopoly, see Sect. 2.2.3.

[181] Faure (2014), p. 695.

government-related factors such as bureaucratic expertise, resource availability, and political constraints.[182] Accordingly, when considering regulatory intervention, one must be wary of the economic effects.

Nevertheless, in certain cases, government intervention can increase social welfare. First, it can be argued that in consumer markets, high transaction costs and unequal bargaining power can impede private bargaining from solving market failures. Second, it is plausible that a market solution will not emerge from the market itself. For example, due to non-competitive market conditions or anti-competitive behavior of the market participants.[183] The government needs then to intervene to provide a solution to the market failure. Third, in some markets, the government can be a more efficient information provider than the market itself. For instance, when the government is already engaged in the collection of information or obtaining information is onerous for private actors due to confidentiality.[184]

In the case that regulatory intervention in the consumer market is justified based on a *cost-benefit analysis* (CBA), one should also look at the distributional effects of regulation. Although protective measures can increase consumer welfare as a whole, the effects can be diverse for different classes of consumers. Three types of distributional effects can be identified: *information-based*, *price-based*, and *enforcement-based effects*.

First, the information-based effects can be seen in the use of mandated disclosures. Several studies have shown that especially middle- and higher-class consumers are better able to familiarize themselves with the information provided.[185] The more sophisticated consumers profit more from the imposed information duties than less sophisticated consumers, which from a *distributive justice perspective* is problematic.[186] Distributive justice refers to the desire to implement policies that will lead to outcomes that are perceived as "fair" or "just".[187] Accordingly, the potential efficiency benefits of regulation can be in tension with distributional considerations.[188]

Second, the price-based effects challenge the desirability of consumer protection policies. Every regulation comes at a price. Increasing consumer protection means

---

182 Guasch and Hahn (1999), p. 152.

183 See for the list of characteristics that may lead to a hypothesis that a market-based solution is unlikely to emerge, Hadfield et al. (1998), p. 155.

184 Hadfield et al. (1998), p. 157 provide a non-exhaustive list of cases in which the government has an informational advantage over the market.

185 See for evidence from consumer credit markets, Angell (1971), product labels, Gage (1979), and the second-hand car market, McNeil et al. (1979).

186 Sophistication refers to consumer sophistication in the online market, consisting of consumers' level of acquired knowledge, experience, and skills which are relevant to being an efficient decision maker. Cfr. Titus and Bradford (1996) for the definition of consumer sophistication in traditional markets.

187 Ogus (2004), pp. 46–51. Of note is that Ogus emphasizes that widely different views are held on what is to be regarded as "fair" or "just".

188 See Mathis (2009) for an elaborate analysis of the ostensible trade-off between efficiency and justice.

that consumer prices will also increase. It could be argued that this price increase is justified because consumers enjoy additional protection. Nonetheless, this overlooks which consumers are benefitting from the increased protection. Regulations can promote higher prices and these increases can have a disproportionally negative effect on low-income households.[189] The reason for this is that lower-income households spend larger proportions of their incomes on heavily regulated goods and services that are prone to sharp price increases. Higher-income households, in contrast, spend smaller proportions of their incomes on heavily regulated goods, which makes them less prone to price increases by sellers. Accordingly, the regulation might constitute a mechanism of cross-subsidization whereby poorer consumers pay for the better protection of richer consumers.[190]

Third, with respect to the enforcement of consumer rights (i.e., enforcement-based effects), it can be argued that, in many cases, going to court is not economically viable. The costs of adjudication are considerable, whereas consumer disputes normally involve small losses.[191] It has been found that in particular the poor, elderly, and less educated are systematically less likely to claim consumer protection because they lack the understanding of information, the sophistication or knowledge to insist on compliance, and the resources to request legal advice or start proceedings.[192] As a consequence, consumer law enforcement will be suboptimal, which threatens the effectiveness of consumer protection devices. A response to this phenomenon has been the emergence of multi-party enforcement by the government, consumer organizations, and litigation funders.[193] It is still a subject of debate, however, to what extent this satisfactorily remedies the enforcement problem in consumer law.

2.3 The Behavioral Law and Economics Approach

The *behavioral law and economics approach* contests the reliance on the rationality assumption by the traditional approach.[194] It argues that the law and economics movement can improve its methodology and policy prescriptions by incorporating insights from cognitive psychology, behavioral sociology, and other behavioral sciences.[195] The rationality assumption is contested by an extensive account of empirical evidence that shows that in many cases individuals do not act rationally or in

[189] Chambers et al. (2019).

[190] Chambers et al. (2019).

[191] Muris (1991), p. 105.

[192] Ben-Shahar and Bar-Gill (2013), p. 115.

[193] Muris (1991), p. 105.

[194] It also contests the self-interest and willpower assumptions.

[195] Korobkin and Ulen (2000).

accordance with the predictions made by RCT.[196] The behavioral law and economics approach offers an economic analysis of law that takes the multitude of biases and heuristics that individuals are subject to into account. This allows for a further explanation of certain behavioral patterns that cannot be explained by rational choice theorists.

The behavioral law and economics approach does not intend to replace the traditional law and economics approach by refuting its core assumption. On the contrary, the behavioral approach aims at refining the law and economics paradigm by including insights from behavioral science.[197] In essence, the behavioral approach is a complement to the traditional approach rather than a critique.[198] As Jolls (2007) puts it: "Behavioral law and economics attempts to improve the predictive power of law and economics by building in more realistic accounts of actors' behavior."[199]

The behavioral law and economics approach offers valuable insights into various areas of law, but it is particularly relevant to the field of consumer law.[200] The rationale behind this statement is that "one might reasonably believe that the impact of cognitive biases is greatest in consumer markets where learning, specializations, and repeat interactions are less likely than in relationships between firms."[201]

In this section, the behavioral law and economics approach will be applied to consumer law. The goal is to highlight the insights that this approach can bring to the analysis of consumer protection policies. In addition, the differences between traditional and behavioral consumer law and economics will become perspicuous. This allows for a better understanding of the different law and economics approaches to consumer law and their corresponding merits.

2.3.1 The Empirical Turn

The development of the behavioral law and economics paradigm is inextricably linked to the increasing demand for empirical research in law and economics. Behavioral law and economics has attacked the rationality assumption of the traditional law and economics paradigm through the extensive use of empirical evidence. Numerous empirical studies showed that individuals do not always act rationally and that, therefore, the rationality assumption can be contested. The extensive use of statistical analyses and experiments in behavioral law and economics boosted an overall demand for the application of empirical methods. Accordingly, empirical

---

[196] This will be further elaborated in the subsections of Sect. 2.3.

[197] Ulen (1998), p. 1748.

[198] Jolls (1998), p. 1654.

[199] Jolls (2007), p. 2.

[200] Faure and Visscher (2018), p. 17.

[201] Wright (2007), p. 474.

evidence could be provided in favor of or against the economic theories that had been developed based on the rationality assumption.[202]

Apart from the behavioral influence, there has also been an increasing demand for the empirical testing of hypotheses that were developed in the traditional law and economics literature. Traditionally, legal rules were primarily analyzed by means of theoretical models that employed several assumptions. Consequently, the model would provide theoretical propositions that could provide clarity as regards ex-ante predicted outcomes of the legal rule in question. This approach was and still is largely popular, perhaps even dominant, in law and economics scholarship.[203] Nonetheless, there is growing attention to the empirical testing of these propositions. By virtue of statistical data, empirical research can provide evidence of how certain legal rules will impact society in practice. This allows the lawmaker to rely on practical evidence rather than ex-ante theoretical predictions. Empirical evidence could be of particular value to the lawmaker due to its focus on factual data.[204]

Hence, the increasing tendency toward the use of empirical research in law and economics indicates an *empirical turn* in the discipline. The empirical turn refers to the *empirical revolution* that has been identified by Klick (2011). He emphasized that empirical work in the field of law and economics has been continuously increasing and that its prospects are promising.[205] New methods from neighboring disciplines are employed to advance the development of methodological standards. In this way, the increasing use of empirical research allows for the development of novel methods that are better able to fit the needs of the discipline.[206]

The emergence of *empirical legal studies* (ELS) supports the empirical revolution that can be seen in law and economics. In short, ELS refers to empirical research on how the legal system works, which helps to inform litigants, policymakers, and society as a whole.[207] In practice, this means that scholars in the field of ELS test positive theories regarding the law or legal institutions by means of empirical research, which can be quantitative but also qualitative.[208] The benefit of conducting these empirical studies is that they contribute to a better and more accurate description and understanding of the legal system. Empirical evidence can reflect the real-life consequences of changes in the legal system, which enables the evaluation of legal changes to promote legal rules that increase fairness and efficiency.[209]

In the field of consumer law, the use of empirical evidence is also emerging. Consumer law utilizes terminology such as the average consumer which embodies a theoretical description of how such a consumer should act in the market.

[202] Cooter and Ulen (2016), p. 50.

[203] Landes (2003).

[204] Faure and Visscher (2018).

[205] Klick (2011).

[206] Engel (2013).

[207] Eisenberg (2004), p. 1741.

[208] Boyd (2015).

[209] Eisenberg (2011).

Nonetheless, it is unclear how an average consumer would behave in practice when facing, for example, certain manipulative marketing strategies. Empirical evidence can provide insights into consumers' beliefs and attitudes. This allows for a deeper understanding of consumer behavior, which enables the refinement of consumer protection laws to improve their reflection of consumer needs.[210] Another illustration of the use of empirical research in consumer law is the interpretation of contracts via surveys and experiments. Through the collection of consumer responses, a statistical analysis can provide relevant evidence regarding the actual interpretation of a contract.[211]

In conclusion, the empirical turn lies at the foundation of behavioral law and economics. Its impact on behavioral research is unequivocal and it has thereby also opened the door for an empirically-backed analysis of consumer protection policies.

2.3.2 Foundations of Behavioral Consumer Law and Economics

Behavioral law and economics can be defined as: "the application of empirical behavioral evidence to the analysis of laws and legal institutions."[212] It investigates how the law impacts actual human behavior rather than hypothesized behavior (i.e., the *homo economicus* response).[213] It thereby accounts for three bounds that aim to explain the systematic departures from the predictions generated by RCT: *bounded rationality*, *bounded willpower*, and *bounded self-interest*.[214]

Bounded rationality refers to the psychological limits of the individual, or in other words, its limited cognitive abilities.[215] This plays a role in individuals' judgment and decision-making, which explains departures from RCT. Due to limited cognitive abilities, such as bounded computational capabilities and flawed memories, in reality, judgments deviate from the predictions of the standard model and actual decisions are not congruent with the axioms of expected utility theory.[216] A related concept that can be used as an example is *information overload*.[217] When consumers face information that exceeds the cognitive abilities of the individual to process all relevant aspects in terms of quantity or complexity, poorer

[210] Luzak (2015).

[211] Ben-Shahar and Strahilevitz (2017).

[212] Parisi (2013), p. 25.

[213] Jolls et al. (1998), p. 1476.

[214] See Jolls (2007) for an extensive elaboration on these three bounds and their workings in various areas of law.

[215] Simon (1955), p. 101.

[216] Jolls et al. (1998), p. 1477.

[217] Jacoby et al. (1974); Eisenberg (1986).

decision-making takes place.[218] A potential consequence of information overload is *decision inertia*, which means that individuals fail to take a decision, leading to non-optimal consequences.[219] An alternative form of decision inertia takes place when individuals repeat previous choices and fail to make new choices, leading to the same outcomes.[220] It is argued, however, that consumers will switch from optimizing to *satisficing* the information.[221] Satisficing means that consumers reduce their set of options by identifying the relevant product characteristics and subsequently screening whether the product complies with the minimum acceptable levels of quality. The consumers are not preoccupied with the other options and accept the "good enough" option. They usually fail to choose the best options when faced with various alternatives for which the costs of acquiring information preclude a full inspection of all information. Alternatively, this can happen when it is too costly to process all relevant information.[222] Satisficing will help the consumer with making a final choice from an unexhaustive search of the options.

Bounded willpower refers to the phenomenon that individuals take actions that promote short-term instead of long-term benefits (e.g., putting off going to the gym). This becomes pivotal when consumers face intertemporal decision-making (e.g., applying for a credit card or not).[223]

Bounded self-interest alludes to the tendency of individuals to not solely care about their own interests but opt for a less self-benefitting option to also take other parties' interests into account (e.g., giving to charity).[224] Bounded self-interest plays a primary role in cases in which consumers care about fairness (e.g., regarding a price as unfair because of price differentiation).

The behavioral law and economics approach does not disregard the economic theories that have been presented by traditional (law and) economics scholars. On the contrary, economic theories provide the framework for behavioral analysis, which is subsequently modified with insights from behavioral science. The importance of this distinction lies in the fact that behavioral law and economics has not yet presented an overarching theory, such as the RCT that is utilized by traditional economists. The degree to which behavioral analysis can serve as the basis for normative policy proposals is disputed since it does not provide an alternative general model of human behavior that is apt to generate testable predictions.[225] The behavioral analysis focuses on the explanation of certain systematic deviations of individuals' behavior from the pattern that has been predicted by conventional economic

[218] Keller and Staelin (1987); Bergstrom and Stoll (1990).

[219] Power et al. (2013).

[220] Jung et al. (2019).

[221] Simon (1956).

[222] Grether et al. (1986). It is worth noting that, in this case, the consumer remains rationally ignorant rather than succumbing to bias.

[223] Jolls et al. (1998), pp. 1479–1480.

[224] Jolls et al. (1998), pp. 1479–1480.

[225] Arlen (1998), p. 1777.

theory. The fact that behavioral analysis does not provide an alternative general theory of behavior does not detract from its value in analyzing discrete legal problems.[226] The lack of an overarching theory is not restrictive for policymaking provided that the relevant decision-making capabilities of the actors in the specific setting are considered.[227]

It is argued that it is more valuable for policymakers to have situation-specific behavioral analyses that can explain individuals' behavior and the effects of changes in legal instruments than a universal theory that lacks sophistication and realism.[228] In practice, individuals often fail to maximize their welfare and err in deciding matters of importance.[229] Behavioral law and economics can provide a deeper understanding of human behavior. In this way, the behavioral approach can contribute to the improvement of law and economic analyses on the effects of legal rules.[230]

The behavioral law and economics methodology is increasingly utilized in various fields of policymaking, among which consumer policy.[231] The insights from behavioral economics are already well-established in consumer research and policymaking.[232] To understand consumer behavior, define consumer problems and their source, and develop effective policy implementation, behavioral insights are particularly useful. As a result of empirical analyses, such as surveys and experiments, consumer behavior and decision-making can be examined and further understood.[233] Moreover, consumer law is centered around the individual, which makes insights from cognitive psychology directly relevant. Consumer law is also inherently paternalistic, which means that it tries to improve consumer decision-making in such a way that consumer welfare is enhanced.[234] In addition, behaviorally-informed consumer policymaking has the potential to provide more target group-specific and problem-tailored solutions.[235] Accordingly, behavioral insights are seen as valuable for the development of effective and efficient behaviorally-informed consumer policy.[236]

All in all, the application of behavioral insights to consumer law issues has marked the emergence of so-called *behavioral consumer law and economics*.

---

[226] Kelman (1998), p. 1586.

[227] Korobkin and Ulen (2000), p. 1058.

[228] Korobkin and Ulen (2000), p. 1073.

[229] Epstein (2006).

[230] Korobkin and Ulen (2000).

[231] Faure and Luth (2011).

[232] Reisch and Zhao (2017), p. 190.

[233] OECD (2017a, b).

[234] Helleringer and Sibony (2017), p. 610.

[235] Reisch and Thøgersen (2017).

[236] Faure and Luth (2011).

2.3.3 *Behavioral Biases and Heuristics*

The three bounds that aim to explain the systematic departures from the predictions generated by RCT cover a wide variety of cognitive biases and heuristics that constitute the behavioral framework. In the behavioral law and economics literature, a myriad of biases and heuristics have been described and applied to legal problems.

In behavioral science, the term *bias* refers to *cognitive biases*, which are defined as "a range of observer effects that cause a systematic error in an agent's assessment of contextual information."[237] A *heuristic*, on the other hand, is a mental shortcut or rule of thumb that individuals employ in their decision-making process.[238] It is based on *attribute substitution* whereby individuals substitute a complex problem with a simpler attribute of the problem to come to a judgment.[239] In other words, a difficult problem is substituted by a simpler one through the elimination of certain factors of the problem that complicate decision-making.

In this section, the biases and heuristics that are most relevant to consumer decision-making will be discussed. The relevance is determined based on the prevalence of the biases and heuristics in behavioral consumer law and economics literature. A survey of the existing literature results in the identification of 14 relevant biases and heuristics. There are, however, more biases that are relevant to consumer-decision making that have been identified and discussed in behavioral science, psychology, and marketing.[240] Nonetheless, most of these biases are scarcely mentioned in consumer law and economics literature. For the scope of this research, a selection is inevitable. For this reason, this list is by no means exhaustive, yet it aims to provide a framework of behavioral insights that will be relevant in later chapters.

2.3.3.1 Self-Serving Bias

The self-serving bias indicates a tendency of individuals to interpret information in a way that fits their self-interests.[241] A corollary of this is the *above-average effect*, whereby individuals regard themselves as being better than average. This *overconfidence* seems to be misplaced in practice.[242]

[237] Parisi (2013), p. 49.

[238] Jolls (2007).

[239] Kahneman and Frederick (2004), pp. 415–416.

[240] See Kamins (2019) for a full list of biases that have been acknowledged in marketing and behavioral science. In addition to the cognitive biases that are being discussed, Kamins presents an overview of social and memory biases that impact consumers-decision making.

[241] Babcock and Loewenstein (1997).

[242] Svenson (1981).

2.3.3.2 Confirmation Bias

Confirmation bias is closely related to self-serving bias in the sense that individuals tend to seek and interpret information in a way that conforms with their prior beliefs.[243] Individuals are, therefore, inclined to relate positive outcomes to their internal skillset and negative outcomes to external forces.[244]

Connected to the confirmation bias is the *cognitive dissonance theory*. According to this theory, individuals strive for internal consistency, which implies that when individuals face inconsistencies, they will try to make them consistent to reduce the feeling of discomfort, even though this amounts to distorted processing of information.[245] Individuals' selective perception of information is congruent with cognitive dissonance. People are eager to dismiss information that is inconsistent with their prior beliefs to remedy emotional distress.[246] When applied to consumer markets, it becomes clear why certain consumer behavior patterns are difficult to break. If consumers are biased toward a certain prior choice, conflicting evidence that might indicate that a switch in brand or product is beneficial could be neglected.

2.3.3.3 Availability Heuristic

The available heuristic is a mental shortcut that individuals employ that helps to estimate the likelihood of, for example, an event by the ease with which an example comes to mind.[247] If an event can be recalled quickly, it must then mean that it is more prominent than alternatives that are less easily recalled.

Related to this heuristic is the *availability cascade* which can be described as the more often a perception is expressed in public discourse, thereby increasing its availability, the higher the likelihood that individuals accept its credibility.[248] The effectiveness of repeating certain messages can be explained by the *mere exposure effect*. The more often individuals are exposed to a certain stimulus, the higher the likelihood that their attitude will change more favorably toward the stimulus.[249] This process occurs on a subliminal level and appears to be effective in manipulating behavior.[250]

---

[243] Nickerson (1998).

[244] Kamins (2019).

[245] Festinger (1957); Festinger (1962).

[246] Kamins (2019).

[247] Tversky and Kahneman (1973), p. 208.

[248] Kuran and Sunstein (1999).

[249] Zajonc (1968), p. 1.

[250] Zajonc (2001).

2.3.3.4 Hindsight Bias

The hindsight bias represents a behavior pattern in which individuals attach exceedingly high probabilities to certain events after they have in fact occurred.[251] In other words, the predictability of the occurrence of an event changes based on the moment when the prediction is made (before or after the event). An adjacent aspect of this is that individuals also tend to have a false memory of their prediction about the likelihood of a certain event.

In the context of terms and conditions, hindsight bias plays a significant role. Before the conclusion of the contract, many contingencies that have been mentioned in the boilerplate seem unlikely to occur. Accordingly, minimal attention is given to the standard form. Nonetheless, after a certain risk has materialized, parties tend to overestimate the probability of certain contingencies in the contract, which also makes them put greater weight on certain terms of the contract after its conclusion than they would have before concluding the contract.

2.3.3.5 Herd Behavior Bias

An alternative term for the term herd behavior is the *bandwagon effect*. It refers to the tendency of individuals to follow trends and adapt their beliefs to the belief system that is adhered to by the majority of people.[252] In essence, consumers let the *wisdom of crowds* influence their decision-making process.[253] A practical example of this is the inclination of consumers to buy products from the market leader. Since most people buy from the market leader, a perception of superior quality compared to the competitors is created.[254]

2.3.3.6 Overoptimism Bias

Individuals tend to believe that they are less likely to be exposed to bad outcomes than others. They miscalculate the probability that a bad risk will materialize since they believe that the probability that the event will happen to others is higher.[255] In combination with the *saliency* of certain effects, risk can be substantially underestimated.[256] To put this in a consumer context, consumers tend to underestimate their future use of credit cards since they miscalculate the probability that certain events will occur that require borrowing. This underestimation of borrowing has opened

[251] Fischhoff (1975).

[252] Kamins (2019).

[253] Surowiecki (2005).

[254] Kamins et al. (2003).

[255] Weinstein (1980).

[256] Jolls et al. (1998), p. 1542.

the door for credit card companies to exploit consumer misperceptions.[257] Another example of overoptimism bias concerns gym memberships. Due to the overoptimism of individuals regarding their future self-discipline to attend the gym, the value of a membership is overestimated in comparison with per-visit gym fees. As a result, individuals are overpaying for a gym membership that they eventually underutilize.[258]

2.3.3.7 Loss Aversion Bias

Loss aversion is an integral part of *prospect theory,* and it indicates the tendency of individuals to weigh losses more heavily than gains in the evaluation of prospects and trades.[259] If individuals have to choose between a fixed certain gain or a higher gain with a probability of losing it, due to their risk aversion, they tend to choose the safe option, albeit the expected value is the same. Conversely, when individuals face a fixed small loss or a probabilistic loss (larger loss or no loss at all), individuals tend to choose the riskier option.[260] In sum, individuals put greater weight on the prevention of losses than on the acquirement of gains. A corollary of the loss aversion bias is the *endowment effect*. This effect refers to the assigned increase in value that individuals give to a good when it becomes part of their endowment.[261] This results in the reluctance of individuals to give up their entitlement although they would not have purchased the entitlement originally.[262] This creates a gap between individuals' *willingness to accept* (WTA) and their *willingness to pay* (WTP). In this sense, the endowment effect can reinforce the loss aversion bias.

2.3.3.8 Status Quo Bias

The status quo bias touches upon the predisposition of individuals to maintain the current situation as it is rather than changing it. In decision-making, this means that individuals stick to their current or previous decision rather than making a new decision. Individuals prefer to not take action rather than pursue a specific course of action. *Status quo framing*, in which one alternative is placed as the status quo choice and the other choices as alternatives to it, can have significant and predictable effects on individuals' decision-making.[263] An alternative manifestation of the

---

[257] Bar-Gill (2004).

[258] DellaVigna and Malmendier (2006); Grubb (2015).

[259] Kahneman and Tversky (1979).

[260] Cooter and Ulen (2016), p. 395.

[261] Kahneman et al. (1990).

[262] Thaler (1980), pp. 43–47.

[263] Samuelson and Zeckhauser (1988).

status quo bias is the *omission bias*. This bias explains the tendency of individuals to prefer omissions over acts of commission.[264]

The prevalence of the status quo and omission bias is evident in contract law. Due to these biases, the transaction costs of changing a course of action are increased. This explains the reluctance to change contract terms even though this could be welfare increasing. For this reason, the setting of default rules in contract law is paramount for efficiency since it is likely that parties will not depart from the default as a result of the status quo and omission biases.[265]

2.3.3.9 Anchoring Bias

The anchoring bias specifies that in decision-making individuals have an internal reference point and by adjusting it they arrive at the final answer. This initial point can be altered by the framing of the decision problem or anticipatory partial calculations.[266] The consequence of this anchoring is that due to insufficient adjustment, decision-making is biased, and it leads to inaccurate probability estimations. Consumers can be effectively influenced through the use of numerical anchors. Consumers' willingness to pay could, for instance, be affected by exposure to a random number.[267] The rationale is that because of value uncertainty, consumers become more susceptible to external influences.[268] This is where the *framing effect* comes into play. The framing effect can be defined as "the ability of an individual to draw different conclusions from identical information depending upon how it is presented or who presents it."[269] Hence, a practical example of the framing effect in relation to the anchoring bias is the practice of restaurants putting an excessively high-priced product on the menu which will make the other products on the menu look lower-priced. This will induce consumers to believe that the overall prices of the restaurant are reasonable.[270]

2.3.3.10 Hyperbolic Discounting

Hyperbolic discounting demonstrates that individuals' impatience for rewards declines as the time horizon becomes longer. In other words, there is a declining *discount rate* that varies in intensity along with the proximity to the present. This implies that individuals' preferences are dynamically inconsistent, which means

---

[264] Ritov and Baron (1990).

[265] Korobkin (1997).

[266] Tversky and Kahneman (1974).

[267] Simonson and Drolet (2004).

[268] Simonson and Drolet (2004), p. 688.

[269] Kamins (2019).

[270] Pearlman (2018).

that the preferences of individuals do not remain stable over time.[271] This bias contrasts with the *exponential discount method* that is preferably utilized by conventional economists.[272]

Empirical research demonstrates that individuals' valuations differ systematically from the predictions made by the exponential discounting model.[273] The behavioral insight of hyperbolic discounting has provided a further explanation of how individuals make intertemporal choices and their corresponding valuation of the future and the present. This bias can, therefore, elucidate why consumers make decisions that are beneficial in the short term, but that are detrimental in the future. In the consumer credit market, it has been found that hyperbolic discounting can make consumers borrow more than the amount that would be preferable regarding their long-term interests. As a result, consumers end up with substantial amounts of debt that, *inter alia,* lead to increasing default rates.[274]

2.3.3.11 Present Bias

The tendencies to value the present or the nearer moment in the future more than the later future are called *present-biased tendencies*. The present bias indicates that individuals tend to postpone actions that have immediate costs but preproperate actions that involve immediate rewards.[275] An alternative term that is used to describe the present bias is *myopia*.[276] In essence, it is directly linked to hyperbolic discounting. It helps to explain the desire of individuals for immediate rather than *delayed gratification*.

2.3.3.12 Sunk Cost Fallacy

According to traditional economic theory, *sunk costs* should not affect a rational actor's decision on the price or quantity of a certain good or service.[277] Sunk costs are costs that have been incurred in the past and are not recoverable. They should, therefore, not impact future decisions.[278] Nonetheless, behavioral economics literature has provided substantial evidence demonstrating that sunk costs do influence

[271] Laibson (1997).

[272] Frederick et al. (2002).

[273] See, for example, Ainslie (1992); Loewenstein and Prelec (1992); Dasgupta and Maskin (2005).

[274] Meier and Sprenger (2007).

[275] Phelps and Pollak (1968).

[276] Strotz (1955).

[277] Posner (2014).

[278] McAfee et al. (2010).

economic decisions.[279] A ramification of the sunk cost fallacy is the proclivity of individuals to take the price they paid for a certain good as the benchmark for the value of the good and determine based on this reference point the price for which the individual is willing to sell the good.[280] This can lead to economic decisions that according to RCT would be characterized as irrational. By not taking sunk costs into account, the rational choice model leads to inaccurate predictions of consumer decision-making. An experiment on *bundling* demonstrates this divergence. Comparing an unbundled and a bundled transaction, which according to RCT should have no effect on consumers, exemplified that the *sunk cost fallacy* does impact consumer decision-making. Consumers found it significantly easier to identify and understand the cost of an individual product when it was presented in an unbundled transaction than within a bundled transaction. Gourville and Soman (2002) state: "The one-to-one relationship between price and benefits in an unbundled transaction makes the cost of that item obvious, creating a strong sunk-cost effect and a high likelihood of consumption."[281]

2.3.3.13 Negativity Bias

Individuals tend to remember and give greater weight to events in the past that created negative emotions in comparison with events that created positive emotions. This proclivity to be more sensitive toward negative information is called negativity bias.[282] Consumers are, therefore, more inclined to let their overall satisfaction and repurchase intention be influenced by negative attributes than positive attributes.[283] A negative reputation can, thus, significantly impact purchasing behavior.[284]

2.3.3.14 The Affect Heuristic

The affect heuristic plays an important role in the field of advertising. This mental shortcut describes a situation in which individuals consult their affective feelings (i.e., emotions) to make a judgment or decision.[285] These effective responses arise quickly and automatically. They aid the individual in the formation of an opinion regarding a certain product or service based on the emotions it invokes and if these are coded as positive or negative. Through advertising, brands can create *affect-*

[279] See Jolls et al. (1998) for a review of the evidence that emphasizes the relevance of sunk costs in decision-making.

[280] Parisi (2013), p. 290.

[281] Gourville and Soman (2002), p. 94.

[282] Ito et al. (1998).

[283] Mittal et al. (1998).

[284] Standifird (2001).

[285] Slovic et al. (2002); Slovic et al. (2007).

laden stimuli that can influence consumer decision-making.[286] More specifically, if brands can evoke positive emotional associations with the product, the likelihood that consumers will feel connected to the brand and their willingness to buy can be significantly increased. In this way, brands that become consumer favorites can dominate the market and inhibit the rational evaluation of product attributes.[287] In other words, successfully evoking emotions can curtail rational thinking.

Finally, it is paramount to put these biases and heuristics in the context of systematic thinking. This enables the identification of the moment where the bias in human thinking occurs. Kahneman (2011) explains *two-system thinking* as follows:

> System 1 operates automatically and quickly, with little or no effort and no sense of voluntary control. System 2 allocates attention to the effortful mental activities that demand it, including complex computations. The operations of System 2 are often associated with the subjective experience of agency, choice, and concentration.[288]

System 1 thinking can be interpreted as automatic processing, emotional, and subconscious, and system 2 thinking can be described as logical, conscious, and calculating.[289] It is not possible to say that by definition one system of thinking is more biased than another. Nonetheless, as will become clear in later chapters, marketing manipulation strategies, among which the use of dark patterns, are aimed at prompting consumers to rely on system 1 rather than system 2 thinking. This is being done to exploit cognitive biases and stimulate consumers into making choices that are inconsistent with their preferences.[290]

2.3.4 Behavioral Insights in Consumer Policy: The Case for Legal Paternalism

Consumer sovereignty plays a central role in traditional law and economics. For this reason, traditional law and economics scholars are skeptical about *paternalistic interventions*. In contrast, the main driver behind paternalistic intervention has been the behavioral law and economics literature that has demonstrated that cognitive errors justify institutional constraints on individual choice.[291] Behavioral scholars demonstrate that three bounds (i.e., bounded rationality, willpower, and self-interest) detract from the efficient working of consumer sovereignty in the market. As a result of the cognitive biases, individuals are unable to maximize their *subjective expected utility* (SEU), which means that social welfare is not maximized. This

[286] Plassmann et al. (2006).

[287] Plassmann et al. (2006).

[288] Kahneman (2011), pp. 19–31.

[289] Kamins (2019).

[290] Luguri and Strahilevitz (2021), p. 44.

[291] Rachlinski (2002), p. 1166.

opens the door for potentially paternalistic interventions.[292] According to Thaler and Sunstein (2009), "a policy is "paternalistic" if it tries to influence choices in a way that will make choosers better off, *as judged by themselves*."[293]

Nonetheless, it can be argued that legislators who will prepare and enforce the intervention will also suffer from the same biases,[294] and due to *consumer heterogeneity*, effective targeting of the regulation will be hampered. In addition, from a *public choice* perspective, it is debatable whether the legislator's purpose will in fact be the maximization of welfare or whether alternative interests put forward by political groups will prevail.[295] Accordingly, *anti-antipaternalism* is advocated, which means that no affirmative case for paternalism is made, but anti-paternalism is not supported either.[296]

Legal paternalism can be found in various areas of law, such as inalienable rights, safety regulation, and the unconscionability doctrine in contracts. A relevant categorization of paternalism refers to the distinction between soft/light and strong/heavy-handed paternalism.[297] *Soft paternalism* is a light intervention that nudges individuals to what are perceived as more beneficial outcomes while "minimizing coercion, maintaining individual autonomy, and maximizing choice to the greatest extent possible."[298] *Strong paternalism* is more interventionistic since its goal is to ensure that individuals' choices that lead to adverse effects are altered or prevented as a whole.[299] In other words, in the former form consumers are informed about their options, whereas in the latter form, their preferences are changed or thwarted.

The notion of interfering with consumer sovereignty through paternalistic intervention is severely criticized since it dismisses the foundations of *free choice*.[300] For this reason, the preferences lie with soft paternalism because it warrants the autonomy of the consumer to a large extent. Soft paternalistic interventions can aid consumers in their decision-making process but leave their sovereignty intact. Examples of soft paternalistic interventions are mandated disclosure duties, default rules, and cooling-off periods.[301]

Three main forms of soft paternalism can be identified in the existing literature: *asymmetric paternalism*, *libertarian paternalism*, and *libertarian welfarism*. Asymmetric paternalism takes place when regulation creates large benefits for individuals who make errors while inflicting minimal harm to those that are fully

---

[292] Korobkin (2009).

[293] Thaler and Sunstein (2008), p. 5.

[294] Glaeser (2006).

[295] Becher and Bar-Gill (2012), p. 24.

[296] Sunstein (1997), p. 1178.

[297] Loewenstein and Haisley (2007).

[298] Loewenstein and Haisley (2007), p. 213.

[299] Van Boom and Ogus (2010), p. 2.

[300] See, for example, Issacharoff (1998); Van den Bergh (2007).

[301] Becher and Bar-Gill (2012), pp. 25–26.

rational.[302] This type of paternalism justifies intervention because the benefits are expected to outweigh the costs. In addition, the *intrusiveness* of the measure is relatively limited since no undue burdens are imposed on individuals that behave rationally.[303] Accordingly, if policies are implemented in compliance with the asymmetric paternalism benchmark, an affirmative case for paternalistic interventions can be made.[304]

Libertarian paternalism is "an approach that preserves freedom of choice but that authorizes both private and public institutions to steer people in directions that will promote their welfare."[305] The emphasis lies on the preservation of freedom of choice. All choice options remain available, which makes the intervention non-intrusive. The difference with asymmetric paternalism is that libertarian paternalism does not restrict itself to asymmetric motivations. That is to say, libertarian paternalistic interventions can be both asymmetric and symmetric.[306]

The libertarian welfarism approach expands the previous two approaches by not solely employing *nudging* "to help individuals maximize their subjective expected utility (SEU), but also to encourage them to produce public goods and otherwise improve overall social welfare, even when doing so is inconsistent with maximizing their utility."[307] The main difference is that paternalistic intervention departs from the individual level. It looks at welfare on a societal level, which justifies interventions that increase overall welfare but do not automatically increase individuals' welfare.

Soft paternalism advocates have proposed three principal intervention strategies: *switching defaults*, *choice architectures*, and the *debiasing of decision-making*. The goal of these interventions is to alter individuals' behavior in a desired and predictable way without limiting the range of options or modifying economic incentives. The so-called *nudging of behavior*.[308]

First, switching defaults refers to the alteration of the status quo option to achieve an alternative outcome. In this way, the decision-making process of the individual is not thwarted, and the freedom of choice is warranted. In essence, the starting point of the decision is changed to arrive at a welfare-increasing outcome.[309] Due to the stickiness of default rules, individuals are not likely to depart from them, which means that more individuals will achieve the welfare-increasing outcome. Accordingly, how the default is set impacts the degree to which social welfare will be optimized.

---

302 Camerer et al. (2003), p. 1212.

303 Camerer et al. (2003), p. 1214.

304 Camerer et al. (2003), p. 1222.

305 Sunstein and Thaler (2003a).

306 Sunstein and Thaler (2003b).

307 Korobkin (2009), p. 1653.

308 Thaler and Sunstein (2008), p. 6.

309 Sunstein (2002).

Second, choice architectures are inextricably related to the concept of *framing*. The way in which choices are presented to individuals impacts their decision-making process significantly. A neutral presentation of a choice is thereby not feasible.[310] The role of a choice architect is to design the context in which individuals make choices.[311] Through the framing of the context, it is possible to nudge behavior in a certain desired direction. A benevolent choice architect has the ability to design a context in such a way that will increase the welfare of the decision-makers.[312]

Third, the debiasing of decision-making consists of nudging individuals to switch from system 1, intuitive thinking, toward system 2, rational thinking. The aim is to take away the effect of the bias or heuristic on the decision-making process.[313] Debiasing through law is at its core a response to the bounded rationality of individuals, which aims to remedy its effects without insulating legal outcomes. An alternative to debiasing is *rebiasing*, whereby the aim is to exchange one bias for another, which will lead to more beneficial outcomes for the individual. The policy-maker can resort to rebiasing rather than debiasing when nudging individuals into rational thinking is more onerous than nudging individuals into the use of other more beneficial biases.[314]

The government decides to implement a paternalistic regulation when it recognizes that consumers face complex choice contexts and will likely make inefficient choices that will make them worse off in terms of welfare.[315] Such an application of legal paternalism that could be justified in consumer law is the remedying of *unintended risks*.[316] These risks are underappreciated by consumers which leads to sub-optimal precaution-taking behavior by this group. For example, despite the warnings on the packaging regarding the use of sunlamps, consumers may fail to anticipate that the warm glow of the light might induce sleep, which could lead to unanticipated burns.[317] If the market does not provide sufficient protection against these unintended risks, a case for welfare-enhancing regulation could be made. It becomes essential to verify if the costs of remedying the risk through additional regulations are lower than the costs of risk materialization. To answer this question, empirical evidence is needed according to behavioral law and economics scholars. In this way, justifiable cases for legal paternalistic interventions can be made.[318]

Nevertheless, two main objections can be raised against this type of paternalistic intervention. First, it interferes with consumers' autonomy to make free choices and

[310] Thaler and Sunstein (2008), p. 3.

[311] Thaler et al. (2013).

[312] For an elaboration these principles see Thaler and Sunstein (2008), chapter 5.

[313] Jolls and Sunstein (2006).

[314] Amir and Lobel (2008).

[315] Burrows (1995), p. 495.

[316] Jolls et al. (1998), p. 1544.

[317] Jolls et al. (1998), p. 1544.

[318] Jolls et al. (1998), p. 1545.

pursue their own preferences.[319] Second, it is debatable to what extent the government is better equipped to determine what is in the consumers' best interests than the consumers themselves. It is argued that freedom of choice is the most reliable manner to increase consumer welfare.[320]

In essence, a trade-off is posited between *consumer autonomy* and *consumer well-being*. Only in cases in which it can be argued that the benefits of increasing consumer well-being outweigh the costs of losing consumer autonomy, legal paternalistic intervention is justified. Assessing this trade-off from a law and economics perspective allows for a cost-benefit analysis that can guide consumer policymakers in their decision-making process.[321]

2.3.5 Law and Economics Approaches to Consumer Law: An Overview

Law and economics is a versatile methodology to study the inefficiencies in consumer markets and investigate the potential effects of regulatory intervention on consumer welfare. The degree to which intervention is desirable depends on the perspective taken. The discussion of the traditional and behavioral approach reveals that consumer policy recommendations can vary, or even diametrically oppose each other, depending on the approach that is being adopted.

The traditional law and economics approach, based on neoclassical economics, with its strong grounding in RCT and complemented with insights from information economics provides the foundation of the economic analysis of consumer law. The economic insights allow for the identification of the effects of legal incentives on consumer behavior and the examination of the welfare effects of legal policy instruments. The economically-informed analysis offers a broader perspective on the effects of consumer policies than a purely legal perspective would provide. Thanks to the traditional law and economics approach, a rationale can be provided for more careful consideration of government intervention in consumer markets. Intervening in the market might lead to adverse economic effects that can be overlooked by a narrow focus on merely enhancing the degree of consumer protection.

Moreover, the traditional law and economics approach considers the presence of a market failure as the starting point for the analysis of potential intervention in the market.[322] Accordingly, if the analysis demonstrates that there is no market failure, intervention is discouraged, which prevents overregulation.

---

319 Van Aaken (2016).

320 Tokeley (2013).

321 Tokeley (2013) provides a detailed description of a multifactored approach to determine the desirability of paternalistic intervention.

322 Van den Bergh (2007).

Under the traditional approach, the market failure of information asymmetries, which leads to imperfectly-informed consumers, is regarded as the sound economic justification for consumer protection policy. This is based on insights from information economics.[323] If there are asymmetric information structures that private mechanisms (e.g., signaling or information intermediaries) cannot remedy, intervention could be warranted.[324] In practice, this leads to the imposition of mandated disclosure duties on the part of the seller that aims to make information available to the consumer, which enables the optimal collection of information.[325]

Nonetheless, the emergence of behavioral research, supported by empirical evidence, has demonstrated that in a vast number of cases the assumptions on which RCT is based do not hold in practice.[326] These deviations from the predictions of the rational choice model cannot solely be explained by the lack of information. Behavioral research has revealed that "people's judgements and decisions are often subject to systematic biases and heuristics and are strongly dependent on the context of the decision."[327] The behavioral law and economics approach shows that in certain cases, biases might justify intervention in consumer markets as opposed to the traditional approach.

Consequently, it can be the case that the traditional analysis of consumer law leads to different policy recommendations compared to the behavioral approach.[328] Where the behavioral approach does justify some type of regulation in consumer markets, the traditional approach is wary of the adverse effects of regulation. Nonetheless, the two approaches are not mutually exclusive, instead, they complement each other in the pursuit of effective consumer policymaking.[329]

It can be argued that, to a certain extent, a transition to behaviorally-informed policymaking is taking place.[330] Governments are increasingly adopting behavioral insights[331] with the conviction that through behaviorally-informed consumer policies, more effective, more efficient, and less intrusive tools can be developed to protect consumers.[332] Nevertheless, despite the developments in behaviorally-informed consumer policy, the lion's share of consumer protection laws is still based on the image of the *sovereign consumer*, or, in other words, the rational

[323] Shapiro (1983).

[324] Stiglitz (2000).

[325] Rischkowsky and Döring (2008), p. 290.

[326] Kahneman et al. (1991); Rabin (1998); Kahneman (2003); Camerer and Loewenstein (2004); Sunstein (2011).

[327] Reisch and Zhao (2017), p. 190.

[328] Bar-Gill and Epstein (2007).

[329] Chetty (2015) argues that "incorporating behavioral features to the extent they help answer core economic questions may be more productive than viewing behavioral economics as a separate subfield that challenges the assumptions of neoclassical models."

[330] Reisch and Zhao (2017).

[331] Whitehead et al. (2014); Sunstein (2016b).

[332] Reisch and Thøgersen (2017).

consumer, that can be empowered through the provision of information.[333] This explains why information duties are still the major policy tools to protect consumers.[334] The effectiveness of these information tools is increasingly contested and the call for more behaviorally-informed consumer policies is getting stronger.[335]

2.4 A New Challenge for Consumer Law and Economics

The starting point of the analysis of potential market intervention should be the presence of a market failure.[336] The existing law and economics approaches offer a comprehensive methodology to analyze market failures in consumer markets. The traditional law and economics approach has scrutinized the well-established market failures, and the behavioral approach has pinpointed the issues that consumers are facing in their decision-making process by identifying relevant consumer biases and heuristics. Nevertheless, the question remains whether the existing framework encompasses all forms of market failures that consumers can encounter in consumer markets.

A field that is known for its innovativeness in finding new ways to research consumer markets and come up with novel strategies to create and extract value is *marketing*.[337] In essence, marketing consists of selling and advertising products and services to customers. Nonetheless, this definition of marketing can be seen as too narrow. Marketing focuses on satisfying consumer needs, whereby selling and advertising are only part of a larger *marketing mix*, which is "the set of tactical marketing tools – product, price, place, and promotion – that the firm blends to produce the response it wants in the target market."[338] The marketing mix aims to "engage customers, satisfy customer needs, and build customer relationships."[339] Kotler and Armstrong (2016) provide a more comprehensive definition of marketing, which describes more accurately the goal of marketing in a modern sense, namely: "The process by which companies create value for customers and build strong customer relationships in order to capture value from customers in return."[340] This process of creating and capturing customer value is also called the *marketing process*, which consists of five steps that together make up the framework of marketing[341]: (1)

[333] See Weber (2020a); Weber (2020b) for an elaboration on the different consumer models in consumer law and their relationship to the information paradigm.

[334] Oehler and Wendt (2017).

[335] Oehler and Wendt (2017); Reisch and Thøgersen (2017); Reisch and Zhao (2017).

[336] Van den Bergh (2007).

[337] See, for instance, Hagen et al. (2020).

[338] Kotler and Armstrong (2016), p. 78.

[339] Kotler and Armstrong (2016), p. 29.

[340] Kotler and Armstrong (2016), p. 29.

[341] Kotler and Armstrong (2016), pp. 30–31.

Understand the marketplace and the customers' needs and wants. (2) Design a customer value-driven marketing strategy. (3) Construct an integrated marketing program that delivers superior value. (4) Build profitable relationships and create customer delight. (5) Capture value from customers to create profits and customer equity. This framework of marketing demonstrates that marketing is much broader than the practices of pricing, branding, selling, and advertising.

Consumers are constantly confronted with marketing tactics in their daily lives. These include the display of different brands in supermarkets, advertisements on television, and the in-store advice of salespeople. However, these also include the provision of loyalty cards that offer personalized benefits, the versioning of products, and differentiated pricing schemes. The impact of marketing on consumer markets should, therefore, not be underestimated.

The insights from behavioral science have enriched the toolbox of marketers.[342] The emergence of data-driven and AI-based technologies have further expanded this toolbox.[343] The threat of employing these technologies to the detriment of the consumer, has, therefore, sparked the discussion about manipulation in consumer markets.

Hanson and Kysar (1999) first introduced the concept of *market manipulation* to indicate "that market outcomes can be influenced, if not determined, by the ability of one actor to control the format of the information, the framing and presentation of choices, and, more generally, the setting within which market transactions occur."[344] Essentially, they described a new market failure by highlighting the influenceability of consumers, which can be targeted by other parties (such as manufacturers and marketers) that will not necessarily lead to an increase in social welfare. They assert: "As a result, the problem of market manipulation seems inescapable in an unregulated consumer product market."[345] Therefore, they argue that preventing substantial harm to consumers requires legal corrections that are inspired by behavioral insights.

Calo (2014) updated the framework of market manipulation by accounting for the developments in technology, which offered companies the possibility to not only exploit general cognitive limitations but also take advantage of consumer frailty at an individual level.[346] Accordingly, taking this into consideration, he proposed a new theory of market manipulation, which he coined *digital market manipulation*. Cognizant of the developments in marketing, Calo (2014) attributed much of the digital market manipulation to data-driven technologies in general.

Kamins (2018) identified that a large part of this digital market manipulation was the result of deliberately designed marketing strategies.[347] He presented an exten-

[342] Walters (2015).

[343] Thaichon and Quach (2022).

[344] Hanson and Kysar (1999), p. 630.

[345] Hanson and Kysar (1999), p. 747.

[346] Calo (2014), p. 995.

[347] Kamins (2019).

sive account of the various methods that are used by marketers to prey on consumers' cognitive, social, and memory-based biases to influence their behavior. Kamins (2018) described this as *marketing manipulation,* thereby referring to the prominent role of marketers as the architects of market manipulation. Kamins' (2018) primary objective was to provide consumers with a survival guide to protect themselves from harmful marketing practices in everyday life. However, as a consequence of the emphasis on the role of self-help against marketing ploys, the harm that marketing manipulation could inflict on consumers faded into the background.

De Geest (2018) affirms that the impact of marketing on markets is significantly larger than one might think.[348] He undertook the first comprehensive study on the relationship between marketing and inequality. De Geest (2018) posits that the rise in inequality since the 1970s can be attributed to advances in marketing. He states that marketers have become better at causing and exploiting market distortions in legal ways and the legal system has not responded adequately.

The goal of this study is to build further on the work of the aforementioned scholars and take on a new challenge that is posed to the consumer law framework and which has become possible due to the developments in AI, namely *personalized marketing.* Personalized marketing touches upon the issues identified by previous scholars, however, it distinguishes itself by its sophistication. The developments in AI have opened the way for marketing strategies to approximate perfect personalization, which means that unseen levels of granularity and sensitivity are reached, elevating the effectiveness of marketing to unprecedented levels.[349] This poses a wide array of challenges to the existing consumer law framework, for which further research is needed.[350] The commonality of personalized marketing techniques is that they have the capacity to exploit consumers by capitalizing on the presence of a *marketing-induced market failure.*[351] In the following section, the concept of a marketing-induced market failure will be further explored.

2.4.1 Marketing-Induced Market Failure

A marketing-induced market failure is *a market failure that has been created by virtue of marketing techniques that are aimed at the extraction of rents, the exploitation of biases and vulnerabilities, and/or the shaping of preferences to the detriment of consumers' autonomy, equity, and welfare.*[352]

[348] De Geest (2018).

[349] Galli (2020), p. 59.

[350] Helberger et al. (2021).

[351] The potential to exploit will be demonstrated in Chaps. 3–5.

[352] The concept of rents will be further discussed in Sect. 2.4.3.

A marketing-induced market failure differentiates itself from the market failure of market manipulation as identified by Hanson and Kysar (1999)[353] or digital market manipulation as defined by Calo (2014).[354] The distinctive character of market-induced market failures is that they fit into the existing market failure framework in law and economics,[355] yet the notion emphasizes that marketing techniques are capable of creating several market failures at the same time. Traditionally, information asymmetry would be seen as the main source of market failure in consumer markets.[356] Nevertheless, the ability of personalized marketing to translate into marketing manipulation challenges this traditional paradigm in consumer law and economics. It is asserted that personalized marketing techniques can result in situations, in which information asymmetry, unequal bargaining power, and prohibitive transaction costs are present at the same time. The materialization of these marketing-induced market failures will be further developed in Chaps. 3–5.

Personalization takes place based on vast amounts of personal (i.e., who users are) and behavioral data (i.e., what users are doing) which enables the profiling of consumers. Accordingly, the potential weaknesses of consumers can be identified on an individual basis, thus enabling businesses to take advantage of consumers' vulnerabilities. Everybody could potentially become a target susceptible to exploitation in a specific online environment architected by data-driven technologies. This refers to the concept of *digital vulnerability*.[357] To further understand this concept, it is necessary to distinguish two states of vulnerability*: dispositional* and *occurrent vulnerability*.[358] Dispositional vulnerabilities are "vulnerabilities that have not yet manifested themselves but that could do so given the underlying circumstances".[359] In other words, potential vulnerabilities. Occurrent vulnerabilities are those dispositional vulnerabilities that manifest themselves. The distinction is important because even though dispositional vulnerabilities seem less imminent, they constitute the specific state of vulnerability that is endangered by data-driven technologies. Not all consumers will by definition become vulnerable, and exploitation thereof is not guaranteed, however, "the mere fact that the digital service holds persuasion profiles of its customers renders those customers *dispositionally* vulnerable to, for instance, manipulation."[360]

AI-driven technologies can continuously learn more about consumers, identify their vulnerabilities, measure their responses, and exploit them accordingly.[361] It has

---

[353] Hanson and Kysar (1999), p. 630.

[354] Calo (2014).

[355] Parisi (2013), p. 178 describes asymmetric information, monopoly and imperfect competition, public goods, and externalities as the main sources of market failures.

[356] Van den Bergh (2007).

[357] Helberger et al. (2022).

[358] There are also three other sources of vulnerability: inherent, situational, and pathogenic. For an extensive elaboration on the concept of vulnerability see Mackenzie et al. (2014).

[359] Helberger et al. (2022), p. 185.

[360] Helberger et al. (2022), p. 185.

[361] Helberger et al. (2022), p. 187.

been found that with the currently available tools, the content of persuasive appeals can be matched to individuals' psychological characteristics causing a significant alteration in online behavior.[362] It has become technically possible to successfully micro-target individuals (i.e., "the ability to reach a specific individual or individuals without their explicit knowledge that they are the only ones an ad reaches"[363]), test individual users' susceptibility to different persuasive strategies,[364] and thereby effectively manipulate individuals on a large scale.[365]

The implication of this is that the traditional concepts of average and vulnerable consumers are not tenable anymore in the digital age.[366] Rather than labeling consumers vulnerable or average based on a pre-determined set of characteristics, vulnerability should be determined in light of the commercial practices in digital environments that can render all consumers potentially vulnerable.[367]

According to Galli (2022), all states of vulnerability come together in the deepest layer of vulnerability in the digital economy, namely the architectural layer.[368] The architectural characteristics of AI technologies give companies access to copious amounts of consumer data that facilitate the creation of a digital environment that is designed to extract value, exploit biases and vulnerabilities, and steer consumption patterns. In essence, the digital market architecture renders the consumer vulnerable. As Galli (2022) describes:

> In this layer, vulnerability affects all consumers, because it does not concern the experience of the individual (as is the case of the privacy layer) but the objective way of being of algorithmic marketing: all consumers, regardless of their status of situation, ultimately find themselves in an unbalanced relationship with traders – an imbalance which depends on the very essence through which algorithmic technologies mediate their transactions.[369]

Personalized marketing enables the simultaneous exploitation of the three market failures in consumer law, namely information asymmetries, transaction costs, and unequal bargaining power.[370] The firm that implements personalization techniques possesses vast amounts of personal and behavioral data from the consumer and has, therefore, a significant informational advantage. Through personalization, it becomes possible to capitalize on the information asymmetry and target the consumer more effectively to extract value. The informational advantage further strengthens the bargaining power of the seller vis-à-vis the buyer.

Moreover, if the information that the consumer receives is hyper-individualized then it becomes significantly more difficult to compare offers, thereby essentially

362 Matz et al. (2017).

363 Faizullabhoy and Korolova (2018).

364 Kaptein et al. (2011).

365 Matz et al. (2017); Faizullabhoy and Korolova (2018).

366 See Sect. 2.2.2.

367 Helberger et al. (2022), p. 194.

368 Galli (2022).

369 Galli (2022), p. 204.

370 See Sect. 2.2.3 for an analysis of these market failures in consumer markets.

increasing transaction costs. Finally, in terms of distributional concerns, personalization will likely lead to regressive distributional effects, because the lack of knowledge, sophistication, and resources of consumers can be leveraged by the firm.[371] In other words, it is easier for businesses to exploit the financially vulnerable, less sophisticated, and less informed.

Furthermore, potentially rendering all consumers vulnerable also opens the door for the exploitation of consumers' privacy. *Privacy harm* is particularly difficult to define and there exists a variety of theories, of which the merits are debatable.[372] Nonetheless, Calo (2014) provides a unified theory of privacy harm and summarizes it as follows:

> the consumer is shedding information that, without her knowledge or against her wishes, will be used to charge her as much as possible, to sell her a product or service she does not need or needs less of, or to convince her in a way that she would find objectionable were she aware of the practice.[373]

There exist two types of privacy harm: *subjective* and *objective privacy harm*. Subjective privacy harm relates to the internal dimension, namely an unwanted feeling of being observed. This includes "unwelcome mental states - anxiety, embarrassment, fear - that stem from the belief that one is being watched or monitored."[374] Objective privacy harm is "the unanticipated or coerced use of information concerning a person against that person. These are negative, external actions justified by reference to personal information."[375] Both types depict, respectively, "the anticipation and consequence of a loss of control over personal information."[376]

Based on this theory, it becomes possible to link the practice of personalized marketing to privacy harm. The collection of personal and behavioral data requires mass surveillance of consumers,[377] which causes a sensation of uneasiness and uncertainty, indicating subjective privacy harm. The actual utilization of privacy-sensitive information to extract value relates to objective privacy harm.

Another type of harm that can occur as a result of the digital vulnerability of consumers is *value-based harm*. Value-based harm comprises the threats to fundamental societal values, such as non-discrimination, consumer autonomy, and human dignity.[378] In particular, personalized marketing strategies that covertly influence consumers' decision-making, exploit biases, and try to target vulnerabilities are hard to be reconciled with the concept of consumer autonomy.[379]

---

[371] Calo (2014), p. 1026.

[372] Solove (2002); Citron and Solove (2022).

[373] Calo (2014), p. 1030.

[374] Calo (2011), p. 1131.

[375] Calo (2011), p. 1131.

[376] Calo (2011), p. 1131.

[377] See Zuboff (2019) for an elaborate discussion of the role of mass surveillance in society.

[378] The relevance of considering this type of harm will be further discussed in Sect. 2.4.4.

[379] See Sect. 2.4.4 for an elaboration on the concept of consumer autonomy.

Consequently, personalized marketing in the digital age poses significant challenges to consumer protection laws, which are not solely troublesome from an economic perspective but also from a distributional and societal perspective.[380]

The notion that certain marketing practices have the potential to create market failures that threaten consumer autonomy, equity, and welfare, provides a *prima facie* justification to explore the possibilities for intervention. In Chaps. 3–5, this will be the premise for the investigation of specific personalized marketing techniques and their possible restrictions, whereby the identification of a market failure, and the analysis of the applicable legal framework will be the main focus. To identify a marketing-induced market failure, however, it is of pivotal importance to incorporate marketing as a relevant factor in the economic analysis of consumer protection.

2.4.2 Insights from Marketing Scholarship for Consumer Policymaking

The digital age has provided marketers with a wide variety of new marketing tools to both create and capture value. As Kotler and Armstrong (2016) describe it:

> In this digital age, along with their tried-and-true traditional marketing methods, marketers have a dazzling set of new customer relationship-building tools—from the Internet, smartphones, and tablets to online, mobile, and social media—for engaging customers anytime, anyplace to shape brand conversations, experiences, and community. If marketers do these things well, they will reap the rewards in terms of market share, profits, and customer equity.[381]

Following this line of thought, the digital age provides a multiplicity of opportunities for marketers to improve customer satisfaction and increase customer value. It is argued, however, that this represents a rosy view of marketing. Unjustly so, marketing is depicted as a tool that merely "serves an educational purpose, informing consumers about the availability, features, qualities, and price of products and thereby allowing consumers to make choices that match their preferences".[382] It is contended that this view neglects the *shadow side* of marketing, in which marketing negatively impacts consumers' autonomy, equity, and welfare to the benefit of sellers.

De Geest (2018) provides an alternative theory of marketing that aims to expose this shadow side of marketing. His *new theory of marketing* is based on two pillars. First, to increase profits in competitive markets, the goal of marketers is to make markets less competitive by utilizing sophisticated marketing strategies that "reduce transparency, separate informed from non-informed consumers, make products less

[380] Wagner and Eidenmüller (2019), p. 608.

[381] Kotler and Armstrong (2016), p. 17.

[382] Trzaskowski (2021), p. 74.

comparable, create lock-in effects, create legal forms of cartels, exploit network externalities, exploit the irrationality of human beings, or make markets fail in numerous other ways."[383] Second, marketing techniques that create market failures "must, at their core, be based on *subtle* forms of fraud, abuse of trust, monopolization, corruption, duress, cartelization, undue influence, or contract breach – subtle enough to fall through the cracks of the legal system."[384]

Hence, there are two views on marketing, whereby, on the one hand, it is claimed that marketing improves economic markets and removes market failures, and, on the other hand, it is asserted that it makes markets fail or it helps to exploit existing market failures.[385] Although opposite views exist, in practice, the negatives of marketing are generally acknowledged by marketers while the positives are also seen by legislators, economists, and legal scholars.[386]

From a legal point of view, the role of marketing is salient in the realm of consumer law. The EU *acquis* provides various definitions of marketing practices, but the most recent and comprehensive definition can be found in the UCPD under the umbrella of *commercial practices*.

Article 2(d) UCPD defines B2C commercial practices as: "any act, omission, course of conduct or representation, commercial communication including advertising and marketing, by a trader, directly connected with the promotion, sale or supply of a product to consumers."

In *marketing law* (i.e., the part of consumer law that specifically deals with marketing practices), the term marketing is used interchangeably with *advertising*, as described in the MCAD,[387] and *commercial communications*, as described in the *E-Commerce Directive*.[388] Nonetheless, these definitions are narrower since they only cover (misleading) information, whereas the UCPD also covers (aggressive) conducts.[389]

Marketing aims to incite *behavior modification*, which means that the marketer is trying to influence the consumer to make a certain decision. Behavior modification can take place in two forms, namely, through *persuasion*, which is the lawful form of influencing behavior, and *manipulation*, which is the unlawful form of influencing, such as deception and coercion.[390] This distinction corresponds with the

383 De Geest (2018), p. 3.

384 De Geest (2018), p. 5.

385 De Geest (2018), pp. 25–26.

386 Kotler and Armstrong (2016), pp. 628–632.

387 Directive 2006/114/EC of the European Parliament and of the Council of 12 December 2006 concerning misleading and comparative advertising (codified version). https://eur-lex.europa.eu/legal-content/EN/TXT/?uri=CELEX%3A32006L0114.

388 Directive 2000/31/EC of the European Parliament and of the Council of 8 June 2000 on certain legal aspects of information society services, in particular electronic commerce, in the Internal Market ('Directive on electronic commerce'). https://eur-lex.europa.eu/legal-content/EN/TXT/?uri=CELEX%3A32000L0031. Referred to as "E-Commerce Directive".

389 Trzaskowski (2021), p. 76.

390 Trzaskowski (2021), p. 12.

distinction between fair and deceptive marketing. In practice, however, the distinction is mainly normative, and a gray area exists in which the difference between lawful persuasion and unlawful manipulation is not conspicuous.

The rationale behind the regulation of marketing stems from the conflicting interests of the seller and the consumer. From a seller's perspective, "marketing serves the legitimate purpose of influencing consumers' preferences – by means of information and conducts – in order to increase profits."[391] This means that there is an incentive for sellers to influence consumers to the extent that profits are optimized. For instance, by highlighting the merits of the product or service, while downplaying the drawbacks. This will attract consumers to buy the product or service, but it will also lead to a partial mismatch between consumers' expectations and preferences, and the product or service in reality. "Consumers, on the other hand, are interested in finding the products and deals that best suit their goals, values, and preferences."[392] In the decision-making process, the consumers collect information from various sources such as their own experience and expertise, available (online) information provided by third parties, and the information provided by the seller, among which the seller's marketing message.

It is in the interest of consumers to make *efficient choices*, that is to say, choosing the product or service that best fits their preferences. Accordingly, to prevent the consumer from making inefficient choices, marketing law aims to "ensure that marketing is not carried out in a way that distorts the consumer's *ability* to make efficient choices, e.g., by means of misleading actions, misleading omissions, or aggressive conduct."[393] Hence, there is a need in the market for the provision of accurate information in the form of truthful marketing.

Consequently, the question arises whether the difference between persuasion and manipulation can be delineated. Since persuasion is lawful, what should then be regarded as unlawful? Sunstein (2016a) describes manipulation as: "A statement or action can be said to be manipulative if it does not sufficiently engage or appeal to people's capacity for reflective and deliberative choice."[394] As a result of manipulation, two problems arise. First, manipulation "fails to respect people's autonomy and is an affront to their dignity."[395] Second, if individuals' choices are "products of manipulation, people's choices might fail to promote their own welfare, and might instead promote the welfare of the manipulator."[396]

In the context of marketing, this would mean that the marketer can modify the behavior of consumers to such an extent that it promotes the welfare of the seller to

[391] Trzaskowski (2021), p. 32.

[392] Trzaskowski (2021), pp. 32, 74.

[393] Trzaskowski (2021), pp. 32, 74.

[394] Sunstein (2016a), p. 213.

[395] Sunstein (2016a), p. 213.

[396] Sunstein (2016a), p. 213.

the detriment of the consumer.[397] The difficulty of ascertaining manipulation is evident since there is great ambiguity concerning the ability to "sufficiently engage or appeal to people's capacity for reflective and deliberative choice."[398] Accordingly, a strong case needs to be made to justify a legal response. As Sunstein (2016a) puts it:

> But as the manipulator's motives become more self-interested or venal, and as efforts to bypass people's deliberative capacities become more successful, the ethical objections to manipulation become very forceful, and the argument for a legal response is fortified.[399]

The added value of adopting a marketing perspective is that the sophistication behind the marketing strategies can be understood, which allows for more accurate detection of marketing manipulation. Subsequently, the necessary legal changes can be made to remedy potential market failures, and, thus, enhance the working of consumer markets.[400] In this sense, a marketing perspective on consumer law can be described as *employing the insights from marketing scholarship to the benefit of consumers.*

2.4.3 Welfare Effects of Marketing-Induced Market Failures

De Geest (2018) argues that one should not only look at the efficiency effects of marketing but also the equity effects because of their implications for income inequality. He states: "When marketers create subtle market failures, they create rents. When marketers get better at this over time, they increase the total amount of rents in the economy, and therefore income inequality."[401] Thus, examining the efficiency and the distributional effects of marketing can lead to a more comprehensive and accurate understanding of the degree to which marketing causes consumer manipulation.

To fully understand the distributional effect of marketing, it is of pivotal importance to understand the concept of *rents*. Economic rents can be defined as artificial profits that could not have been made in a perfectly competitive market.[402] These profits can be obtained by extracting consumer surplus and transferring it to the seller.

The theory of rents has been propounded by Ricardo (1817), and he defined rents as "that portion of the produce of the earth which is paid to the landlord for the use

---

[397] See Sect. 3.2.3 for an application of the persuasion-manipulation debate in the context of personalized advertising.

[398] Sunstein (2016a), p. 216 describes extensively the difficulty with determining if there is manipulation in an individual case due to the idiosyncrasy of the context.

[399] Sunstein (2016a), p. 213.

[400] Andrews (2001).

[401] De Geest (2018), p. 27.

[402] De Geest (2018), p. 2.

of the original and indestructible powers of the soil."[403] Thus, rents go to the landlord rather than the worker on the land because the farmer owns the land, even though the latter performs the labor. This is plausible based on two grounds, namely, land is scarce in absolute terms, and it is divided arbitrarily. The legal system then determines how high the rents will be. These rents are solely caused by the scarcity of land and, therefore, have been named *Ricardian rents*.

Although Ricardo was the first to coin the term rents, the importance of rents in the economy became apparent after the publication of the works by Tullock (1967)[404] and Krueger (1974).[405] Krueger (1974) introduced the term *rent-seeking*, which describes the activities that are undertaken to obtain rents. The idea was already formulated by Tullock in the field of monopolies but was further developed and formalized in his work "Efficient Rent-Seeking",[406] which discussed rent-seeking through lobbying.

In essence, rent-seeking is a socially costly activity, because it destroys wealth by wasting valuable resources. Rent-seeking does not produce welfare; it merely seeks to redistribute it. This distinguishes it from profit-seeking, which can be seen as productive since it generates new products or services and it allocates resources to the highest-valuing users.[407] Through lobbying, interest groups try to manipulate the political environment in return for favors that will transfer wealth to them without them needing to contribute to overall productivity. In other words, surplus from other groups is extracted without any compensation.

In Tullock's work, the emphasis lies on political rent-seeking, which was assumed to occur in legal and illegal ways, such as corruption and bribery. Accordingly, the concept of rents has received a prominent place in *public choice theory*. Nevertheless, rent-seeking does not only apply to a political economy setting. Rent-seeking also takes place in the private economy, and there is empirical evidence that this practice adds up to substantial amounts of social costs.[408] It is estimated that rents amount to 35% of the economy and it is argued that marketing has played a significant role in the creation and distribution of these rents.[409] In this sense, the concept of rents obtains a different meaning from the one utilized in public choice theory. In the context of marketing, rent-seeking entails the efforts of marketers to obtain artificial profits that cannot have been made in a perfectly competitive market. This is done in two ways: employing marketing techniques that

[403] Ricardo (1817), p. 39.

[404] Tullock (1967).

[405] Krueger (1974).

[406] Tullock (1980).

[407] Tullock (1980).

[408] Tollison (2012).

[409] See De Geest (2018) for the extensive calculation of the magnitude of rent-seeking in the economy.

facilitate the exploitation of existing market failures or the creation of new market failures.[410]

The more successful companies are in extracting consumer surplus, the larger the distortionary effect of marketing in terms of distributive justice, which refers to the desire to implement policies that will lead to outcomes that are perceived as fair or just.[411] In this sense, the potential efficiency effects can be in tension with distributional considerations.[412]

2.4.4 Broadening the Analysis: A Consumer Policy Perspective

The examination of the traditional and behavioral law and economics approaches demonstrated that both approaches are not mutually exclusive. Instead, they can complement each other to explain a consumer issue.[413] However, as the previous sections made clear, personalized marketing touches upon many aspects that go beyond a total welfare analysis, in which efficiency denotes the criterion for maximizing welfare.[414] Consumer policy aims to empower consumers, enhance their welfare, and protect them.[415] However, the role of consumer policy is more than merely protecting consumer rights; it also aims to promote consumer interests.[416] To achieve this goal, a variety of tools are used, giving consumer policy a broad scope of application. Nevertheless, the orientation of consumer policy seems geared toward the *consumer sovereignty model*, which means that welfare-maximizing outcomes in the market can be facilitated by ensuring that the consumer can make well-informed choices.[417] This explains the prominence of the information paradigm in consumer policy.[418] As demonstrated in Sect. 2.3, the behavioral law and economics approach criticized this view. Although the behavioralist approach emphasizes the irrationality of consumers and moves beyond reliance on mandated disclosure,[419] sovereignty continues to serve as the normative baseline for consumer law and economics.

However, from a consumer policy perspective, there is a call for a more pluralistic perspective, whereby more values related to consumer protection are taken into

410 De Geest (2018).

411 Ogus (2004), pp. 46–51.

412 See Mathis (2009).

413 Pomar and Golobardes (2018), p. 123.

414 Parisi (2013), p. 319.

415 See Sect. 2.2.2.

416 See Sect. 2.2.2 for an elaboration on this distinction.

417 Herrine (2022).

418 Esposito (2017).

419 Esposito (2017).

account.[420] The need for a reconsideration of consumer protection laws is spurred on by the technological advancements in the digital age.[421] Consumer markets have changed: the market shaping power of online service providers is significantly larger, there is a deepened information asymmetry due to advanced data collection and processing, and the bargaining power of the consumer vis-à-vis the trader has deteriorated. Consumer law has showed to be maladapted to the rapid changes in online commercial practices. As a consequence, there is more at stake for consumers, which requires a broader scope of application for consumer policy.[422]

Personalized marketing is one of the developments in the digital age that has a far-reaching impact on fundamental societal values.[423] There is a multiplicity of values that is pertinent to consumer protection[424]; however, in this study, the focus lies on two substantive values that consumer policy should consider: autonomy and equity.[425]

2.4.4.1 Autonomy

Mik (2016) clearly connected the combined, mutually enforcing effect of online technologies (e.g., personalized marketing) with the erosion of consumer autonomy.[426] In consumer law, there is a strong emphasis on consumers' ability to make free choices in order to advance their interests, i.e., consumer autonomy.[427] Personalization techniques that negatively interfere with consumers' choices affect their autonomy. Autonomy is limited when consumers are restricted in their ability to choose from the full range of options.[428] The sophistication and opacity behind AI-driven technologies have the capacity to circumvent consumer protection legislation while manipulating consumer choices.[429] As Mik (2016) describes: "In sum, there is nothing new in the fact that businesses try to influence consumption choices. It is the differences in the available tools and in the characteristics of the online environment that warrant legal attention."[430]

---

[420] See, for example, Domurath (2013); Davies (2016); Guttentag (2019); Van Loo (2019); Herrine (2022); Raghavan (2022); Van Loo (2023); Wu (2023); Brenncke (2024).

[421] Fletcher et al. (2023).

[422] Fletcher et al. (2023).

[423] Helberger et al. (2021); Trzaskowski (2021).

[424] Davies (2016); Herrine (2022); Van Loo (2023).

[425] Cfr. Willis (2015). According to Willis, consumer law should focus on three metagoals: autonomy, welfare, and fairness.

[426] The concept of autonomy was introduced in Sect. 2.4.1. This section emphasizes its importance in the context of consumer policy.

[427] This is, for example, visible in the provisions of the UCPD.

[428] This refers to the availability of choices, not the assumption that more is better, see Zarsky (2002).

[429] Wu (2023).

[430] Mik (2016), p. 24.

Consumer autonomy, however, lacks proper conceptualization in EU consumer law and further elaboration on the concept in an AI context is strongly needed.[431] However, by drawing upon various definitions from marketing, legal, and philosophical literature, it becomes possible to identify its fundamental characteristics.[432] Hyman et al. (2023) demonstrate, after extensively reviewing the marketing ethics literature, that true consumer autonomy consists of control over choice, matching wills/desires with product choices, and the opportunity for self-reflection.[433]

Anker (2020) discerns consumer autonomy in internal (i.e., cognitive, and volitional aspects) and external components (i.e., market conditions).[434] He argues that when the internal or external components impede consumers' ability to exercise autonomy and make informed decisions, the ethical justification of marketing as a social system is threatened.[435]

Sax et al. (2018) discuss the concept of consumer autonomy from a consumer law perspective and conclude that three requirements need to be fulfilled to speak of autonomy in a digital context, namely: *independence*, *authenticity*, and *options*.[436] Independence indicates the extent to which persons have control over their own life, authenticity relates to individuals' relationship to their own values, desires, and goals, and options refer to the adequate range of choices.[437] Accordingly, consumer autonomy refers to "consumers' ability to make and enact decisions on their own, free from external influences imposed by other agents."[438]

Fassiaux (2023) reviewed the different definitions of consumer autonomy and placed them in the context of AI-driven marketing.[439] He argues that AI marketing can only maintain its legitimacy when consumer autonomy is preserved. The conception of consumer autonomy is reliant on four requirements: (1) *choice*, (2) *privacy*, (3) *independence*, and (4) *reciprocity*.[440] To specify, choice has a structural and granular element. Structurally, there needs to be sufficient competition in the market and, granularly, there needs to be a true set of options for consumers, which are not manipulated by professionals. Privacy refers to the vast collection and processing of personal data, which can lead to large-scale privacy violations and the manipulation of consumers in the market. Independence indicates the control that consumers have

---

[431] Jabłonowska et al. (2018).

[432] In this chapter, the focus lies on consumer autonomy. For a general discussion on the concept of autonomy in philosophy, see, for instance, Christman (2020) who defines individual autonomy as "the capacity to be one's own person, to live one's life according to reasons and motives that are taken as one's own and not the product of manipulative or distorting external forces, to be in this way independent."

[433] Hyman et al. (2023).

[434] Anker (2020).

[435] Anker (2020), p. 528.

[436] Sax et al. (2018).

[437] Sax et al. (2018), p. 109.

[438] Wertenbroch et al. (2020), p. 430.

[439] Fassiaux (2023).

[440] Fassiaux (2023), p. 713.

in acting in accordance with their preferences and desires while avoiding manipulation. Reciprocity relates to the capacity of consumers to interact on the same level playing field with professionals using AI-driven market techniques, which means that they can decide themselves to engage with the services or opt out.[441]

Based on this framework, it can be determined to what extent marketing techniques infringe on consumer autonomy. It can be argued that personalized marketing techniques that lead to the extraction of value, the exploitation of biases, and/or the shaping of preferences, conflict with the requirements of consumer autonomy. There is a mismatch between first-order (i.e., desire for a certain action) and second-order motivations (i.e., desire to act in a certain way).[442] If through marketing efforts, there is no coherence between the different motivations, a consumer is impeded from acting autonomously.[443] In other words, the "true" preferences of the consumer do not correspond to the product choice. In addition, the privacy of consumers is not respected when their consent leads to the collection of large amounts of personal data that are employed to target vulnerabilities and shape preferences to the benefit of the seller.

Marketing strategies that structurally exploit biases, steer consumption patterns, and extract value cannot be regarded as respecting the independent decision-making capacity of the consumer. One cannot speak of a reciprocal relationship if through sophisticated marketing techniques, the seller can unilaterally determine the position of consumers and deny consumers to have a say in the matter. It is, therefore, argued that "the current situation in consumer markets allows "autonomy capture" by professionals using AI systems at the expense of consumers."[444] This does not mean that the technology in itself is detrimental to consumer autonomy; however, it implies that AI-driven marketing has the potential to be a threat in specific cases.[445]

Esposito (2022) argues that adhering to the consumer welfare hypothesis leads to the institutionalization of consumer autonomy. This means there can also be a market failure when, through the reduction of consumer welfare, consumer autonomy is overthrown, although net total welfare might not be reduced.[446]

Nevertheless, Brenncke (2024) explains that losses in autonomy are not necessarily related to welfare losses. He states that "autonomy in a welfare framework has value only as far as it is preferred by individuals."[447] Non-economic losses of autonomy, for example, violations of personal autonomy[448] (ability to make one's own choices) that can be attributable to fairness, dignity, or moral wrongness considerations are not regarded as welfare losses in this framework. Consequently,

---

[441] Fassiaux (2023), p. 714.

[442] Frankfurt (1971).

[443] Anker et al. (2010).

[444] Fassiaux (2023), p. 714.

[445] These cases will be further discussed in Chaps. 3–5.

[446] Hutt (1940); Esposito (2022), p. 33.

[447] Brenncke (2024), p. 148.

[448] Bigwood (2003).

autonomy considerations fall outside the scope of the economic efficiency analysis.[449] It is, therefore, argued that autonomy should become a key element in consumer policy assessments to determine to what extent marketing strategies lead to legally unacceptable levels of transactional exploitation.[450]

The exploitation of vulnerabilities is inextricably linked to the concept of autonomy. As discussed before, personalized marketing allows for the targeting of different sources and triggers of vulnerability.[451] In the digital age, all consumers can be rendered vulnerable because individual characteristics, biases, and circumstances can be exploited through profiling.[452] It is of note, however, that this does not mean that consumers are vulnerable by definition. In contrast, it is the *digital asymmetry* that makes consumers vulnerable. Digital asymmetry refers to the structural power imbalances and online choice architectures that are designed to exploit vulnerabilities.[453]

The vulnerability of consumers effectively translates into "the power or ability of commercial actors to affect the decisions, desires, and behaviour of the consumer in ways that the consumer, all things considered, does not condone, but also is not in a position to prevent."[454] In other words, exploiting vulnerability is a direct infringement of consumers' autonomy in the market. The structural component of the asymmetry cannot simply be resolved by providing more information to consumers. A solution needs to be found that does not focus on protection by extending the sources of vulnerability but on identifying the commercial practices that render consumers vulnerable.[455] Accordingly, from a consumer policy perspective, vulnerability needs to be explicitly considered in the analysis of commercial practices. Exploitation can then become a valuable consideration for regulation.[456] Riefa and Gamper (2020) explain that behavioral economics can help identify the exploitation of biases and vulnerabilities, yet for the sake of consumer protection, a broader perspective that encompasses vulnerability in the regulatory assessment is needed.[457]

[449] Brenncke (2024), p. 148.

[450] Mik (2016), p. 11; André et al. (2018) emphasize the importance of analyzing consumer choice and autonomy in the age of AI and big data.

[451] See Sect. 2.4.1.

[452] Newman (2014) demonstrates how, for example, financial ignorance can be exploited through profiling.

[453] Helberger et al. (2021).

[454] Helberger et al. (2021), p. 15.

[455] Helberger et al. (2021), pp. 25–51.

[456] Fletcher et al. (2023).

[457] Riefa and Gamper (2020), p. 24.

2.4.4.2 Equity

Mathis (2009) emphasizes the prominent role of the equity-efficiency trade-off in law and economics, whereby the trade-off shows how much justice sometimes (not always) needs to be sacrificed to achieve more efficiency.[458] Equity seems to be the counterpart of efficiency in policy development. Okun (1975) describes it as "our biggest socioeconomic tradeoff, and it plagues us in dozens of dimensions of social policy."[459] The traditional law and economics view is that efficiency and equity should be separated.[460] Mathis (2009), however, states that this separation should be rejected.[461] Instead, an integrated view of various policy goals needs to be taken, in which the efficiency analysis is complemented with additional considerations. Mathis (2009) states:

> Efficiency and justice are by no means mutually exclusive; in fact, they stand in a complex interrelationship. Although this relationship is not without its strains, it is reasonable to conclude that the endeavour to realize both goals need not always be a competitive trade-off, and can in fact be undertaken cooperatively to large extent.

Various consumer protection scholars share this view.[462] Therefore, the role of equity should not be overlooked in consumer policy. The main problem, however, when analyzing policies from an equity perspective is that a variety of terms come to mind when trying to formulate a definition, such as (distributive) justice, fairness, and ethicality.

In the field of economics, when justice is considered, the type of justice in question is *distributive justice*, which "is applied in the allocation of benefits by the state. On this principle, rights are distributed to the people in accordance with their honour, i.e. according to their social status and their merit to the community."[463] The concept of distributive justice, however, has been studied to a much greater extent. For example, there is a significant difference between the static concept of distributive justice (i.e., the ideal type of distribution) and the dynamic concept (i.e., the establishment of institutions that aid individuals in the fulfillment of their potential, whereby the outcome of the distribution is less relevant).[464]

In law and economics, distributive justice is expressed in the *distribution of surplus*. In other words, "efficiency corresponds to the "size of the pie," while equity has to do with how it is sliced."[465] Nevertheless, equity is not confined to the discus-

---

[458] Mathis (2009), p. 185. The terms justice and equity are used interchangeably.

[459] Okun (1975), p. 2.

[460] Polinsky (1989); Posner (1990); Kaplow and Shavell (2001). This argument will be further explored in Sect. 4.4.3.

[461] Mathis (2009), p. 201.

[462] See, for example, Guttentag (2019); Markovits et al. (2022); Raghavan (2022); Van Loo (2023). The rationale will be further explained in this section.

[463] Mathis (2009), p. 186.

[464] Mathis (2009), p. 189.

[465] Polinsky (1989), p. 7.

sion of surplus. A broader perspective of equity allows for the consideration of additional values, including fairness and human dignity.[466] Consequently, this study will define equity based on three elements: distributive justice, fairness, and ethical considerations.

The starting point will be distributive justice, which is manifested in the form of an equitable distribution of surplus. Guttentag (2019) highlights the need to consider the role of surplus in consumer protection law.[467] With the advent of big data analytics, companies' extraction of surplus will become increasingly important. Rent-seeking is not a phenomenon that only applies to the public choice context; it is relevant in the broader market context.[468] The law can then be an effective tool to tackle distributional concerns.[469]

Van Loo (2019) provides empirical evidence showing that algorithmic pricing can lead to substantial overcharge, which deepens inequality, and suggests that "consumer law, despite prominent critiques of its shortcomings, can reduce overcharge when designed well."[470] This does not mean, however, that redistribution through law should be a primary goal. The idea is that the consumer protection analysis is incomplete when distributional issues are not considered.[471] A pluralist approach that includes distributional equity is, therefore, advocated.[472] Correspondingly, Guttentag (2019) argues that consumer law scholars should extend their view beyond the traditional information asymmetry and behavioral market failure arguments and explore distributional concerns to justify regulatory intervention. In his words: "Failing to include questions related to law and surplus in the consumer law context is an opportunity missed."[473]

The second element of equity relates to fairness considerations. Consumers can be treated differently for reasons that can be justified from an efficiency perspective (e.g., price differentiation[474]), but is it also considered fair? The concept of fairness can be defined as: "A judgment of whether an outcome and/or the process to reach an outcome is reasonable, acceptable, or just."[475] Fairness has a prominent place in consumer law but also in adjacent fields of law, such as competition and data protection law.[476] However, fairness considerations fall outside the economic efficiency analysis.[477] It is argued that incorporating fairness considerations is vital for con-

---

466 Mathis (2009).

467 Guttentag (2019).

468 Guttentag (2019), p. 621. See also Sect. 2.4.3.

469 Markovits et al. (2022).

470 Van Loo (2019), p. 211.

471 Esposito and Grochowski (2022).

472 Liscow (2018); Raghavan (2022).

473 Guttentag (2019), p. 660.

474 Algorithmic pricing will be further examined in Chap. 4.

475 Xia et al. (2004), p. 1.

476 Graef et al. (2018).

477 Beckerman (2017), pp. 68–70.

sumer policy, and making fairness judgments more explicit can serve consumer interests.[478] Fairness can play a motivating role in intervention and should, therefore, complement economic considerations.[479]

Lastly, the concept of equity encompasses considerations from an ethical perspective. Equity also relates to the equitable treatment of individuals, which means that discussions regarding discrimination, social sorting,[480] and human dignity are pivotal. Trzaskowski (2021) emphasizes the interplay between data-driven marketing and the protection of fundamental rights, such as human dignity and non-discrimination.[481] In this context, it is argued that persuasive technologies can undermine human dignity.[482] However, before it can be analyzed how human dignity is put at risk, it is vital to define it. The definition of human dignity has been a subject of study since it acquired philosophical relevance within the ancient Roman world. Accordingly, there exists a plethora of definitions of human dignity.[483] Remarkably, even though many legal provisions of the EU legal framework refer to human dignity and derive rights from it, there is no explicit definition of human dignity in EU law.[484] The meaning of human dignity is enshrined in EU law by its many functions, applications, and corresponding jurisprudence, but there is no single definition.

Recognizing that dignity has *dual-faced character* helps to establish a definition. On the one hand, dignity refers to the special position of humans because of their natural endowment with it. On the other hand, dignity is a value that can be endangered if not protected.[485] Human dignity represents a fundamental value that all individuals possess. In the words of Lebech (2004): "When 'human' and 'dignity' are used in conjunction they form the expression 'human dignity, which means the status of human beings entitling them to respect, a status which is first and to be taken for granted."[486] The concept of dignity has an absolute value (i.e., all human beings possess it) and a relative value (i.e., the value can be acquired or lost by actions).[487] With this concept in mind, it becomes possible to see how the relative value can be endangered in the context of personalization. The shaping of preferences, steering of behavior, and undermining of choices compromises human agency and their right to be treated ethically. Accordingly, pressing ethical concerns

---

[478] Herrine (2022).

[479] Fletcher et al. (2023).

[480] This will be further explained in Sects. 3.5.3.3 and 4.4.3.3, but in short, social sorting refers to the classification of people according to varying criteria to separate one group from another.

[481] Trzaskowski (2021).

[482] Trzaskowski (2021).

[483] See for an extensive study on human dignity and its relation to law, Becchi and Mathis (2019).

[484] Becchi and Mathis (2019), pp. 943–967.

[485] Becchi and Mathis (2019), pp. 2–7.

[486] Lebech (2004), p. 1.

[487] Becchi and Mathis (2019), pp. 2–7.

regarding human dignity, and other fundamental values such as non-discrimination, should also be included in consumer policy discussions.

The final step is to determine how to include all these considerations in the analysis of personalized marketing. The law and economics approach in this study is characterized by a cost-benefit analysis (CBA), which can be a valuable tool "to weigh the advantages and disadvantages of projects in a clear and systematic way, unlike more complex decision procedures."[488] However, the CBA, in this study, will deliberately avoid putting monetary values on the benefits and downsides. As Mathis (2009) describes:

> But attention should also be given to this method's weaknesses: the insistence on monetarization means that a financial value must be attached to all impacts, even those for which no market prices are available. Whilst it is relatively easy to evaluate costs in monetary terms, benefits must often be assessed using ad hoc reference data and rough approximations. These uncertainties produce valuations with rather broad scope for interpretation, which can cast doubt on the meaningfulness of the results.[489]

For this reason, the goal of the CBA in this study will be to provide a comprehensive evaluation of the arguments that contribute to the overall assessment of each analyzed personalized marketing practice.[490] This also opens up the way for the inclusion of considerations that can be raised in terms of consumer autonomy and equity.[491] This approach reflects the complexity of consumer policy by recognizing that values such as consumer welfare, autonomy, and equity coexist and often resist direct trade-offs or singular weighting systems. While assigning explicit relative weights to economic and non-economic arguments might appear to offer precision, it can be counterproductive in consumer policy, where overlapping goals, such as empowering consumers, enhancing welfare, and protecting them, are not easily reduced to a single metric.[492] Accordingly, a layered methodology is adopted, beginning with an efficiency analysis focused on consumer welfare and progressively broadening the scope to incorporate autonomy and equity. This progression ensures a comprehensive evaluation that captures the diverse interests involved and addresses the multifaceted nature of personalized marketing in the digital age.

In conclusion, from a consumer policy perspective, there is a need for a pluralistic approach, in which there is room to take both economic and non-economic arguments into account. The core methodology of this study is grounded in law and economics.[493] However, to provide a comprehensive assessment of personalized marketing that can contribute to improving consumer policy in the digital age, addi-

---

[488] Adler and Posner (1999), p. 245.

[489] Mathis (2009), p. 205.

[490] Applications of this type of cost-benefit analysis can be found in the existing literature. See, for example, Moewe (1971) in the field of advertising, Rekaiti and Van den Bergh (2000) in the field of consumer protection, and Seele et al. (2021) in the field of algorithmic pricing.

[491] Adler and Posner (1999) advocate that CBA allows for the incorporation of nonwelfarist concerns.

[492] This is in accordance with the goals of EU consumer policy as described in Sect. 2.2.2.

[493] See Sect. 1.4.

tional considerations that pertain to consumers' interests will be incorporated. Including the values of autonomy and equity will not detract from the law and economics methodology; instead, it will *broaden the analysis*.[494]

2.5 Conclusion

This chapter reviewed the law and economics of consumer law. The disquisition of the traditional and behavioral law and economics approaches demonstrated the versatility of the methodology. The economic insights allow for the identification of the effects of legal incentives on consumer behavior and the examination of the welfare effects of legal policy instruments.

The traditional law and economics approach investigates, on the basis of RCT, how legal structures affect human behavior and how legal rules can be engineered to maximize total welfare or reduce total societal costs. The law and economics approach advocates that the presence of a market failure should be taken as the starting point for the analysis of potential intervention in the market. Accordingly, if the analysis demonstrates that there is no market failure, intervention is discouraged, which prevents overregulation.

There exist three main economic justifications for regulatory intervention in consumer markets, namely information asymmetries, transaction costs, and unequal bargaining power (which refers to market power). To correct these market failures, several traditional devices have been employed in consumer law. Five prominent devices include mandated disclosure, cooling-off periods, mandatory legal warranties, default rules, and boilerplate regulation. The economic analysis of their merits demonstrated that each device generates positive, but also adverse effects. In the traditional consumer law and economics literature, the adverse effects are emphasized and market solutions to the market failures are highlighted. Private provision of information, insurance, reputation, ratings, relational contracts, consumer learning, and consumer-based innovations constitute the proof of a market that can effectively self-remedy its market failures.

Nonetheless, a substantial body of empirical evidence shows that in various cases the market is not able to correct itself. This raises the question: To what extent is governmental intervention desirable? Due to the versatile character of government regulation, an ex-ante cost-benefit analysis of the proposed regulation is necessary before its implementation. To perform an accurate assessment of the regulation, it is of pivotal importance to take distributional and welfare effects into account. Consequently, a more complete and economically-sound analysis of the effects of the proposed regulation can be provided.

Although the traditional law and economics approach helps to improve the level of consumer protection while accounting for the welfare effects of regulation, its

[494] Guttentag (2019).

reliance on the rationality assumption has been contested by behavioral law and economics scholars. According to the behavioral perspective, the law and economics movement can improve its methodology and policy prescriptions by incorporating insights from cognitive psychology, sociology, and other behavioral sciences. Rather than substituting the traditional paradigm, behavioral law and economics aims to refine the paradigm with empirical insights. By means of empirical analyses, the behavioral paradigm postulates that it can more accurately describe how the law impacts human behavior. It accounts for three bounds (i.e., bounded rationality, willpower, and self-interest) that explain the systematic deviations from the predictions generated by RCT. They cover a variety of biases and heuristics that all provide a partial answer to the question of why individuals fail to maximize their subjective expected utility. As a result, the door has been opened for paternalistic interventions. Yet, a critical evaluation of these interventions remains advocated by both traditional and behavioral law and economics scholars.

The exploration of both approaches revealed that each approach has its advantages and disadvantages, which inhibit a full reliance on one approach. The approaches complement each other. In this chapter, the concept of marketing-induced market failures was introduced, which poses a new challenge to consumer law and economics. Personalized marketing has the capacity to cause several market failures simultaneously and lead to substantial consumer harm through the exploitation of vulnerabilities, which are reinforced by the digital environment in which consumers operate.

Broadening the law and economics analysis with additional considerations that are pertinent to consumers' interests can provide a more comprehensive consumer policy assessment. This study advocates the consideration of autonomy and equity as fundamental values.

In addition, this chapter found that a contribution to the improvement of consumer protection can be made by incorporating marketing insights into the analysis. Employing a marketing perspective allows for the reconsideration of the dividing line between persuasive and manipulative marketing, which has been blurred by the AI-driven technologies, but which is necessary to clarify in order to safeguard consumer autonomy, equity and welfare in digital markets.

References

Adler MD, Posner EA (1999) Rethinking cost-benefit analysis. Yale Law J 109(2):165–248

Ainslie G (1992) Picoeconomics: the strategic interaction of successive motivational states within the person. Cambridge University Press, Cambridge

Akerlof GA (1970) The market for "lemons": quality uncertainty and the market mechanism. Q J Econ 84(3):488–500

Amir O, Lobel O (2008) Stumble, predict, nudge: how behavioral economics informs law and policy. Colum Law Rev 108:2098–2138

André Q, Carmon Z, Wertenbroch K, Crum A, Frank D, Goldstein W et al (2018) Consumer choice and autonomy in the age of artificial intelligence and big data. Cust Needs Solut 5:28–37

Andrews JC (2001) The use of marketing knowledge in formulating and enforcing consumer protection policy. In: Bloom PN, Gundlach GT (eds) The handbook of marketing and society. Sage Publications, Thousand Oaks, pp 1–33

Angell FJ (1971) Some effects of the truth-in-lending legislation. J Bus 44(1):78–85

Anker T (2020) Autonomy as license to operate: establishing the internal and external conditions of informed choice in marketing. Mark Theory 20(4):527–545

Anker TB, Kappel K, Sandøe P (2010) The liberating power of commercial marketing. J Bus Ethics 93:519–530

Arlen J (1998) Comment: the future of behavioral economic analysis of law. Vand Law Rev 51(6):1765–1788

Arrow K (1982) Risk perception in psychology and economics. Econ Inq 20(1):1–9

Ayres I, Gertner R (1989) Filling gaps in incomplete contracts: an economic theory of default rules. Yale Law J 99(1):87–130

Babcock L, Loewenstein G (1997) Explaining bargaining impasse: the role of self-serving biases. J Econ Perspect 11(1):109–126

Bar-Gill O (2004) Seduction by plastic. Northwest Univ Law Rev 98(4):1373–1434

Bar-Gill O, Ben-Shahar O (2016) Optimal defaults in consumer markets. J Leg Stud 45(S2):137–161

Bar-Gill O, Epstein RA (2007) Consumer contracts: behavioral economics vs. neoclassical economics. Minn Law Rev 92:1–63

Beales H, Craswell R, Salop SC (1981) The efficient regulation of consumer information. J Law Econ 24(3):491–539

Bebchuk LA, Posner RA (2006) One-sided contracts in competitive consumer markets. Mich Law Rev 104(5):827–836

Becchi P, Mathis K (2019) Handbook of human dignity in Europe. Springer, Cham

Becher SI, Bar-Gill O (2012) Consumer protection. Harv Public Law Working Paper No. 18-42:1–49

Beckerman W (2017) Economics as applied ethics: fact and value in economic policy, 2nd edn. Palgrave Macmillan, London

Ben-Shahar O (2010) One-way contracts: consumer protection without law. Eur Rev Contract Law 6(3):221–249

Ben-Shahar O, Bar-Gill O (2013) Regulatory techniques in consumer protection: a critique of European consumer contract law. Common Mark Law Rev 50:109–126

Ben-Shahar O, Posner EA (2011) The right to withdraw in contract law. J Leg Stud 40(1):115–148

Ben-Shahar O, Schneider CE (2014) More than you wanted to know: the failure of mandated disclosure. Princeton University Press, Princeton

Ben-Shahar O, Strahilevitz L (2017) Interpreting contracts via surveys and experiments. New York Univ Law Rev 92(6):1753–1827

Bergstrom JC, Stoll JR (1990) An analysis of information overload with implications for survey design research. Leisure Sci 12(3):265–280

Bigwood R (2003) Exploitative contracts. Oxford University Press, Oxford

Board O (2009) Competition and disclosure. J Ind Econ 57(1):197–213

Boo EF, Low KY, Soh X, Lim M (2007) Assurance versus insurance: a study of consumer receptiveness in an e-commerce setting. Account Horiz 21(4):331–350

Borges G, Irlenbusch B (2007) Fairness crowded out by law: an experimental study on withdrawal rights. J Inst Theor Econ 163(1):84–101

Boulding W, Kirmani A (1993) A consumer-side experimental examination of signaling theory: do consumers perceive warranties as signals of quality? J Consum Res 20(1):111–123

Bourgoignie T (1992) Characteristics of consumer law. J Consum Policy 14(3):293–315

Boyd CL (2015) In defense of empirical legal studies. Buff Law Rev 63(2):363–378

Brenncke M (2024) Regulating dark patterns. Notre Dame J Int Comp Law 14(1):39–79

Bridgeman C (2006) Misrepresented intent in the context of unequal bargaining power. Mich State Law Rev 2006(4):993–1010

Brodley JF (1987) The economic goals of antitrust: efficiency, consumer welfare, and technological progress. New York Univ Law Rev 62(5):1020–1053

Burrows P (1995) Analyzing legal paternalism. Int Rev Law Econ 15(4):489–508

Busch C (2016) Crowdsourcing consumer confidence: how to regulate online rating and review systems in the collaborative economy. In: De Franceschi A (ed) Eur contract law digit single market. Intersentia, Antwerp, pp 223–245

Calabresi G (1968) Transaction costs, resource allocation and liability rules: a comment. J Law Econ 11(1):67–73

Calo R (2011) The boundaries of privacy harm. Indiana Law J 86(3):1131–1162

Calo R (2014) Digital market manipulation. Geo Wash Law Rev 82(4):995–1051

Camerer CF, Loewenstein G (2004) Behavioral economics: past, present, future. In: Camerer CF, Loewenstein G, Rabin M (eds) Advances in behavioral economics. Princeton University Press, Princeton, pp 3–51

Camerer CF, Issacharoff S, Loewenstein G, O'Donoghue T, Rabin M (2003) Regulation for conservatives: behavioral economics and the case for "asymmetric paternalism.". Univ Pa Law Rev 151(3):1211–1254

Chambers D, Collins CA, Krause A (2019) How do federal regulations affect consumer prices? An analysis of the regressive effects of regulation. Public Choice 180(1):57–90

Chetty R (2015) Behavioral economics and public policy: a pragmatic perspective. Am Econ Rev 105(5):1–33

Christman J (2020) Autonomy in moral and political philosophy. Stanford Encyclopedia of Philosophy. https://plato.stanford.edu/entries/autonomy-moral/

Citron DK, Solove DJ (2022) Privacy harms. Boston Univ Law Rev 102(3):793–864

Clemons EK (2007) An empirical investigation of third-party seller rating systems in e-commerce: the case of buy SAFE. J Manag Inf Syst 24(2):43–71

Coase RH (1960) The problem of social cost. J Law Econ 3(1):1–44

Conlisk J (1996) Why bounded rationality? J Econ Lit 34(2):669–700

Cooter R, Ulen T (2016) Law and economics, 6th edn. Berkeley Law Books, Berkeley

Craswell R (2006) Taking information seriously: misrepresentation and nondisclosure in contract law and elsewhere. Va Law Rev 92(4):565–632

Cseres KJ (2006) The controversies of the consumer welfare standard. Compet Law Rev 3(2):121–173

Darby MR, Karni E (1973) Free competition and the optimal amount of fraud. J Law Econ 16(1):67–88

Dasgupta P, Maskin E (2005) Uncertainty and hyperbolic discounting. Am Econ Rev 95(4):1290–1299

Davies GT (2016) The consumer, the citizen and the human being. In: Leczykiewicz D, Weatherill S (eds) The images of the consumer in EU law. Hart Publishing, Oxford, pp 325–338

De Geest G (1994) Economische analyse van het contracten- en quasi-contractenrecht: Een onderzoek naar de wetenschappelijke waarde van de rechtseconomie. Maklu, Antwerp

De Geest G (2016) Signing without Reading. In: Marciano A, Ramello GB (eds) Encyclopedia of law and economics. Springer, Cham, pp 1–8

De Geest G (2018) Rents: how marketing causes inequality. Beccaria Books, Leuven

DellaVigna S, Malmendier U (2006) Paying not to go to the gym. Am Econ Rev 96(3):694–719

Demsetz H (1968) The cost of transacting. Q J Econ 82(1):33–53

Domurath I (2013) The case for vulnerability as the normative standard in European consumer credit and mortgage law–an inquiry into the paradigms of consumer law. J Eur Consum Mark Law 2(3):124–137

Easterbrook FH, Fischel DR (1984) Mandatory disclosure and the protection of investors. Va Law Rev 70(4):669–715

Eisenberg MA (1986) Text anxiety. S Cal. Law Rev 59(2):305–312

Eisenberg T (2004) Why do empirical legal scholarship. San Diego Law Rev 41(4):1741–1746

Eisenberg T (2011) The origins, nature, and promise of empirical legal studies and response to concerns. Univ Ill Law Rev 2011(5):1713–1738

Engel C (2013) Behavioral law and economics: empirical methods. MPI Collect Goods Preprint 2013/1:1–22

Epstein RA (2006) Behavioral economics: human errors and market corrections. Univ Chicago Law Rev 73(1):111–132

Epstein RA (2008) The neoclassical economics of consumer contracts. Minn Law Rev 92(3):803–835

Esposito F (2017) A dismal reality: behavioural analysis and consumer policy. J Consum Policy 40:193–216

Esposito F (2022) The consumer welfare hypothesis in law and economics: towards a synthesis for the 21st century. Edward Elgar Publishing, Cheltenham

Esposito F, Grochowski M (2022) The consumer benchmark, vulnerability, and the contract terms transparency: a plea for reconsideration. Eur Rev Contract Law 18(1):1–31

Everson M (2006) Legal constructions of the consumer. In: Trentmann F (ed) The making of the consumer: knowledge, power and identity in the modern world. Berg Publishers, Oxford, pp 99–121

Faizullabhoy I, Korolova A (2018) Facebook's advertising platform: new attack vectors and the need for interventions. arXiv preprint arXiv:1803.10099:1–6

Fassiaux S (2023) Preserving consumer autonomy through European Union regulation of artificial intelligence: a long-term approach. Eur J Risk Regul 14:710–730

Faure MG (2014) The complementary roles of liability, regulation and insurance in safety management: theory and practice. J Risk Res 17(6):689–707

Faure MG, Luth HA (2011) Behavioural economics in unfair contract terms. J Consum Policy 34(3):337–358

Faure MG, Visscher LT (2018) Rechtseconomie en privaatrecht in de Lage Landen. In: Dirix E, Falconis J (eds) Interdisciplinariteit in het recht: Law and...-bewegingen in het privaatrecht. Intersentia, Antwerp, pp 15–39

Festinger L (1957) A theory of cognitive dissonance, vol 2. Stanford University Press, Stanford

Festinger L (1962) Cognitive dissonance. Sci Am 207(4):93–106

Fischhoff B (1975) Hindsight is not equal to foresight: the effect of outcome knowledge on judgment under uncertainty. J Exp Psychol Hum Percept Perform 1(3):1–34

Fishman MJ, Hagerty KM (2003) Mandatory versus voluntary disclosure in markets with informed and uninformed customers. J Law Econ Organ 19(1):45–63

Fletcher A, Crawford GS, Crémer J, Dinielli D, Heidhues P, Luca M, Salz T, Schnitzer M, Scott Morton FM, Seim K, Sinkinson M (2023) Consumer protection for online markets and large digital platforms. Yale J Regul 40(3):875–914

Frankfurt HG (1971) Freedom of the will and the concept of a person. J Philos 68(1):5–20

Frederick S, Loewenstein G, O'Donoghue T (2002) Time discounting and time preference: a critical review. J Econ Lit 40(2):351–401

Gage RJ (1979) The discriminating use of information disclosure rules by the Federal Trade Commission. UCLA Law Rev 26(5):1037–1083

Galli F (2020) AI and consumers manipulation: what is the role of EU fair marketing law? Catolica Law Rev 4(2):35–64

Galli F (2022) Algorithmic marketing and EU law on unfair commercial practices. Springer Nature, Cham

Glaeser EL (2006) Paternalism and psychology. Univ Chicago Law Rev 73(1):133–156

Gourville J, Soman D (2002) Pricing and the psychology of consumption. Harv Bus Rev 80(9):90–96

Graef I, Clifford D, Valcke P (2018) Fairness and enforcement: bridging competition, data protection, and consumer law. Int Data Privacy Law 8(3):200–223

Grether DM, Schwartz A, Wilde LL (1986) The irrelevance of information overload: an analysis of search and disclosure. South Calif Law Rev 59(2):277–304

Grossman SJ (1981) The informational role of warranties and private disclosure about product quality. J Law Econ 24(3):461–483

Grubb MD (2015) Overconfident consumers in the marketplace. J Econ Perspect 29(4):9–36

Guasch JL, Hahn RW (1999) The costs and benefits of regulation: implications for developing countries. World Bank Res Obs 14(1):137–158

Guttentag MD (2019) Law and surplus: opportunities missed. Utah Law Rev 2019(3):607–660

Hadfield GK, Howse R, Trebilcock MJ (1998) Information-based principles for rethinking consumer protection policy. J Consum Policy 21(2):131–169

Hagen L, Uetake K, Yang N, Bollinger B, Chaney AJ, Dzyabura D, Zhu Y (2020) How can machine learning aid behavioral marketing research? Mark Lett 31(4):361–370

Hanson JD, Kysar DA (1999) Taking behavioralism seriously: the problem of market manipulation. New YorkUniv Law Rev 74(3):630–749

Hart O, Moore J (1988) Incomplete contracts and renegotiation. Econometrica 56(4):755–785

Helberger N, Lynskey O, Micklitz HW, Rott P, Sax M, Strycharz J (2021) EU consumer protection 2.0: structural asymmetries in digital consumer markets. Joint report from EUCP2.0 Project BEUC, pp 1–207

Helberger N, Sax M, Strycharz J, Micklitz HW (2022) Choice architectures in the digital economy: towards a new understanding of digital vulnerability. J Consum Policy 45(2):175–200

Helleringer G, Sibony A (2017) European consumer protection through the behavioral lens. Columbia J Eur Law 23(3):607–646

Herrine L (2022) What is consumer protection for? Loy Consum Law Rev 34(2):1–50

Heymann LA (2011) The law of reputation and the interest of the audience. Boston Coll Law Rev 52(4):1341–1440

Hillman RA, Barakat I (2008) Warranties and disclaimers in the electronic age. Yale J Law Technol 11(1):1–69

Hillman RA, Rachlinski JJ (2002) Standard-form contracting in the electronic age. New York Univ Law Rev 77(2):429–495

Howells GG, Wilhelmsson T (2017) EC consumer law. Routledge, London

Hutt WH (1940) The concept of consumers' sovereignty. Econ J 50(197):66–77

Hyman MR, Kostyk A, Trafimow D (2023) True consumer autonomy: a formalization and implications. J Bus Ethics 183(3):841–863

Issacharoff S (1998) Can there be behavioral law and economics? Vanderbilt Law Rev 51(6):1729–1746

Ito TA, Larsen JT, Smith NK, Cacioppo JT (1998) Negative information weighs more heavily on the brain: the negativity bias in evaluative categorizations. J Pers Soc Psychol 75(4):887–900

Jabłonowska A, Kuziemski M, Nowak AM, Micklitz HW, Pałka P, Sartor G (2018) Consumer law and artificial intelligence: challenges to the EU consumer law and policy stemming from the business' use of artificial intelligence. Final report of the ARTSY project. EUI Department of Law Research Paper (2018/11):1–79

Jacoby J, Morrin M (2015) Consumer psychology. In: Wright JD (ed) International encyclopedia of the social & behavioral sciences, vol 4, 2nd edn. Elsevier, pp 738–743

Jacoby J, Speller DE, Kohn CA (1974) Brand choice behavior as a function of information load. J Mark Res 11(1):63–69

Jolls C (1998) Behavioral economics analysis of redistributive legal rules. Vand Law Rev 51(6):1653–1678

Jolls C (2007) Behavioral law and economics. NBER Work Pap Ser Work Pap 12879:1–45

Jolls C, Sunstein CR (2006) Debiasing through law. J Leg Stud 35(1):199–242

Jolls C, Sunstein CR, Thaler RH (1998) A behavioral approach to law and economics. Stan Law Rev 50(5):1471–1550

Jung D, Erdfelder E, Bröder A, Dorner V (2019) Differentiating motivational and cognitive explanations for decision inertia. J Econ Psychol 72:30–44

Kahneman D (2003) Maps of bounded rationality: psychology for behavioral economics. Am Econ Rev 93(5):1449–1475

Kahneman D (2011) Thinking, fast and slow. Macmillan, New York
Kahneman D, Frederick S (2004) Attribute substitution in intuitive judgment. In: Augier M, March JG (eds) Models of a man: essays in memory of Herbert A. Simon. MIT Press, pp 411–432
Kahneman D, Tversky A (1979) Prospect theory: an analysis of decision under risk. Econometrica 47(2):363–391
Kahneman D, Knetsch JL, Thaler RH (1990) Experimental tests of the endowment effect and the Coase theorem. J Polit Econ 98(6):1325–1348
Kahneman D, Knetsch JL, Thaler RH (1991) Anomalies: the endowment effect, loss aversion, and status quo bias. J Econ Perspect 5(1):193–206
Kamins M (2019) Marketing manipulation: a consumer's survival manual. World Scientific Publishing, Singapore
Kamins MA, Alpert FH, Perner L (2003) Consumers' perception and misperception of market leadership and market pioneership. J Mark Manag 19(7–8):807–834
Kaplow L, Shavell S (2001) Fairness versus welfare. Harv Law Rev 114(4):961–1389
Kaptein M, Duplinsky S, Markopoulos P (2011) Means based adaptive persuasive systems. Proceedings of the SIGCHI Conference on Human Factors in Computing Systems, pp 1–10
Keller KL, Staelin R (1987) Effects of quality and quantity of information on decision effectiveness. J Consum Res 14(2):200–213
Kelman M (1998) Behavioral economics as part of rhetorical duet: response to Jolls, Sunstein, and Thaler. Stan Law Rev 50(5):1577–1592
Kessler F (1943) Contracts of adhesion—some thoughts about freedom of contract. Colum Law Rev 43(5):629–642
Kim JC (1985) The market for "lemons" reconsidered: a model of the used car market with asymmetric information. Am Econ Rev 75(4):836–843
Kinsey J, McAlister R (1981) Consumer knowledge of the costs of open-end credit. J Consum Aff 15(2):249–270
Klick J (2011) The empirical revolution in law and economics. Eleven International Publishing, The Hague
Korobkin R (1997) Status quo bias and contract default rules. Cornell Law Rev 83(3):608–687
Korobkin R (2009) Libertarian welfarism. Calif Law Rev 97(6):1651–1685
Korobkin RB, Ulen TS (2000) Law and behavioral science: removing the rationality assumption from law and economics. Calif Law Rev 88(4):1051–1144
Kotler P, Armstrong G (2016) Principles of marketing, 16th edn. Pearson, London
Krueger AO (1974) The political economy of the rent-seeking society. Am Econ Rev 64(3):291–303
Kuran T, Sunstein CR (1999) Availability cascades and risk regulation. Stan Law Rev 51(4):683–768
Laibson D (1997) Golden eggs and hyperbolic discounting. Q J Econ 112(2):443–478
Landes WM (2003) The empirical side of law & economics. Univ Chicago Law Rev 70(1):167–180
Lebech M (2004) What is human dignity? Maynooth Philos Pap 2:59–69
Li X, Hitt LM (2010) Price effects in online product reviews: an analytical model and empirical analysis. MIS Q 34(4):809–832
Liscow Z (2018) Is efficiency biased? Univ Chicago Law Rev 85(7):1649–1718
Loebbecke C, Hornig V (2001) Increasing trust in e-commerce: Concepts and examples of insurance solutions. Proc Int Electron Commer Conf Bled Slovenia:1–18
Loewenstein G, Haisley EC (2007) The economist as therapist: methodological ramifications of 'light' paternalism. In: Caplin A, Schotter A (eds) The foundations of positive and normative economics: a handbook. Oxford University Press, Oxford, pp 210–245
Loewenstein G, Prelec D (1992) Anomalies in intertemporal choice: evidence and an interpretation. Q J Econ 107(2):573–597
Luguri J, Strahilevitz LJ (2021) Shining a light on dark patterns. J Leg Anal 13(1):43–109
Luth HA (2010) Behavioural economics in consumer policy: the economic analysis of standard terms in consumer contracts revisited. Erasmus University Rotterdam, Rotterdam
Luzak JA (2015) Empirical evidence in consumer law cases: what are 'up to' claims up to? Amsterdam Law Sch Res Pap:1–19

Mackenzie C, Rogers W, Dodds S (2014) Introduction: what is vulnerability, and why does it matter for moral theory? In: Mackenzie C, Rogers W, Dodds S (eds) Vulnerability: new essays in ethics and feminist philosophy. Oxford University Press, Oxford, pp 1–29

Maitre-Ekern E, Dalhammar C (2016) Regulating planned obsolescence: a review of legal approaches to increase product durability and reparability in Europe. Rev Eur Comp Int Environ Law 25(3):378–394

Mak V (2011) Standards of protection: in search of the 'average consumer' of EU law in the proposal for a consumer rights directive. Eur Rev Priv Law 19(1):25–42

Mandell L (1973) Consumer knowledge and understanding of consumer credit. J Consum Aff 7(1):23–36

Markovits D, Richman BD, Van Loo R (2022) Consumer law as an axis of economic inequality. Boston Univ Law Rev 102(4):1169–1184

Mathis K (2009) Efficiency instead of justice? Searching for the philosophical foundations of the economic analysis of law. Springer, Dordrecht

Mathis K, Burri PA (2016) Nudging in Swiss contract law? In: Mathis K, Tor A (eds) Nudging—possibilities, limitations and applications in European law and economics. Springer, Cham, pp 121–151

Matz SC, Kosinski M, Nave G, Stillwell DJ (2017) Psychological targeting as an effective approach to digital mass persuasion. Proc Natl Acad Sci USA 114(48):12714–12719

McAfee RP, Mialon HM, Mialon SH (2010) Do sunk costs matter? Econ Inq 48(2):323–336

McNeal J (2007) On becoming a consumer. Routledge, London

McNeil K, Nevin JR, Trubek DM, Miller RE (1979) Market discrimination against the poor and the impact of consumer disclosure laws: the used car industry. Law Soc Rev 13(3):695–720

Meier S, Sprenger C (2007) Impatience and credit behavior: evidence from a field experiment. Fed Reserve Bank Boston Work Pap No 07-3:1–42

Mik E (2016) The erosion of autonomy in online consumer transactions. Law Innov Technol 8(1):1–38

Mittal V, Ross WT Jr, Baldasare PM (1998) The asymmetric impact of negative and positive attribute-level performance on overall satisfaction and repurchase intentions. J Mark 62(1):33–47

Mitts J (2014) How much mandatory disclosure is effective? Available at SSRN: https://ssrn.com/abstract=2404526

Moewe JA (1971) Consumers, class actions and costs: an economic perspective on deceptive advertising. UCLA Law Rev 18(3):592–615

Muris TJ (1991) Economics and consumer protection. Antitrust Law J 60(1):103–122

Narciso M (2017) Review mechanisms in online marketplaces and adverse selection: a law and economics analysis. Maastricht Eur Priv Law Inst Work Pap (2017/2):1–27

Narciso M (2022) The unreliability of online review mechanisms. J Consum Policy 45(3):349–368

Nash JF Jr (1950) The bargaining problem. Econometrica 18(2):155–162

Nelson P (1970) Information and consumer behavior. J Polit Econ 78(2):311–329

Newman N (2014) Search, antitrust, and the economics of the control of user data. Yale J Regul 31(2):401–454

Nickerson RS (1998) Confirmation bias: a ubiquitous phenomenon in many guises. Rev Gen Psychol 2(2):175–220

Noll J (2003) Does one size fit all? A note on the harmonization of national warranty law as a tool of consumer protection. Eur J Law Econ 16(2):219–231

OECD (2017a) Use of behavioural insights in consumer policy. OECD Sci Technol Innov Policy Pap No. 36:1–48

OECD (2017b) Behavioural insights and public policy: lessons from around the world. OECD Publ, Paris

Oehler A, Wendt S (2017) Good consumer information: the information paradigm at its (dead) end? J Consum Policy 40(2):179–191

Ogus AI (2004) Regulation: legal form and economic theory. Bloomsbury Publishing, London

Okun AM (1975) Equality and efficiency: the big tradeoff. Brookings Inst, Washington, DC
Pacces AM, Visscher LT (2011) Methodology of law and economics. In: Van Klink B, Taekema S (eds) Law and method: interdisciplinary research into law. Mohr Siebeck, Tübingen, pp 85–107
Parisi F (2004a) Positive, normative and functional schools in law and economics. Eur J Law Econ 18(3):259–272
Parisi F (2004b) The harmonization of legal warranties in European sales law: an economic analysis. Am J Comp Law 52(2):403–432
Parisi F (2013) The language of law and economics. Cambridge Books, Cambridge
Pearlman A (2018) May we suggest: restaurant menus and the art of persuasion. Agate Publishing, Evanston
Pee LG (2016) Customer co-creation in B2C e-commerce: does it lead to better new products? Electron Commer Res 4(6):1–27
Pelkmans J (1984) Consumer interests in the EC competition regime: an economic perspective. In: Goyens M (ed) EC competition policy and the consumer interest. Cabay, Leuven, pp 21–69
Phelps ES, Pollak RA (1968) On second-best national saving and game-equilibrium growth. Rev Econ Stud 35(2):185–199
Pindyck R, Rubinfeld D (2013) Microeconomics, 9th edn. Pearson, Boston
Plassmann H, Kenning P, Deppe M, Kugel H, Schwindt W, Ahlert D (2006) How brands twist heart and mind: neural correlates of the affect heuristic during brand choice. University of Muenster, Muenster
Polinsky AM (1989) An introduction to law and economics, 2nd edn. Little, Brown & Co, Boston
Pomar FG (2001) Directive 1998/44/EC on certain aspects of the sale of consumer goods and associated guarantees: An economic perspective. InDret:1–23
Pomar FG, Golobardes MA (2018) Rational choice and behavioral approaches to consumer issues. In: Micklitz HW, Sibony AL, Esposito F (eds) Research methods in consumer law. Edward Elgar Publication, Cheltenham, pp 119–164
Posner RA (1990) The problems of jurisprudence. Harvard University Press, Cambridge, MA
Posner RA (2014) Economic analysis of law. Wolters Kluwer, New York
Power N, Alison L, Ralph J (2013) Decision inertia: defining its meaning and dichotomizing its context as a latent and emergent variable. In: International Conference on Naturalistic Decision Making, Marseille, France, pp 261–264
Priest GL (1981) A theory of the consumer product warranty. Yale Law J 90(6):1297–1352
Rabin M (1998) Psychology and economics. J Econ Lit 36(1):11–46
Rachlinski JJ (2002) The uncertain psychological case for paternalism. Nw Univ Law Rev 97(3):1165–1226
Raghavan V (2022) Consumer law's equity gap. Utah Law Rev 2022(3):511–571
Rakoff TD (1983) Contracts of adhesion: an essay in reconstruction. Harv Law Rev 96(6):1173–1284
Ramsay I (2012) Consumer law and policy: text and materials on regulating consumer markets. Bloomsbury Publ, London
Ranchordás S (2018) Online reputation and the regulation of information asymmetries in the platform economy. Crit Anal Law 5(1):127–147
Rawls JB (1971) A theory of justice. Belknap Press, Cambridge, MA
Reisch LA, Thøgersen JB (2017) Behaviorally informed consumer policy: Research and policy for "humans.". In: Keller M, Halkier B, Wilska TA, Truniger M (eds) Routledge handbook on consumption. Routledge, London, pp 242–253
Reisch LA, Zhao MIN (2017) Behavioural economics, consumer behaviour and consumer policy: state of the art. Behav Public Policy 1(2):190–206
Rekaiti P, Van den Bergh R (2000) Cooling-off periods in the consumer laws of the EC member states: a comparative law and economics approach. J Consum Policy 23(4):371–408
Ricardo D (1817) On the principles of political economy and taxation. Batoche Books, Kitchener
Riefa C, Gamper H (2020) Economic theory and consumer vulnerability: exploring an uneasy relationship. In: Riefa C, Saintier S (eds) Vulnerable consumers and the law. Routledge, London, pp 17–30

Rischkowsky F, Döring T (2008) Consumer policy in a market economy: considerations from the perspective of the economics of information, the new institutional economics, and behavioral economics. J Consum Policy 31(3):285–313
Ritov I, Baron J (1990) Reluctance to vaccinate: omission bias and ambiguity. J Behav Decis Mak 3(4):263–277
Šajn N (2021) Vulnerable consumers. Eur Parl Res Serv, Doc No. PE 690.619. https://www.europarl.europa.eu/RegData/etudes/BRIE/2021/690619/EPRS_BRI(2021)690619_EN.pdf
Salop SC (2010) Question: what is the real and proper antitrust welfare standard? Answer: the true consumer welfare standard. Loy Consum Law Rev 22(3):336–353
Samuelson W, Zeckhauser R (1988) Status quo bias in decision making. J Risk Uncertain 1(1):7–59
Sax M, Helberger N, Bol N (2018) Health as a means towards profitable ends: mHealth apps, user autonomy, and unfair commercial practices. J Consum Policy 41:103–134
Schaub M (2017) How to make the best of mandatory information requirements in consumer law. Eur Rev Priv Law 25(1):25–44
Seele P, Dierksmeier C, Hofstetter R, Schultz MD (2021) Mapping the ethicality of algorithmic pricing: a review of dynamic and personalized pricing. J Bus Ethics 170(4):697–719
Shapiro C (1983) Consumer protection policy in the United States. J Inst Theor Econ 139(3):527–544
Shenkar O, Yuchtman-Yaar E (1997) Reputation, image, prestige, and goodwill: an interdisciplinary approach to organizational standing. Hum Relat 50(11):1361–1381
Simon HA (1955) A behavioral model of rational choice. Q J Econ 69(1):99–118
Simon HA (1956) Rational choice and the structure of the environment. Psychol Rev 63(2):129–138
Simonson I, Drolet A (2004) Anchoring effects on consumers' willingness-to-pay and willingness-to-accept. J Consum Res 31(3):681–690
Slovic P, Finucane ML, Peters E, MacGregor DG (2002) Rational actors or rational fools: implications of the affect heuristic for behavioral economics. J Socio-Econ 31(4):329–342
Slovic P, Finucane ML, Peters E, MacGregor DG (2007) The affect heuristic. Eur J Oper Res 177(3):1333–1352
Smits JM (2011) Rethinking the usefulness of mandatory rights of withdrawal in consumer contract law: the right to change your mind. Penn State Int Law Rev 29(3):671–684
Solove DJ (2002) Conceptualizing privacy. Calif Law Rev 90(4):1087–1155
Sovern J (2006) Toward a new model of consumer protection: the problem of inflated transaction costs. William Mary Law Rev 47(5):1635–1710
Standifird SS (2001) Reputation and e-commerce: eBay auctions and the asymmetrical impact of positive and negative ratings. J Manag 27(3):279–295
Stiglitz JE (2000) The contributions of the economics of information to twentieth-century economics. Q J Econ 115(4):1441–1478
Strotz RH (1955) Myopia and inconsistency in dynamic utility maximization. Rev Econ Stud 23(3):165–180
Stuart C (1977) Consumer protection in a market where sellers have better information than buyers. In: Skogh G (ed) Law and economics. Juridiska Föreningen, Lund, pp 155–164
Stuyck J (2000) European consumer law after the treaty of Amsterdam: consumer policy in or beyond the internal market? Common Mark Law Rev 37(2):367–400
Sunstein CR (1997) Behavioral analysis of law. Univ Chicago Law Rev 64(4):1175–1196
Sunstein CR (2002) Switching the default rule. New York Univ Law Rev 77(1):106–134
Sunstein CR (2011) Empirically informed regulation. Univ Chicago Law Rev 78(4):1349–1430
Sunstein CR (2016a) Fifty shades of manipulation. J Mark Behav 1(3–4):213–244
Sunstein CR (2016b) The council of psychological advisers. Annu Rev Psychol 67:713–737
Sunstein CR, Thaler RH (2003a) Libertarian paternalism. Am Econ Rev 93(2):175–179
Sunstein CR, Thaler RH (2003b) Libertarian paternalism is not an oxymoron. Univ Chicago Law Rev 70(4):1159–1202
Surowiecki J (2005) The wisdom of crowds. Anchor, New York

Svenson O (1981) Are we all less risky and more skillful than our fellow drivers? Acta Psychol 47(2):143–148

Thaichon P, Quach S (2022) Artificial intelligence for marketing management. Taylor & Francis, London

Thaler RH (1980) Toward a positive theory of consumer choice. J Econ Behav Organ 1(1):39–60

Thaler RH, Sunstein CR (2008) Nudge: improving decisions about health, wealth, and happiness. Yale University Press, New Haven

Thaler RH, Sunstein CR, Balz JP (2013) Choice architecture. In: Shafir E (ed) The behavioral foundations of public policy. Princeton University Press, Princeton, pp 428–439

Titus PA, Bradford JL (1996) Reflections on consumer sophistication and its impact on ethical business practice. J Consum Aff 30(1):170–194

Tokeley K (2013) Consumer law and paternalism: a framework for policy decision-making. In: Frankel S, Ryder D (eds) Recalibrating behaviour: smarter regulation in a global world. LexisNexis, Wellington, pp 265–304

Tollison RD (2012) The economic theory of rent seeking. Public Choice 152(1):73–82

Trebilcock MJ (1997) The limits of freedom of contract. Harvard University Press, Cambridge

Trzaskowski J (2021) Your privacy is important to us! Restoring human dignity in data-driven marketing. Ex Tuto, Copenhagen

Tullock G (1967) The welfare costs of tariffs, monopolies, and theft. Econ Inq 5(3):224–232

Tullock G (1980) Efficient rent-seeking. In: Buchanan J, Tollison RD, Tullock G (eds) Toward a theory of the rent-seeking society. Texas A&M University Press, College Station

Tversky A, Kahneman D (1973) Availability: a heuristic for judging frequency and probability. Cognit Psychol 5(2):207–232

Tversky A, Kahneman D (1974) Judgment under uncertainty: heuristics and biases. Science 185(4157):1124–1131

Ulen TS (1998) Growing pains of behavioral law and economics. Vand Law Rev 51(6):1747–1764

Valant J (2015) Consumer protection in the EU. Policy overview. Policy Dept Econ Sci Qual Life Policies, EPRS. https://aei.pitt.edu/96092/1/consumer.1.pdf

Van Aaken A (2016) Constitutional limits to paternalistic nudging: a proportionality assessment. In: Kemmerer A, Möllers C, Steinbeis M, Wagner G (eds) Choice architecture in democracies. Hart-Nomos, Oxford, pp 161–195

Van Boom WH, Ogus AI (2010) Introducing, defining, and balancing autonomy vs. paternalism. Erasmus Law Rev 3(1):1–6

Van den Bergh RJ (1997) Wer schützt die europäischen Verbraucher vor dem Brüsseler Verbraucherschutz? In: Ott C, Schäfer HB (eds) Effiziente Verhaltenssteuerung und Kooperation in Zivilrecht. Mohr Siebeck, Tübingen, pp 77–102

Van den Bergh RJ (2000) Averechts recht. Intersentia, Antwerpen

Van den Bergh RJ (2007) Economische analyse van het consumentenrecht. In: Weterings WTC (ed) De economische analyse van het recht. Boom Juridische Uitgevers, Den Haag, pp 119–140

Van den Bergh RJ, Heremans D (1987) Recht en economie. Tijdschr Econ Manag 32(2):139–164

Van Heusden A (2023) The law and economics of consumer law. In: Baumann AGC, Nobel P, Aliverti E (eds) Law and Economics in all seinen Facetten: Festschrift zu Ehren von Klaus Mathis. Duncker & Humblot, Berlin, pp 525–565

Van Loo R (2019) Broadening consumer law: competition, protection, and distribution. Notre Dame Law Rev 95(1):211–262

Van Loo R (2023) The public stakes of consumer law: the environment, the economy, health, disinformation, and beyond. Minn Law Rev 107(5):2039–2114

Varian HR (2009) Intermediate microeconomics: a modern approach, 8th edn. W. W. Norton & Company, New York

Waddington L (2013) Vulnerable and confused: the protection of "vulnerable" consumers under EU law. Eur Law Rev 6:757–782

Wagner G, Eidenmüller H (2019) Down by algorithms: siphoning rents, exploiting biases, and shaping preferences: regulating the dark side of personalized transactions. Univ Chicago Law Rev 86(2):581–610
Walters D (2015) Behavioral marketing: delivering personalized experiences at scale. Wiley, Hoboken
Wan Y, Ma B, Pan Y (2018) Opinion evolution of online consumer reviews in the e-commerce environment. Electron Commer Res 18(2):291–311
Weber F (2020a) Das Verbraucherleitbild des Verbrauchervertragsrechts–Im Wandel? Verbraucher und Recht 35(1):9–15
Weber F (2020b) Verbraucherleitbilder im Spiegel der Verbraucherverhaltensforschung. Z Rechtspolitik 53(4):98–101
Weinstein ND (1980) Unrealistic optimism about future life events. J Pers Soc Psychol 39(5):806–820
Wertenbroch K, Schrift RY, Alba JW, Barasch A, Bhattacharjee A, Giesler M, Zwebner Y (2020) Autonomy in consumer choice. Mark Lett 31:429–439
Whitehead M, Jones R, Howell R, Lilley R, Pykett J (2014) Nudging all over the world: assessing the impacts of the behavioural sciences on public policy. ESRC Negotiating Neuroliberalism Project Report. http://changingbehaviours.wordpress.com
Williamson OE (1979) Transaction-cost economics: the governance of contractual relations. J Law Econ 22(2):233–261
Willis LE (2015) Performance-based consumer law. Univ Chicago Law Rev 82(3):1309–1409
Wright JD (2007) Behavioral law and economics, paternalism, and consumer contracts: an empirical perspective. New York Univ J Law Liberty 2(3):470–511
Wu JJX (2023) Beyond free markets and consumer autonomy: rethinking consumer financial protection in the age of artificial intelligence. J Intellect Prop Entertain Law 13(1):56–134
Xia L, Monroe KB, Cox JL (2004) The price is unfair! A conceptual framework of price fairness perceptions. J Mark 68(4):1–15
Zajonc RB (1968) Attitudinal effects of mere exposure. J Pers Soc Psychol 9(2p2):1–27
Zajonc RB (2001) Mere exposure: a gateway to the subliminal. Curr Dir Psychol Sci 10(6):224–228
Zarsky TZ (2002) Mine your own business: making the case for the implications of the data mining of personal information in the forum of public opinion. Yale J Law Technol 5:1–56
Zuboff S (2019) The age of surveillance capitalism: the fight for a human future at the new frontier of power. Profile Books, London

Chapter 3
Online Consumer Manipulation: A Law and Economics Analysis of Personalized Advertising

Abstract This chapter investigates personalized advertising from a law and economics perspective, highlighting its potential benefits and harms. The analysis incorporates consumer perceptions and ethical considerations to provide a comprehensive view. The merits of personalized advertising are examined through the lenses of total welfare, consumer welfare, equity, and consumer autonomy. Subsequently, a legal analysis evaluates whether the existing regulatory framework is adequately equipped to safeguard consumers' welfare, autonomy, and equity in the face of personalized advertising practices.

3.1 Introduction

A tailored ad for each individual. That is the utopia of advertisers. However, as this chapter will demonstrate, society is getting closer and closer to such a scenario, and the associated consequences should not be underestimated. The extent to which ads can be personalized as of today has never been seen before, and the developments in AI, *machine learning* (ML), and *deep learning* (DL) are opening up new possibilities.[1]

Online advertising is a booming business. Ad spending in digital advertising was predicted to reach 616 billion US dollars in 2022, which would account for 67% of global ad spending.[2] Online (also labeled as digital) advertising has surpassed traditional advertising by a substantial margin. The growth of online advertising is not expected to stop anytime soon. The *compound annual growth rate* (CAGR) of the online advertising market is estimated to be 14.3% over the period 2022–2027.[3] The key driver behind this growth is the transition of consumers from the offline to the online world. Time on the Internet has overtaken people's time on alternative media,

---

[1] Chintalapati and Pandey (2022).

[2] Statista (2022).

[3] Mordor Intelligence (2022).

A. J. van Heusden, *The Law and Economics of Personalization*, Economic Analysis of Law in European Legal Scholarship 20,
https://doi.org/10.1007/978-3-032-01468-9_3

mainly due to the increasing use of mobile devices.[4] The digitalization of society has enabled the collection of vast amounts of data, which offers a plethora of possibilities for data-driven marketing, including personalization.

Personalized advertising is the fastest-growing and "trendiest" form of online advertising.[5] The value of personalized advertising is continuously increasing, and it has become the largest contributor to the growth of online advertising.[6] Marketers have widely recognized the potential of personalized advertising, and it has become the most well-known personalized marketing practice among the general public.[7]

Personalization could give rise to new challenges for which the current consumer protection laws might not be sufficiently equipped.[8] As a result of personalization, traditional marketing, which has extensively been regulated by marketing and consumer protection laws over the years, is being transformed into highly innovative and effective AI-driven marketing that can circumvent the existing legal framework.

Personalization offers new opportunities to target consumer biases and vulnerabilities, differentiate between the sophisticated and the unsophisticated,[9] and exploit consumers accordingly.[10] In addition, the challenges consumers face due to personalization are exacerbated by the thriving use of dark patterns, which have the potential to reinforce the effectiveness of personalized ads. Connecting an established set of dark patterns to personalization makes marketing a more powerful tool for exploiting consumer vulnerabilities.[11]

The focus of this chapter is to analyze the practice of personalized advertising from a law and economics perspective. By employing a law and economics approach, it becomes possible to understand the mechanism behind personalized advertising, identify the economic benefits and harms, and determine to what extent legal intervention is required. The analysis is deliberately broadened by including consumer perceptions, privacy, and ethical considerations.

The structure of the chapter is as follows. First, an introduction to data-driven business models is given to understand how these models enable personalization. Subsequently, the practice of personalized advertising will be explored. In addition, the complementary role of dark patterns will be examined. The economic analysis of personalized advertising will take place with the consideration of consumer perceptions, privacy, and ethical concerns. Finally, the current legal framework that addresses personalized advertising and dark patterns will be reviewed to see if a marketing-induced market failure is present that justifies further regulatory intervention.

---

[4] DataReportal (2022).

[5] Lombo and Evas (2020).

[6] Boudet et al. (2019).

[7] European Commission (2016), pp. 34–40.

[8] Galli (2022).

[9] This refers to consumers' sophistication in the online market, see Sect. 2.2.6.

[10] Galli (2022), p. 104.

[11] Helberger et al. (2021), p. 110.

3.2 Data-Driven Business Models: An Introduction

The advent of big data alludes to the increasingly prominent role that data plays in people's daily lives. Big data refers to the "large data sets that can be analysed, interrogated and processed in order to provide new meaning, value, and understanding."[12] Four fundamental characteristics need to be mentioned concerning big data, also called "the four V's", namely *volume*, *variety*, *velocity*, and *veracity*. In short, 1) volume relates to the large scale of data that is involved, 2) variety refers to the multiplexity of options that enables the recombination of disparate data sets to create new data sets and extract value from them, 3) velocity is the rate with which data is generated and moved, and 4) veracity refers to the accuracy and the trustworthiness of the data.[13]

With respect to business development, big data has spurred on innovation in many realms of human endeavor, such as organizational decision-making and strategizing,[14] improving products and services, and developing business models.[15] The latter is of particular interest since the emergence of *data-driven business models* has enabled the creation and extraction of value in the form of data-driven marketing, which will be further explained in Sect. 3.2.2.

A business model is data-driven when its core activity necessitates digital data.[16] In other words, a key element of a data-driven business model is the processing of data, which is required for its value proposition.[17] The value creation of data-driven business models relies on monetizing three key factors: 1) *surveillance*, 2) *attention*, and 3) *behavior modification*.[18]

First, surveillance refers to the act of searching for and collecting personal (i.e., data about the personal characteristics of an individual) and behavioral data (i.e., data about individuals' interaction with the business) by data-driven businesses.[19] Through the collection of personal data, profiling can be improved, enabling businesses to personalize their marketing. Consequently, personalization allows for the extraction of so-called *behavioral surplus*.[20] That is to say, vast amounts of data are processed to accurately predict consumer behavior and influence it with the goal of obtaining revenue.

Second, to be able to collect data, it is of paramount importance that the individual interacts with the business. To spur the interaction, businesses need to grab individuals' attention. Attention is a scarce resource in an information-rich world;

---

[12] Wilson (2019), p. 4.

[13] Wilson (2019), p. 7.

[14] Chen et al. (2012).

[15] Engelbrecht et al. (2016).

[16] Engelbrecht et al. (2016), p. 5.

[17] The value created and offered to consumers, see Chesbrough and Rosenbloom (2002), p. 533.

[18] Trzaskowski (2021), p. 9.

[19] Zuboff (2019).

[20] Acquisti et al. (2016), p. 460.

therefore, attention has value.[21] It is in the interest of data-driven businesses to capture consumers' attention and subsequently monetize it.[22] The capturing of consumer attention takes place by means of marketing, in particular advertising.

Traditionally, advertising is defined as: "Any paid form of nonpersonal presentation and promotion of ideas, goods, or services by an identified sponsor."[23] As will become apparent from Sect. 3.3, this definition does not hold up in this day and age. An advertising strategy is employed to achieve a specific objective, which can be divided into three categories: *informative*, *persuasive*, and *reminder advertising*.[24] If the exposure to an ad enables the capture of consumers' attention, it opens up the way for value extraction. In other words, if consumers can be engaged by advertising, it becomes possible, through the interaction process, to obtain valuable and monetizable personal and behavioral data from the individual.

Third, the possession of consumers' data facilitates marketing strategies aimed at preference formation and behavior modification to the benefit of the seller.[25] As explained in Chap. 2, behavior modification occurs in two manners: through persuasion and manipulation. The emergence of data-driven marketing has blurred this distinction between lawful persuasion and unlawful manipulation.[26]

3.2.1 *The Monetization of Data*

Data-driven business models enable, in principle, a mutually beneficial interaction between the seller and the consumer. The interaction provides the seller with valuable data that can be monetized in the form of ads, which in turn enables the consumer to gain access to certain services, usually for "free" (e.g., YouTube). Apart from interacting with consumers, businesses can also obtain valuable data by purchasing data from third-party data brokers. Data monetization is facilitated by the developments in AI. The concept and the corresponding definition of AI have been and still are the subject of a vast array of research.[27] In this study, the focus lies on what AI means for marketing.

A definition of AI that can be found in the marketing literature is:

> AI, frequently coined machine intelligence, is the demonstration by computers (machines) to complete tasks normally associated to humans, traditionally requiring human involvement

---

[21] Simon (1971).

[22] Cfr. Gösser et al. (2021).

[23] Kotler and Armstrong (2016), p. 474.

[24] Kotler and Armstrong (2016), pp. 475–476.

[25] Galli (2022), p. 100.

[26] Trzaskowski (2021), p. 12.

[27] McCarthy et al. (2006); Nilsson (2009); Aghion et al. (2019); Cockburn et al. (2019).

> and intelligence. AI can cover many things such as problem-solving, learning from new data sets, as well as prescribing actions and meaning from new data.[28]

In this study, when the term AI is used, it comprises the use of big data, algorithms, machine learning (ML), and deep learning (DL) for marketing purposes.[29] This corresponds to the notion of *algorithmic marketing*.[30]

Algorithms can be defined as "computer systems that are able to replicate the logic, approach, expertise and reasoning behind processing information for problem-solving."[31] Machine learning can be described as "a field of AI which relies upon statistical driven processes, functions and techniques to enable a computer to learn from new and changing data. It's the automated (self)learning without explicit programming that is core to ML."[32]

Deep learning is, simply put, a sub-category of ML, in which the system integrates context sensitivity and improves by learning autonomously from its past performance. In other words, in the case of DL, the machine can teach itself to transform data points into valuable knowledge. In contrast, in ML, the developer must instruct the machine to learn from the data.[33]

The advent of the digital age has caused a wave of digitalization in society, substantially increasing the amount of data being collected. Through far-reaching surveillance, more data about individuals can be obtained than ever before.[34] Algorithms can self-improve and self-update through the continuous input of data, which allows the algorithm to learn and improve its prediction accuracy.

3.2.2 Data-Driven Marketing

In the realm of marketing, AI can be utilized to optimize marketing effectiveness by making more accurate predictions of future consumer behavior.[35] This gave rise to the term *data-driven marketing*. In essence, data are the critical driver behind marketing strategies.[36]

The data-driven marketing analysis consists of three key elements: *tracking*, *targeting*, and *forecasting*.[37] The analysis of consumers' personal and behavioral data allows for the identification of specific correlations from which individuals'

---

[28] Wilson (2019), p. 10.

[29] In correspondence with Trzaskowski (2021), p. 16.

[30] Galli (2022), p. 18.

[31] Wilson (2019), p. 10.

[32] Wilson (2019), p. 10.

[33] Agrawal et al. (2019).

[34] Agrawal et al. (2019), pp. 12–13.

[35] Dimitrieska et al. (2018).

[36] Tripathi et al. (2021).

[37] Kumar et al. (2006); Kakatkar and Spann (2019); Shah and Murthi (2021).

preferences and (predicted) behaviors can be inferred. One of the significant advantages of self-learning algorithms is that they can approximate future behavior with ever-improving accuracy.[38] In the mobile network operator market, it has been found that data-driven marketing, based on ML, leads to conversion rates (i.e., an indicator of effectiveness) that are significantly higher than the ones that result from traditional best-practice marketing strategies (e.g., the marketing team's experience and gut feeling).[39]

The rationale behind data-driven marketing is that due to sophisticated AI-based technologies, it becomes possible to understand, predict, and influence consumer behavior more accurately. This opens the door for data experimentation in order to find the most effective way of personalization to reach the goal set by a business. Galli (2022) states:

> The configuration of content, product, or any campaign is not determined by considering the real needs and desires of consumers but is performed through a continuous process of predicting and measuring the impact of business micro-decisions in pursuit of a specific business objective, calculated with the appropriate metrics.[40]

3.2.3 Persuasion or Manipulation?

The potential to shape consumer preferences and steer behavior raises the question to what degree AI-driven marketing still falls within the domain of persuasion rather than manipulation. The difference between persuasive and manipulative marketing has briefly been introduced in Chap. 2. As a refresher, persuasion is using marketing lawfully to convince consumers to buy a product or service. Conversely, manipulation occurs when an action or statement "does not sufficiently engage or appeal to people's capacity for reflective and deliberative choice."[41]

As a result of manipulation, consumers' autonomy and dignity are endangered, and consumers might fail to promote their welfare and instead promote the welfare of the manipulator.[42] The challenge lies in determining whether a marketing strategy is persuasive or manipulative.[43] In essence, both persuasive and manipulative marketing aim to influence human decision-making. Marketing has incorporated insights from behavioral science to understand how to influence consumer behavior. The *Cialdini's principles of persuasion* are a manifestation of these insights.[44] Cialdini (2021) asserts that if one or more of the seven levers of influence are

---

[38] Trzaskowski (2021), p. 18.

[39] Sundsøy et al. (2014).

[40] Galli (2022), p. 95.

[41] Sunstein (2016), p. 213.

[42] Sunstein (2016), p. 213.

[43] Sunstein (2016), p. 216.

[44] Cialdini (2021).

employed in a marketing strategy,[45] consumers will likely be persuaded to respond positively to the message conveyed by marketers.[46] Consequently, incorporating behavioral insights can lead to effective, persuasive marketing strategies. Moreover, the digital age offers marketers technological tools to help foster the automatization, upscaling, and personalization of persuasive marketing strategies.[47]

Two key features of persuasive marketing can be identified. First, *diminishing friction* to facilitate cognitive ease.[48] In practice, this amounts to curating a reality for consumers in which they can be nudged into taking the action that is most profitable to the seller. This relates to the design of consumer online experiences, which will be further scrutinized in Sect. 3.4. Second, the emphasis on *motivation*, *ability*, and *prompts* (MAP). "Motivation is your desire to do the behavior. Ability is your capacity to do the behavior. And prompt is your cue to do the behavior."[49]

Advancements in digital technology allow marketers to personalize marketing activities to the individual's needs and characteristics, which increases the individual's ability (i.e., taking away friction by creating an effortless buying experience), and prompts them to take action. The collection of vast amounts of personal and behavioral data facilitates *persuasion profiling*, which creates the possibility for targeted persuasion.[50] Persuasion profiling takes place when firms collect the expected effects of different influence strategies on an individual (i.e., the predicted responses) and make adjustments to determine which strategy or which combination of strategies give the best results.[51]

An essential element of persuasive marketing is the use of *emotions*.[52] Marketers are able to evoke emotions by displaying social cues in an online environment, which can subsequently be detected by digital technologies (e.g., facial expression analysis). To illustrate, an experiment concerning emotional contagion on Facebook has demonstrated that: "Emotional states can be transferred to others via emotional contagion, leading people to experience the same emotions without their awareness."[53]

By manipulating the amount of emotional content in a newsfeed, it was found that "when positive expressions were reduced, people produced fewer positive posts and more negative posts; when negative expressions were reduced, the opposite pattern occurred."[54] The experiment provided clear evidence for massive-scale

[45] It must be noted that this does not mean that these tactics are legal *per se*. This needs to be determined on a case-by-case basis.

[46] The seven levers of influence are reciprocation, liking, social proof, authority, scarcity, commitment and consistency, and unity.

[47] Trzaskowski (2021), p. 143.

[48] Kahneman (2011), p. 67.

[49] Fogg (2019).

[50] Kaptein and Eckles (2010).

[51] Kaptein et al. (2011), pp. 5–6.

[52] For an elaborate analysis on the use of emotions in AI-driven marketing, see Galli (2022).

[53] Kramer et al. (2014), p. 8788.

[54] Kramer et al. (2014), p. 8788.

contagion via social networks. It also showed the far-reaching effects of the online digital environment on an individual's state of mind and behavior. Accordingly, these virtual realities can detect emotions and evoke, amplify, and change them. This is directly related to *engagement*, which is essential for optimizing profit-maximizing marketing strategies. Therefore, it is conceivable that emotions are "a driver of engagement, habits and addictive behavior."[55] It can be profitable for companies to influence consumers' emotions to encourage specific desired behavior. However, it can be argued that at this point the boundary between persuasion and manipulation is being transgressed.[56]

Continuous and practical exposure to personalized marketing can make the persuasive effect so overwhelming that consumers are tricked into making decisions that promote the welfare of the seller rather than their own. Akerlof and Shiller (2015) see this as a form of manipulation and deception and coined the term *phishing for phools*. In essence, "phishing" means getting people to act for the other party's benefit rather than their own. The "phool" is the one that falls for the artificial lure.

3.3 Personalization of Advertising

Advertising is a key aspect of the marketing mix[57] that has undergone significant change. The collection of vast amounts of personal and behavioral data coupled with sophisticated analytical methods have transformed standardized offline promotional efforts into cost-effective and powerful targeted online advertising.[58] In traditional marketing, the ability to show consumers ads that are specifically tailored to each individual sounded like a marketer's dream; however, online advertising has enabled the personalization of ads on a massive scale in real time. In other words, the theoretical scenario has become a real-life practice.

A key component of personalized advertising is *online behavioral advertising* (OBA). OBA has been defined as "the practice of monitoring people's online behavior and using the collected information to show people individually targeted advertisements."[59] When speaking of online behavior, it aims to include, *inter alia*, web browsing, search queries, consumption data, purchases, social media content, click-through rates, and communication content.[60]

Online personalized advertising is broader than OBA alone. Where OBA is based on the consumer's behavioral data, personalized advertising can also include

[55] Trzaskowski (2021), p. 153.

[56] Trzaskowski (2021); Galli (2022).

[57] See Sect. 2.4.2.

[58] OECD (2019).

[59] Boerman et al. (2017), p. 364.

[60] Boerman et al. (2017), p. 364.

consumer's personal data (i.e., relating to the individual's characteristics). It must be noted, however, that, in practice, AI systems fueled by behavioral data are able to profile consumers with such accuracy that it eventually will lead to the same outcome as if they were fueled by personal data.[61] Simply put, even limited amounts of data points regarding what an individual does online will paint a highly accurate picture of who that individual is.

To function properly, OBA relies on tracking consumer behavior online to develop highly detailed consumer profiles. For this purpose, it needs to rely on tracking technology. Three tracking methods are well-known in marketing. First, the use of *cookies*, which is "a small piece of code embedded in a website that places a unique identifier in a user's browser whenever they visit a particular advertiser's website."[62] These cookies can have a first-party origin, i.e., placed by the website the consumer is viewing, or a third-party origin, i.e., set by a party unknown to the consumer.[63] The latter case is possible based on the *retargeted advertising mechanism*. The cookie allows the ad agency or advertiser to track browsing behavior on the first party's website and subsequently put up the records thereof for auction to all available ad agencies. The highest bidder wins the auction and can display the ad. This process is repeated and happens in real-time. As a result, the consumer is shown a mix of products and services they have viewed in the past.[64] The automated process of buying and selling advertising space to communicate a marketing message to the consumer is called *programmatic advertising*.[65]

Another method is *deterministic tracking*, which "involves tying unique devices to a common persistent identifier—such as a name or email address."[66] In other words, tracking based on consumer-identifying characteristics, which can, for example, be provided by the consumers themselves in the form of credentials to access a website. In this way, companies can leverage the identifying information by correlating user activity across devices where the same credentials are being used. This allows for *cross-device tracking*.[67]

The third method is *probabilistic tracking*, which "works by first uniquely identifying various devices (for example, through a cookie, hardware identifier, or device fingerprint), and then comparing collected information about those devices for shared attributes to infer a likelihood of whether those devices are used by the same person."[68] An example of such an identifier is an IP address. Deterministic and probabilistic techniques are often combined to further improve the accuracy of

---

[61] Bock (2016).

[62] Aziz and Telang (2016).

[63] Miyazaki (2008), p. 22.

[64] Aziz and Telang (2016).

[65] Galli (2022), p. 85. For an in-depth discussion on the workings of programmatic advertising, see White and Samuel (2019); Lee and Cho (2020); Samuel et al. (2021).

[66] Brookman et al. (2017).

[67] Brookman et al. (2017), p. 116.

[68] Brookman et al. (2017), p. 115.

cross-device tracking models.[69] As a result of these tracking methods, ads can be more accurately targeted, consumer interactions with the ads can be measured, and advertising expenditures can be optimized.[70]

3.3.1 *The Development of Advertising*

Traditionally, advertising had a signaling function that incentivized sellers to increase product quality. Advertising, in a way, fulfilled the same role as warranties.[71] High advertising expenditures were perceived as high-quality signals.[72] Since firms made substantial investments in advertising campaigns, it would be financially detrimental if the quality were below consumers' expectations. Nowadays, due to the vast amount of information that is available online, the informational and signaling functions of advertising can be disputed.[73]

In economic literature, advertising is seen as a tool to convey helpful information to consumers.[74] That way, it enables sellers to create demand for their products and signal quality.[75] Nonetheless, the digital age has made the provision of information through advertising obsolete.[76] The development of the Internet has enabled consumers to get product information from various sources and become less dependent on advertising. For instance, consumers are strongly influenced by social media and influencer marketing,[77] and consumers heavily rely on online reviews before making a purchase rather than the information provided by the seller.[78]

Digital technologies facilitate new ways to promote products and services via advertisements, and they "provide for interactive and individually tailored advertising in a way that no other medium has before, using the vast amounts of personal data collected online."[79] Due to the decreased advertising costs in the marketplace, the quality signaling function of advertising can be contested. Accordingly, advertising in the digital age has reinforced the persuasive power of the marketing message, whereas the quality signaling power has primarily lost its value.[80]

---

[69] Brookman et al. (2017), p. 117.

[70] OECD (2019), p. 11.

[71] Noll (2004).

[72] Moorthy and Zhao (2000).

[73] Woodcock (2018).

[74] Bagwell (2007).

[75] Nelson (1974).

[76] Woodcock (2018), p. 2274.

[77] Hutter et al. (2013); Bharucha (2018); Voramontri and Klieb (2019).

[78] Hu et al. (2008); Jiménez and Mendoza (2013); Zhang et al. (2014).

[79] OECD (2019), p. 11.

[80] Woodcock (2018).

3.3.2 *Types of Online Advertising*

Various forms of online advertising exist, but in general, they can be classified into five categories: *display advertising*, *search advertising*, *social media advertising*, *native advertising*, and *classified advertising*. The goal of this section is to provide an overview of the main categories of advertising. In this way, it becomes possible to understand how the advertising landscape has changed, but more importantly, to what extent data-driven marketing has led to new forms of advertising that have a greater potential to influence, persuade, but also manipulate consumers.

3.3.2.1 Display Advertising

Display advertising, also known as *contextual advertising*, is a form of advertising that has been around for decades. In the traditional sense, display advertising meant using giant billboards, television commercials, or flyers to attract consumers' attention. Nonetheless, the developments in digital technology have pushed the frontiers of advertising, and nowadays, highly innovative display advertising methods can be found online. The state-of-the-art form of display advertising is called *digital display advertising*, defined as "advertisements that are displayed on websites or applications in various forms. It includes social media advertising, video advertisements, and banner advertisements."[81]

There are two forms of display advertising: non-intrusive and intrusive. In the case of *non-intrusive display advertising*, the ad that the consumer sees online has no or little connection to the consumer's behavior. A thematically related ad that pops up when consumers are in an online session is regarded as being "fairly innocuous from a privacy perspective."[82] However, advertisements based on large amounts of data, such as the use of search engines or the scanning of emails, amount to *intrusive display advertising*.[83] For example, if consumers speak about a specific topic in their emails (assuming consumers have a Gmail account), Google will be able to display an ad about the topic the next time consumers visit a website.

3.3.2.2 Search Advertising

The largest category of online advertising is search advertising.[84] Firms pay search engine operators to link their websites (on which they sell products or services) to users' search results. When a user enters a search query, the specific advert (or

[81] Fourberg et al. (2021).

[82] Nill and Aalberts (2014), p. 128.

[83] Nill and Aalberts (2014), p. 128.

[84] According to Statista (2022), the market's largest segment is search advertising with a market volume of US $260bn in 2022.

sponsored link) is then shown together with the organic search results."[85] The organic search results are the "unpaid results returned by the search engine's algorithm based on their relevance to a consumer's query."[86] The prominence and ranking of the ads are determined by an auction in which advertisers can bid for the highest rank. This process of paying for an improved position in consumers' search results falls under the umbrella of *sponsored ranking*.[87]

3.3.2.3 Social Media Advertising

Social media advertising is gaining popularity as a strategy to target consumers. The rationale is that social media have become significantly more important in people's daily lives. People spend increasing amounts of time on social media, creating opportunities for advertisers to attract attention, increase engagement, and magnify ad exposure. Accordingly, more effective and targeted ads can be developed through the collection of both personal and behavioral data provided by social media users and their networks.[88] The ads can then be shown in the social (e.g., Meta and TikTok) and business networks (e.g., LinkedIn) of the users by embedding them in their individualized newsfeed. Social media companies have become key actors in advertising by collecting massive amounts of data about consumers' profiles, interactions, and browsing activities while using social media services.[89]

3.3.2.4 Native Advertising

Native advertising falls within "a spectrum of new online advertising forms that share a focus on minimizing disruption to a consumer's online experience by appearing in-stream."[90] The disruption can be minimized through optimal placement and blending into the surrounding content. Native advertising is appealing to advertisers since it offers a solution to overcome *ad blindness,* which is consumers' antipathy to advertisement exposure. That is to say, consumers tend to dislike intrusive advertising.[91]

Native advertising can be defined as "a new marketing technique for unobtrusively integrating paid advertising into editorial content."[92] In essence, the advertiser intentionally uses the credibility of the content publisher by imitating the format

[85] Fourberg et al. (2021), p. 16.

[86] OECD (2019), p. 16.

[87] ACM (2021).

[88] OECD (2019), p. 18.

[89] Fourberg et al. (2021), p. 17.

[90] Campbell and Marks (2015), p. 600.

[91] Levi (2015).

[92] Levi (2015), p. 647.

and location of the content.[93] It deliberately makes it more demanding for consumers to identify the message as advertising. In this light, native advertising is a misleading marketing technique involving consumer deception.[94] Accordingly, native advertising has quickly achieved the infamous status of being the *black sheep* of the marketing family.[95]

The act of concealing the commercial nature of ads is paramount since its recognition generally leads to negative consumer evaluations of the company that advertises the products and the publisher of the editorial content. Therefore, the credibility and accuracy of the information are essential for consumer decision-making and the corresponding decision satisfaction. It is, therefore, questionable to what extent improved consumer reach comes at the cost of loss of goodwill for the advertising company.[96]

3.3.2.5 Classified Advertising

The smallest category of advertising is classified advertising. In this case, advertisers purchase an advertising slot directly from a publisher's website to target a specific group of users.[97] Examples of classified advertising are advertisements with the titles "for sale" or "wanted" in (online) newspapers. The pricing mechanism behind this type of advertisement is comparatively more transparent, and the impact on consumers is moderate.[98]

Noteworthy, another subcategory of online advertising is advertising by email and text messages. In this case, advertisers obtain, in principle, the consumer's consent to send manual or automated marketing messages (e.g., by signing up for a newsletter when visiting the webpage or when signing up for marketing communications to obtain a discount). If the messages are sent without consent, they are seen as *spam*. As a result of technological developments, this seemingly traditional form of advertising has been reinvented because of the possibility of personalization at a relatively low cost.[99]

---

[93] Wojdynski and Golan (2016).

[94] Hoofnagle and Meleshinsky (2015).

[95] Taylor (2017).

[96] Wojdynski and Evans (2016).

[97] Fourberg et al. (2021), p. 18.

[98] Fourberg et al. (2021), p. 18.

[99] Martin et al. (2003); Sahni et al. (2018).

3.3.3 *Targeting Strategies*

The development of different online advertising strategies has enabled different targeting strategies. In essence, these strategies can be classified into four groups: *contextual, segmented, behavioral,* and *personalized targeting.* The order reflects the level of intrusiveness, from low to high, of the data tracking method that facilitates the targeting.

3.3.3.1 Contextual Targeting

In the case of contextual targeting, relatively little data is needed to display a targeted ad to the consumer. The targeted ad is based on the search query or the website that a consumer is visiting.[100] For example, if consumers enter the query "Valencia, Spain", they are directed to a travel website, after which the website will display banner ads that are promoting hotels or rental cars in Valencia. Accordingly, the ad's content is not based on specific information about the consumer but on the website the consumer is visiting. In this regard, the degree of intrusiveness could be classified as low.

3.3.3.2 Segmented Targeting

Under segmented targeting, the ads are tailored based on the information the user voluntarily discloses. This occurs, for instance, when platforms or websites require the consumer to create an account for which they need to provide their personal information, such as name, address, gender, contact information, and information related to their personal interests.[101] Based on this information, the consumer can be accurately identified. However, it does not mean that the consumer can be perfectly targeted. More information about the consumer's behavior and personal interests are needed for more precise targeting.[102] In addition, the mechanism entirely relies on the information the user provides. If the user discloses relatively limited or erroneous information, the effectiveness of the targeting is restricted. For this reason, the degree of intrusiveness of segmented targeting could be seen as moderate.

---

[100] Article 29 Data Protection Working Party (2010), pp. 4–5.

[101] Article 29 Data Protection Working Party (2010), pp. 4–5.

[102] Fourberg et al. (2021), p. 18.

3.3.3.3 Behavioral Targeting

To generate behaviorally-targeted ads, the actual online behavior of the consumer needs to be tracked, which includes, *inter alia*, the individuals' usage of a platform, search history, browsing history, purchase history, technological information such as the device that is being used, and the IP-address. Accordingly, sophisticated tracking technologies are employed to construct an adequate consumer profile. Three examples of these tracking technologies are *browser-based*, *stealth browser-based*, and *Internet service provider-based tracking*.[103]

Browser-based tracking "allows the collection of data across several webpages and over multiple online sessions."[104] This means that a consumer profile can be built by collecting data about the consumer's browsing behavior in different contexts and times.[105] This is usually done using cookies that mark a particular browser and track if a consumer goes to another website. A potential remedy against this type of tracking is the installation of cookie blockers or deleting cookies after each session.

Stealth-browser-based tracking is a more advanced form of browser-based tracking because it can circumvent cookie blockers that inhibit the placement of "regular" cookies. Under stealth-browser-based tracking, tracking tools can be installed in the software code of local shared objects (commonly known as *Flash cookies*), which are used by multimedia software platforms such as Adobe Flash. In essence, this technology can collect historical behavioral data, even if the user has deleted the cookie history. This practice is also called *respawning*.[106] This tracking software is generally not detected by common anti-spy software, and it is highly demanding for consumers to become aware that this tracking is taking place.[107]

The most advanced and intrusive form of tracking is Internet service provider-based tracking. In this case, an Internet service provider keeps log files of an individual that track each and every move on the Internet utilizing an individuals' unique IP address.[108] Advertisers are willing to pay substantial amounts of money to Internet service providers to obtain these log files, enabling them to assemble a more precise, actual, and complete consumer profile. There is an incentive to collect large amounts of data about the consumer since there is a positive relationship between the amount of available data and the degree of targeting. For this reason, the degree of intrusiveness of this type of targeting can be classified as high. When looking at the other two forms of tracking in behavioral targeting, the distinguishing factor of Internet service provider-based tracking is that it can collect information about all user web transactions. That is to say, it is not bound by websites that use

[103] Nill and Aalberts (2014), p. 129.

[104] Nill and Aalberts (2014), p. 129.

[105] Manny (2010).

[106] Soltani et al. (2010); McDonald and Cranor (2012).

[107] Howart (2010).

[108] Nill and Aalberts (2014), p. 129.

cookies. This implies that the consumer cannot remedy this tracking by blocking cookies or deleting its history.[109]

3.3.3.4 Personalized Targeting

Personalized targeting combines all aforementioned types of targeting, but also makes use of personal data for profiling based on AI. This leads to the most granular and intrusive form of targeting. Galli (2022) states: "Based on multiple data, AI enables different types of computations on consumers' data and act on that knowledge to make decisions at the individual level and in real time."[110]

Personalized ads are significantly more effective than non-personalized ads.[111] In particular, combining highly personalized behavioral targeting with less personalized contextual targeting can be highly effective, i.e., higher ad click-through rates.[112] However, as indicated before, highly personalized ads can be experienced by consumers as being too intrusive, which leads to less engagement.[113] Accordingly, to work effectively, personalized ads are continuously evaluated based on real-time consumer feedback.[114] Through reinforcement learning, the targeting mechanism can be fine-tuned to deliver optimal engagement scores.[115] In essence, *programmatic creative optimization* takes place, which means that advertisements can be modified in real time to specific consumers in order to obtain the highest conversation rates.[116] In other words, an infinite number of ad variations can be created to *micro-target* a consumer most effectively, which leads to a situation of *hyper-targeting*.[117]

3.3.4 *Personalized Advertising in Practice*

The digital advertising market is continuously growing and expanding at a higher rate than the advertising sector as a whole.[118] A driving force behind the growth of digital adverting is marketing personalization. Big data has made personalization one of the most indispensable marketing strategies among B2B and B2C marketers

---

[109] Nill and Aalberts (2014), p. 129.

[110] Galli (2022), p. 83.

[111] Tam and Ho (2006).

[112] Lu et al. (2016).

[113] Tucker (2014); Aguirre et al. (2015).

[114] Bakpayev et al. (2022).

[115] Van Noort et al. (2020).

[116] Chen and Gallego (2019).

[117] Semerádová and Weinlich (2019).

[118] Zenith (2021).

worldwide.[119] In the realm of digital advertising, personalized marketing plays a key role. In Europe, for example, behavioral advertising revenues alone were estimated to grow by 106% between 2016 and 2020, reaching a value of €21.4 billion.[120] It has been found that behavioral advertising is significantly more effective than standard advertising. For instance, the click-through rates of behavioral advertising are 5.3 times higher than for standard advertising, and in the case of retargeting (i.e., customers that have shown previous interest in the product), the click-through rates are 10.8 times higher.[121] Since personalized advertising is more-encompassing and powerful than behavioral targeting, its effectiveness has been found to be even higher.[122]

Since personalized advertising is a data-intensive technology that can improve its accuracy if more data can be collected, it is no surprise that it is highly prevalent in social media.[123] It has been established that social media significantly impacts consumer behavior and, therefore, is a profitable channel for advertisers to promote their products and services.[124] For the sake of illustration, Meta's targeting strategy will be discussed to demonstrate how personalized advertising works in practice.

The choice for Meta can be justified based on three reasons. First, Meta is the worldwide leading social media advertising company. It has a market share of 75% to 80% in Europe and the US, and the expectations are that its advertisement effectiveness and revenue will increase significantly over the coming years.[125] Second, being the largest *social network site* (SNS), the platforms' advertising activities have been extensively scrutinized in the existing literature.[126] In particular, numerous privacy concerns have been raised as a result of Meta's activities, which have given rise to a plethora of studies and reports.[127] Third, Meta is well-known for its personalization of advertisements targeting its global community of users. Meta possesses vast amounts of personal and behavioral data about its users.[128] Personal data is given by the user during the registration process and the creation of a user profile. Meta uses tracking technology that allows the platform to track specific behavioral information about a particular individual across various websites, also

[119] Statista (2023).

[120] IHS Markit (2017).

[121] IHS Markit (2017).

[122] See, for example, Milošević et al. (2017); Zhang et al. (2019); Mitrović et al. (2022).

[123] Gregurec et al. (2011); Tucker (2014); Wirtz et al. (2017).

[124] Voramontri and Klieb (2019).

[125] Statista (2021a).

[126] Van den Broeck et al. (2020).

[127] See Debatin et al. (2009) for an extensive review of the troublesome relationship between Meta and privacy protection.

[128] Van den Broeck et al. (2020).

called *third-party tracking*.[129] This can even occur when the user is not logged into the service account.[130]

To be able to show a tailored ad, it is essential to collect as much information about a user as possible to create an adequate personal profile. This can be information about "likes", personal preferences, social connections, and location.[131] These data are also shared with (i.e., sold) *third-party services*, which allows Meta to monetize collected data. Subsequently, personalized ads are embedded in the user's interface, or more specifically, newsfeed. In the so-called *Meta News Feed*, ads are shown adjacent to the content a user is interested in. That way, users are obliged to tolerate the advertisement if they want to use the platform. The combination of displaying a personal ad in an individual's newsfeed causes the line between commercial and non-commercial content to blur. This is a key characteristic of *social media newsfeed advertising*.[132]

Accordingly, Meta can employ large datasets to optimize the targeting and placement of advertisements. The question of whether this optimization strategy is effective and profitable for Meta can be answered positively. In 2021, Meta generated 114.93 billion U.S. dollars in ad revenues, which accounts for virtually all of the social network's revenue.[133]

3.4 Deceived by Design: Dark Patterns and Advertising

A key element of advertising is the manner in which the ad is presented to the consumer. The consumer's perception of the advertisement and consequent decision-making are dependent on the framing of the advertisement. The context in which consumers make their decisions has a significant influence on the final decision they will make.[134] This has given rise to the concept of *choice architecture*.[135]

In marketing, choice architecture is paramount for many aspects of the marketing mix, that is, the presentation of the product, the prices, the product placement, and the advertising (i.e., promotion). It has been found that the context in which consumers make decisions can be manipulated to *nudge* consumers into making a specific choice. A nudge is defined as "any aspect of the choice architecture that alters people's behavior in a predictable way without forbidding any options or significantly changing their economic incentives."[136] It is argued that in digital contexts,

[129] Gomer et al. (2013).

[130] Puglisi et al. (2017).

[131] Roosendaal (2012).

[132] Youn and Shin (2020).

[133] Statista (2021b).

[134] Thaler and Sunstein (2008), pp. 81–100.

[135] Thaler and Sunstein (2008).

[136] Thaler and Sunstein (2008), p. 6.

the effect of nudges is stronger due to their ubiquity and the ability to adapt to each consumer.[137]

The role of online choice architectures has been extensively researched in existing literature. Under the umbrella of *dark patterns*, digital nudges are used to capitalize on the information about the consumers to influence their decisions.[138] An individual can encounter a plethora of dark patterns while surfing the web. A full review of all existing dark patterns falls outside the scope of this study. However, the specific relationship between dark patterns and personalized advertising merits further attention. This section focuses on the application of dark patterns in online advertising to identify to what extent the manipulation of consumer experiences through choice architecture can reinforce the effectiveness of online advertising.

3.4.1 Dark Patterns: An Exploration

To understand the applications and consequences of dark patterns, it is vital to define them and point out their objectives. *Dark patterns* are "user interfaces whose designers knowingly confuse users, make it difficult for users to express their actual preferences, or manipulate users into taking certain actions."[139] In other words, they tend to discourage deliberative decision-making and thwart users' preferences. The typical objective of dark patterns is "to manipulate the consumer into doing something that is inconsistent with her preferences, in contrast to marketing efforts that are designed to alter those preferences."[140] In this context, consumers are prompted to either purchase goods or services that they are not inclined to purchase or give personal information they would otherwise not share. In the context of two-system thinking,[141] it can be stated that dark patterns push consumers from system 2 deliberative decision-making into system 1 impulsive decision-making.

The mechanism behind dark patterns is based on the use of *sludges*.[142] Where nudges try to help people make better choices as judged by themselves, sludges push people in the opposite direction, i.e., making wise and informed decision-making more difficult. This is done by increasing friction, thereby making it harder to follow the desired course of action.

Dark patterns are also described as a subcategory of *market manipulation*. In this sense, market manipulation refers to user interface designs that work against the user.[143] In practice, there exists a multiplicity of dark patterns. Brignull et al. (2023),

[137] Susser (2019); Yeung (2019).

[138] Weinmann et al. (2016), p. 433.

[139] Luguri and Strahilevitz (2021), p. 44.

[140] Luguri and Strahilevitz (2021), p. 44.

[141] Kahneman (2011), see Sect. 2.3.3.

[142] Thaler (2018); Sunstein (2019).

[143] Calo (2014), p. 1006.

Table 3.1 Types of dark patterns[a]

Type	Description
Trick questions	While filling in a form you respond to a question that tricks you into giving an answer you didn't intend. When glanced upon quickly the question appears to ask one thing, but when read carefully it asks another thing entirely.
Sneak into basket	You attempt to purchase something, but somewhere in the purchasing journey, the site sneaks an additional item into your basket.
Roach motel	You get into a situation very easily, but then you find it hard to get out of it (e.g., a premium subscription).
Privacy zuckering	You are tricked into publicly sharing more information about yourself than you intended to. Named after Meta's CEO Mark Zuckerberg.
Price comparison prevention	The retailer makes it hard for you to compare the price of an item with another item, so you cannot make an informed decision.
Misdirection	The design purposefully focuses your attention on one thing in order to distract your attention from another.
Hidden costs	You get to the last step of the checkout process, only to discover some unexpected charges have appeared, e.g., delivery charges, tax, etc.
Bait and switch	You set out to do one thing, but a different, undesirable thing happens instead.
Confirmshaming	The act of guilting the user into opting for something. The option to decline is worded in such a way as to shame the user into compliance.
Disguised ads	Adverts are disguised as other kinds of content or navigation, in order to get you to click on them.
Forced continuity	When your free trial with a service comes to an end and your credit card silently starts getting charged without any warning. In some cases, this is made even worse by making it difficult to cancel the membership.
Friend spam	The product asks for your email or social media permissions under the pretense it will be used for a desirable outcome (e.g., finding friends), but then spams all your contacts in a message that claims to be from you.

[a] Brignull et al. (2023)

the first to coin the term "dark pattern", provide a simplified taxonomy of dark patterns found online.[144] Table 3.1 illustrates the taxonomy of Brignull et al. (2023), which was later extended and formalized by various scholars.[145] Of note is that many more dark patterns exist. Table 3.1 only exemplifies the variety of online dark patterns consumers can encounter.

Subsequently, the question arises: To what extent are these dark patterns prevalent in online consumer markets? It has been found that in a survey of 53.000 product pages from 11.000 shopping sites, more than 11 percent employed dark

[144] Harry Brignull is a user experience (UX) specialist, who is a professional that researches and streamlines technology products to optimize a user's experience when interacting with the product in a digital environment.

[145] See for an extensive review of dark patters in practice and corresponding taxonomies Conti and Sobiesk (2010); Bösch et al. (2016); Gray et al. (2018); Lacey and Caudwell (2019); Mathur et al. (2019); Commission Nationale de l'Informatique et des Libertés (CNIL) (2020).

patterns.[146] Noteworthy, the more popular the website, the higher the likelihood they used dark patterns. In mobile apps, it was discovered that 95% of Android apps in the US Google Play Store used dark patterns.[147] The tendency to use dark patterns was also confirmed in the context of social network sites.[148]

Gray et al. (2018) summarize dark pattern strategies into five general categories: *nagging*, *obstruction*, *sneaking*, *interface interference*, and *forced action*.[149] Nagging occurs when users are repeatedly asked to perform a task unrelated to the course of action they want to take.[150] For example, pop-ups such as cookie banners or the request to turn on notifications.[151]

Obstruction is making an interaction more than difficult than it needs to be to discourage the individual from taking a specific action.[152] This occurs, for instance, when the user is required to register and create an account to use the website's services or if the user needs to buy a special package to obtain better system functionality as is the case with Spotify and YouTube Premium.

Sneaking refers to the "attempt to hide, disguise, or delay the divulging of information that has relevance to the user."[153] Consequently, users can be misled into carrying out actions that they would not have performed in the case of complete information. A typical example of sneaking is the placement of one-sided terms in the fine print with the knowledge that people will most likely not read the general terms and conditions.

Interface interference is defined as "any manipulation of the user interface that privileges specific actions over others, thereby confusing the user or limiting discoverability of important action possibilities."[154] Interface interference is the prominent strategy for user experience manipulation, and it comes in three forms: *hidden information*, *pre-selection*, and *aesthetic manipulation*. In the case of hidden information, information relevant to the user is not made accessible in a conspicuous manner, requiring additional effort. Under pre-selection, default choices are made to benefit the seller rather than the user. Finally, aesthetic manipulation occurs when the user interface's presentation (i.e., the aesthetic characteristics) redirects the user's attention from the aspects that interest the consumer to the elements the seller wants the consumer to focus on.[155]

---

[146] Mathur et al. (2019). They note that "these numbers represent a lower bound on the total number of dark patterns on these websites, since our automated approach only examined text-based user interfaces on a sample of product pages per website."

[147] Di Geronimo et al. (2020).

[148] Kelly and Rubin (2022).

[149] Gray et al. (2018).

[150] Gray et al. (2018).

[151] Hung (2021), pp. 2487–2490.

[152] Gray et al. (2018), p. 5.

[153] Gray et al. (2018), p. 6.

[154] Gray et al. (2018), p. 7.

[155] Gray et al. (2018), p. 7.

Table 3.2 Classifying deceptive designs

Dark pattern strategies	Deceptive design
Nagging	N/A
Obstruction	Roach motel, price comparison prevention
Sneaking	Forced continuity, sneak into basket, bait and switch, hidden costs
Interface interference	Confirmshaming, disguised ads, trick questions, misdirection
Forced action	Privacy zuckering, friend spam

Forced action relates to "any situation in which users are required to perform a specific action to access (or continue to access) specific functionality."[156] The most well-known example is the obligation to install a certain update to continue using a specific service (e.g., Microsoft Windows operating system updates). Instead of being presented with the options "accept" or "reject", the available options are "accept" or "install later". Following the categorization by Gray et al. (2018), it is possible to identify each of the deceptive design patterns presented by Brignull et al. (2023).[157] Table 3.2 provides a schematic overview.

Luguri and Strahilevitz (2021) provide clear evidence regarding the effectiveness of dark patterns. According to them, dark patterns are "strikingly effective in getting consumers to do what they would not do when confronted with more neutral user interfaces."[158] More specifically, they found that *mild dark patterns* (i.e., moderately intrusive) doubled the percentage of consumers signing up for the service in the experiment compared to a neutral interface. In contrast, in the case of *aggressive dark patterns* (i.e., highly intrusive), this percentage quadrupled.[159] It is worth noting that although the aggressive dark patterns were more effective, they generated more consumer backlash. The mild dark patterns, however, could go under the radar, which gives reason for concern. In practice, subtle dark patterns are more appealing to firms because they are effective in changing consumers' behavior without facing a substantial risk of getting caught by consumers.[160]

The experiment found that the most effective dark pattern strategies were hidden information, obstruction, trick questions, social proof, loaded questions, and acceptance by default. The least effective dark pattern strategies were countdown timers and recommended choice labels. Surprisingly, an increase in prices did not mitigate the effectiveness of dark patterns, which means that dark patterns exert influence to such an extent that higher prices do not affect acceptance rates.[161] Finally, a result that was found to be particularly problematic was that dark patterns seem to prey on the most vulnerable individuals in society. Their effectiveness seems to be stronger

[156] Gray et al. (2018), p. 8.

[157] Brignull et al. (2023).

[158] Luguri and Strahilevitz (2021), p. 46.

[159] Luguri and Strahilevitz (2021), p. 47.

[160] Luguri and Strahilevitz (2021), p. 47.

[161] Luguri and Strahilevitz (2021), p. 64.

on more vulnerable groups of society as defined by their education, age, gender, and race.[162]

3.4.2 Dark Patterns and Consumer Biases

The success of dark patterns is dependent on the ability to exploit consumers' biases.[163] By targeting behavioral biases, consumers can be subconsciously influenced, and their decisions can be manipulated. Dark patterns can exploit a myriad of biases. However, a complete one-on-one analysis would go beyond the scope of this section.[164] For this reason, an exemplary review of certain biases will be conducted to demonstrate the interrelationship between dark patterns and consumer biases.

Mathur et al. (2019) establish that the most prevalent dark patterns can be related to six main biases: the *anchoring effect*, *bandwagon effect*, *default effect*, *framing effect*, *scarcity bias*, and the *sunk cost fallacy*.[165]

The anchoring effect relates to the influence of initial values, the anchor, on individuals' decision-making process.[166] A pressured selling tactic based on the anchoring effect is selecting the most expensive option as the point of comparison (i.e., subtractive option-framing—consumers need to delete options for a lower price). As a result, consumers tend to end up with a higher-priced option compared to the selection of the least-expensive option (additive option-framing—consumers need to add options, which will increase the price commensurately).[167]

The bandwagon effect (also known as the herd behavior effect) refers to the tendency of individuals to adapt their beliefs to the belief system that is adhered to by most people.[168] Social proof is the category of dark patterns based on the bandwagon effect. Social proof is used to indicate to the individual what other users are doing, which will create psychological pressure. Two forms of social proof are activity messages and testimonials.

The default effect describes the tendency of individuals to stick with the option presented to them as the default. This effect is caused by the status quo bias, which refers to the predisposition of individuals to maintain the current situation as it is rather than change it.[169] The dark pattern of *bad defaults* employs the default effect

---

[162] Luguri and Strahilevitz (2021), pp. 70–71.

[163] See Sect. 2.3.3 for a review of the heuristics and cognitive biases related to consumer decision-making.

[164] See Lewis (2014) for an extensive analysis of dark patterns using psychological theories of intrinsic motivation, behavioral psychology, and behavioral economics. Lewis created a library of 27 motivational design patterns with corresponding real-world examples of how they work.

[165] Mathur et al. (2019), p. 6.

[166] Tversky and Kahneman (1974).

[167] Park et al. (2000).

[168] Sherif (1936); Kamins (2019).

[169] Samuelson and Zeckhauser (1988).

to induce consumers to choose the standard option of sharing more personal information than they initially wanted to. In combination with *privacy zuckering*, which makes privacy settings deliberately more complex for consumers to understand, the service provider can prevent consumer switching and increase the number of users that maintain the privacy-intrusive default.[170] Besides, the *sneak-into-basket* dark patterns use the default effect to add products surreptitiously and automatically to consumers' shopping carts. If consumers do not actively take out the added product (i.e., going against the default), the consumer will, perhaps unconsciously, buy the added product.

The framing effect refers to the proclivity of individuals to draw different conclusions from the same information depending on how it is presented or by whom.[171] Together with the default effect, the framing effect is a key tool for designing user interfaces that aim to benefit the service provider in terms of data collection.[172] By misdirecting the users through confirmshaming, trick questions, and aesthetic manipulation, they can be steered in a certain direction. In the case of confirmshaming, the options can be framed as "accept" or "I do not mind paying the full price" to cause a feeling of unease among consumers that choose the latter option.

In line with confirmshaming, trick questions aim to confuse the user into making certain choices that counter consumers' propensity to opt out of privacy-intrusive marketing tools. This is commonly done by asking questions with double negatives or making consumers actively opt in.[173] Aesthetic manipulation takes place by virtue of *visual interference*, which is the tactical use of style and visual presentation to direct the attention of the user to a certain choice. This can be done, for example, by making one option stand out with a specific font size and color while presenting the other options in a neutral fashion.[174]

Related to the framing effect is the loss aversion bias, whereby individuals weigh losses more heavily than gains in their decision-making process.[175] Through confirmshaming, the advertiser can create the feeling among consumers that they are missing out on something if they decide not to follow the option that is recommended by and favorable to the advertiser. The options are then presented as gains or losses, for instance, "I like to earn reward points" or "I do not care about saving money".

The scarcity bias refers to the propensity of individuals to attach greater subjective value to a good or service based on the mere fact that it is scarce.[176] Creating a sense of urgency can appeal to the scarcity bias of users. Two examples of urgency dark patterns are countdown timers or limited-time messages. Alternatively, the

[170] Bösch et al. (2016), p. 248.

[171] Kahneman and Tversky (1984); Tversky and Kahneman (1981); Johnson et al. (2002).

[172] Norwegian Consumer Council/Forbrukerrådet (2018).

[173] Mathur et al. (2019), p. 17.

[174] Mathur et al. (2019), p. 17.

[175] Kahneman and Tversky (1979).

[176] Mittone and Savadori (2009).

scarcity of the good or service can also be addressed directly through low-stock, high-demand messages or pop-ups. In this way, a *fear of missing out* (FOMO) can be evoked in consumers, which can incite them to take immediate action.[177]

Lastly, the sunk cost fallacy concerns individuals' tendency to consider past investments when evaluating options in the current decision-making process. This means that individuals might decide to continue a course of action simply because they have invested resources, although, from a rational perspective, it would be better to make an alternative decision.[178] The dark pattern of *hidden costs* takes advantage of the sunk cost fallacy. In this case, the user is confronted with unexpected additional costs at the last step of completing the checkout process. These can, for instance, include reservation costs, service fees, shipping fees, or handling costs. At this stage of the checkout process, the user has already invested resources in completing the process, such as deciding on the specific product, providing the required personal information, and filling out the shipping and billing address. Accordingly, the user will most likely want to avoid the loss of the invested resources, and, therefore, the sunk costs will influence the decision to proceed with the purchase.

All in all, this overview illustrates the intertwined relationship between cognitive biases and dark patterns. Many more dark patterns that fall outside these categories can be classified in this way. However, the common denominator of these dark patterns is that they are designed based on behavioral insights. The exploitation of behavioral biases enables firms to optimize the extraction of value from consumers.[179]

3.4.3 Using Dark Patterns for Advertising Purposes

Dark patterns are applied in various contexts, such as online shopping,[180] online interactions,[181] privacy choices,[182] video games,[183] and social media.[184] The role of dark patterns in advertising is twofold: they contribute to collecting large quantities of data, enabling personalized advertising, and affecting the advertisements' design.

---

[177] Mathur et al. (2019), p. 14.

[178] Arkes and Blumer (1985).

[179] Gabaix and Laibson (2006); Ellison and Wolitzky (2012).

[180] Mathur et al. (2019).

[181] Greenberg et al. (2014).

[182] Bösch et al. (2016); Norwegian Consumer Council/Forbrukerrådet (2018).

[183] Zagal et al. (2013).

[184] Kelly and Rubin (2022).

3.4.3.1 Leverage for Data Collection and Processing

To target consumers with personalized advertisements, vast amounts of personal data need to be collected, facilitating the creation of individualized consumer profiles. Under the *General Data Protection Regulation* (GDPR),[185] firms are only permitted to gather data for profiling purposes if it is deemed necessary for business activities, authorized by law, or based on explicit *consumer consent*.[186] The exact role of the GDPR will be further discussed in Sect. 3.6, but the point of this reference to the GDPR is that consumer consent is the driving force behind the collection and processing of personal data. In principle, if consent is provided freely, genuinely, and sufficiently informed, it would be a valid legal instrument.[187] However, this is where the dark patterns come into play.

As a result of dark patterns, consumers can subtly be induced to consent to the collection and processing of their data.[188] In addition, through misleading interfaces, consumers can be prevented from choosing privacy-preserving options.[189] An investigation of the practices by tech giants in the field of digital services demonstrated that various dark patterns are employed to manipulate users and nudge consumers into choosing the privacy-intrusive options, which will allow for the maximal collection and processing of personal data.[190] Several prominent dark patterns that are being employed by Meta, Google, and Microsoft are "privacy intrusive default settings, misleading wording, giving users an illusion of control, hiding away privacy-friendly choices, take-it-or-leave-it choices, and choice architectures where choosing the privacy friendly option requires more effort for the users."[191]

Dark patterns are prominently used in consent forms requiring permission to process personal and behavioral data. The consent options are designed in such a way that they nudge consumers into making a decision that is against their own interest, i.e., providing more data than they actually want and allowing the firm to share the data with a large number of third parties. Combined with lengthy and complex privacy policies, dark patterns effectively inhibit consumers from giving informed consent.[192]

The paradox that underlies the role of consent is that the reasons not to provide consent are placed in the non-salient general terms and conditions or privacy notices, whereas the triggers to give consent are designed and promoted by expert

[185] Regulation 2016/679. Regulation (EU) 2016/679 of the European Parliament and of the Council of 27 April 2016 on the protection of natural persons with regard to the processing of personal data and on the free movement of such data, and repealing Directive 95/46/EC (General Data Protection Regulation). https://eur-lex.europa.eu/eli/reg/2016/679/oj. Referred to as "GDPR".

[186] OECD (2019), p. 39.

[187] Gil González and De Hert (2019).

[188] Sartor (2020), p. 23.

[189] Sartor (2020), p. 36.

[190] Norwegian Consumer Council/Forbrukerrådet (2018).

[191] Norwegian Consumer Council/Forbrukerrådet (2018), p. 3.

[192] OECD (2021), p. 5.

advertisers and user interface specialists to make them stand out more.[193] The framing of a choice has a significant impact on consumers' decision-making. Framing consent positively (i.e., ostensibly more protective of consumer privacy) will lead to a higher willingness to consent and vice versa.[194]

The role of linguistic patterns in framing should not be underestimated. The language chosen to describe the consent choice can nudge consumers in a specific direction. To specify, to persuade the consumer that consent is a beneficial choice, the positive implications of consent in terms of, for example, functionality and customer experience are highlighted. In contrast, the negative privacy implications are downplayed or disregarded. In this way, the consent notice functions as a *double-edged sword.*

On the one hand, it fulfills mandated disclosure requirements by providing a user with information. On the other hand, the linguistic patterns of the consent form work as persuasion tools.[195] If the design and content of the consent notices are optimized, it can significantly impact how people interact with the notices.[196] From the advertiser's perspective, obtaining consent to the fullest extent possible would be optimal, enabling numerous possibilities for advertising and corresponding personalization.

3.4.3.2 The Design of Advertisements

In 2020, the Hungarian Competition Authority (GVH) imposed a fine of 2.5 billion Hungarian forints on Booking.com for unfair commercial practices, including misleading advertisements and undue psychological pressure on consumers to make early bookings.[197] A closer look at the case of Booking.com demonstrates that dark patterns facilitated the misleading tactics employed on their website. The company emphasized the option "free cancellation", which was highlighted. This option was only provided for a limited period of time. Notably, consumers would pay more for the accommodation that included this feature. In other words, the free cancellation was surreptitiously included in the price.

Furthermore, Booking.com exerted undue psychological pressure on consumers by adopting pressuring selling tactics in the user interface of the booking process. Various dark patterns could be identified in the interface such as aesthetic manipulation (e.g., highlighting specific features with different colors and font sizes), social proof (e.g., activity message—other people are watching this accommodation), and scarcity (e.g., informing consumers about the limited availability). Together, these dark patterns distorted the consumers' decision-making process.

---

[193] Matzner et al. (2016), p. 297.

[194] Adjerid et al. (2013).

[195] Pollach (2005).

[196] Utz et al. (2019).

[197] Hungarian Competition Authority (2020).

The Hungarian case concerning Booking.com is an example of how dark patterns can be used in advertising. The key factor that makes the use of dark patterns in online advertising particularly alarming is the ability to improve its effectiveness continuously. Through data analytics such as A-B testing, user interfaces can be constantly adapted, refined, and perfected to make dark patterns as effective as possible.[198] In addition, developments in personalization have opened up the possibility of personalizing dark patterns, to make them even more powerful against consumers.[199] This raises concerns because, to work effectively, the dark pattern must successfully exploit consumers' behavioral biases. By exploiting biases, consumers can be nudged into behaviors beneficial to advertisers and third parties but detrimental to their own welfare.[200]

Big data has enabled businesses to continuously collect vast amounts of data that facilitate personalization. As a consequence, advertising techniques, as well as marketing in general, can be constantly improved, leading to the maximization of conversation rates and sales. In that regard, dark patterns can also be personalized, focusing on identifying personal behavioral biases and the subsequent exploitation thereof. That is to say, rather than designing dark patterns on the basis of generally-known biases, dark patterns can be tailored to each individual.[201]

In the realm of advertising, there is a myriad of application possibilities for dark patterns. Three dark patterns are commonly perceived in relation to advertising. First is the *roach motel*, whereby it is easy for consumers to get into a certain situation but very difficult to get out.[202] For example, when clicking on an ad (deliberately or accidentally), there is an immediate redirection to the advertisers' webpage with the ad's display. Yet, it is particularly cumbersome to go back or get out (e.g., due to a hidden 'X' or an 'X' that only appears after a certain amount of time to close or stop the ad's display).

Second, *bait-and-switch* techniques aim to make the user believe that a certain result will occur when a particular action is undertaken. Still, it leads to a different, likely undesired, result.[203] For instance, when browsing through a website or the newsfeed on a social media platform, clicking on an "X" to close an ad leads to the actual opening of the advertisement. The actual closing button was located elsewhere in an inconspicuous place.

Third, the *disguised ad,* which is closely related to the previous dark pattern of bait and switch. In the case of a disguised ad, adverts are concealed as other kinds of content or navigation tools, which transform into a "real" ad when you click on

198 Luguri and Strahilevitz (2021), p. 103.

199 Stigler Center (2019), pp. 240–242.

200 Fourberg et al. (2021), p. 34.

201 OECD (2021), p. 6.

202 Gray et al. (2018), p. 6.

203 Gray et al. (2018), p. 6.

them. For example, when clicking on a specific website feature, such as a download button, another page is loaded with an advertisement.[204]

Noteworthy, deceptive design patterns are being frequently applied to promote, *inter alia*, fraudulent advertising that incites consumers to buy counterfeit and other illicit products.[205] It is, therefore, no surprise that the use of dark patterns has a broad scope of application, which can vary from lawful persuasion to unlawful manipulation.

3.4.4 The "Dark" Implications for Consumers

Due to the analysis of dark patterns, it has become possible to identify manipulative user interfaces. However, the question arises: What are the consequences of these dark patterns for consumers? From a law and economics perspective, several effects are prominent. This section will provide a non-exhaustive overview of potential "dark" implications.

First, a reduction in consumer welfare. If dark patterns nudge consumers into making decisions that do not reflect their true preferences but are to the seller's benefit, they will incur financial losses. The rationale is that consumers will be induced to spend more than they initially anticipated.[206] The dark patterns impair consumers' ability to act rationally, which sets them up for behavioral exploitation that reduces their welfare.[207]

Second, price obfuscation. To make an informed decision, consumers need to be able to collect the optimal amount of information. This information includes transparency about the price. Through dark patterns, transparency can be decreased.[208] This can be done, for example, by means of hidden prices or price comparison prevention. In this sense, it also contributes to financial losses.

Third, hampering competition. Firms can use dark patterns to attract consumers and lock them in, for example, through obstruction, although a cheaper and better alternative might be available. This can be done by increasing switching costs without actually offering a better product than the competitors. Consequently, dark patterns empower firms to extract consumer value and build market power without the challenges that come into play when competing for the market.[209]

Fourth, reduction of consumer trust in the market. If consumers feel that firms are manipulating them through dark patterns, it could undermine consumer trust in the market. If overall trust goes down, it automatically means that honest sellers are

[204] Gray et al. (2018), p. 7.

[205] TRACIT and AAFA (2020).

[206] Mathur et al. (2021), p. 13.

[207] Day and Stemler (2020).

[208] Mathur et al. (2021), p. 16.

[209] Day and Stemler (2020), pp. 36–39.

harmed by the behavior of malicious companies that employ dark patterns.[210] Accordingly, it can lead to anticompetitive effects and a loss of welfare for both sellers and consumers. From a law and economics perspective, this strongly indicates the presence of an adverse selection problem.[211]

Fifth, the more vulnerable groups of society, in terms of education, age, gender, and race, are potentially more at risk of falling subject to a dark pattern.[212] Dark patterns can affect specific groups of vulnerable consumers disproportionally. In the digital world, the concept of vulnerable consumers is not fixed or easy to determine. To a certain extent, each person can be vulnerable depending on the online context.[213] As Helberger et al. (2021) state:

> In the digital economy, consumer vulnerability is not simply a vantage point from which to assess some consumers' lack of ability to activate their awareness of persuasion. Instead, digital vulnerability describes a universal state of defencelessness and susceptibility to (the exploitation of) power imbalances that result from the increasing automation of commerce, datafied consumer–seller relations, and the very architecture of digital marketplaces.[214]

Sixth, it interferes with individuals' *decisional privacy*, which refers to the ability of an individual to decide without coercion.[215] Dark patterns can subtly and persuasively influence consumers' decisions about their privacy. Consequently, serious concerns about consumers' privacy can be raised: 1) Dark patterns enable the extraction of consumer value because they facilitate the collection of personal and behavioral data that can be monetized.[216] 2) Firms will be able to incite consumers to choose privacy-unfriendly options, which enables the exploitation of their privacy.[217] 3) Dark patterns can obfuscate interface elements that could aid consumers in protecting their privacy, thereby exposing them to further privacy exploitation.[218]

Lastly, consumer autonomy is undermined.[219] The manipulation of online interfaces threatens individuals' ability to act for their own reasons.[220] The agency of consumers is compromised through choice architecture, and conscious, self-aware decision-making is subverted.[221] Hence, it can be stated that dark patterns are

---

210 Mathur et al. (2021), p. 16.

211 Akerlof (1970).

212 Luguri and Strahilevitz (2021), p. 47.

213 See Sect. 2.4.1.

214 Helberger et al. (2022).

215 Day and Stemler (2020), p. 2.

216 Conti and Sobiesk (2010), p. 271.

217 Bösch et al. (2016), p. 241.

218 Waldman (2020), p. 107.

219 Susser et al. (2019), pp. 35–39.

220 Susser et al. (2019), p. 39.

221 Susser et al. (2019), p. 16.

inciting people to take actions that they would otherwise not have taken in the absence of the modified choice architecture,[222] which is a reason for concern.[223]

In conclusion, dark patterns entail several negative implications for consumers. Apart from threats to consumer welfare, dark patterns pose challenges to consumer privacy, autonomy and equity. The effectiveness of personalized advertising is strongly facilitated by the developments in dark pattern designs. Based on these findings, the focus can shift to the economic assessment of personalized advertising as a whole.

3.5 Economic Analysis of Personalized Advertising

In his seminal work on the economic analysis of advertising, Bagwell (2007) states: "By its very nature, advertising is a prominent feature of economic life."[224] Advertising permeates consumer markets, and its purpose is to evoke consumer response. Advertising can be used to complement the needs of consumers by matching a product with the identified set of preferences that a consumer has, but it can also be employed to alter consumers' tastes and persuade them to take specific actions.[225] On the one hand, consumers can receive valuable information about products' attributes through advertising, which helps to partially remedy information asymmetries in consumer markets.[226] On the other hand, information can be provided to mislead consumers, which deteriorates the information asymmetry problem in consumer markets. The effects of advertising can, therefore, be ambiguous and lead to conflicting evaluations of its value to consumers.

In existing literature, the potential social benefits and costs of advertising are well documented.[227] Nonetheless, due to the advent of the digital age, consumers spend increasingly more time on the Internet and therefore, traditional advertising has largely evolved into online advertising. As a result of technological advancements, the cost of targeting has decreased drastically, opening the way for large-scale personalized targeting.[228] Consequently, this requires a revisited assessment of the social welfare implications of advertising in the context of online personalization.

[222] Susser et al. (2019), pp. 38–39.

[223] Westin and Chiasson (2019).

[224] Bagwell (2007).

[225] Bagwell (2007), p. 1705.

[226] Bagwell (2007), p. 1706.

[227] Bagwell (2007), p. 1724 provides an overview of the main considerations regarding the impact of advertising on social welfare.

[228] Goldfarb (2014), p. 116.

3.5.1 *Traditional Law and Economics Analysis*

From a traditional law and economics perspective, several benefits and drawbacks of personalized advertising can be identified. The economic benefits can be subdivided into two categories: consumer benefits and business benefits.

3.5.1.1 Consumer Benefits

First and foremost, personalized advertising leads to more targeted and tailored ads. As the word personalized indicates, an ad will be more relevant to the consumer.[229] Personalization leads to a more accurate matching of consumer preferences.[230] By reducing the amount of information and cognitive load, preferences can be formed more easily, which leads to increased consumer convenience. In this sense, personalization aids consumer decision-making.[231] Capitalizing on these effects, the effectiveness of targeted advertising can be optimized by fostering higher click-through rates.[232]

Self-reference is an essential element of personalization, whereby personalized content is related to the self, in other words, the being of a user.[233] If content is closely targeted to an individual, a user will pay more attention to content in comparison with non-self-referent content. Combined with content relevance (i.e., congruence with the user's goals), it will lead to more recall, acceptance of offers, and higher evaluations.[234] Improved targeting provides more useful and relevant information and prevents consumers from being exposed to random ads.[235]

Second, the timing of an ad can be improved, which reduces transaction costs.[236] Consumers will be exposed to products that match their preferences, which reduces search costs (i.e., the invested time, money, and energy trying to find the right product) and increases demand.[237] Besides, timely advertising allows consumers to stay up to date regarding the products or services of their interest. This positive effect can be reinforced by coupling personalized ads with a personalized discount offer and vice versa. Consequently, consumers could potentially profit from lower prices.[238]

Third, advertising plays a key role in providing "free" services to consumers. Due to the effectiveness of personalized advertising, firms are willing to pay

[229] Montgomery and Smith (2009).
[230] Vesanen (2007).
[231] Tam and Ho (2006).
[232] Ansari and Mela (2003).
[233] Tam and Ho (2006), p. 870.
[234] Tam and Ho (2006), p. 884.
[235] Ham (2017).
[236] OECD (2019), p. 23.
[237] European Commission (2016), pp. 251–252.
[238] OECD (2019), p. 23.

platforms to, for example, display an advertisement, thereby generating substantial advertising revenues. This, in turn, enables the platform to provide their services for free to the consumer.[239]

3.5.1.2 Business Benefits

First of all, personalized advertising is a highly profitable strategy for businesses.[240] Personalization increases the profitability of direct marketing efforts at an unprecedented scale.[241] For instance, it has been found that personalized advertisements are nearly twice as effective as standardized advertisements.[242] Nonetheless, it must be noted that some of the benefits are offset by the necessity to invest in technology. Although advertising costs are reduced by improved targeting, substantial investments in tracking and personalization technologies are still required. However, the net effect is positive for firms since the effectiveness of personalized ads significantly outperforms standardized ads, which means higher click-through rates and, therefore, higher revenues.[243]

According to the *long tail of the Internet argument*, targeted advertising is highly valuable because it aids niche firms and consumers.[244] To specify, under traditional advertising, it is only cost-efficient to advertise for firms that have a large target audience since they can spread the costs over many potential customers. Niche firms, however, are practically excluded from these traditional ad channels because their target market is too small to make advertising cost-efficient. Under sophisticated targeted advertising, niche firms can reach their target audience, and the consumers who belong to this group can profit from it.[245]

Furthermore, personalized advertising can lead to a competitive advantage. AI-driven personalization techniques allow for consumer profiling through the collection and analysis of data, the matching of consumers' preferences, and the evaluation of strategy effectiveness. By improving this personalization process, firms can gain a competitive edge compared to firms that do not personalize or do it to a lesser degree.[246]

Lastly, precise targeting enables firms to eliminate otiose advertising to consumers that are not interested in the promoted product or service (i.e., mismatch in preferences and product attributes) and focus on consumers who could become

---

[239] The extent to which these services can be considered "free" are subject to ongoing debate. See, for example, Helman (2019); Custers and Malgieri (2022).

[240] Johnson (2013), p. 129.

[241] Rossi et al. (1996); Zhang and Wedel (2009).

[242] Tucker (2014).

[243] Beales (2010).

[244] Johnson (2013), p. 129.

[245] Anderson (2006).

[246] Murthi and Sarkar (2003).

potential buyers.[247] This is efficiency-enhancing since it leads to a more optimal allocation of advertising resources.[248]

3.5.1.3 Economic Drawbacks for Consumers

Personalized advertising also entails several drawbacks. Although it could be argued that personalized advertising could negatively impact businesses, for instance, due to reputation loss as a result of a personalized ad that is perceived to be deceptive,[249] marketers generally promote the development of personalized advertising. It is becoming an increasingly important method in online advertising.[250] In this section, the focus will, therefore, lie on the economic drawbacks for consumers.

First of all, there is a problem of information asymmetry. The personalization of advertising utilizes innovative tracking and data processing techniques that are beyond the comprehension of the average consumer. Nonetheless, consumers are expected to be well-informed through consent notices, although reality shows that this is not the case. In practice, consumers cannot always identify specific forms of advertising, let alone understand the mechanisms behind them. For instance, in the case of influencer marketing, it can be complicated for consumers to identify the commercial nature of the message.[251] When influencers promote a product, it can be hard to determine if they are providing an unbiased opinion (i.e., without financial incentives) or if they are simply a mouthpiece of the advertising company. In addition, determining the financial incentives behind an ad can be onerous because social influencers might not get monetary compensation, but free products that are theirs to keep after creating promotional content.

Furthermore, it leads to increased transaction costs. To prevent economic harm from the systematic leveraging of consumers' bias and vulnerabilities, consumers can be incentivized to use ad avoidance techniques. That is to say, a certain number of consumers targeted by personalized advertising will become aware of the potential manipulation, and these consumers will try to escape this by means of *advertising avoidance tools*.[252] This behavior generates transaction costs because consumers spend scarce resources to circumvent the advertising techniques. The overall effect is that the increase in transaction costs decreases overall market efficiency.[253]

To illustrate, when consumers are looking for a flight ticket and they know that their browsing behavior is being tracked, they might use a different computer, a

---

[247] Iyer et al. (2005).

[248] Rust and Chung (2006).

[249] Rao and Wang (2017).

[250] See, for example, Liu-Thompkins (2019) who elaborates on the increasing importance and relevance of personalization in online advertising and the evolution of academic research in this field.

[251] Trzaskowski (2018).

[252] Johnson (2013).

[253] Calo (2011), p. 1132.

foreign IP address, or ask a friend to book the ticket because they believe the tracking will lead to higher prices. If this belief is shared and represents a general tendency, it would signal to consumers that they will be overcharged if they do not employ such avoidance techniques. In this example, ad avoidance and increased transaction costs go hand in hand.

The effect of increased transaction costs has also been found in the context of social media networks.[254] This occurs when consumers enter into an agreement with the platform. When, later on, they are confronted with unanticipated transaction costs relating to understanding the consequences of using the service and the difficulties with leaving the platform, they might delete their profile entirely. As a result, a misalignment of interests impedes cost-efficient transacting, leading to market inefficiency.[255]

In addition, although consumers are targeted with more relevant ads under personalized advertising, the overall number of ads will increase due to their effectiveness and low cost, which decreases the marginal value of ads to consumers. In other words, the continuous increase in ads will reduce the value consumers attach to them, making consumers lose the gains from advertising.[256] The rationale is that due to the excess of advertisements, the high-value messages will be crowded out by low-value messages, and since consumers have limited attention, the social benefits derived from advertising will be negatively affected.[257]

Moreover, improved targeting can result in consumers being exposed to ads that they dislike more than the ads they would see when targeting is less precise.[258] The rationale is that improved targeting will lead to the receipt of niche advertisements only, while it could be that consumers prefer the receipt of mainstream ads. In essence, micro-targeting causes an adverse effect that offsets the benefit of the long tail of the Internet argument. That is to say, consumers would not be exposed to ads that do not match their preferences or profile, although that could be beneficial for their personal development.[259]

Finally, the reduction of trust in consumer markets. If consumers feel manipulated by personalized advertising or are too closely monitored, it can damage consumer trust. The ability to generate consumer trust depends on how the public sees the practice. This will be further explored in Sect. 3.5.3. In general, it has been found that consumers' concerns regarding online personalized advertising lead to a

---

[254] Whittington and Hoofnagle (2012).

[255] Whittington and Hoofnagle (2012), p. 1333.

[256] Johnson (2013), pp. 129, 133.

[257] Van Zandt (2004); Anderson and De Palma (2009).

[258] Johnson (2013), p. 129. Of note is that this also has its effect on the business since the conversion rates will be lower.

[259] Helberger (2012).

decrease in trust.[260] The decline in trust is detrimental to social welfare and economic prosperity.[261]

Noteworthy, personalized advertising is strongly related to personalized pricing, which will be the focus of Chap. 4. Firms are able to apply differential pricing to extract the greatest amount of consumer surplus or overprice all consumers for a substantial aggregate gain. If the share of overcharged consumers is larger than the share of consumers who get a discount, the differential pricing scheme is profitable to the company. Consequently, it has been found that personalized pricing in combination with personalized advertising boosts firms' profits compared to uniform pricing combined with mass advertising, whereas the majority of consumers is worse off.[262]

3.5.2 Behavioral Law and Economics Analysis

The potential of personalized advertising to enhance ad effectiveness lies in its ability to alter consumers' preferences.[263] It has been found that personalized targeting can affect consumers' self-perception, which induces them to change their behavior to match the desired behavior proposed by the ad.[264] This effect is caused by the implied *social label* of the ad. A social label is an explicit characterization of an individual formed on the basis of their behavior, beliefs, and personality.[265] Accordingly, this characterization influences consumers' self-perception and the evaluation of their behavior with the label as their benchmark. Applying this to advertising means that consumers tend to match the suggested behavior of the ad because they recognize that the advertiser has made an inference about their identity to tailor the ad to them individually. They feel the need, whether that be consciously or unconsciously, to match the label for the sake of consistency. More specifically, receiving a personalized ad signals to the consumer some information about their identity, which signifies that the consumer is expected to like the featured product.[266]

For instance, if a personalized ad proposes a new self-improvement book written for conscientious, motivated, and successful people and the consumer is exposed to this ad, the consumer might derive from this information that she is viewed as such a person (or that she could potentially become one). It can then be considerably more challenging for the consumer to say no to such an ad and reject this implied image about her compared to the case in which a book would be recommended that

[260] OECD (2019), p. 27.

[261] See, for example, Zak and Knack (2001); Roy (2016); Weitzner (2018).

[262] Esteves and Resende (2019).

[263] European Commission (2016), p. 251.

[264] Summers et al. (2016).

[265] Summers et al. (2016), derived from Goffman (1963).

[266] Summers et al. (2016), p. 158.

has no relevance to her persona. Through the implied social label, the ad can successfully persuade consumers to match the suggested behavior.

The psychological effects of advertising make personalized advertising significantly more effective than traditional advertising.[267] More specifically, persuasive and psychologically-tailored advertising that matches consumers' characteristics results in substantially higher click-through rates and purchases. Matz et al. (2017) found that psychological targeting can result in up to 40% more clicks and up to 50% more purchases compared to non-personalized targeting, indicating a significant alteration of consumer behavior.[268]

Personalized advertising can lead to the exploitation of consumer biases and vulnerabilities.[269] Consumers can be encouraged to buy products they initially did not want. This can be done by virtue of persuasion profiling,[270] whereby consumer attitudes, motivations, and vulnerabilities can be detected, enabling advertisers to change the ad in real time to make it most effective in its persuasion.[271] Consequently, exploiting consumer vulnerabilities allows for extracting value at the expense of consumer welfare. It should be noted that dark patterns exacerbate this exploitation. In combination with personalized advertising, dark patterns can reinforce the persuasive nature of messages to the extent that they become manipulative.[272]

Moreover, an extension can be made of the argument Bar-Gill (2018) presented on the topic of algorithmic pricing. He argues that algorithmic pricing is based not only on the perception of potential benefits but also on misperceptions.[273] Through demand-inflated perceptions, which can be induced through marketing efforts, consumers can be persuaded to buy a product they should not buy (actual costs are higher than perceived benefits) or to overpay for certain products.[274] Consequently, the practice leads to more harm to consumers and decreases overall efficiency.[275] This argument can be applied analogously to personalized advertising. The personalized ad can inflate the product's perceived benefits, which convinces consumers to buy a product they cannot pay for, do not need, or do not want. As a consequence, products are purchased based on misperceptions, which creates efficiency losses that need to be borne completely by the consumers.[276] In sum, personalized ads can create losses on the consumer side by steering them toward products or services that

[267] Summers et al. (2016), p. 171.

[268] Matz et al. (2017).

[269] Clifford (2017); Matz et al. (2017).

[270] See Sect. 3.2.3.

[271] Calo (2014), p. 1017.

[272] See Sect. 3.4.

[273] Bar-Gill (2018).

[274] Bar-Gill (2018), p. 3.

[275] Bar-Gill (2018), p. 3.

[276] Bar-Gill (2018) proves this by presenting a behavioral model that depicts the changes in surplus, the loss in efficiency, and the harm to the consumer. Four combinations of misperceptions and price discrimination are constructed (2 × 2 matrix) and analyzed.

do not optimally match their needs or aim to extract the maximal amount of consumer surplus (i.e., matching their reservation price).[277]

3.5.3 *Broadening the Analysis: Additional Considerations for Consumer Policy*

As part of the analysis, three specific aspects of personalized advertising will be considered that are essential to consumer policy. The perceptions of consumers, the effect on privacy, and ethical concerns.

3.5.3.1 Consumer Perceptions

Surveying consumers' perceptions regarding personalized advertising allows for a broader identification of potential problems that would not be conspicuous from a purely economic perspective. For instance, consumers might experience concerns or doubts that might not relate to their welfare but perhaps to their well-being. Therefore, it is also paramount to consider these views for a comprehensive analysis.

Personalized advertising is plagued by a *personalization paradox*, which indicates that "personalization can be both an effective and an ineffective marketing strategy, depending on the context."[278] There are several causes for this personalization paradox in advertising. An increasing degree of personalization causes a twofold effect in terms of consumer (dis)comfort. On the one hand, more personalization leads to higher levels of attention (i.e., consumers spend more time looking at an ad). On the other hand, it leads to significantly higher levels of discomfort caused by the unease of surveillance. Hence, there is a trade-off between attention and discomfort. Therefore, advertisers aim to create an optimal balance between these values by identifying valuable data points that create noticeable ads that grab consumers' attention while minimizing discomfort.[279]

Consumer trust is highly relevant to the effectiveness of personalization. If consumers feel more vulnerable (assuming they are aware), they are less prone to react positively to the personalized ad. Openness about the personalization process can influence the degree of trust. To specify, click-through rates (i.e., a key indicator of ad effectiveness) are higher when consumers are overtly informed about their data collection. The opposite is the case when firms engage in covert data collection.[280] In particular, when the consumer is given no justification for personalization and the

[277] European Commission (2016), p. 249.

[278] Aguirre et al. (2015), p. 35.

[279] Malheiros et al. (2012).

[280] Aguirre et al. (2015), p. 41.

corresponding use of their data, higher personalization leads to lower effectiveness.[281]

Remarkably, combining high visibility of ads (i.e., *obtrusiveness*) with individual targeting evokes negative consumer perceptions. This explains a certain type of bifurcation in current advertising, i.e., plain text being highly targeted and highly visible ads being relatively less targeted.[282] To illustrate, if consumers encounter a virtually striking ad because of its graphic content and notice that it is highly targeted to them personally, this could evoke privacy concerns. These concerns with corresponding irritation can lead to increased ad avoidance.[283] In contrast, when the seller makes privacy protection information more accessible and salient, consumers are more willing to deal with the seller.[284]

Turow et al. (2009) contrast the views between privacy advocates, who severely criticize personalized advertising because it leads to the undermining of consumers' rights, and marketers, who state that personalized advertising gives consumers what they want because the ads are specifically tailored to match their interests. Turow et al. (2009) identified with which group American consumers side. It was found that in the United States, consumers stand with the privacy advocates. 66% of the respondents did not want to be exposed to personalized ads. After informing them about the mechanism behind personalization, this percentage rose to 73%–86% (the latter figure comprised the responses of young adults).[285] Part of this result can be explained by the phenomenon called *personalization reactance,* which refers to the psychological resistance of individuals to (subjectively) inappropriate personalization.[286] This reactance is triggered when consumers feel they are being observed too closely by a firm and want to break free from this surveillance. Consumers seem to follow a *utility-maximizing principle*, which in the context of personalized advertising means that consumers "appear willing to incur the psychological "costs" of highly personalized messages only to the extent they perceive net benefits that offset these costs."[287]

In 2016, the EC conducted an extensive market study on consumers' awareness and perceptions of personalized practices to understand the formation of their attitudes and perspectives in more depth.[288] The relevant points of the survey can be summarized as follows: 1) Awareness of personalized advertising was higher than that of personalized pricing; 2) more vulnerable consumers, in terms of age, finances, age, education, and experience, report lower awareness of online personalization; 3) increasing transparency led to higher awareness and a more accurate

[281] Aguirre et al. (2015), p. 44.

[282] Goldfarb and Tucker (2011).

[283] Beak and Morimoto (2012).

[284] Tsai et al. (2011).

[285] Turow et al. (2009).

[286] White et al. (2008).

[287] White et al. (2008), p. 48.

[288] European Commission (2016).

perception of personalized practices; 4) higher reported self-declared awareness did not imply that consumers actually recognized personalization practices when confronted with them in an online environment. In the experiment, less than 50% of the consumers were able to identify personalized ads.[289]

In terms of benefits and drawbacks of targeted advertising, the respondents mentioned as main benefits: more interesting advertised products, fewer irrelevant ads, and the funding of free content. The main concerns were the use of data for alternative purposes, profiling, and the unwanted installation of cookies on their computer. Overall, 29% of the respondents only saw disadvantages of targeted advertising, whereas between 8% and 9% only saw benefits. Approximately half of the respondents, the majority, saw both the advantages and the disadvantages of personalization and advertising in particular.[290]

In addition, the EC conducted an experiment to measure the influence of personalization on consumer behavior.[291] The results can be summarized as follows. The motivation to continue with a purchase, although personalization took place and consumers were informed, was based on the belief that products were better targeted, which led to a reduction in search time. Conversely, the inclination to not proceed with the purchase was based on the belief that they would pay higher prices than under normal conditions, the data was used for customer profiling purposes, and the choice of products offered would be more limited in the case of targeted advertising. Surprisingly, increasing the transparency regarding the collection and processing of personal data did not significantly change consumers' purchasing behavior in the experiment.[292]

Ham (2017) conducted a study on this subject a year later and tried to interpret and understand consumer attitudes toward personalized advertising by employing a *persuasion knowledge model* (PKM),[293] a well-known framework in the marketing literature to interpret and understand how consumers cope with covert persuasion tactics.[294] The PKM states that consumers use their knowledge of persuasion strategies. This knowledge develops over time, and is being used to interpret, evaluate, and respond to influence attempts from advertisers.[295] According to Ham (2017), consumers are more likely to avoid personalized advertising when they obtain more knowledge about the persuasion tactics behind it. This is caused by an increased understanding of the potential risks. Overall, consumers find targeted advertising more harmful than beneficial. It is emphasized that privacy concerns play a crucial role in consumers' decisions to avoid personalized targeting.[296]

---

[289] European Commission (2016), p. 167.

[290] European Commission (2016), pp. 168–169.

[291] European Commission (2016).

[292] European Commission (2016), p. 248.

[293] Friestad and Wright (1994).

[294] Ham (2017).

[295] Friestad and Wright (1994).

[296] Ham (2017), pp. 650–652.

Noteworthy, if the benefits of personalized advertising are framed in terms of reciprocal exchange (e.g., consumers repay the website for the benefits they have received by accepting personal ads), consumers have more positive perceptions of the practice.[297] The result significantly differs when utilitarian arguments are used to convince the consumer (i.e., highlighting higher relevance and better functionality). This type of argument is considerably less effective in changing consumer perceptions.

In conclusion, although the exact benefits and downsides of personalized advertising are perceived differently by consumers, and the general perceptions vary per study, a common trend can be seen. There seems to be a consensus that consumers can identify and appreciate the benefits personalized advertising brings. Still, privacy concerns override the positive perceptions, leading to a generally unfavorable perception among consumers of personalized advertising.[298]

3.5.3.2 Privacy Harm

Privacy harm is conceptualized as the negative consequence that follows from privacy violations. Privacy harm can fall into two categories: subjective and objective.[299] In short, subjective privacy harm relates to the negative perception of being monitored, or so-called unwanted observation, which relates to the individual's internal state. Objective privacy harm refers to the negative, external actions that are performed against a person based on the corresponding personal data that has been collected.[300] Applying this theory to advertising, it becomes clear that personalized ads can generate subjective harm by creating a sense of unease among consumers in relation to their behavior being tracked and their personal information being collected. This is exacerbated by the lack of certainty surrounding companies' potential uses of data.[301] While this subjective harm does not typically result in direct economic losses, it can reduce consumer utility and, by extension, negatively impact social welfare. Objective harm occurs when the personal data about the consumer is used to extract consumer surplus to the largest extent possible, which indicates a tangible economic loss on the consumer side.[302]

Furthermore, personalized targeting jeopardizes consumers' autonomy.[303] The rationale behind this argument is twofold. One the hand one, tracking technologies

---

[297] Schumann et al. (2014).

[298] Further studies on this tendency are Ur et al. (2012); Moore et al. (2015); Gironda and Korgaonkar (2018); Strycharz et al. (2019).

[299] See Sect. 2.4.1.

[300] Calo (2011), p. 1132.

[301] Calo (2014), p. 1029.

[302] Calo (2014), p. 1029. Economic loss, in this context, refers to a reduction in welfare, including direct financial harm and indirect impacts on utility or social welfare, caused by privacy violations or the misuse of personal data.

[303] Hoofnagle et al. (2012), p. 291.

are resistant to privacy protection mechanisms, thereby taking away consumer choice. As a result, new anti-track technologies are developed through consumer initiatives, which innovative tracking technologies used by advertisers try to circumvent.[304]

On the other hand, tracking technologies undermine the fundamental privacy principle of *selective revelation*. According to this principle, consumers should be able to select themselves with which companies they want to share their data. This provides them with a certain degree of control over their data.[305] This principle is also embodied in the GDPR.[306] However, new tracking technologies enable companies to aggregate consumer information in ways consumers are unlikely to comprehend, thereby complicating their decision-making process.[307] Data can be used for purposes that diverge significantly from what consumers expected when giving their initial consent. This is also called *context creep*, which refers to "the reuse of the data in new contexts."[308] As a consequence, consumers are not fully aware of what they are consenting to and what the long-term effects will be of their consent.[309]

Although consumers technically consent to share their data with third parties in the privacy notice, companies now also buy data from other companies about their active users.[310] In this way, companies can match up data and override the selective sharing of data to which the consumer consented. It becomes particularly challenging to foresee the consequences of the given consent since inferences can be made from the data provided, of which the consumer has no awareness or control.[311] Consequently, these innovative tracking technologies can undermine consumer autonomy and circumvent consumer choice to an extent that is worrisome. It has been found that, in practice, this worry is shared by consumers. Consumers are reluctant to share their data for personalization purposes, whether for personalized advertising or contracted services.[312]

3.5.3.3 Ethical Concerns

To enrich the analysis, this section incorporates some of the most prominent concerns that have been raised from an ethical perspective. The purpose of this section is to provide an illustration of the societal concerns that circulate in the debate regarding personalized advertising. This will be done by highlighting three of the

[304] Hoofnagle et al. (2012), p. 294.
[305] Hoofnagle et al. (2012), p. 293.
[306] Articles 6 and 7 GDPR.
[307] Smit et al. (2014).
[308] Galli et al. (2022), p. 499.
[309] Helberger et al. (2021), p. 31.
[310] Hoofnagle et al. (2012), p. 293.
[311] Wachter and Mittelstadt (2019).
[312] Leszczynska and Baltag (2024).

most pressing concerns. First of all, there is a concern that personalized advertising will circumvent anti-discrimination laws. It has been found that personalized advertising does actually target traits based on sensitive categories of data for which regulatory prohibitions are in place, such as religion, ethnicity, health, and sexual orientation.[313] Advertisers target the aspects of individuals that are most valuable in economic terms, even though some of these traits are banned as targeting criteria. Accordingly, individuals can be identified as being potentially valuable consumers or not. As claimed by Turow (2011), people will be classified by marketers as "targets" or "waste".[314] In practice, it will likely lead to narrowed options and social discrimination.[315]

Second, personalized advertising will lead to *social sorting*,[316] which refers to the practice whereby a surveillance system (e.g., tracking technology) "obtains personal and group data in order to classify people and populations according to varying criteria, to determine who should be targeted for special treatment, suspicion, eligibility, inclusion, access, and so on."[317] In essence, consumers get a *social score* that determines their value for targeting. As a result, consumers will be divided into a strong market (i.e., high-value consumers) and a weak market (i.e., low-value consumers). Inevitably, the low-value market will face different treatment than the high-value market (e.g., inferior services since it will be a less profitable market for businesses to be active in). This will most likely amount to exploitation and aggravation of existing biases, the reflection of power disparities, and, ultimately, discrimination.[318]

Third, human dignity is endangered. Hoofnagle et al. (2012) define the problem as follows: "This combination of disguised tracking technologies, choice-invalidating techniques, and models to trick the consumers into revealing data suggests that advertisers do not see individuals as autonomous beings."[319] In other words, personalization seems to compromise human dignity.[320] The harm to human dignity can be seen in five different ways: 1) Consumers are paying with their human dignity since their privacy and agency are invaded for the purpose of behavior modification that will result in financial gain for marketers.[321] 2) Continuous exposure to ads appropriates consumers' attention and makes them more prone to manipulation with potentially harmful effects on human well-being in terms of health, safety, and economic interests.[322]

---

[313] Carrascosa et al. (2015).

[314] Turow (2011), p. 88.

[315] Turow (2011), p. 89.

[316] This concept is also relevant in the context of algorithmic pricing, see Sect. 4.4.3.3.

[317] Lyon (2003), p. 20.

[318] Turow (2008); Nissenbaum (2009).

[319] Hoofnagle et al. (2012), p. 294.

[320] See Sect. 2.2.4 for the definition of human dignity.

[321] Trzaskowski (2021), p. 223.

[322] Trzaskowski (2021), pp. 224–226.

3) The battle for attention superficializes social interactions because of its focus on inciting emotional behavior, individualization (which causes loneliness), and commodification of relationships.[323] 4) Consumers are engaged through addictions spurred on by dopamine-centered interactions. These are interactions shaped by persuasive technologies that are designed to trigger the automatic release of dopamine in the consumer's brain. To illustrate, many of the popular platforms are designed to keep the users engaged (e.g., scrolling) by using behavioral insights (e.g., affecting moods, giving rewards, and emphasizing the fear of missing out).[324] 5) Services are made exceedingly complex to comprehend in order to thwart deliberate thinking and decision-making.[325] In other words, pushing consumers from system 2 toward system 1 thinking.

Trzaskowski (2021) provides a succinct summary of the risk to human dignity: "In the context of data-driven business models human beings may be observed as programmable and hackable algorithms, as we react predictably (in probabilistic terms) to external stimuli that may be delivered through the technology we use."[326] Consequently, the commercialization of human attention and agency takes place to facilitate behavior modification, ultimately undermining human dignity.[327]

3.5.4 An Overall Assessment

The law and economics analysis of personalized advertising has demonstrated that the practice impacts consumer markets in various aspects. Determining the merits of personalized advertising depends on the perspective taken, viz. traditional, behavioral, or a broadened analysis perspective. Various consumer benefits can be pinpointed, among which: more relevant ads, better timing, and the provision of "free" services. In addition, there are numerous business benefits, which include increased profits, competitive advantages, and more effective targeting. However, the analysis also demonstrated several drawbacks related to personalized advertising. It leads to the exploitation of consumer biases and vulnerabilities, exacerbation of information asymmetries, increased transaction costs, economic privacy harm, decreasing marginal value of ads, reduced consumer trust, and the extraction of consumer surplus.

If the analysis would end with a comparison of the economic benefits and drawbacks of personalized advertising, it would amount to a crude counting of pros and cons to determine if the practice is desirable or not. However, this would amount to

[323] Becher and Dadush (2021).

[324] Alter (2017).

[325] Cialdini (2021).

[326] Trzaskowski (2021), p. 221.

[327] Trzaskowski (2021), p. 222 provides a comprehensive study on the relationship between data-driven marketing and human dignity in all its facets.

a severely incomplete analysis. The economic arguments do not encompass an inherent weighing of the underlying evidence. To specify, the statement that personalized advertising could lead to the exploitation of consumer biases does not imply by any means that this harm to consumers will be larger in magnitude than the benefits that would accrue to them because of better-tailored ads. Similarly, the argument that business benefits are significant does not automatically mean that they are greater than the harms inflicted on consumers. Accordingly, the extent to which the benefits outweigh the negative effects, or vice versa, is open to discussion.[328] The economic balancing of the benefits and harms seems to give a mixed result.[329] The impact can be context-specific, which makes it unfeasible to draw an unambiguous conclusion about the exact effects on total welfare.[330]

The welfare impact also depends on the type of consumer in question. Sophisticated consumers are expected to find their way around personalization. In contrast, the less sophisticated, vulnerable consumers will most likely be harmed.[331] Accordingly, this chapter has tried to broaden the economic analysis by incorporating equity considerations, consumer perceptions, and ethical concerns. This opens the way for a more meaningful answer to the question of whether personalized advertising is a practice that needs further regulation.

The assessment of personalized advertising in all its facets demonstrated that from a total welfare perspective, the desirability of the practice is debatable. If the consumer welfare hypothesis is followed,[332] a convincing argument can be made that from an efficiency perspective, personalized advertising is detrimental to consumer welfare. From an equity perspective, personalized advertising is problematic because of its regressive effects. Through the exploitation of biases and the steering of preferences, consumer surplus can be more effectively extracted. The economic harm seems to be particularly troublesome for the more vulnerable groups of society, and the use of dark patterns exacerbates these effects.

Moreover, from a consumer perspective, the practice of personalized advertising evokes privacy concerns that override positive perceptions, leading to a generally unfavorable attitude toward personalized advertising. In addition, the practice seems to be particularly detrimental to fundamental societal values such as consumer autonomy, non-discrimination, and human dignity.

Based on this broadened analysis of personalized advertising, it can be argued that an exploration of the regulatory avenue for the sake of consumer protection is warranted. Consequently, the next step will be analyzing the current legal framework concerning personalized advertising (and dark patterns) to assess its effectiveness and determine if additional regulation is justified.

---

328 Cfr. Acquisti et al. (2016) in the context of privacy protection. They found that the economic analysis of privacy does not provide a straightforward answer to the question of whether privacy protection entails a net positive or negative in purely economic terms.

329 Wagner and Eidenmüller (2019), pp. 586–588.

330 Cfr. Acquisti et al. (2016), p. 448.

331 European Commission (2016), p. 249.

332 See Sect. 1.4.

3.6 Legal Framework

A patchwork of regulations regulates the practice of personalized advertising. This section aims to analyze to what extent the current legal framework is sufficiently equipped to deal with personalized advertising and the corresponding use of dark patterns. An extensive review of each regulation falls outside the scope of this chapter. The focus, therefore, lies on ascertaining how personalized advertising could be tackled with the legal tools that are currently available. In this way, the current state of affairs can be determined, and the extent to which the regulatory avenue should be further explored can be established.

3.6.1 Market-Based Solutions

The market has responded to personalized advertising by developing technological tools that aid consumers in protecting their privacy and limit their exposure to ads. Browser software or incognito modes allow consumers to delete cookies or inhibit the working of cookies. Similarly, consumers can turn off cookies in their browser settings. In this way, no or less data about a consumer can be collected, which impedes exposure to personalized ads.[333] A related tool is the use of *proxy servers*, which act as an intermediary between the user and the Internet by hiding the user's IP address and safeguarding the user's anonymity.[334]

Furthermore, reputation is of pivotal importance to companies in the online world. Due to the existence of review mechanisms and rating services, companies are exposed to the risk of causing consumer backlash if they create the impression that customer data is being exploited.[335] Accordingly, reputational concerns work as a constraint on the activities of an advertising firm.[336] In line with this, firms might be incentivized to build a reputation of being privacy-conscious to attract consumers.

The self-regulatory actions of the advertising industry can take away the need for governmental intervention. Through sound practice principles and strict rules of conduct, the sector can independently see to the development of marketing strategies that warrant transparency, awareness, and professional diligence. This way, advertisers can be steered into law-abiding, compliant behavior, which enables the self-regulatory framework to function as a valuable enforcement tool.[337] A strong feature of self-regulation compared to public regulation is the low administrative costs involved, which makes it an attractive market-based solution.[338]

---

[333] Balebako et al. (2012).

[334] Kumar et al. (2020).

[335] See Sect. 2.2.5.

[336] Rao and Wang (2017).

[337] Weber (2014), p. 5.

[338] Weber (2014), p. 15.

An example of a self-regulatory tool is the adoption of the *ICC Advertising and Marketing Communications Code*.[339] This code includes rules particularly suitable for personalized advertising and digital advertising in general. The rules provide guidance in terms of, for example, decency, honesty, social responsibility, identification, transparency, and privacy. The code aims to complement national and international regulation and acts as a driver of compliance with the legal framework.

There are, however, several problems with these market-based solutions. Primarily, not all consumers are aware of the existence of these technological tools, or they do not know how to use them. In other words, there is a problem of awareness and skill.[340] It is questionable to what extent consumers will be in a position to use the available tools effectively. In particular, vulnerable consumers in online environments are less likely to profit from the benefits of technological tools to protect their privacy.[341]

Second, data analytics companies have developed technologies that can circumvent many of the tools that consumers have at their disposal. For example, disabling flash cookies or circumventing advanced tracking technologies is a particularly complex mechanism.[342]

In addition, if the consumer successfully disables all cookies and tracking mechanisms, the functionality of the websites is often lowered, which increases transaction costs as well.

Third, the constraint imposed on firms by reputational concerns is not expected to preclude the implementation of personalization strategies.[343] Due to the lack of awareness regarding tracking technologies and data analytics, the actual threat of causing consumer backlash might be lower than one would expect from a theoretical point of view. The chances of getting exposed by consumers are low due to this lack of awareness and the degree of sophistication needed to understand the mechanism behind personalized advertising.[344] It is, therefore, not plausible that reputational concerns would remedy most, let alone all, potential harms concerning personalized advertising.[345]

Lastly, concerning self-regulation, the close link to the advertising industry might lead to *regulatory capture*, which refers to the perception that regulatory agencies do not meet public interest goals because they are "subverted by pressure, influence, and 'bribery' to protect the interests of those who were the subjects of the regulation."[346] Accordingly, the self-regulatory framework needs to be designed carefully, and the incentives of the involved parties and the optimal allocation of

[339] International Chamber of Commerce (ICC) (2018).

[340] Cranor (2012); Ur et al. (2012).

[341] European Commission (2016), section 4.9.

[342] Soltani et al. (2010); McDonald and Cranor (2012).

[343] Office of Fair Trading (2010), p. 45.

[344] Helberger et al. (2021), p. 141.

[345] Office of Fair Trading (2010), p. 45.

[346] Ogus (2004), p. 57.

risks must be considered. Self-regulation cannot be a self-sufficient enforcement mechanism in itself and should be combined with public regulation and enforcement. This gives rise to *co-regulation*, which integrates various enforcement mechanisms for optimal compliance rates.[347]

All in all, it can be asserted that market-based solutions provide consumers with some degree of protection, but the market cannot cure itself. Thus, market failures persist in the absence of legal intervention.

3.6.2 *Regulation of Personalized Advertising*

Under the current EU legal framework, no regulation specifically deals with personalized advertising. The *Omnibus Directive*[348] has not proposed any amendments that have changed the status quo. Nonetheless, several regulations are in place that could provide partial protection. These legal instruments deal with more general concepts concerning advertising, communications, and commercial practices. However, the CJEU has stated that these instruments can be interpreted broadly to deal with newer practices.[349] The regulations can roughly be distinguished into four groups: data protection, consumer protection, digital regulation, anti-discrimination laws. Although these regulations complement each other, the four groups of regulations will be analyzed separately for the sake of clarity.

3.6.2.1 Data Protection Law

The collection of vast amounts of personal data from consumers facilitates personalization. To improve the accuracy of personalization, the algorithms underlying the mechanism need to be fed substantial amounts of data continuously. In other words, the more data is collected, the higher the degree of personalization. For the collection and processing of personal data to be deemed lawful, companies must adhere to the GDPR requirements.

In accordance with Articles 5(1)(a) and 5(1)(b) of the GDPR, personal data shall be "processed lawfully, fairly and in a transparent manner in relation to the data subject ('lawfulness, fairness and transparency')" and "collected for specified,

[347] Weber (2014), p. 16.

[348] Directive (EU) 2019/2161 of the European Parliament and of the Council of 27 November 2019 amending Council Directive 93/13/EEC and Directives 98/6/EC, 2005/29/EC and 2011/83/EU of the European Parliament and of the Council as regards the better enforcement and modernisation of Union consumer protection rules. https://eur-lex.europa.eu/eli/dir/2019/2161/oj. Referred to as "Omnibus Directive".

[349] Case C-657/11, Belgian Electronic Sorting Technology NV tegen Bert Peelaers en Visys NV, ECLI:EU:C:2013:516. The Court of Justice of the European Union. https://curia.europa.eu/juris/liste.jsf?language=nl&num=C-657/11, para 35.

explicit and legitimate purposes and not further processed in a manner that is incompatible with those purposes." This gives consumers a certain degree of control over their data and constrains companies' collection and processing possibilities.

Article 6 GDPR provides legitimate grounds for lawful processing, such as the data subject's consent, the necessity for contract performance, compliance with a legal obligation, protection of the data subject's vital interests, the performance of a task in the public interest, and/or legitimate interest. Deciding which legal basis to use for personalization is a challenge. Three legal bases are relevant for the purpose of personalization: *consent*, *necessity for contract performance*, and *legitimate interest*.[350]

A landmark case that clarified the relationship between personalized advertising and the GDPR is *Meta v Bundeskartellamt*.[351] The CJEU analyzed the legal bases for Meta's processing activities in depth. The Court illuminated the concept of contractual necessity and stated that personalized advertising does not fall under this legal ground since Meta's services failed to satisfy the criterion of being "objectively indispensable for a purpose that is integral to the contractual obligation intended for the data subjects."[352] The services can also be provided in an equivalent non-personalized manner, making personalization unnecessary for the contract.[353]

In addition, personalized advertising was not found to be covered under the exception of legitimate interest.[354] Although Recital 47 of the GDPR states that the "processing of personal data for direct marketing purposes may be regarded as carried out for a legitimate interest of the controller", users cannot reasonably expect that their data will be processed, without their consent, for the purpose of personalized advertising.[355] The Court argues that the data subject's interests in such circumstances override the data controller's interests (*balancing provision*), which means that the processing of personal data for personalized advertising cannot take place on the basis of legitimate interest.[356] It is of note that the balancing provision is an open norm susceptible to varying interpretations and, from case law, it is not evident how the sphere of application should be delineated.[357]

Thus, it can be argued that consent is the only legal basis for processing personal data for personalized advertising.[358] The Court clarifies that consent needs to be freely given, specific, informed, and unambiguous, in an affirmative manner, and

---

[350] Zuiderveen Borgesius and Poort (2017), p. 359.

[351] Case C-252/21, Meta Platforms v. Bundeskartellamt, ECLI:EU:C:2023:537. The Court of Justice of the European Union. https://eur-lex.europa.eu/legal-content/EN/TXT/?uri=CELEX%3A62021CJ0252.

[352] Paras 98, 102, 104, and 117.

[353] Para 102.

[354] Para 117.

[355] Para 117.

[356] Para 117.

[357] European Commission (2010), p. 72; Traung (2012), p. 41; Irion and Luchetta (2013), p. 53.

[358] Steppe (2017), pp. 778–781; Zuiderveen Borgesius and Poort (2017), p. 360.

with a genuine or free choice to refuse or withdraw without detriment.[359] A relevant observation is that the Court states that to corroborate users' free choice, they need to be offered "if necessary for an appropriate fee, an equivalent alternative not accompanied by such data processing operations."[360] In other words, users should still be able to use the services offered without being obliged to consent to the processing of their data for personalization purposes.

The outcome of the *Meta v Bundeskartellamt* case is in harmony with the decision made by the *Irish Data Protection Commission* (DPC), who announced on January 4, 2023, that it fined Meta Ireland 210 million euros for breaches of the GDPR relating to its Facebook service and 180 million euros for breaches in relation to its Instagram service.[361] The decision was made after the *European Data Protection Board* (EDPB) issued its determinations on December 5, 2022, in which it rejected Meta's assertion that users agree, through their consent to the standard terms and conditions, to receive ads based on their personal data because they enter into a contract that provides a legal basis for the processing activities. In other words, the EDPB found that Meta Ireland was not allowed to rely on the contractual approach to satisfy Article 6 of the GDPR for the purpose of personalized advertising.[362] Consequently, the DPC imposed a total fine of 390 million euros, thereby reflecting the EDPB's views on Meta Ireland's breaches of its obligations in relation to the fair and transparent processing of users' personal data.

This decision by the DPC, backed by the EDPB, has been a notable development concerning personalized advertising. The fact that the CJEU followed a similar reasoning in its judgment and considerably restricted Meta's personal data processing by strictly interpreting the legal bases under the GDPR is promising for the future protection of consumers against personalized advertising. Nonetheless, more cases are needed to set a solid precedent for future proceedings based on data protection laws that challenge companies that employ personalization strategies. To specify, it can be argued that companies can still rely on the necessity for contract performance when they call attention to the fact that personalization services are the main subject matter of the contract.[363] This rationale, for example, can be applicable to streaming platforms that process personal data to personalize movie or music recommendations, which is a defining feature of the service they provide (e.g., Netflix or Spotify). The collection and processing of personal data takes place when consumers sign up for the service and accept the terms and conditions.[364] In other words, case law made it clear how the legal bases apply to personalized advertising; however, this is less evident for other personalization practices.[365]

---

[359] Meta Platforms v. Bundeskartellamt, paras 142–143.

[360] Para 150.

[361] Irish Data Protection Commission (2023).

[362] The Guardian (2023).

[363] Leszczynska and Baltag (2024).

[364] Leszczynska and Baltag (2024), pp. 349–350.

[365] Leszczynska and Baltag (2024), p. 346.

In its current form, it can be argued that the strict interpretation of the legal bases under the GDPR offers a promising approach for protecting consumers against personalized advertising but is still far from being a panacea for the potential harms that have been identified in this chapter. Because the legal bases of the GDPR are narrowly interpreted, it is expected that companies will shift toward a consent-based approach to make their processing of personal data GDPR-compliant.[366]

Obtaining consent is far from an insurmountable obstacle under the current legal framework. *The notice and choice approach*[367] that is followed in data protection law is nowhere near being effective in protecting consumers against marketing practices, such as personalized advertising. The approach entails "that consumers be informed of what firms are doing with personal information so they can make their own choices about how and whether that data should be used."[368] Thus, rational consumers would decide based on the presented information if they want to consent to the processing of their data. This approach would respect consumers' preferences and values. However, there is a significant signing-without-reading problem: less than 1% of consumers read privacy notices and are not aware of what they are consenting to.[369] The relationship between what the consumer is consenting to and the actual practice is particularly non-transparent due to the complex and technical nature of the data processing activities. It is not reasonable to expect consumers to understand how their personal data will be used for personalized advertising and comprehend the associated risks by simply reading the privacy notice.[370] Consent notices are known to be lengthy, complex, and full of legalese, hampering consumers' ability to understand what they are consenting to and lowering their propensity to read them.[371]

Consequently, the notice and choice approach can be regarded as a largely insufficient tool to protect consumers against personalized advertising.[372] Correspondingly, it is proffered that the current consent mechanism in EU law needs to be revised to ensure the freedom and fairness of individuals' consent and prevent the massive ongoing collection of personal data.[373]

Against this backdrop, it also becomes clear why Articles 21(2) and 22(2)(c) of the GDPR will not be particularly useful in addressing personalized advertising. Article 21(2) GDPR gives consumers the right to object to the processing of their personal data for direct marketing purposes, including profiling. This allows consumers to decline any personalization services from advertisers, thereby shifting the control into the hands of the consumer. However, according to Article 22(2)(c)

[366] Finck (2021), p. 2.

[367] Stigler Center (2019).

[368] Stigler Center (2019), p. 217.

[369] Bakos et al. (2014).

[370] Stigler Center (2019), p. 209; Finck (2021).

[371] McDonald and Cranor (2008).

[372] De Geest (2016), p. 2.

[373] Briefing European Parliament (2021).

GDPR, firms can collect and process consumers' personal data when they obtain *explicit consent*.

Even though explicit consent is not directly mentioned in the GPDR, it is different from "regular" consent. Both types of consent need to be freely given, specific, informed, and unambiguous. Nevertheless, the difference lies in the manner in which the consent is given. According to Article 4(11) GDPR, consent needs to be given through a statement or by a clear affirmative action. Explicit consent is required when it concerns serious data protection risks and, consequently, a higher level of control over the data processing is needed.[374] Correspondingly, explicit consent needs to be more than a statement or a clear affirmative action.[375] Therefore, it cannot be given through pre-ticked boxes and should be actively and specifically given to be considered an express statement of consent.[376] This could be done by means of a written statement, including electronic means, or an oral statement.[377] In the digital context, the requirement can be fulfilled by filling out online forms, sending an email, scanning a written and signed statement, or by using an electronic signature.[378] More practically, explicit consent will be validly obtained when the user is presented with a consent pop-up or message that offers an accept or reject option (various alternatives are feasible, for example, ticking a "Yes" or "No" box), whereby the users' consent is clearly expressed.[379] In spite of the fact that a more active behavior of the consumer is envisioned, *consent desensitization* is lurking. Consumers will be exposed to numerous explicit consent notices, which leads to *consent overload* and eventually might still result in consumers simply agreeing to the request without making an active, informed choice.[380] Even though Article 22 refers to explicit consent, it essentially points again at the same flaw in the legislation. In short, the GDPR does not provide a robust protection mechanism due to the issues identified with consent notices.[381]

Another legal instrument is the *ePrivacy Directive*.[382] Pursuant to Article 3(1), the Directive applies to "the processing of personal data in connection with the pro-

---

[374] Article 29 Data Protection Working Party (2018); European Data Protection Board (EDPB) (2020), p. 20.

[375] Hordern (2019), section 7.3.1.

[376] Case C-673/17, Bundesverband der Verbraucherzentralen und Verbraucherverbände - Verbraucherzentrale Bundesverband e.V. v Planet49 GmbH, ECLI:EU:C:2019:801, The Court of Justice of the European Union. https://curia.europa.eu/juris/liste.jsf?num=C-673/17.

[377] Recital 32 GDPR.

[378] Article 29 Data Protection Working Party (2018), p. 18; Hordern (2019), section 7.3.1; European Data Protection Board (EDPB) (2020), p. 21.

[379] Article 29 Data Protection Working Party (2018), p. 19; European Data Protection Board (EDPB) (2020), p. 21.

[380] Schermer et al. (2014).

[381] Briefing European Parliament (2021); Finck (2021).

[382] Directive 2002/58/EC of the European Parliament and of the Council of 12 July 2002 concerning the processing of personal data and the protection of privacy in the electronic communications sector (Directive on privacy and electronic communications). https://eur-lex.europa.eu/legal-content/EN/TXT/?uri=celex%3A32002L0058. Referred to as the "ePrivacy Directive".

vision of publicly available electronic communications services in public communications networks in the Community." In essence, this also applies to companies that market their products or services via, for example, websites, making the Directive pertinent to personalized advertising. The relevant provision of the ePrivacy Directive is Article 5(1), which requires consent from the user for the surveillance technologies utilized for, *inter alia*, personalized advertising.[383] This provision complies with the requirements of the GDPR.[384] However, this also implies that the same problem that is encountered under the GDPR applies to the protection provided by the ePrivacy Directive; namely, the fact that the consent-and-choice approach falls short. As Finck (2021) puts it: "Indeed, the focus on informational self-determination on which consent is based has proven to have serious limitations in today's complex data ecosystems."[385] The ePrivacy Directive does not provide, therefore, additional safeguards that could benefit consumers.

In a nutshell, although the data protection regulations are able to limit the practice of personalized advertising to a considerable extent, the consent-and-choice approach still provides companies with enough leeway to implement the practice successfully.[386] For this reason, attention needs to be shifted to the safeguards that consumer protection regulations can offer.

3.6.2.2 Consumer Protection Law

In the realm of consumer protection, the term *marketing law* is used interchangeably with the term consumer law.[387] Marketing law aims to ensure fair commercial practices in the market to protect consumers and competitors from unfair practices.[388] On a European level, marketing law is subsumed into the working sphere of UCPD. The Directive aims to protect consumers' economic interests.[389] The UCPD proved to be a powerful instrument for addressing harms that arise from consumer profiling in digital markets.[390] Accordingly, the UCPD is argued to be the most prominent legal instrument for addressing personalized advertising.[391]

The UCPD has a three-tier structure, which guides how the Directive should be applied.[392] The assessment of a commercial practice starts by checking Annex 1,

---

383 Article 29 Data Protection Working Party (2010), p. 8.

384 Article 29 Data Protection Working Party (2010), p. 10.

385 Finck (2021), p. 6.

386 Bietti (2019).

387 Nielsen (2002).

388 Trzaskowski (2011), p. 386.

389 Nielsen (2002).

390 Goanta (2024), p. 74.

391 Galli (2020, 2021, 2022).

392 Goanta (2024), p. 75. In essence, the steps go from blacklisted practices (1) to specific clauses (2) to a general clause (3), which functions as a safety net when the two previous steps are not suitable to address the practice in question.

which contains all the practices that are under all circumstances deemed unfair. The Annex does not cover the practice of personalized advertising or personalized marketing in general. Therefore, the analysis can continue with the second step: assessing whether personalized advertising falls under the tests of Articles 6–9, which include *misleading* and *aggressive* commercial practices. Misleading commercial practices relate to the provision of information (or its omission), and aggressive commercial practices refer to the conduct of traders in the course of business (i.e., impairing the freedom of choice or conduct of the consumer).[393]

Article 6 covers misleading actions (false information), and Article 7 covers misleading omissions (leaving out material information for informed decision-making). Arguably, the lack of transparency in personalized advertising could amount to a misleading omission under Article 7. A personalized ad uses consumers' data to individualize the content and address them directly. Article 7 UCPD does not contain an obligation to disclose all information about the practice to the consumer. Nevertheless, it prohibits traders from omitting material information that the average consumer needs in order to make a transactional decision. Material information for the consumer would consist of a clear explanation of which personal data is being collected, how the profile has been established, and what specific characteristics (or vulnerabilities) are being targeted in the presented ad. Therefore, it can be argued that solely informing the consumer that an ad has been personalized is insufficient. Nonetheless, CJEU case law gives the impression that the Court is not, at the moment, willing to interpret Article 7 in such a broad manner.[394] Further litigation or legislative complements would be needed to accommodate such broadened interpretations of the UCPD.[395]

Also of note, the Danish Consumer Ombudsman determined that Meta was guilty of an unfair commercial practice because it targeted individuals interested in gambling with payday loans. The Ombudsman figured this out because Meta adopted a tool in which they clarified why the advertisement was shown to users. This openness about the practice enabled the Consumer Ombudsman to conclude that Meta's type of targeting was unfair.[396] This case demonstrates that more transparency would allow for more effective enforcement and a more successful invocation of the UCPD to address personalized advertising.

Alternatively, personalized advertising could be seen as an aggressive commercial practice in line with Articles 8 and 9 UCPD if it can be proven that by harassment, coercion, including the use of physical force or undue influence, the average consumer's freedom of choice or conduct has been significantly impaired, which led to a transactional decision that the consumer would not have taken otherwise. In contrast to misleading practices, the focus of an aggressive practice lies on the

[393] Article 7 and 8 UCPD.

[394] Helberger et al. (2021), p. 143.

[395] Galli (2022).

[396] Trzaskowski (2021), p. 246; Danish Consumer Ombudsman/Forbrugerombudsmanden (2022), p. 16.

infringement of consumers' freedom to act or choose instead of the ability to make an informed decision.[397] These aggressive practices represent a compromise between the national contract law systems of the Member States, which share a relatively equivalent interpretation of the doctrines of coercion, harassment, and undue influence.[398]

The UCPD does not further define the concepts of coercion and harassment. Thus, it is argued that the UCPD fails to provide further guidance on how these doctrines should be read in the context of the legislation.[399] However, examining how the concepts are interpreted in the national legal systems of the Member States reveals that harassment and coercion refer to the most blatant forms of aggressive selling techniques.[400] Undue influence seems, therefore, better suited to navigate the subtle line between legitimate persuasion and unfairly influencing consumers' transactional decisions,[401] which characterizes personalized advertising.

The concept of undue influence is further defined in the UCPD by Article 2(j), which states:

> 'undue influence' means exploiting a position of power in relation to the consumer so as to apply pressure, even without using or threatening to use physical force, in a way which significantly limits the consumer's ability to make an informed decision;

In the *Wind Tre*[402] and *Orange Polska*[403] cases, the CJEU explained that an aggressive practice based on undue influence should affect both consumers' freedom of choice and conduct. The mere withholding of information to make a choice (*Wind Tre*) or the presence of a courier (or trader, for that matter) (*Orange Polska*) is not sufficient; there must be *additional practices* that have a pressuring effect on the consumer, thereby affecting the freedom of choice.

In the *Orange Polska* case, the CJEU clarifies that a practice:

> constitutes an aggressive commercial practice through the exertion of undue influence where the trader or its courier adopt unfair conduct, the effect of which is to put pressure on the consumer such that his freedom of choice is significantly impaired, such as conduct that makes that consumer feel uncomfortable or confuses his thinking concerning the transactional decision to be taken.[404]

---

[397] Recital 16 UCTD.

[398] Howells et al. (2016), p. 168.

[399] Howells et al. (2016), p. 169.

[400] Schulze and Schulte-Nölke (2003).

[401] Schulze and Schulte-Nölke (2003), p. 37.

[402] Case C-54/17, Autorità Garante della Concorrenza e del Mercato v Wind Tre SpA and Vodafone Italia SpA, ECLI:EU:C:2018:710. The Court of Justice of the European Union. https://curia.europa.eu/juris/liste.jsf?language=en&num=C-54/17.

[403] Case C 628/17, Prezes Urzędu Ochrony Konkurencji i Konsumentów v Orange Polska S.A., ECLI:EU:C:2019:480. The Court of Justice of the European Union. https://curia.europa.eu/juris/liste.jsf?language=en&num=C-628/17.

[404] Para 49.

Furthermore, according to Article 2(j), there must be a position of power, which is not further defined in the UCPD. However, considering the factors that are mentioned in Article 9 to define a practice as aggressive, for example, time, location, persistence, language, behavior, or threats, the position of power should not be interpreted in terms of economic market power, which leads to an unequal standing between consumers and sellers. Instead, it refers to a situational context in which additional pressure is put on the consumer, taking away the ability to reflect on the decision and thus impeding the ability to make a free choice.[405] The consumers are, in essence, at the trader's mercy, leading to a type of domination that hinders the assessment of the transaction's risks and benefits.[406] An example of this is high-pressure selling, which makes the consumer feel like there is no escape.

Alternatively, sellers can exploit consumers' misfortunes or their personal circumstances of such gravity that they impair consumers' judgment pursuant to Article 9(c), which creates a position of power. The element of "such gravity" is traditionally interpreted as encompassing tragic or traumatic events, such as illnesses or accidents.[407] Although there is reason to believe that the criterion is comprehensive because the CJEU clarified that psychological effects also fall under this provision,[408] it is highly doubtful that this criterion can be extended to cover the digital asymmetry between consumers and sellers caused by the exploitation of digital vulnerabilities and/or circumstances.

The bottleneck of applying the undue influence provision to personalized advertising is that it is exceedingly difficult to define the boundary between legitimate persuasion and aggressive selling.[409] On the one hand, "all kinds of advertising are *per definitionem* aimed at influencing the transactional decisions of potential customers."[410] On the other hand, it is hard to prove that this happens by pressuring consumers to such an extent that their freedom of choice is significantly impaired, thereby making them feel uncomfortable and second-guess the transactional decision taken.

The personalization mechanism is characterized by its ability to subtly but effectively influence consumers.[411] It does not exert pressure on consumers in the sense that it has been interpreted in the context of Articles 8 and 9 of the UCPD. Accordingly, it can be argued that the doctrine of undue influence will not be of practical relevance to addressing personalized advertising.[412]

---

405 Willett (2010), p. 260.

406 Willett (2010), pp. 260–261.

407 Galli (2022).

408 Case C-428/11, Purely Creative Ltd and Others v Office of Fair Trading, ECLI:EU:C:2012:651. The Court of Justice of the European Union. https://curia.europa.eu/juris/liste.jsf?num=C-428/11&language=EN.

409 Howells et al. (2016), p. 168.

410 Schulze and Schulte-Nölke (2003), p. 36.

411 Sibony (2014), p. 925.

412 Mik (2016).

Overall, in the way that Articles 8 and 9 are currently interpreted, their scope is limited to commercial practices that clearly limit consumers' ability to make a free choice. Using the provisions on aggressive commercial practices to address personalized advertising will be complex. Personalized marketing exerts an influence based on soft intrusion and cannot be regarded as foreclosing options.[413] The sophistication and subtlety of personalized advertising make it difficult to prove that an ad significantly impairs or is likely to significantly impair the average consumer's freedom of choice or conduct. Only in cases of outright harassment, coercion, or undue influence would such an appeal succeed.[414]

The last step is to see if the commercial practice can be addressed via the general unfairness clause of Article 5. Under Article 5(2) UCPD, a commercial practice is deemed unfair when:

> (a) it is contrary to the requirements of professional diligence
> and
> (b) it materially distorts or is likely to materially distort the economic behaviour with regard to the product of the average consumer whom it reaches or to whom it is addressed, or of the average member of the group when a commercial practice is directed to a particular group of consumers.

Professional diligence refers to "the standard of special skill and care which a trader may reasonably be expected to exercise towards consumers, commensurate with honest market practice and/or the general principle of good faith in the trader's field of activity."[415] This notion encompasses principles such as honest and good market practices and good faith, although they are not explicitly mentioned in the UCPD.[416] These principles underscore the normative values that pertain to a specific field of business activity.[417] In essence, this means that businesses are expected not to engage in commercial practices that manipulate consumers and harm their interests.[418]

In addition, the commercial practice needs to *materially distort* the *economic behavior* of the *average* consumer (or the average member of the group) that it addresses. Three elements underlie this provision. Pursuant to Article 2(e) materially distort means appreciably impairing consumers' ability to make an informed decision, which causes them to take a transactional action they would not have taken otherwise. The economic behavior refers to the transactional action, which, according to the CJEU, should be broadly interpreted, as became clear from the *Trento Sviluppo srl* case.[419] The Court states that the definition "covers not only the decision whether or not to purchase a product, but also the decision directly related to

[413] Galli (2022).

[414] Helberger et al. (2021), p. 142.

[415] Article 2(h) UCPD.

[416] European Commission (2021), section 2.7.

[417] European Commission (2021), section 2.7.

[418] Goanta (2024), p. 75.

[419] Case C-281/12, Trento Sviluppo srl and Centrale Adriatica Soc. coop. arl v Autorità Garante della Concorrenza e del Mercato, ECLI:EU:C:2013:859. The Court of Justice of the European Union. https://curia.europa.eu/juris/liste.jsf?num=C-281/12&language=EN.

that decision, in particular the decision to enter the shop."[420] According to Guidance on the UCPD,[421] this also includes spending more time on a purchasing process, deciding not to switch providers, clicking on a link or advertisement, or continuing to use a service by browsing or scrolling. It is not required to demonstrate that economic behavior has been distorted. Instead, an assessment is needed to see if a commercial practice will likely have such an impact. The relevance of this consideration is that marketing techniques fall under the ambit of the UCPD, and it allows for the assessment of the potential impact that they can have on the average or targeted consumer. Accordingly, the manipulative character of a marketing technique can be evaluated by its ability to affect behavior (e.g., limiting consumer choice), whereby manipulation of the consumer's economic behavior implies consumer harm.[422]

Nevertheless, the benchmark to assess the impact of the commercial practice is the average consumer, "who is reasonably well-informed and reasonably observant and circumspect, taking into account social, cultural and linguistic factors".[423] Notably, the average consumer test is not statistical. National authorities and courts must exercise their own faculty of judgment to determine the typical average consumer's reaction while taking the case law of the CJEU into account.[424]

Article 5(2)(b) UCPD further develops the average consumer test by looking at specifically targeted consumers within a group. When a specific group is targeted, the average member of that group functions as the benchmark to assess the practice. However, it could be said that a different level of knowledge is expected from members of a specific group (e.g., a car enthusiast group is expected to know more about commercial practices in an automotive context). Thus, to a certain extent, the provision does not provide more protection to this group. In contrast, Article 5(3) ensures a higher level of protection for consumers that belong to one of the groups that are particularly vulnerable due to their mental or physical infirmity, age, or credulity. The practice then needs to be assessed from the perspective of the average member of that particularly susceptible group.[425]

The existing literature heavily criticizes the average consumer test of the UCPD for failing to reflect consumers' actual behavior adequately.[426] The test's practical workability is limited due to its emphasis on the consumer's theoretical rational behavior, which disregards the insights put forward by cognitive psychology and behavioral (law and) economics.[427] In addition, empirical evidence could provide

[420] Para 36.

[421] European Commission (2021), section 2.4.

[422] Trzaskowski (2016).

[423] Recital 18 UCPD. See also Case C-210/96, Gut Springenheide and Rudolf Tusky v. Oberkreisdirektor des Kreises Steinfurt, ECLI:EU:C:1998:369. The Court of Justice of the European Union. https://eur-lex.europa.eu/legal-content/EN/TXT/?uri=CELEX%3A61996CJ0210.

[424] Recital 18 UCPD.

[425] Recital 19 UCPD.

[426] See, for example, Cohen (2019); Riefa and Gamper (2020); Duivenvoorde (2023).

[427] Incardona and Poncibò (2007); Galli (2022).

valuable insights into how consumers actually behave and help assess commercial practices' effective impact.[428]

Moreover, the current notion of vulnerability in the UCPD is not fit to address the exploitation of vulnerability as it is facilitated by algorithmic personalization technologies.[429] Nevertheless, according to the Guidance on the UCPD,[430] the concept is broader than the characteristics listed in Article 5(3). It should also include context-dependent vulnerabilities that are present in digital environments, which are also influenced by socio-demographic, personal, and psychological characteristics. In other words, it concerns a dynamic and situational concept, which can, in highly personalized circumstances, be formulated from the perspective of a single person who was addressed by the commercial practice.[431] Although this interpretation sounds promising to tackle personalization,[432] it must be noted that, in practice, it has led to a more traditional enumeration of demographic characteristics and has still not materialized into a concept that can capture vulnerability in online markets, which is characterized by a digital asymmetry between traders and consumers.[433]

Accordingly, applying Article 5(2) UCPD to personalized advertising could be functional when it can be proven that the marketing practices go against the trader's professional diligence and materially distort the consumer's behavior from the average consumer's perspective. Concerning professional diligence, it would need to be argued that, in light of honest trading and good faith, traders have an obligation to investigate whether the marketing practice does not violate consumers' fundamental rights and the duty to provide clarity regarding the mechanism behind the practice.[434] Such an interpretation of professional diligence would require a broad interpretation of the definition under the UCPD, which is yet to be made in case law and remains a recommendation for the moment.[435]

In addition, the personalized ad would need to materially distort consumers' behavior to cause them to make a transactional decision they would not have made otherwise.[436] The difficulty with proving this is that the material distortion is proven by looking at the transactional decision made. This presumes that average consumers have pre-set preferences regarding a range of options, which, due to the trader's behavior, are distorted and leads to an unwanted transactional decision that does not maximize their preferences.[437] In other words, it presumes exogenously given pref-

[428] Luzak (2015).

[429] See Sect. 2.4.1.

[430] European Commission (2021), section 2.6.

[431] European Commission (2021), section 4.2.7.

[432] It is of note that the Guidance on the UCPD is not binding and does not equate the position of the CJEU or prejudge further developments in case law.

[433] Helberger et al. (2021); Goanta (2024).

[434] Helberger et al. (2021), p. 143.

[435] Helberger et al. (2022), p. 196.

[436] Although the wording of Article 5(2) differs from those in Articles 6, 7, and 8, the material distortion requirement should be interpreted similarly, see European Commission (2021), section 2.4.

[437] Galli (2022).

erences. This, however, overlooks the preference-shaping ability of personalized advertising, which emphasizes the endogenous character of preferences.[438]

Through the collection of large amounts of consumer data and the building of consumer profiles, marketers can anticipate preferences, shape them (e.g., filtering information or options[439]), and guide the behavior of a consumer in a specific direction. This does not amount to a distortion of behavior but rather to a shaping of consumer behavior, which could, in principle, correspond with consumers' preferences.[440] It is far from evident that personalized advertising will lead to consumers' preferences being entirely ignored and overruled by businesses' interests. The personalization mechanism is subtle, which means that the effectiveness does not lie in contradicting consumers but in guiding them to options that match their preferences in a way that extracts more value to the seller's benefit.[441]

To illustrate, an ad that promotes meat products to vegetarians is unlikely to be effective (i.e., mismatched preferences). Instead, targeting vegetarians with a personalized ad that promotes tasty vegetarian meals is likely more effective (matching preferences). However, targeting the same vegetarians, while they are hungry and stressed, with an ad that promotes exactly those options of meals that approximate their maximum willingness to pay (i.e., reservation price) and can be delivered within 30 minutes, does not only match their preferences,[442] but also guides their behavior to choose an option that will be most beneficial to the seller (extracting most or all consumer surplus).[443]

In this regard, Recital 6 of the UCPD is of particular relevance:

> Further, this Directive does not affect accepted advertising and marketing practices, such as legitimate product placement, brand differentiation or the offering of incentives which may legitimately affect consumers' perceptions of products and influence their behaviour without impairing the consumer's ability to make an informed decision.

It will then be difficult to demonstrate that consumers' behavior was materially distorted, and a transactional decision was made that they would not have been made otherwise. The subtlety of the personalization mechanism can circumvent the materiality requirement while still being significantly more effective in steering consumers than traditional non-personalized advertising.[444] Even though the harm can be minor on an individual level, it can be substantial on the market level.

Lastly, the assessment of material distortion is inextricably linked to the debate about the average consumer test. The current differentiation between average and vulnerable consumers is not suitable for tackling the identified digital vulnerability

---

[438] Sunstein (1993); Porat (2021).

[439] Pariser (2011).

[440] Galli (2022).

[441] This corresponds to the notion of marketing-induced market failures.

[442] In this case, it could be argued that there is a mismatch between first-order and second-order motivations, see Sect. 2.4.4.

[443] Chapter 4 will further elaborate on the power of combining personalized advertising and pricing.

[444] Galli (2022).

that each consumer faces in the context of personalization.[445] The interpretation of the benchmarks would need to be significantly stretched to cover the harms identified by personalization. Although it can be the case that the CJEU will follow a broader interpretation of the benchmarks, as advocated in the Guidance on the UCPD,[446] there is no evidence for such a movement, which means that a revision of the UCPD would be needed in this regard.[447]

All things considered, Article 5 of the UCPD, which functions as the safety net for practices not covered by Annex 1 and Articles 6 to 9, is also conceptually unfit to address personalized advertising. In fact, considering the complete analysis of the UCPD, it can be concluded that the UCPD, as it stands, is not able to offer adequate protection to consumers against the harms identified with personalized advertising.[448] Many of its provisions would require reinterpretation and further development.[449]

Next, the UCTD[450] could be used to address personalized advertising. Pursuant to Article 3(1):

> A contractual term which has not been individually negotiated shall be regarded as unfair if, contrary to the requirement of good faith, it causes a significant imbalance in the parties' rights and obligations arising under the contract, to the detriment of the consumer.

Accordingly, if the standard form allows a firm to develop a data exploitation strategy by obtaining consumers' consent, the standard contract terms that make this possible should be submitted to the *fairness test* under the UCTD.[451] The rationale behind this is that consumers are in a weaker negotiation position and are consenting to a term that will have significant consequences at a later stage, of which they might not be aware at the time of the conclusion of the contract.[452] This situation could be regarded as unfair, but it requires a broad interpretation of the provision, which includes other consumer interests, such as protecting privacy and consumer autonomy.

A broader interpretation of fairness, in which other social policies or entitlements from fundamental rights that fall under the EU *acquis* would be considered, could reinforce the ability of the UCTD to tackle personalized advertising. To specify, the *good faith* element of the UCTD could allow for the consideration of a more

---

[445] Helberger et al. (2022), p. 195.

[446] European Commission (2021).

[447] In Chap. 6, regulatory proposals will be discussed.

[448] Cfr. Helberger et al. (2022).

[449] Leiser and Caruana (2021) discuss various possible extensions of the UCPD, among others, to combat unfair commercial practices and dark patterns; Galli (2020, 2021, 2022).

[450] Council Directive 93/13/EEC of 5 April 1993 on unfair terms in consumer contracts. https://eur-lex.europa.eu/legal-content/EN/TXT/?uri=celex%3A31993L0013. Referred to as the "UCTD".

[451] Helberger et al. (2021), p. 47.

[452] Helberger (2016), p. 146.

equitable treatment of consumers under the contract.[453] For instance, it could be argued that consent to terms that enable data exploitation to the detriment of the consumer, which could be in terms of loss of welfare and fundamental rights, leads to a case of contractual unfairness.[454]

In the context of standard-form contracting, consumers are often unaware of the implications of consent, the workings of the mechanism, and the underlying cost structure. Concerning the latter, the concept of "give data to get service" is often advocated by companies. That is to say, because consumers give their data, many services can be provided for free, indicating an equal exchange. However, it is complicated for consumers to assess the actual costs and benefits of sharing their data. Correspondingly, there is no benchmark to determine if significantly more data is requested from the consumer than would be necessary to cover the service's costs.[455] In this sense, there is a significant imbalance in the parties' rights and obligations under the contract. The UCTD could be used as a remedy for imbalanced counter-performances by excluding the validity of consent when the requested data are excessive compared to the service's value, particularly when the provider enjoys superior market power.[456]

Nevertheless, the pitfall is that Article 4(2) UCTD removes the fairness assessment of the main subject matter of the contract and the price, provided that they are drafted in plain intelligible language. The value of data as a counter-performance could be regarded as a matter relating to the price dimension of the contract and will *prima facie* be excluded from the assessments. Only excessive imbalances relating to the exchange of data could be remedied under the UCTD.[457] Besides, the seller could design the contract in a way that such an assessment could be circumvented, for example, by making service personalization the main subject matter.[458] It is, therefore, arguable to what extent the UCTD will effectively be able to address personalized advertising.

The ability to tackle personalized advertising by virtue of the UCTD could be strengthened by harmonizing the outcomes of the fairness tests of the GDPR, UCPD, and UCTD. In other words, consent to unfair terms should also entail the constitutive elements of an unfair commercial practice (under the UCPD) and vice versa.[459] This proposes the hypothesis that data exploitation strategies will be seen as infringements of unfairness under all three regulations.[460] This way, the regulations would mutually reinforce each other, leading to more effective enforcement. Nevertheless, this rationale is not followed by the CJEU, which stated that a viola-

[453] Wilhelmsson and Willett (2018).

[454] Helberger (2016), p. 148.

[455] Helberger (2016), p. 148.

[456] Sartor and Galli (2022), p. 509.

[457] Hacker (2019), p. 22.

[458] Zardiashvili and Sears (2023), p. 833.

[459] Orlando (2011).

[460] Helberger et al. (2021), p. 61.

tion of the UCPD does not automatically imply unfairness of the contested terms under the UCTD.[461] Hence, a specific contested term must be considered on its own in relation to all relevant circumstances of the case. Nevertheless, if a commercial practice is found to be unfair, it must be regarded as one of the elements of the unfairness test under the UCTD. Accordingly, there is room for integrating value judgments under the three regulations.[462]

Apart from the primary consumer protection tools, the UCPD and the UCTD, there exists a variety of additional relevant instruments that have a bearing on the practice of personalized advertising. These include the *P2B regulation*,[463] the *E-Commerce Directive*,[464] the *Audiovisual Media Services Directive* (AVMS),[465] the MCAD,[466] and the *Consumer Rights Directive* (CRD).[467]

Each of these regulations addresses only certain aspects of personalized advertising and often indirectly in a manner that requires wide interpretations. Although these regulations have a different scope of application, a common denominator in their approach to online advertising techniques, including personalized advertising, allows for summarization. The regulations collectively impose rules that require transparency.[468]

Nonetheless, these more specific regulations do not provide additional protections to tackle personalized advertising, which are not already accounted for by the GDPR, UCPD, and the UCTD. Under the currently existing consumer protection law framework, no legal obligation exists that fosters clear and comprehensible

---

[461] Case C-453/10, Pereničová and Perenič, ECLI:EU:C:2012:144. The Court of Justice of the European Union. https://curia.europa.eu/juris/liste.jsf?num=C-453/10&language=EN, paragraphs 43–44.

[462] Helberger et al. (2021), p. 61.

[463] Regulation (EU) 2019/1150 of the European Parliament and of the Council of 20 June 2019 on promoting fairness and transparency for business users of online intermediation services. https://eur-lex.europa.eu/legal-content/EN/TXT/?uri=celex%3A32019R1150. Referred to as "P2B Regulation".

[464] Directive 2000/31/EC of the European Parliament and of the Council of 8 June 2000 on certain legal aspects of information society services, in particular electronic commerce, in the Internal Market ('Directive on electronic commerce'). https://eur-lex.europa.eu/legal-content/EN/TXT/?uri=CELEX%3A32000L0031. Referred to as "E-Commerce Directive".

[465] Directive 2010/13/EU of the European Parliament and of the Council of 10 March 2010 on the coordination of certain provisions laid down by law, regulation or administrative action in Member States concerning the provision of audiovisual media services (Audiovisual Media Services Directive) (codified version). https://eur-lex.europa.eu/eli/dir/2010/13/oj. Referred to as "AVMS".

[466] Directive 2006/114/EC of the European Parliament and of the Council of 12 December 2006 concerning misleading and comparative advertising (codified version). https://eur-lex.europa.eu/legal-content/EN/TXT/?uri=CELEX%3A32006L0114.

[467] Directive 2011/83/EU of the European Parliament and of the Council of 25 October 2011 on consumer rights, amending Council Directive 93/13/EEC and Directive 1999/44/EC of the European Parliament and of the Council and repealing Council Directive 85/577/EEC and Directive 97/7/EC of the European Parliament and of the Council. https://eur-lex.europa.eu/legal-content/EN/TXT/?uri=celex%3A32011L0083. Referred to as the "Consumer Rights Directive".

[468] Fourberg et al. (2021), p. 73.

information for the consumer, which means that meaningful and manageable consent is still impeded, thereby allowing processing operations to continue that are likely to lead to individual and social harm.[469]

3.6.2.3 Digital Regulation

There have been new legislative developments on the EU level concerning digital regulations pertinent to personalized advertising. First and foremost, the *Digital Services Act* (DSA)[470] presents new comprehensive rules on online advertising, including personalized advertising. The DSA focuses on *digital intermediary services,* particularly *very large online platforms* (VLOPs) and *very large online search engines* (VLOSEs). It aims to set out "harmonised rules for a safe, predictable and trusted online environment that facilitates innovation and in which fundamental rights enshrined in the Charter, including the principle of consumer protection, are effectively protected."[471] This provision demonstrates that the DSA addresses societal concerns associated with platforms' operations, and explicitly highlights the role of consumer protection.

The DSA introduces several provisions that are relevant to personalized advertising. To start with, the DSA aims to increase the level of transparency regarding targeting. Article 26(1) DSA states:

> Providers of online platforms that present advertisements on their online interfaces shall ensure that, for each specific advertisement presented to each individual recipient, the recipients of the service are able to identify, in a clear, concise and unambiguous manner and in real time, the following:
>
> (a) that the information is an advertisement, including through prominent markings, which might follow standards pursuant to Article 44;
> (b) the natural or legal person on whose behalf the advertisement is presented;
> (c) the natural or legal person who paid for the advertisement if that person is different from the natural or legal person referred to in point (b);
> (d) meaningful information directly and easily accessible from the advertisement about the main parameters used to determine the recipient to whom the advertisement is presented and, where applicable, about how to change those parameters.

Recital 68 further clarifies Article 26(1)(d) by stating that:

> recipients of the service should have information directly accessible from the online interface where the advertisement is presented, on the main parameters used for determining that a specific advertisement is presented to them, providing meaningful explanations of the logic used to that end, including when this is based on profiling.

---

[469] Briefing European Parliament (2021).

[470] Regulation (EU) 2022/2065 of the European Parliament and of the Council of 19 October 2022 on a Single Market For Digital Services and amending Directive 2000/31/EC (Digital Services Act). https://eur-lex.europa.eu/legal-content/EN/TXT/?uri=celex%3A32022R2065. Referred to as "DSA".

[471] Article 1(1) DSA.

Article 26 empowers consumers since they will better understand why content is suggested to them and based on what grounds, allowing them to take appropriate action. Before the DSA, such an obligation to be transparent about targeting did not exist in EU consumer law. Therefore, the DSA marks a significant change in terms of transparency in online advertising, which can be regarded as an enhancement of consumer protection.[472]

In addition, the DSA takes measures to counteract far-reaching profiling. The DSA does not encompass a ban on personalized advertising, but it does include a prohibition to target advertising based on sensitive personal data. More specifically, Article 26(3) prohibits advertising that is based on the profiling (as defined in Article 4(4) GDPR) of sensitive personal data (Article 9(1) GDPR). Following Recital 69 of the DSA, the provision is meant to tackle the adverse effects of personalized advertising that appeal to consumer vulnerabilities. In principle, this provision offers further protection to consumers not offered by the GDPR, which does allow for profiling based on sensitive personal data, provided that data subjects have given their express consent.

Article 26(3) DSA, however, cannot remedy all the concerns surrounding the practice of personalized advertising.[473] The exploitation of consumer vulnerabilities can still take place in the forms of, for example, the targeting of irrationality or external factors that influence the consumer's decision-making process. Accordingly, although the provision extends the protection of consumers, its scope is limited (i.e., it only targets profiling based on sensitive personal data).[474] As a consequence, tackling exploitative personalized advertising practices will predominantly still have to take place under the UCPD, which, as has become clear, is only of limited effectiveness.

Noteworthy, Article 28(2) DSA provides further protection to minors. Pursuant to this provision, all targeting of minors based on profiling is prohibited, which, thus, also includes personalized advertising based on profiling.

Article 39 DSA requires further transparency from VLOPs and VLOSEs by demanding the establishment of a publicly available repository that contains more detailed information about the advertisements they present (e.g., the content, principal, period of display, targeting mechanism, commercial communications, and the recipients). This provision reinforces the transparency obligation of Article 26(1)(c) and offers enforcement authorities a tool to go after VLOPs and VLOSEs that conduct harmful personalized advertising. Nevertheless, it is questionable to what extent the provided data will be sufficient to determine if consumer exploitation is taking place, which warrants further action.

In addition to these provisions, the DSA can be relevant to personalized advertising through its rules on illegal content. Pursuant to Article 3(h):

---

[472] Duivenvoorde and Goanta (2023), p. 8.

[473] See Sect. 3.5.

[474] Duivenvoorde and Goanta (2023), p. 11.

> 'illegal content' means any information that, in itself or in relation to an activity, including the sale of products or the provision of services, is not in compliance with Union law or the law of any Member State which is in compliance with Union law, irrespective of the precise subject matter or nature of that law;

In this sense, a violation of EU consumer law can qualify an advertisement as illegal content. Recital 12 mentions "the sale of products or the provision of services in infringement of consumer protection law." Accordingly, the DSA encompasses a broader meaning of illegality that exceeds the confines of criminal law.[475] This means that the DSA reinforces the enforcement of consumer protection laws, such as the UCPD. Advertising qualified as unfair under the UCPD would qualify as illegal content under the DSA. Nevertheless, this does entail that a case-by-case analysis under the UCPD will still be necessary since there is no specific provision for personalized advertising in the UCPD. For this reason, it can be argued that linking the provision of illegal content with the consumer *acquis* will not automatically contribute to remedying consumer harm from exploitative online advertising practices.

In essence, the DSA strengthens user rights with respect to online advertising. Personalized ads based on sensitive data are prohibited, and clear disclosure is required. This disclosure will enable consumers to understand better why they are targeted and help distinguish between sponsored and regular content. Besides, the encouragement by the EC to the platforms to draft voluntary codes of conduct for online advertising (Article 46) can further contribute to transparency beyond the requirements of Articles 26 and 39.

Nonetheless, whether these transparency requirements will effectively protect consumers from online exploitation through personalized advertising is questionable. Apart from the limited effectiveness of mandated disclosure,[476] it is doubtful whether information regarding the parameters and how to change them will foster a deeper understanding of targeted advertising and the corresponding impact. In light of Article 26(1)(c) DSA, it can be expected that platforms will comply with the requirements by merely indicating based on what characteristics in the database the consumers have been targeted instead of explaining why certain characteristics have been chosen.[477] Then, the mechanism behind targeted advertising remains unclear, particularly concerning the aspects that are relevant to protecting consumers' vulnerabilities. Understanding the intention behind, and the reasons for, the targeting is fundamental for consumers to protect themselves against personalized advertising. Transparency is equally essential for enforcement authorities in order to detect strategies that are built on the exploitation of vulnerabilities.[478]

Overall, the DSA seems to be a valuable contribution to the consumer law framework. Concerning personalized advertising, it imposes further transparency

---

[475] Duivenvoorde and Goanta (2023), pp. 5–6.

[476] See Chap. 2.

[477] Duivenvoorde and Goanta (2023), p. 8.

[478] Helberger et al. (2021), p. 111.

obligations that can enhance consumer protection and provide valuable enforcement tools. However, serious concerns remain as to the extent to which the DSA can offer an effective mechanism to tackle personalized advertising.

On the one hand, the DSA provides harmonized rules for a safe, predictable, and trustworthy online environment (Recital 3). However, it remains to be seen how new disclosure duties for platforms will improve consumers' position in online markets, especially considering the long-standing key role mandated disclosure played in consumer protection, which was found to be severely limited in its effectiveness.[479] Time will show how these duties will be interpreted and complemented in relation to the existing consumer *acquis*.

On the other hand, considering the consumer harms identified in this chapter, it is implausible that the DSA will effectively hamper exploitative personalized advertising practices. Although the DSA does provide protection for profiling based on sensitive personal data, its scope of application is limited, especially taking the versatility of personalized advertising into account.

In summary, reliance on further disclosure duties and limited targeting bans will most likely not fully empower consumers in practice.[480] Although the DSA is a valuable new regulatory tool that will partly address the impact of online advertising, it is unlikely to provide a cure-all for the adverse effects associated with personalized advertising.

The second relevant digital regulation is the *Digital Markets Act* (DMA).[481] The DMA specifically targets gatekeepers of core platform services, which include advertising services,[482] for the sake of improving fairness and contestability in the digital sector.[483] The DMA is a comprehensive legislation with various obligations for gatekeepers. A full review of the regulation falls outside the scope of this study, but the provisions pertinent to personalized advertising, or personalized marketing in general, will be discussed.

The first provision of the DMA that aims to benefit end-users (i.e., consumers) is Article 5(2), in which gatekeepers are prohibited to:

(a) process, for the purpose of providing online advertising services, personal data of end users using services of third parties that make use of core platform services of the gatekeeper;
(b) combine personal data from the relevant core platform service with personal data from any further core platform services or from any other services provided by the gatekeeper or with personal data from third-party services;

---

479 Ben-Shahar and Schneider (2014).

480 Duivenvoorde and Goanta (2023), p. 13.

481 Regulation (EU) 2022/1925 of the European Parliament and of the Council of 14 September 2022 on contestable and fair markets in the digital sector and amending Directives (EU) 2019/1937 and (EU) 2020/1828 (Digital Markets Act). https://eur-lex.europa.eu/eli/reg/2022/1925/oj. Referred to as "DMA".

482 Article 2(2)(j) DMA.

483 Article 1(1) DMA.

(c) cross-use personal data from the relevant core platform service in other services provided separately by the gatekeeper, including other core platform services, and vice versa; and
(d) sign in end users to other services of the gatekeeper in order to combine personal data,

unless the end user has been presented with the specific choice and has given consent within the meaning of Article 4, point (11), and Article 7 of Regulation (EU) 2016/679.

Essentially, the provision aims to tackle the practice of combining personal data.[484] In this way, the DMA aims to provide consumers with a "real choice" and places "an indirect limit on consumer exploitation by extractive targeted advertising and personalised pricing."[485]

Furthermore, Recitals 36 and 37 indicate that gatekeepers should not undermine the contestability of core platform services and that they are obliged to offer less personalized but equivalent service alternatives, enabling consumers to freely decide to opt in or out. This means that the use of the service or its corresponding functionalities cannot be conditional upon end users' consent, and not giving consent should be as easy as giving consent. The latter should be achieved by requiring gatekeepers to "proactively present a user-friendly solution to the end user to provide, modify or withdraw consent in an explicit, clear and straightforward manner."[486] In this way, the DMA makes a significant step forward in tackling the take-it-or-leave-it feeling consumers experience when faced with consent decisions.

Moreover, in Recital 45, the opacity of online advertising nowadays is explicitly acknowledged, which justifies the call for more transparency obligations. In Articles 5(9) and (10), gatekeepers are obliged to provide advertisers and publishers, upon their request and free of charge, with information regarding the price and fees paid, remuneration received, and the metrics on which each of the prices, fees, and remunerations are calculated. Similarly, Article 6(8) DMA requires gatekeepers to provide advertisers and publishers, as well as third parties authorized by them, upon their request and free of charge, with access to the performance measuring tools that are used by the gatekeeper and the information that is essential for them to conduct their independent verification of the ad inventory. Although there are several more obligations, it can be deduced from these provisions that the DMA aims to shed light on the advertising mechanism governed by gatekeepers, which is characterized by its non-transparency.

Article 15 DMA imposes the obligation on a gatekeeper to submit an audit to the EC concerning any techniques used for consumer profiling, which must be updated at least once a year. The Commission will transmit that audited description to the European Data Protection Board. This is an important provision to achieve more transparency regarding profiling practices, which can eventually aid enforcement.[487]

---

[484] Petit (2021).

[485] Petit (2021), p. 536.

[486] Recital 37.

[487] In correspondence with recital 72 DMA.

The last piece of relevant regulation is the *Artificial Intelligence Act* (AI Act).[488] The AI Act lays down a legal framework for the development, placing on the market, putting into service, and use of AI systems in accordance with the EU's values.[489] The AI Act needs to be addressed since AI is the main driver behind personalized advertising. Due to the scope of the AI Act, it is not feasible to provide a comprehensive overview of the entire regulation. Only the aspects that pertain to personalized advertising, or personalized marketing on a more general level, will be reviewed.

Recital 29 provides the first relevant consideration for personalized advertising by stating:

> AI-enabled manipulative techniques can be used to persuade persons to engage in unwanted behaviours, or to deceive them by nudging them into decisions in a way that subverts and impairs their autonomy, decision-making and free choices. The placing on the market, the putting into service or the use of certain AI systems with the objective to or the effect of materially distorting human behaviour, whereby significant harms, in particular having sufficiently important adverse impacts on physical, psychological health or financial interests are likely to occur, are particularly dangerous and should therefore be prohibited.

This text reminisces of the UCPD provisions on unfair commercial practices, a relation which is confirmed later on in the recital:

> The prohibitions for such AI practices are complementary to the provisions contained in Directive 2005/29/EC of the European Parliament and of the Council (17), in particular unfair commercial practices leading to economic or financial harms to consumers are prohibited under all circumstances, irrespective of whether they are put in place through AI systems or otherwise.

The complementarity between the AI Act and the UCPD becomes more apparent when examining Article 5 of the AI Act, which discusses prohibited AI practices. Article 5(1)(a) and (b) are particularly relevant.

Article 5(1)(a) explicitly prohibits:

> the placing on the market, the putting into service or the use of an AI system that deploys subliminal techniques beyond a person's consciousness or purposefully manipulative or deceptive techniques, with the objective, or the effect of materially distorting the behaviour of a person or a group of persons by appreciably impairing their ability to make an informed decision, thereby causing them to take a decision that they would not have otherwise taken in a manner that causes or is reasonably likely to cause that person, another person or group of persons significant harm;

---

[488] Regulation (EU) 2024/1689 of the European Parliament and of the Council of 13 June 2024 laying down harmonised rules on artificial intelligence and amending Regulations (EC) No 300/2008, (EU) No 167/2013, (EU) No 168/2013, (EU) 2018/858, (EU) 2018/1139 and (EU) 2019/2144 and Directives 2014/90/EU, (EU) 2016/797 and (EU) 2020/1828 (Artificial Intelligence Act). https://eur-lex.europa.eu/legal-content/EN/TXT/?uri=CELEX:32024R1689. Referred to as "AI Act".

[489] Recital 1.

This provision strongly resembles the unfairness test of Article 5(2)(b) UCPD.[490] Article 5(1)(b) of the AI Act, which addresses the targeting of vulnerabilities, as defined by age, disability, or a specific social or economic situation, corresponds to Article 5(3) UCPD. Goanta (2024) compared the two provisions and concluded that the Articles could be regarded as *regulatory siblings*, a concept used to define similar or identical rules across regulatory instruments.[491]

Therefore, Article 5 of the AI Act seems to be most relevant in the context of personalized advertising. It could be argued that the provision prohibits AI systems that facilitate the use of manipulative dark patterns and advertisements that induce consumers to make transactional decisions they would not have otherwise made. In this sense, the AI Act provides the tools to specifically tackle the AI component of personalization, which could press for more effective enforcement against manipulative marketing practices. This offers another layer of protection for consumers. However, it remains to be seen how Article 5 will be interpreted in the context of Recital 29, which at the end states "common and legitimate commercial practices, for example in the field of advertising, that comply with the applicable law should not, in themselves, be regarded as constituting harmful manipulative AI-enabled practices."

Moreover, following Article 6 in combination with Annex III of the AI Act, AI systems employed for marketing are likely not classifiable as high-risk.[492] This means that the more robust protection that the AI Act offers against high-risk AI systems will not apply, and only limited transparency obligations will be imposed on, for example, AI systems that are intended to interact directly with natural persons.[493]

Veale and Zuiderveen Borgesius (2021) argue that although there are differences in scope and terminology, in the context of what the AI Act can do to address manipulative practices, it seems to offer essentially the same protection as the UCPD and is of little added value for the regulatory framework.[494]

In addition, Goanta (2024) highlights the considerable overlap between the AI Act and the UCPD, the interaction with existing data protection and digital service legislation, and the lack of guidance on how to interpret the interplay and complementarity between the different regulations. Accordingly, Goanta (2024) foresees that it will take "strenuous and long-lasting interpretation cycles to delineate this overlap even if courts take terminological similarities as a starting point."[495] Further guidelines by the EC and case law will be strongly needed to determine to what extent the AI Act can contribute to regulating manipulative algorithmic marketing.[496]

[490] See Sect. 3.6.2.2.

[491] Goanta (2024).

[492] Li (2022), p. 16.

[493] Article 50 AI Act.

[494] Veale and Zuiderveen Borgesius (2021).

[495] Goanta (2024), p. 87.

[496] Goanta (2024), p. 88.

Of note is that Article 5(1)(c) of the AI Act can be a valuable provision to address algorithmic discrimination and tackle the problem of social sorting.[497] Article 5(1)(c) prohibits:

> the placing on the market, the putting into service or the use of AI systems for the evaluation or classification of natural persons or groups of persons over a certain period of time based on their social behaviour or known, inferred or predicted personal or personality characteristics, with the social score leading to either or both of the following:
>
> (i) detrimental or unfavourable treatment of certain natural persons or groups of persons in social contexts that are unrelated to the contexts in which the data was originally generated or collected;
> (ii) detrimental or unfavourable treatment of certain natural persons or groups of persons that is unjustified or disproportionate to their social behaviour or its gravity;

Accordingly, this provision could further strengthen the enforcement against threats of discrimination and social scoring in personalized advertising or marketing in general, which is a step in the right direction.

3.6.2.4 Anti-discrimination Law

Anti-discrimination laws, *inter alia,* the *Charter of Fundamental Rights of the European Union* (CFR),[498] *European Convention on Human Rights* (ECHR),[499] *Universal Declaration of Human Rights* (UDHR),[500] *International Convention on the Elimination of All Forms of Racial Discrimination* (ICERD),[501] and TFEU, complement the legal framework by ensuring that discrimination of individuals, based on, for example, sex, race, ethnicity, religion, and political belief, is prohibited.

However, it has been found that algorithms have the capacity to circumvent the prohibited categories of discrimination and still lead to discriminatory outcomes.[502] In this case, there is no direct discrimination, but indirect discrimination through factors that are not explicitly prohibited by law, for instance, credit scores or place of residence, that leads to the same outcomes as with direct discrimination.[503] This means that there is a pivotal role to play for the programmers of the algorithms, although it is debatable to what extent the machine learning aspect will undermine the programming efforts. If companies can demonstrate that the personalized ads

---

[497] See Sect. 3.5.3.3.

[498] Charter of Fundamental Rights of the European Union (OJ C 83:389-403). European Union. https://eur-lex.europa.eu/LexUriServ/LexUriServ.do?uri=OJ:C:2010:083:0389:0403:en:PDF.

[499] Convention for the Protection of Human Rights and Fundamental Freedoms (Council of Europe Treaty Series 005). Council of Europe. https://rm.coe.int/1680063765.

[500] Universal Declaration of Human Rights. https://digitallibrary.un.org/record/666853?v=pdf.

[501] International Convention on the Elimination of All Forms of Racial Discrimination. Treaty Series, 660, 195. https://treaties.un.org/doc/Publication/UNTS/Volume%20660/volume-660-I-9464-English.pdf.

[502] Bock (2016); Hacker (2018).

[503] Schreurs et al. (2008), p. 261.

are not based on discriminatory categories that have been explicitly prohibited by law, there is a limited role for anti-discrimination laws to play.[504]

Anti-discrimination laws could be complemented by the *principles of fairness* and *transparency* in the GDPR (Article 5).[505] To specify, it could be the case that some commercial activities are unfair but do not pass the threshold of discrimination. Then, the principles of fairness and transparency could be invoked to argue that there is a lack of sufficient information about a firm's tracking activities, which violates the duty of transparent data processing or contravenes consumers' reasonable expectations.[506]

Alternatively, the principle of fairness could be linked to the principle of legality.[507] However, this requires a broad interpretation of Article 5(1) GDPR, which might need to be extended to comply with other branches of law (i.e., lawfulness, meaning compliance with the EU legal framework as a whole).[508] The major problem with coupling data protection law with anti-discrimination law to determine what is considered unfair is that further case law is needed that supports such interpretations of the law.[509]

3.6.3 Regulation of Dark Patterns

Dark patterns play a pivotal role in the presentation of the ads displayed to the consumer. The online setting and the design of the ad have a significant influence on the perception of the consumer. Dark patterns have the potential to exploit the cognitive biases and heuristics of consumers, opening the way for exploitation. In essence, dark patterns can make use of behavioral biases and heuristics to incite consumers to make certain decisions that they would not have taken in the absence of the modified choice architecture.[510] In the current EU legal framework, dark patterns are regulated by a patchwork of directives. Additionally, the EDPB guidelines[511] address dark patterns but they are not binding and remain an instrument of soft law.

Although personalized advertising and dark patterns are inextricably linked, it is argued that the regulation of dark patterns merits a separate analysis. There are

[504] Schreurs et al. (2008), p. 264.

[505] Zuiderveen Borgesius (2020).

[506] Helberger et al. (2021), pp. 133–134.

[507] Helberger et al. (2021), pp. 133–134.

[508] Helberger et al. (2021), p. 135.

[509] Helberger et al. (2021), p. 135 call for *sectional coherence* and refer to the Finnish national supervision authority, which made the link between data protection and anti-discrimination law and found that the method with which a firm was establishing credit scores discriminated against individuals with a very low or high age (i.e., automatic rejection). See Lynskey (2020), p. 36 for further details.

[510] Susser et al. (2019), pp. 38–39.

[511] European Data Protection Board (EDPB) (2022).

certain peculiarities of dark patterns that trigger specific provisions of the existing legal framework, which depart from the analysis in Sect. 3.6.2, and could eventually lead to more adequate consumer protection in comparison with personalized advertising.[512]

The first legal instrument to address dark patterns is also advocated by the EDPB guidelines, namely the GDPR. In the context of dark patterns, it could be argued that dark patterns infringe both the principles of fairness and transparency (Article 5(1)(a) GDPR and 12(1) GDPR) through their information (i.e., content-based dark patterns) or interface design (i.e., interface-based dark patterns). Consumers are placed in a position where they do not, or with increasing difficulty, understand how their personal data is processed, and are constrained to exercise control.[513]

A practical example of enforcement based on the infringement of transparency requirements is the case brought forward by the *Commission Nationale de l'Informatique et des Libertés* (CNIL) against Google.[514] CNIL issued a fine of 50 million euros against Google for failing to meet the objectives of accessibility, clarity, and intelligibility laid down in Article 12 GDPR. Google did not provide certain information made mandatory by Article 13 GDPR.[515] This case is particularly relevant to dark patterns because Google's user interface failed to comply with the *easily accessible* requirement by excessively spreading relevant information across several documents, thus forcing users to increase the number of clicks necessary.[516] The forced multiplication of actions, coupled with a choice of non-explicit titles, failed to satisfy the requirements of transparency and accessibility of information.[517] *Per analogiam*, this would mean that the dark patterns based on obstruction, sneaking, interface interference, and forced action (Sect. 3.4.1) would also fail to meet this criterion.

Furthermore, dark patterns that incite consumers to provide more data than necessary by nagging[518] them to consent to a new purpose of processing (i.e., continuous prompting) go against the *principle of purpose limitation* (Article 5(1)(b) GDPR). Similarly, dark patterns that push consumers into sharing more personal data than what is strictly necessary infringe the *principle of data minimization* (Article 5(1)(c) GDPR). Moreover, the inherent nature of dark patterns directly violates the principles of data protection *by design and default* (Article 25 GDPR). Rather than designing user interfaces in a manner that maximizes privacy protection, dark patterns maximize data collection to the benefit of the service provider. Lastly, in accordance with Articles 4(11) and 7 GDPR, consent should be given

[512] It must be noted that the regulation of dark patterns is a topic of on its own. In this section, the regulation of dark patterns that is relevant to personalized advertising will be discussed. For a full discussion on the regulation of dark patterns, see, for instance, Brenncke (2024).

[513] European Commission (2022), p. 76.

[514] Commission Nationale de l'Informatique et des Libertés (CNIL) (2019).

[515] Commission Nationale de l'Informatique et des Libertés (CNIL) (2019), para 88.

[516] Commission Nationale de l'Informatique et des Libertés (CNIL) (2019), paras 96–97.

[517] Commission Nationale de l'Informatique et des Libertés (CNIL) (2019), paras 102–103.

[518] See, for instance, Hung (2021).

freely, specifically, informed, and unambiguously. Dark patterns that manipulate consumers into giving consent fail the requirements of valid consent in the GDPR.[519]

The degree to which the principles of the GDPR are infringed depends on the specific type of dark pattern and the corresponding purpose. Therefore, the assessment needs to take place on a case-by-case basis and with the consideration of all relevant circumstances. Hence, specific dark patterns could be tackled under the GDPR; however, they can only be tackled if they violate data protection standards. Manipulative dark patterns that violate consumer rights on grounds other than data protection standards remain unchallenged. In addition, only using the GDPR will put the protection of consumers against dark patterns entirely in the hands of data protection authorities, and, to date, such vigorous enforcement that has effectively restricted the use of dark patterns in online markets has failed to materialize. For these reasons, the GDPR needs to be complemented by other legal instruments to tackle dark patterns effectively.[520]

The second instrument is the UCPD. Dark patterns are not legally defined under the UCPD. Still, in the Guidance on the UCPD,[521] it is stated that the UCPD can be used to challenge the fairness of dark patterns, in addition to other instruments in the EU legal framework. Depending on the dark pattern that is applied, if it materially distorts (or is likely to distort) the economic behavior of an average or vulnerable consumer, the provisions of the UCPD can be used. At the same time, it is emphasized that intent is not required but the requirements of professional diligence entail the obligation of the traders to take appropriate measures to ensure that the interface design does not distort consumers' transactional decisions.[522] Dark patterns have the capacity to deceive consumers by their design. In this sense, Articles 6 and 7 regarding misleading commercial practices could apply.

It can also be argued that dark patterns developed through data-driven techniques constitute aggressive commercial practices (Articles 8 and 9). Especially when pressure, for example by triggering emotions through confirmshaming, is applied, it can be asserted that undue influence impairs consumers' decision-making.[523] Dark patterns are designed to exploit consumer biases and vulnerabilities optimally. Arguably, the use of data analytics to see what circumstances can be optimized (i.e., user interface design) to induce consumers into taking certain actions that are most beneficial to the seller falls under the sphere of this provision.[524]

Some of the dark patterns that are being utilized can be coupled with blacklisted practices of Annex 1 of the UCPD. Annex 1 includes all commercial practices that are, in all circumstances, considered unfair. For example, practices 5 and 6 (invitation to purchase a product while intending to promote another product) refer

[519] European Commission (2022), pp. 77–78.

[520] European Data Protection Board (EDPB) (2022), p. 7.

[521] European Commission (2021), section 4.2.7.

[522] European Commission (2021), section 4.2.7.

[523] European Commission (2021), section 4.2.7.

[524] BEUC (2022), p. 8.

explicitly to the bait-and-switch dark pattern. Practice 7 refers to the false indication of limited availability or time to elicit an immediate decision and deprive consumers of sufficient opportunity or time to make an informed choice. This can be seen in countdown timers or announcements that several people are currently looking at the same scarce product or service. Other dark patterns that can be coupled are nagging with practice 26 (sending persistent and unwanted messages), disguised ads with practice 11 (using editorial content without making the promotional intent clear to the consumer), forced registration with practice 24 (the consumer cannot leave until the contract is accepted), sneak into basket with practice 29 (inertia selling), and urgency with practice 18 (passing on materially inaccurate information on market conditions).

It is then the task of enforcement to demonstrate the links between prohibited practices and dark patterns. It must be noted, however, that the list is severely limited and that many dark patterns do not fall under one of the listed practices. Actions have been taken to extend the list with new practices. For instance, the *Omnibus Directive* has added point 11a, which prohibits paid ranking without disclosure; point 23a, reselling with automated means; and point 23b, using reviews that have not been checked or the submission/commissioning of false reviews or endorsements. However, only through Directive amendments is it possible to add new practices; Member States cannot add additional practices independently.[525]

Equivalent to the application of the UCPD to personalized advertising, the average and vulnerable consumer benchmarks pose an obstacle to addressing dark patterns. The assumed rationality of average consumers implies that they are not behaviorally biased in their decision-making.[526] For this reason, it is argued that the rational consumer is not susceptible to the exploitation of their cognitive biases, thereby limiting the UCPD's utility.[527] It is an ongoing debate about the extent to which the average consumer benchmark can incorporate the findings from behavioral science in the consumer law framework.[528] As a consequence, the vigor of the UCPD as an instrument to tackle dark patterns is limited.

Overall, the UCPD proves to be a broad and flexible instrument for addressing dark patterns. Various manipulative dark patterns can be covered through broad interpretations of Articles 5–9 of the UCPD and case-by-case assessments. Nonetheless, further amendments or elaborations are needed to tackle newer and more subtle forms of dark patterns and personalization practices.[529]

The next instrument is the CRD. It could be argued that dark patterns nullify the CRD's objective of safeguarding consumers' right to information and right to withdraw. It is then up to the courts and authorities to demonstrate that dark patterns

[525] European Commission (2022), p. 71.

[526] Incardona and Poncibò (2007); Mak (2016); Riefa and Gamper (2020).

[527] Brenncke (2024), p. 47.

[528] Cohen (2019); Galli (2022); Duivenvoorde (2023).

[529] European Commission (2022), p. 73.

breach the CRD's objectives.[530] This could be done by linking some of the provisions of the CRD with specific dark patterns. To specify, the CRD provides additional safeguards to protect consumers from obligations for which the traders have obtained consent by using default options (the consumer must actively reject to avoid them), such as additional payments (Article 22) or inertia selling (Article 27). With respect to the former, the dark patterns of hidden costs or pre-selection are applicable and concerning the latter (the case in which consent is obtained because a consumer has not responded to an unsolicited supply of goods or services), the sneak into basket dark pattern comes to mind. In accordance with Article 7 UCPD, in particular 7(5), a breach of duty to inform consumers in compliance with the requirements laid down by Articles 5–8 of the CRD amounts to an unfair commercial practice, which opens the way for enforcement actions.[531] Nevertheless, this also implies that the same challenges encountered in analyzing the UCPD as a legal instrument will apply to the CRD.

The *Directive on Financial Services Contracts Concluded at a Distance*[532] provides additional protection regarding online interfaces and inserted Article 16e into the CRD. This new provision prevents traders from using dark patterns in their online interfaces by explicitly protecting consumers' autonomy and ability to make a free and informed choice, devoid of deception and manipulation. In this sense, it offers additional protection to consumers online, yet it only applies when consumers conclude financial services contracts at a distance.

Another possibility is using the UCTD to nullify consumers' consent to standard forms that creates a significant imbalance in the parties' rights and obligations and/or when consent is obtained through a manipulative exchange, which the use of dark patterns has facilitated.[533] However, it is precisely the manipulative aspect that is particularly difficult to ascertain. The most problematic subset of dark patterns, but also the most effective ones,[534] is the one that could fall under the umbrella of *subtle* or *mild dark patterns*. These dark patterns are designed to pass through the cracks of the current legal framework. They are regarded as non-deceptive; however, they actually warrant legal intervention due to their negative impact on consumers' welfare.[535] The effectiveness of the aforementioned instruments in protecting consumers from dark patterns strongly depends on pro-consumer and creative interpretations of the Directives, for which there is currently scarce evidence in EU case law.

530 European Commission (2022), pp. 71, 74.

531 European Commission (2022), pp. 71, 74.

532 Directive (EU) 2023/2673 of the European Parliament and of the Council of 22 November 2023 Amending Directive 2011/83/EU as Regards Financial Services Contracts Concluded at a Distance and Repealing Directive 2002/65/EC. https://eur-lex.europa.eu/legal-content/EN/ALL/?uri=CELEX%3A32023L2673.

533 Stigler Center (2019), p. 253.

534 Luguri and Strahilevitz (2021).

535 Stigler Center (2019), p. 249.

The DMA and *Data Act*[536] provide valuable tools to address dark patterns. On the one hand, the DMA introduced the *anti-circumvention rule* (Article 13), which could be regarded as a general ban on dark patterns.[537] Article 13(4) DMA states that:

> The gatekeeper shall not engage in any behaviour that undermines effective compliance with the obligations of Articles 5, 6 and 7 regardless of whether that behaviour is of a contractual, commercial or technical nature, or of any other nature, or consists in the use of behavioural techniques or interface design.

Since dark patterns are basically technical tools that use design alterations to circumvent the obligations of gatekeepers or make the exercise of rights or choices unduly difficult, the practice of using dark patterns could be seen as being non-compliant with the DMA. This corresponds to Recital 37, which states that: "Gatekeepers should not design, organise or operate their online interfaces in a way that deceives, manipulates or otherwise materially distorts or impairs the ability of end users to freely give consent."

Consequently, the DMA could complement the UCPD, whereby UCPD provisions are applied concurrently or additionally by covering the types of platforms or practices not regulated by the DMA.[538]

The Data Act provides a novel approach to tackling dark patterns. The Data Act has been adopted with the goal of "ensuring fairness in the allocation of value from data among actors in the data economy and fostering fair access to and use of data in order to contribute to establishing a genuine internal market for data".[539] The Data Act is consistent with the GDPR and the ePrivacy Directive and could be seen as a complementary tool. Of particular relevance is Recital 38, which relates to the data minimization principle of the GDPR and, in essence, states that third parties or data holders should not rely on dark patterns in designing their digital interfaces.

In addition, Article 4(4) of the Data Act phrases the prohibition of dark patterns as follows:

> Data holders shall not make the exercise of choices or rights under this Article by the user unduly difficult, including by offering choices to the user in a non-neutral manner or by subverting or impairing the autonomy, decision-making or choices of the user via the structure, design, function or manner of operation of a user digital interface or a part thereof.

With the explicit mentioning of dark patterns in Recital 38, the Data Act makes a major step forward in protecting consumers with this prohibition.[540] It aims to complement the UCPD, CRD, and the UCTD to promote "the interests of consumers and ensure a high level of consumer protection, and to protect their health, safety

---

[536] Regulation (EU) 2023/2854 of the European Parliament and of the Council of 13 December 2023 on harmonised rules on fair access to and use of data and amending Regulation (EU) 2017/2394 and Directive (EU) 2020/1828 (Data Act). https://eur-lex.europa.eu/eli/reg/2023/2854.

[537] European Commission (2022), p. 82.

[538] European Commission (2022), p. 83.

[539] Recital 119 Data Act.

[540] The prohibition also applies to third-parties pursuant to Article 6.

and economic interests".[541] The Data Act appears to be promising in terms of protecting consumers against dark patterns. However, since the Data Act was recently adopted on December 13, 2023, and will apply from September 12, 2025, it remains to be seen how effective it will be in practice as an instrument to challenge dark patterns.

Finally, the DSA also offers a direct prohibition of dark patterns. Article 25(1) DSA states:

> Providers of online platforms shall not design, organise or operate their online interfaces in a way that deceives or manipulates the recipients of their service or in a way that otherwise materially distorts or impairs the ability of the recipients of their service to make free and informed decisions.

This offers consumers more protection when navigating online platforms such as social media, content-sharing websites, and online marketplaces. Although this provision seems to mark a significant step in the direction of protecting consumers against dark patterns, it must be noted that Article 25(2) clearly states that the prohibition does not apply to practices covered by the UCPD and GDPR. Thus, it remains to be seen how the prohibitions will materialize in practice and to what extent dark patterns will be sufficiently addressed to protect consumers. Besides, the scope of this prohibition is limited to providers of online platforms, which means that a substantial part of the market is not covered.

Nevertheless, it can be concluded that the new regulatory developments, particularly the digital regulations (the DMA, Data Act, and DSA), seem to provide promising tools to combat dark patterns in online interfaces. In this sense, the regulations go further in tackling dark patterns compared to personalized advertising, offering consumers better protection and reducing the need for more substantive regulation.

3.6.4 Current State of Affairs

The analysis of the legal framework raises the question: To what extent is personalized advertising addressed by the current legal framework?[542]

The market has responded to personalized advertising with technological tools that aid consumers in protecting their privacy, such as browser software, proxy servers, and cookie disablers. In addition, online review mechanisms have strengthened the role of seller reputation, and through self-regulatory actions, the advertising industry is trying to encourage law-abiding, compliant behavior by advertisers. Nonetheless, a lack of awareness of these tools reduces their effectiveness, particularly among vulnerable consumers. Besides, the advertising industry has found ingenious technologies to circumvent privacy-protecting tools.

---

[541] Article 1(9) Data Act.

[542] See Sect. 3.5.4 for the overall assessment of personalized advertising, which justified the exploration of the regulatory road.

Moreover, too much emphasis on self-regulation could lead to regulatory capture. It should, therefore, be combined with public regulation and enforcement, which leads to co-regulation.

The current legal framework partly remedies the shortcomings of market-based solutions. However, the EU legal framework does not contain a regulation that deals explicitly with personalized advertising. Personalized advertising is covered by a patchwork of directives.

First, concerning the GDPR, it can be stated that as a result of the *Meta v Bundeskartellamt* case, it will become particularly challenging for online companies to justify their data collection and processing for the purpose of personalized advertising based on the necessity for the performance of a contract or legitimate interest (in correspondence with the legal bases of Article 6). The role of consent is, therefore, expected to become increasingly important. However, the extent to which this will benefit consumers is questionable. In short, consent notices cannot remedy the problems associated with personalized advertising due to the signing-without-reading problem, which negatively impacts their effectiveness in protecting consumers.

Consumer law provides additional safeguards through two principal instruments: the UCPD and the UCTD. On the one hand, the UCPD could potentially cover personalized advertising; however, this would require a broad interpretation of the provisions, which needs to materialize in CJEU case law. Further litigation or legislative reforms that advocate consumer-friendly interpretations would be needed. On the other hand, under the UCTD, it could be stated that standard terms that allow for the development of data exploitation strategies should be submitted to the fairness test. Nonetheless, to be effective, the CJEU would need to follow a broadened interpretation of fairness, in which other social policies or entitlements from fundamental rights that fall under the EU *acquis* would be considered. In this way, the ability of the UCTD to tackle personalized advertising would be reinforced. Nevertheless, the shortcoming of this solution is that Article 4(2) UCTD excludes the fairness assessment relating to the main subject matter of the contract and the price, provided that these terms are transparently drafted. The value of data as a counter-performance could be regarded as relating to the price dimension of the contract. Thus, it will *prima facie* be excluded from the assessment. Only excessive imbalances relating to the exchange of data could be remedied under the UCTD, which severely limits the effectiveness of the regulation.

Personalized advertising is also partly addressed by the P2B regulation, the E-Commerce Directive, the AVMS, the MCAD, and the CRD. The core of these regulations is that they impose rules on transparency; however, these rules essentially correspond to the obligations laid down in the GDPR, UCPD, and UCTD, and are, therefore, of limited added value in the context of personalized advertising.

Nonetheless, the DSA, DMA, and the AI Act appear to put forward promising regulatory tools. In short, the DSA imposes obligations on digital service intermediaries to increase transparency and elucidate the targeting mechanism behind advertising. Profiling based on sensitive personal data is also prohibited. This scope of application did not exist before in the EU legal framework, indicating an enhancement in consumer protection.

The DMA challenges the dominance of gatekeepers to promote fair and contestable markets. For consumers, the objective to tackle the combination of personal data, the emphasis on consumer choice, and the mandatory audit of consumer profiling techniques is highly beneficial. In addition, the obligation for gatekeepers to provide financial and performance-based information to advertisers and publishers upon request can tackle the opacity surrounding online advertising. The focus on transparency can put external pressure on gatekeepers to scale back on consumer profiling and go for differentiation through the provision of more consumer-friendly privacy guarantees.[543] Nonetheless, the limited scope of the DMA (i.e., gatekeepers), its focus on market competition, and the key role of consent raise doubts about the regulation's capacity in improving consumer protection against personalized advertising.

Lastly, the AI Act prohibits AI-practices that drive consumer manipulation, which can tackle part of the identified harms that are inflicted on consumers. Nevertheless, the AI Act does not appear to be offering more protection than the UCPD does. It can work as a valuable complement; however, more guidelines and case law are needed to see to what extent it leads to synergy benefits instead of cannibalization between the legal instruments.

The regulation of personalized advertising is inextricably linked to the regulation of dark patterns. Although the regulation of dark patterns resembles the regulation of personalized advertising to a large extent, there are some notable differences. To start with, dark patterns can be tackled under the GDPR if, on a case-by-case basis, it can be determined that a specific dark pattern infringes one or more principles of the GDPR. It must be emphasized that only the violation of the data protection standards could be remedied and that a significant burden would be placed on the data protection authorities to ensure vigorous enforcement that provides a sufficient degree of protection to consumers.

The UCPD could complement the GDPR. The UCPD is a broad and flexible instrument that can address dark patterns. Various manipulative dark patterns can be covered through broad interpretations of Articles 5–9 and the linking of dark patterns to the prohibited practices of Annex 1 of the UCPD. Nonetheless, further amendments or elaborations are needed to tackle newer and more subtle forms of dark patterns. The CRD can be a valuable complement to open the way for enforcement actions.

The DMA can inhibit gatekeepers' circumvention of their legal obligations and work in a complementary manner to the UCPD. The Data Act appears to adequately address dark patterns by explicitly denouncing the use of deceptive designs in Recital 38 and the prohibitions of dark patterns in Articles 4 and 6. The Data Act bodes well for the future of consumer protection; however, at the moment, it is unclear how it will eventually take form in practice.

[543] Cfr. Recital 72 DMA.

Finally, the DSA offers a promising tool to address dark patterns through Article 25, which effectively provides consumers with more protection when navigating online platforms and using online search engines.

Taking everything into consideration, it can be argued that, although improvements can be made,[544] the regulation of dark patterns is more comprehensive compared to the regulation of personalized advertising. Accordingly, only with respect to the latter is it justified, based on the legal analysis, to conclude that further complementary regulatory action is needed.[545] The existing regulations do not sufficiently remedy the potential consumer harm caused by personalized advertising. It is, therefore, expected that if no changes to the current legal framework are made, the adverse effects for consumers, which have been previously discussed in this chapter, can continue to materialize.

3.7 Conclusion

The personalization of advertising has opened the way for effective behavior modification and subsequent value extraction. In combination with dark patterns, the effectiveness of personalized ads can even be further improved. Consequently, the question needed to be answered as to what extent personalized advertising is expected to be problematic for consumers' autonomy, equity, and welfare. The law and economics analysis demonstrated the various benefits and harms that personalized advertising entails. From a purely efficiency perspective, it is unfeasible to conclude unambiguously whether personalized advertising is economically desirable or detrimental or to ascertain its precise effects on total welfare. However, from a consumer welfare hypothesis perspective, it can be stated that the practice of personalized advertising will negatively impact consumers.

To enrich the discussion and clarify the need for intervention, the economic analysis has been broadened by incorporating equity considerations, consumer perceptions, and ethical concerns. It was found that pursuant to the broadened analysis, personalized advertising is problematic. In terms of equity, the practice causes regressive effects through the exploitation of biases and the steering of preferences to extract consumer surplus to the benefit of the seller. The exploitation effects seem to be particularly troublesome for the more vulnerable groups of society, which the use of dark patterns exacerbates. From a consumer perspective, personalized advertising raises significant privacy concerns that override positive perceptions, resulting in a generally unfavorable attitude toward it. From an ethical point of view, personalized advertising carries the potential to allow for discrimination, social sorting, and the endangerment of human dignity.

---

[544] Brenncke (2024).

[545] Fourberg et al. (2021), p. 97.

The overall assessment of personalized advertising shows that although the total welfare arguments might be inconclusive, the consumer welfare, the distributive, and ethical concerns justify the exploration of legal remedies.

Based on the current state of affairs, it can be concluded that the existing legal framework is not sufficiently equipped to adequately address personalized advertising in a way that safeguards consumers' autonomy, equity, and welfare. Further regulation is needed to supplement the legal framework with provisions that shield consumers from the negative effects of personalized advertising. In Chap. 6, the regulation of personalized marketing practices will be further discussed, and several policy proposals to enhance consumer protection in the digital age will be presented.

References

Acquisti A, Taylor C, Wagman L (2016) The economics of privacy. J Econ Lit 54:442–492

Adjerid I, Acquisti A, Brandimarte L, Loewenstein G (2013) Sleights of privacy: framing, disclosures, and the limits of transparency. Symp Usable Priv Secur (SOUPS):1–17

Aghion P, Jones BF, Jones CI (2019) Artificial intelligence and economic growth. In: Agrawal A, Gans J, Goldfarb A (eds) The economics of artificial intelligence: an agenda. University of Chicago Press, Chicago, pp 237–282

Agrawal A, Gans J, Goldfarb A (2019) The economics of artificial intelligence: an agenda. University of Chicago Press, Chicago

Aguirre E, Mahr D, Grewal D, De Ruyter K, Wetzels M (2015) Unraveling the personalization paradox: the effect of information collection and trust-building strategies on online advertisement effectiveness. J Retailing 91(1):34–49

Akerlof GA (1970) The market for "lemons": quality uncertainty and the market mechanism. Q J Econ 84(3):488–500

Alter A (2017) Irresistible: the rise of addictive technology and the business of keeping us hooked. Penguin, London

Anderson C (2006) The long tail: why the future of business is selling less of more. Hachette UK, London

Ansari A, Mela CF (2003) E-customization. J Mark Res 40(2):131–145

Arkes HR, Blumer C (1985) The psychology of sunk cost. Organ Behav Hum Decis Process 35:124–140

Article 29 Data Protection Working Party (2010) Opinion 2/2010 on online behavioural advertising (Report No. 00909/10/EN WP 171). Art 29 WP. https://ec.europa.eu/justice/article-29/documentation/opinion-recommendation/files/2010/wp171_en.pdf

Article 29 Data Protection Working Party (2018) Article 29 Working Party Guidelines on consent under Regulation 2016/679 (Report No. 17/EN WP259 rev.01). Art 29 WP. https://ec.europa.eu/newsroom/article29/items/623051/en

Autoriteit Consument & Markt (ACM) (2021) Sponsored ranking: an exploration of its effects on consumer welfare. ACM. https://www.acm.nl/sites/default/files/documents/sponsored-ranking-study-acm.pdf

Aziz A, Telang R (2016) What is a digital cookie worth? SSRN. https://doi.org/10.2139/ssrn.2757325

Bagwell K (2007) The economic analysis of advertising. In: Armstrong M, Porter R (eds) Handbook of industrial organization, vol 3. North Holland, Amsterdam, pp 1701–1844

Bakos Y, Marotta-Wurgler F, Trossen DR (2014) Does anyone read the fine print? Consumer attention to standard-form contracts. J Leg Stud 43(1):1–35

Bakpayev M, Baek TH, van Esch P, Yoon S (2022) Programmatic creative: AI can think but it cannot feel. Australas Market J 30(1):90–95
Balebako R, Leon P, Shay R, Ur B, Wang Y, Cranor L (2012) Measuring the effectiveness of privacy tools for limiting behavioral advertising. Web 2.0 Secur Priv Workshop 1–10
Bar-Gill O (2018) Algorithmic price discrimination: when demand is a function of both preferences and (mis)perceptions. Univ Chic Law Rev 86(2):1–30
Beak TH, Morimoto M (2012) Stay away from me. J Advert 41(1):59–76
Beales H (2010) The value of behavioral targeting. Network Advert Initiat 1:1–24
Becher SI, Dadush S (2021) Relationship as product: transacting in the age of loneliness. Univ Illinois Law Rev 2021(5):1547–1604
Ben-Shahar O, Schneider CE (2014) More than you wanted to know: the failure of mandated disclosure. Princeton University Press, Princeton
BEUC (2022) "Dark patterns" and the EU consumer law acquis: recommendation for better enforcement and reform (Report No. BEUC-X-2022-013). BEUC. https://www.beuc.eu/sites/default/files/publications/beuc-x-2022-013_dark_patters_paper.pdf
Bharucha J (2018) Social media and young consumers behavior. Int J Supply Chain Manage 7(6):72–81
Bietti E (2019) Consent as free pass: platform power and the limits of the informational turn. Pace Law Rev 40(1):310–398
Bock C (2016) Preserve personal freedom in networked societies. Nature 537(7618):9
Boerman SC, Kruikemeier S, Zuiderveen Borgesius FJ (2017) Online behavioral advertising: a literature review and research agenda. J Advert 46(3):363–376
Bösch C, Erb B, Kargl F, Kopp H, Pfattheicher S (2016) Tales from the dark side: privacy dark strategies and privacy dark patterns. Proc Priv Enhanc Technol 2016(4):237–254
Boudet J, Gregg B, Rathje K, Stein E, Vollhardt K (2019) The future of personalization—and how to get ready for it. McKinsey & Co. https://www.mckinsey.com/capabilities/growth-marketing-and-sales/our-insights/the-future-of-personalization-and-how-to-get-ready-for-it#/
Brenncke M (2024) Regulating dark patterns. Notre Dame J Int Comp Law 14(1):39–79
Briefing European Parliament (2021) Regulating targeted and behavioural advertising in digital services. How to ensure users' informed consent. Report No. PE 696.967. Policy Department for Citizens' Rights and Constitutional Affairs. https://www.europarl.europa.eu/RegData/etudes/BRIE/2021/696967/IPOL_BRI(2021)696967_EN.pdf
Brignull H, Leiser M, Santos C, Doshi K (2023) Deceptive patterns – user interfaces designed to trick you. https://www.deceptive.design/types
Brookman J, Rouge P, Alva A, Yeung C (2017) Cross-device tracking: measurement and disclosures. Proc Priv Enhanc Tools 2017(2):113–128
Calo R (2011) The boundaries of privacy harm. Indiana Law J 86(3):1131–1162
Calo R (2014) Digital market manipulation. Geo Wash Law Rev 82(4):995–1051
Campbell C, Marks LJ (2015) Good native advertising isn't a secret. Bus Horiz 58(6):599–606
Carrascosa JM, Mikians J, Cuevas R, Erramilli V, Laoutaris N (2015) I always feel like somebody's watching me: measuring online behavioural advertising. In: Proc 11th ACM Conf Emerg Netw Exp Technol, pp 1–13
Chen N, Gallego G (2019) Welfare analysis of dynamic pricing. Manag Sci 65(1):139–151
Chen H, Chiang RH, Storey VC (2012) Business intelligence and analytics: from big data to big impact. MIS Q 36(4):1165–1188
Chesbrough H, Rosenbloom RS (2002) The role of the business model in capturing value from innovation: evidence from Xerox corporation's technology spin-off companies. Ind Corp Change 11(3):529–555
Chintalapati S, Pandey SK (2022) Artificial intelligence in marketing: a systematic literature review. Int J Market Res 64(1):38–68
Cialdini RB (2021) Influence, new and expanded: the psychology of persuasion. Harper Collins, New York

Clifford D (2017) Citizen-consumers in a personalised galaxy: emotion influenced decision-making, a true path to the dark side? In: Edwards L, Schafer B, Harbinja E (eds) Future law: emerging technology, regulation and ethics. Edinburgh University Press, Edinburgh, pp 79–130
Cockburn IM, Henderson R, Stern S (2019) The impact of artificial intelligence on innovation. In: Agrawal A, Gans J, Goldfarb A (eds) The economics of artificial intelligence: an agenda. University of Chicago Press, Chicago, pp 115–152
Cohen J (2019) Bringing down the average: the case for "less sophisticated" reasonableness standard in US and EU consumer law. Loy Consum Law Rev 32(1):1–44
Commission Nationale de l'Informatique et des Libertés (CNIL) (2019) Deliberation of the Restricted Committee SAN-2019-001 of 21 January 2019 pronouncing a financial sanction against GOOGLE LLC. CNIL, Paris. https://www.cnil.fr/sites/default/files/atoms/files/san-2019-001.pdf
Commission Nationale de l'Informatique et des Libertés (CNIL) (2020) Shaping choices in the digital world. IP Reports No. 06. CNIL, Paris. https://www.cnil.fr/sites/cnil/files/2023-06/cnil_ip_report_06_shaping_choices_in_the_digital_world.pdf
Conti G, Sobiesk E (2010) Malicious interface design: exploiting the user. Proc 19th Int Conf World Wide Web:271–280
Cranor LF (2012) Can users control online behavioral advertising effectively? IEEE Secur Priv 10(2):93–96
Custers B, Malgieri G (2022) Priceless data: why the EU fundamental right to data protection is at odds with trade in personal data. Comput Law Secur Rev 45:105683
Danish Consumer Ombudsman/Forbrugerombudsmanden (2022) Forbrugerombudsmanden Årsberetning 2021/21. Stibo Complete. https://www.forbrugerombudsmanden.dk/media/56760/forbrugerombudsmandens-aarsberetning-2020-2021.pdf
DataReportal (2022) Digital 2022: global overview report. We Are Social & Hootsuite. https://datareportal.com/reports/digital-2022-global-overview-report
Day G, Stemler A (2020) Are dark patterns anticompetitive? Ala Law Rev 72(1):1–46
De Geest G (2016) Signing without reading. In: Marciano A, Ramello GB (eds) Encyclopedia of law and economics. Springer, Cham, pp 1–8
Debatin B, Lovejoy JP, Horn AK, Hughes BN (2009) Facebook and online privacy: attitudes, behaviors, and unintended consequences. J Comput-Mediat Commun 15(1):83–108
Di Geronimo L, Braz L, Fregnan E, Palomba F, Bacchelli A (2020) UI dark patterns and where to find them: a study on mobile applications and user perception. Proc 2020 CHI Conf Human Factors Comput Syst:1–14
Dimitrieska S, Stankovska A, Efremova T (2018) Artificial intelligence and marketing. Entrepreneurship 6(2):298–304
Duivenvoorde B (2023) Redesigning the UCPD for the age of personalised marketing. J Eur Consum Mark Law 12(5):177–184
Duivenvoorde B, Goanta C (2023) The regulation of digital advertising under the DSA: a critical assessment. Comput Law Secur Rev 51:105870
Ellison G, Wolitzky A (2012) A search cost model of obfuscation. RAND J Econ 43(3):417–441
Engelbrecht A, Gerlach J, Widjaja T (2016) Understanding the anatomy of data-driven business models towards an empirical taxonomy. Proc 24th Eur Conf Inf Syst, Istanbul, Turkey:1–15
Esteves RB, Resende J (2019) Personalized pricing and advertising: who are the winners? Int J Ind Organ 63:239–282
European Commission (2010) Comparative study on different approaches to new privacy challenges, in particular in the light of technological developments (Report No. JLS/2008/C4/011–30-CE-0219363/00-28). Publications Office of the European Union. https://op.europa.eu/en/publication-detail/-/publication/9c7a02b9-ecba-405e-8d93-a1a8989f128b
European Commission (2016) Consumer market study on online market segmentation through personalised pricing/offers in the European Union (Report No. Request for specific services 2016 85 02 for the implementation of framework Contract EAHC/2013/CP/04, final report).

Publications Office of the European Union. https://op.europa.eu/en/publication-detail/-/publication/ed9ce056-c2cf-11e8-9424-01aa75ed71a1/language-en
European Commission (2021) Commission Notice: Guidance on the Interpretation and Application of Directive 2005/29/EC of the European Parliament and of the Council Concerning Unfair Business-to-consumer Commercial Practices in the Internal Market. https://eur-lex.europa.eu/legal-content/EN/TXT/?uri=CELEX%3A52021XC1229%2805%29
European Commission (2022) Behavioural study on unfair commercial practices in the digital environment: dark patterns and manipulative personalization (Final report). Publications Office of the European Union. https://op.europa.eu/en/publication-detail/-/publication/606365bc-d58b-11ec-a95f-01aa75ed71a1/language-en
European Data Protection Board (EDPB) (2020) Guidelines 05/2020 on consent under Regulation 2016/679 (Version 1.1). EDPB. https://www.edpb.europa.eu/our-work-tools/our-documents/guidelines/guidelines-052020-consent-under-regulation-2016679_en
European Data Protection Board (EDPB) (2022) Guidelines 3/2022 on Dark patterns in social media platform interfaces: how to recognise and avoid them (Version 1.0). EDPB. https://www.edpb.europa.eu/our-work-tools/documents/public-consultations/2022/guidelines-32022-dark-patterns-social-media_en
Finck M (2021) The limits of the GDPR in the personalisation context. Max Planck Inst Innov Compet Res Pap No 21-11:1–14
Fogg BJ (2019) Tiny habits: the small changes that change everything. Eamon Dolan Books, Boston
Fourberg N, Taş S, Wiewiorra L, Godlovitch I, De Streel A, Jacquemin H, Hill J, Nunu M, Bourguigon C, Jacques F, Ledger M, Lognoul M (2021) Online advertising: the impact of targeted advertising on advertisers, market access and consumer choice (Report No PE 662.913). European Parliament, Luxembourg. https://www.europarl.europa.eu/RegData/etudes/STUD/2021/662913/IPOL_STU(2021)662913_EN.pdf
Friestad M, Wright P (1994) The persuasion knowledge model: how people cope with persuasion attempts. J Consum Res 21(1):1–31
Gabaix X, Laibson D (2006) Shrouded attributes, consumer myopia, and information suppression in competitive markets. Q J Econ 121(2):505–540
Galli F (2020) AI and consumers manipulation: what is the role of EU fair marketing law? Catolica Law Rev 4(2):35–64
Galli F (2021) Online behavioural advertising and unfair manipulation between the GDPR and the UCPD. In: Ebers M, Gamito MC (eds) Algorithmic governance and governance of algorithms: legal and ethical challenges. Springer Nature, Cham, pp 109–135
Galli F (2022) Algorithmic marketing and EU law on unfair commercial practices. Springer Nature, Cham
Galli F, Lagioia F, Sartor G (2022) Consent to targeted advertising. Eur Bus Law Rev 33(4):485–512
Gil González E, De Hert P (2019) Understanding the legal provisions that allow processing and profiling of personal data: an analysis of GDPR provisions and principles. ERA Forum 2019(4):597–621
Gironda JT, Korgaonkar PK (2018) iSpy? Tailored versus invasive ads and consumers' perceptions of personalized advertising. Electron Commer Res Appl 29:64–77
Goanta C (2024) Regulatory siblings: the Unfair Commercial Practices Directive roots of the AI Act. In: Graef I, van der Sloot B (eds) The legal consistency of technology regulation in Europe. Hart Publishing, Oxford, pp 71–88
Goffman E (1963) Stigma. Penguin, London
Goldfarb A (2014) What is different about online advertising? Rev Ind Organ 44(2):115–129
Goldfarb A, Tucker C (2011) Online display advertising: targeting and obtrusiveness. Mark Sci 30(3):389–404
Gomer R, Rodrigues EM, Milic-Frayling N, Schraefel MC (2013) Network analysis of third party tracking: user exposure to tracking cookies through search. 2013 IEEE/WIC/ACM Int Joint Conf Web Intell (WI) Intell Agent Technol (IAT):549–556

Gösser N, Gürer K, Haucap J, Meyring B, Michailidou A, Schallbruch M, Thorwarth S (2021) Total consumer time: a new approach to identifying digital gatekeepers. DICE Discussion Paper No. 369:1–38
Gray CM, Kou Y, Battles B, Hoggatt J, Toombs AL (2018) The dark (patterns) side of UX design. Proc 2018 CHI Conf Hum Factors Comput Syst:1–14
Greenberg S, Boring S, Vermeulen J, Dostal J (2014) Dark patterns in proxemic interactions: a critical perspective. Proc 2014 Conf Designing Interact Syst:523–532
Gregurec I, Vranešević T, Dobrinić D (2011) The importance of database marketing in social network advertising. Int J Manag Cases 13(4):165–172
Hacker P (2018) Teaching fairness to artificial intelligence: existing and novel strategies against algorithmic discrimination under EU Law. Common Mark Law Rev 55(4):1143–1186
Hacker P (2019) Regulating the economic impact of data as counter-performance: from the illegality doctrine to the unfair contract terms directive. 5th Münster Colloquium EU Law Digit Econ:1–23
Ham CD (2017) Exploring how consumers cope with online behavioral advertising. Int J Advert 36(4):632–658
Helberger N (2012) Exposure diversity as policy goal. J Media Law 4(1):65–92
Helberger N (2016) Profiling and targeting consumers in the Internet of Things—a new challenge for consumer law. In: Schulze R, Staudenayer D (eds) Digital revolution: challenges for contract law in practice. Nomos, Baden-Baden, pp 135–164
Helberger N, Lynskey O, Micklitz HW, Rott P, Sax M, Strycharz J (2021) EU consumer protection 2.0: structural asymmetries in digital consumer markets. Joint report from EUCP2.0 Project BEUC, pp 1–207
Helberger N, Sax M, Strycharz J, Micklitz HW (2022) Choice architectures in the digital economy: towards a new understanding of digital vulnerability. J Consum Policy 45(2):175–200
Helman L (2019) Pay for (privacy) performance: holding social network executives accountable for breaches in data privacy protection. Brooklyn Law Rev 84(2):523–570
Hoofnagle CJ, Meleshinsky E (2015) Native advertising and endorsement: schema, source-based misleadingness, and omission of material facts. Technol Sci 2015121503:1–23
Hoofnagle CJ, Soltani A, Good N, Wambach DJ (2012) Behavioral advertising: the offer you can't refuse. Harv Law Policy Rev 6(2):273–296
Hordern V (2019) Lawful processing criteria. In: Ustaran E, Lovells H (eds) European data protection: law and practice. IAPP, Chapter 7
Howart B (2010) How far will behavioral targeting go? B&T Mag 60(2724):24–29
Howells G, Micklitz HW, Wilhelmsson T (2016) European fair trading law: the Unfair Commercial Practices Directive. Routledge, London
Hu N, Liu L, Zhang JJ (2008) Do online reviews affect product sales? The role of reviewer characteristics and temporal effects. Inf Technol Manag 9(3):201–214
Hung A (2021) Keeping consumers in the dark: addressing "nagging" concerns and injury. Columbia Law Rev 121(8):2483–2520
Hungarian Competition Authority (2020) Gigantic fine imposed on Booking.com by the GVH. Hungarian Competition Authority. https://www.gvh.hu/en/press_room/press_releases/press-releases-2020/gigantic-fine-imposed-on-booking.com-by-the-gvh
Hutter K, Hautz J, Dennhardt S, Füller J (2013) The impact of user interactions in social media on brand awareness and purchase intention: the case of MINI on Facebook. J Prod Brand Manag 22(5/6):342–351
IHS Markit (2017) The economic value of behavioural targeting in digital advertising. Data-Driven Advertising. https://datadrivenadvertising.eu/the-economic-value-of-behavioural-targeting-in-digital-advertising
Incardona R, Poncibò C (2007) The average consumer, the unfair commercial practices directive, and the cognitive revolution. J Consum Policy 30(1):21–38
International Chamber of Commerce (ICC) (2018) ICC advertising and marketing communications code. ICC. https://iccwbo.org/publication/icc-advertising-and-marketing-communications-code

Irion K, Luchetta G (2013) Online personal data processing and EU data protection reform. CEPS Task Force Rep CEPS Digit Forum:1–93

Irish Data Protection Commission (2023) Data Protection Commission announces conclusion of two inquiries into Meta Ireland. Data Protection Commission. https://www.dataprotection.ie/en/news-media/data-protection-commission-announces-conclusion-two-inquiries-meta-ireland

Iyer G, Soberman D, Villas-Boas JM (2005) The targeting of advertising. Mark Sci 24(3):461–476

Jiménez FR, Mendoza NA (2013) Too popular to ignore: the influence of online reviews on purchase intentions of search and experience products. J Interact Mark 27(3):226–235

Johnson JP (2013) Targeted advertising and advertising avoidance. RAND J Econ 44(1):128–144

Johnson EJ, Bellman S, Lohse GL (2002) Defaults, framing and privacy: why opting in–opting out. Mark Lett 13(1):5–15

Kahneman D (2011) Thinking, fast and slow. Macmillan, New York

Kahneman D, Tversky A (1979) Prospect theory: an analysis of decision under risk. Econometrica 47(2):363–391

Kahneman D, Tversky A (1984) Choices, values, and frames. Am Psychol 39(4):341–350

Kakatkar C, Spann M (2019) Marketing analytics using anonymized and fragmented tracking data. Int J Res Mark 36(1):117–136

Kamins M (2019) Marketing manipulation: a consumer's survival manual. World Scientific Publishing, Singapore

Kaptein M, Eckles D (2010) Selecting effective means to any end: futures and ethics of persuasion profiling. Int Conf Persuas Technol:82–93

Kaptein M, Duplinsky S, Markopoulos P (2011) Means based adaptive persuasive systems. Proc SIGCHI Conf Hum Factors Comput Syst:1–10

Kelly D, Rubin VL (2022) Dark pattern typology: how do social networking sites deter disabling of user accounts? Proc Int Conf Social Media Soc 12:1–5

Kotler P, Armstrong G (2016) Principles of marketing, 16th edn. Pearson, London

Kramer AD, Guillory JE, Hancock JT (2014) Experimental evidence of massive-scale emotional contagion through social networks. Proc Natl Acad Sci USA 111(24):8788–8790

Kumar V, Shah D, Venkatesan R (2006) Managing retailer profitability—one customer at a time! J Retail 82(4):277–294

Kumar K, Bright Keswani D, Jaglan V (2020) Privacy protection in personalized web search using obfuscation. Int J Emerg Trends Eng Res 8(4):1410–1416

Lacey C, Caudwell C (2019) Cuteness as a 'dark pattern' in home robots. Proc ACM/IEEE Int Conf Hum-Robot Interact 14:374–381

Lee H, Cho CH (2020) Digital advertising: present and future prospects. Int J Advert 39(3):332–341

Leiser MR, Caruana M (2021) Dark patterns: light to be found in Europe's consumer protection regime. J Eur Consum Mark Law 10(6):237–251

Leszczynska M, Baltag D (2024) "Can I have it non-personalised?" An empirical investigation of consumer willingness to share data for personalized services and ads. J Consum Policy 47:345–372

Levi L (2015) A Faustian pact: native advertising and the future of the press. Ariz Law Rev 57(3):647–713

Lewis C (2014) Irresistible apps: motivational design patterns for apps, games, and web-based communities. Apress, New York

Li Z (2022) Affinity-based algorithmic pricing: a dilemma for EU data protection law. Comput Law Secur Rev 46:105705

Liu-Thompkins Y (2019) A decade of online advertising research: what we learned and what we need to know. J Advert 48(1):1–13

Lombo N, Evas T (2020) Digital service act: European added value assessment. European Parliamentary Research Service (EPRS), Report No. PE 654.180. https://www.europarl.europa.eu/RegData/etudes/STUD/2020/654180/EPRS_STU(2020)654180_EN.pdf

Lu X, Zhao X, Xue L (2016) Is combining contextual and behavioral targeting strategies effective in online advertising? ACM Trans Manag Inf Syst 7(1):1–20

Luguri J, Strahilevitz LJ (2021) Shining a light on dark patterns. J Leg Anal 13(1):43–109

Luzak JA (2015) Empirical evidence in consumer law cases: what are 'up to' claims up to? Amsterdam Law Sch Res Pap:1–19

Lynskey O (2020) General report topic 2: the new EU data protection regime. In: Rijpma J (ed) The new EU data protection regime: setting global standards for the right to personal data protection. Eleven, The Hague, pp 23–78

Lyon D (2003) Surveillance as social sorting: computer codes and mobile bodies. In: Lyon D (ed) Surveillance as social sorting. Routledge, London, pp 13–30

Mak V (2016) The consumer in European regulatory private law. In: Leczykiewicz D, Weatherill S (eds) The image of the consumer in EU law: legislation, free movement and competition law. Hart Publishing, Oxford, pp 381–400

Malheiros M, Jennett C, Patel S, Brostoff S, Sasse MA (2012) Too close for comfort: a study of the effectiveness and acceptability of rich-media personalized advertising. Proc SIGCHI Conf Hum Factors Comput Syst:579–588

Manny C (2010) Online behavioral targeting: efforts to limit unfair information practices. Bus Law Rev 43(1):91–111

Martin BA, Van Durme J, Raulas M, Merisavo M (2003) Email advertising: exploratory insights from Finland. J Advert Res 43(3):293–300

Mathur A, Acar G, Friedman MJ, Lucherini E, Mayer J, Chetty M, Narayanan A (2019) Dark patterns at scale: findings from a crawl of 11K shopping websites. Proc ACM Hum-Comput Interact 3(CSCW):1–32

Mathur A, Kshirsagar M, Mayer J (2021) What makes a dark pattern… dark? Design attributes, normative considerations, and measurement methods. Proc 2021 CHI Conf Hum Factors Comput Syst:1–18

Matz SC, Kosinski M, Nave G, Stillwell DJ (2017) Psychological targeting as an effective approach to digital mass persuasion. Proc Natl Acad Sci USA 114(48):12714–12719

Matzner T, Masur PK, Ochs C, Pape TV (2016) Do-It-yourself data protection—empowerment or burden? In: Gutwirth S, Leenes R, De Hert P (eds) Data protection on the move: current developments in ICT and privacy/data protection. Springer, Dordrecht, pp 277–305

McCarthy J, Minsky ML, Rochester N, Shannon CE (2006) A proposal for the Dartmouth summer research project on artificial intelligence, August 31, 1955. AI Mag 27(4):12–14

McDonald AM, Cranor LF (2008) The cost of reading privacy policies. I/S J Law Policy 4(3):540–565

McDonald AM, Cranor LF (2012) Survey of the use of Adobe Flash local shared objects to respawn HTTP cookies. I/S J Law Policy Inf Soc 7(3):639–690

Mik E (2016) The erosion of autonomy in online consumer transactions. Law Innov Technol 8(1):1–38

Milošević M, Živić N, Andjelković I (2017) Early churn prediction with personalized targeting in mobile social games. Expert Syst Appl 83:326–332

Mitrović K, Jakšić A, Bošković D, Milić B, Spajić J (2022) An effective personalized targeting—The case of loyalty programs. Proc 10th Int Conf Mass Customization Personalization–Community Eur (MCP–CE 2022):102–106

Mittone L, Savadori L (2009) The scarcity bias. Appl Psychol 58(3):453–468

Miyazaki AD (2008) Online privacy and the disclosure of cookie use: effects on consumer trust and anticipated patronage. J Public Policy Mark 27(1):19–33

Montgomery AL, Smith MD (2009) Prospects for personalization on the Internet. J Interact Mark 23(2):130–137

Moore RS, Moore ML, Shanahan KJ, Horky A, Mack B (2015) Creepy marketing: three dimensions of perceived excessive online privacy violation. Mark Manag 25(1):42–53

Moorthy S, Zhao H (2000) Advertising spending and perceived quality. Mark Lett 11(3):221–233

Mordor Intelligence (2022) Online advertising market—growth, trends, COVID-19 impact, and forecasts (2022–2027). Mordor Intelligence. https://www.mordorintelligence.com/industry-reports/online-advertising-market

Murthi BPS, Sarkar S (2003) The role of the management sciences in research on personalization. Manage Sci 49(10):1344–1362

Nelson P (1974) Advertising as information. J Polit Econ 82(4):729–754

Nielsen ADB (2002) Harmonisation of EU marketing law: analysis of advantages and disadvantages regarding regulating of marketing law in EU. Nordic Council of Ministers, Copenhagen

Nill A, Aalberts RJ (2014) Legal and ethical challenges of online behavioral targeting in advertising. J Curr Issues Res Advert 35(2):126–146

Nilsson NJ (2009) The quest for artificial intelligence. Cambridge University Press, Cambridge

Nissenbaum H (2009) Privacy in context. Stanford University Press, Stanford

Noll J (2004) Comparing quality signals as tools of consumer protection: are warranties always better than advertisements to promote higher product quality? Int Rev Law Econ 24(2):227–239

Norwegian Consumer Council/Forbrukerrådet (2018) Deceived by design: how tech companies use dark patterns to discourage us from exercising our rights to privacy. Forbrukerrådet. https://storage02.forbrukerradet.no/media/2018/06/2018-06-27-deceived-by-design-final.pdf

OECD (2019) Online advertising: trends, benefits and risks for consumers. OECD Digit Econ Pap No. 272:1–43

OECD (2021) Roundtable on dark commercial patterns online—Summary of discussion. Org Econ Co-Oper Dev, Doc No. DSTI/CP(2020)23/FINAL. https://one.oecd.org/document/DSTI/CP(2020)23/FINAL/En/pdf

Office of Fair Trading (OFT) (2010) Online targeting of advertising and pricing: a market study. Crown, Doc No. OFT1231. https://webarchive.nationalarchives.gov.uk/ukgwa/20140402142426/http://www.oft.gov.uk/shared_oft/business_leaflets/659703/OFT1231.pdf

Ogus AI (2004) Regulation: legal form and economic theory. Bloomsbury Publishing, London

Orlando S (2011) The use of unfair contractual terms as an unfair commercial practice. Eur Rev Contract Law 7(1):25–56

Pariser E (2011) The filter bubble: what the Internet is hiding from you. Penguin UK, London

Park CW, Jun SY, MacInnis DJ (2000) Choosing what I want versus rejecting what I do not want: an application of decision framing to product option choice decisions. J Mark Res 37(2):187–202

Petit N (2021) The proposed digital markets act (DMA): a legal and policy review. J Eur Compet Law Pract 12(7):529–541

Pollach I (2005) A typology of communicative strategies in online privacy policies: ethics, power and informed consent. J Bus Ethics 62(3):221–235

Porat A (2021) Changing people's preferences by the state and the law. Theor Inq Law 22(2):215–246

Puglisi S, Rebollo-Monedero D, Forné J (2017) On web user tracking of browsing patterns for personalized advertising. Int J Parallel Emerg Distrib Syst 32(5):502–521

Rao A, Wang E (2017) Demand for "healthy" products: false claims and FTC regulation. J Mark Res 54(6):968–989

Riefa C, Gamper H (2020) Economic theory and consumer vulnerability: exploring an uneasy relationship. In: Riefa C, Saintier S (eds) Vulnerable consumers and the law. Routledge, London, pp 17–30

Roosendaal A (2012) We are all connected to Facebook… by Facebook! In: Gutwirth S, Leenes R, De Hert P, Poullet Y (eds) European data protection: in good health? Springer, Dordrecht, pp 3–19

Rossi PE, McCulloch RE, Allenby GM (1996) The value of purchase history data in target marketing. Mark Sci 15(4):321–340

Roy SK (2016) Consumer justice: a symbol of economic prosperity and social progressiveness. Hasanuddin Law Rev 1(2):170–181

Rust RT, Chung TS (2006) Marketing models of service and relationships. Mark Sci 25(6):560–580

Sahni NS, Wheeler SC, Chintagunta P (2018) Personalization in email marketing: the role of non-informative advertising content. Mark Sci 37(2):236–258

Samuel A, White GR, Thomas R, Jones P (2021) Programmatic advertising: an exegesis of consumer concerns. Comput Hum Behav 116:106657
Samuelson W, Zeckhauser R (1988) Status quo bias in decision making. J Risk Uncertain 1(1):7–59
Sartor G (2020) New aspects and challenges in consumer protection. Eur Parl Res Serv, Doc No. PE 648.790. https://www.europarl.europa.eu/RegData/etudes/STUD/2020/648790/IPOL_STU(2020)648790_EN.pdf
Sartor G, Galli F (2022) Consent to targeted advertising. Eur Bus Law Rev 33(4):485–512
Schermer BW, Custers B, Van der Hof S (2014) The crisis of consent: how stronger legal protection may lead to weaker consent in data protection. Ethics Inf Technol 16(2):171–182
Schreurs W, Hildebrandt M, Kindt E, Vanfleteren M (2008) Cogitas, ergo sum. The role of data protection law and non-discrimination law in group profiling in the private sector. In: Hildebrandt M, Gutwirth S (eds) Profiling the European citizen. Springer, Dordrecht, pp 241–270
Schulze R, Schulte-Nölke H (2003) Analysis of national fairness laws aimed at protecting consumers in relation to commercial practices. European Commission. https://lirias.kuleuven.be/bitstream/123456789/204413/1/unfair_practices_en.pdf
Schumann JH, Von Wangenheim F, Groene N (2014) Targeted online advertising: using reciprocity appeals to increase acceptance among users of free web services. J Mark 78(1):59–75
Semerádová T, Weinlich P (2019) Computer estimation of customer similarity with Facebook lookalikes: advantages and disadvantages of hyper-targeting. IEEE Access 7:153365–153377
Shah D, Murthi BPS (2021) Marketing in a data-driven digital world: implications for the role and scope of marketing. J Bus Res 125:772–779
Sherif M (1936) The psychology of social norms. Harper & Brothers Publishing, New York
Sibony AL (2014) Can EU consumer law benefit from behavioural insights? An analysis of the Unfair Practices Directive. Eur Rev Private Law 22(6):901–942
Simon HA (1971) Designing organizations for an information-rich world. In: Greenberger M (ed) Computers, communications, and the public interest. Johns Hopkins University Press, Baltimore, pp 37–72
Smit EG, Van Noort G, Voorveld HA (2014) Understanding online behavioural advertising: user knowledge, privacy concerns, and online coping behaviour in Europe. Comput Hum Behav 32:15–22
Soltani A, Canty S, Mayo Q, Thomas L, Hoofnagle CJ (2010) Flash cookies and privacy. 2010 AAAI Spring Symp Ser, pp 158–163
Statista (2021a) Digital advertising report 2021—Social media advertising. Statista. https://www.statista.com/study/36294/digital-advertising-report-social-media-advertising/
Statista (2021b) Meta's (formerly Facebook Inc.) advertising revenue worldwide from 2009 to 2021. Statista. https://www.statista.com/statistics/271258/facebooks-advertising-revenue-worldwide/
Statista (2022) Digital advertising – Worldwide. Statista. https://www.statista.com/outlook/dmo/digital-advertising/worldwide
Statista (2023) Marketing personalization worldwide – Statistics & facts. Statista. https://www.statista.com/topics/4481/personalized-marketing/
Steppe R (2017) Online price discrimination and personal data: a General Data Protection Regulation perspective. Comput Law Secur Rev 33(6):768–785
Stigler Center (2019) Stigler committee on digital platforms (Final report). Chicago Booth. https://www.chicagobooth.edu/-/media/research/stigler/pdfs/digital-platforms%2D%2D-committee-report%2D%2D-stigler-center.pdf
Strycharz J, van Noort G, Smit E, Helberger N (2019) Consumer view on personalized advertising: overview of self-reported benefits and concerns. In: Bigne E, Rosengren S (eds) Advances in advertising research. Springer, Wiesbaden, pp 53–66
Summers CA, Smith RW, Reczek RW (2016) An audience of one: behaviorally targeted ads as implied social labels. J Consum Res 43(1):156–178
Sundsøy P, Bjelland J, Iqbal AM, Pentland A, Montjoye YAD (2014) Big data-driven marketing: how machine learning outperforms marketers' gut-feeling. In: Kennedy WG, Agarwal N, Jay

Yang S (eds) Social computing, behavioral-cultural modeling, and prediction. Springer, Cham, pp 367–374
Sunstein CR (1993) Endogenous preferences, environmental law. J Leg Stud 22(2):217–254
Sunstein CR (2016) Fifty shades of manipulation. J Mark Behav 1(3–4):213–244
Sunstein CR (2019) Sludge and ordeals. Duke Law J 68(8):1843–1884
Susser D (2019) Invisible influence: artificial intelligence and the ethics of adaptive choice architectures. AAAI/ACM Conf AI Ethics Soc 2019:403–408
Susser D, Roessler B, Nissenbaum H (2019) Online manipulation: hidden influences in digital world. Georgetown Law Technol Rev 4(1):1–46
Tam KY, Ho SY (2006) Understanding the impact of web personalization on user information processing and decision outcomes. MIS Q 30(4):865–890
Taylor CR (2017) Native advertising: the black sheep of the marketing family. Int J Advert 36(2):207–209
Thaler RH (2018) Nudge, not sludge. Science 361(6401):431–431
Thaler RH, Sunstein CR (2008) Nudge: improving decisions about health, wealth, and happiness. Yale University Press, New Haven
The Guardian (2023) Meta dealt blow by EU ruling that could result in data use ‘opt-in.’ Guardian. https://www.theguardian.com/technology/2023/jan/04/meta-dealt-blow-eu-ruling-data-opt-in-facebook-instagram-ads
TRACIT & AAFA (2020) Fraudulent advertising online: emerging risks and consumer fraud. TRACIT. https://www.tracit.org/uploads/1/0/2/2/102238034/tracit_fraudulentadvertisingonline_july21_2020_final.pdf
Traung P (2012) The proposed new EU general data protection regulation. Comput Law Rev Int 13(2):33–49
Tripathi A, Bagga T, Sharma S, Vishnoi SK (2021) Big data-driven marketing enabled business performance: a conceptual framework of information, strategy, and customer lifetime value. In: 2021 11th Int Conf Cloud Comput Data Sci Eng (Confluence), pp 315–320
Trzaskowski J (2011) Behavioural economics, neuroscience, and the unfair commercial practices directive. J Consum Policy 34(3):377–392
Trzaskowski J (2016) Lawful distortion of consumers’ economic behaviour–collateral damage under the Unfair Commercial Practices Directive. Eur Bus Law Rev 27(1):25–49
Trzaskowski J (2018) Identifying the commercial nature of ‘influencer marketing’ on the Internet. Scand Stud Law 65:81–100
Trzaskowski J (2021) Your privacy is important to us! Restoring human dignity in data-driven marketing. Ex Tuto, Copenhagen
Tsai JY, Egelman S, Cranor L, Acquisti A (2011) The effect of online privacy information on purchasing behavior: an experimental study. Inf Syst Res 22(2):254–268
Tucker CE (2014) Social networks, personalized advertising, and privacy controls. J Mark Res 51(5):546–562
Turow J (2008) Niche envy: marketing discrimination in the digital age. MIT Press, Cambridge
Turow J (2011) The daily you: how the new advertising industry is defining your identity and your worth. Yale University Press, New Haven
Turow J, King J, Hoofnagle CJ, Bleakley A, Hennessy M (2009) Americans reject tailored advertising and three activities that enable it. SSRN Electron J. https://doi.org/10.2139/ssrn.1478214
Tversky A, Kahneman D (1974) Judgment under uncertainty: heuristics and biases. Science 185(4157):1124–1131
Tversky A, Kahneman D (1981) The framing of decisions and the psychology of choice. Science 211(4481):453–458
Ur B, Leon PG, Cranor LF, Shay R, Wang Y (2012) Smart, useful, scary, creepy: perceptions of online behavioral advertising. In: Proc Eighth Symp Usable Privacy Secur, pp 1–15
Utz C, Degeling M, Fahl S, Schaub F, Holz T (2019) (Un)informed consent: studying GDPR consent notices in the field. In: Proc 2019 ACM Sigsac Conf Comput Commun Secur, pp 973–990

Van den Broeck E, Poels K, Walrave M (2020) How do users evaluate personalized Facebook advertising? An analysis of consumer-and advertiser-controlled factors. Qual Mark Res 23(2):309–327
Van Noort G, Himelboim I, Martin J, Collinger T (2020) Introducing a model of automated brand-generated content in an era of computational advertising. J Advert 49(4):411–427
Van Zandt T (2004) Information overload in a network of targeted communication. RAND J Econ 35(3):542–560
Veale M, Zuiderveen Borgesius F (2021) Demystifying the Draft EU Artificial Intelligence Act—analysing the good, the bad, and the unclear elements of the proposed approach. Comput Law Rev Int 22(4):97–112
Vesanen J (2007) What is personalization? A conceptual framework. Eur J Mark 41(5/6):409–418
Voramontri D, Klieb L (2019) Impact of social media on consumer behaviour. Int J Inf Decis Sci 11(3):209–233
Wachter S, Mittelstadt B (2019) Right to reasonable inferences: re-thinking data protection law in the age of big data and AI. Columbia Bus Law Rev 2019(2):494–620
Wagner G, Eidenmüller H (2019) Down by algorithms: Siphoning rents, exploiting biases, and shaping preferences: regulating the dark side of personalized transactions. Univ Chic Law Rev 86(2):581–610
Waldman AE (2020) Cognitive biases, dark patterns, and the 'privacy paradox'. Curr Opin Psychol 31:105–109
Weber F (2014) The law and economics of self-regulation in advertising. J Eur Consum Mark Law 3(1):5–16
Weinmann M, Schneider C, Brocke JV (2016) Digital nudging. Bus Inf Syst Eng 58:433–436
Weitzner DJ (2018) Promoting economic prosperity in cyberspace. Ethics Int Aff 32(4):425–439
Westin F, Chiasson S (2019) Opt out of privacy or "go home" understanding reluctant privacy behaviours through the FoMO-centric design paradigm. Proc New Secur Paradigms Workshop 57–67
White GR, Samuel A (2019) Programmatic advertising: forewarning and avoiding hype-cycle failure. Technol Forecast Soc Change 144:157–168
White TB, Zahay DL, Thorbjørnsen H, Shavitt S (2008) Getting too personal: reactance to highly personalized email solicitations. Mark Lett 19(1):39–50
Whittington J, Hoofnagle CJ (2012) Unpacking privacy's price. North Carolina Law Rev 90(5):1327–1370
Wilhelmsson T, Willett C (2018) Unfair terms and standard form contracts. In: Howells G, Ramsay I, Wilhelmsson T, Kraft D (eds) Handbook of research on international consumer law, 2nd edn. Edward Elgar, Cheltenham, pp 139–171
Willett C (2010) Fairness and consumer decision making under the Unfair Commercial Practices Directive. J Consum Policy 33:247–273
Wilson L (2019) Data-driven marketing content: a practical guide. Emerald Publishing, Bingley
Wirtz BW, Göttel V, Daiser P (2017) Social networks: usage intensity and effects on personalized advertising. J Electron Commer Res 18(2):103–123
Wojdynski BW, Evans NJ (2016) Going native: effects of disclosure position and language on the recognition and evaluation of online native advertising. J Advert 45(2):157–168
Wojdynski BW, Golan GJ (2016) Native advertising and the future of mass communication. Am Behav Sci 60(12):1403–1407
Woodcock RA (2018) The obsolescence of advertising in the information age. Yale Law J 127(8):2270–2341
Yeung K (2019) 'Hypernudge': Big Data as a mode of regulation by design. In: Beer D (ed) The social power of algorithms. Routledge, London, pp 118–136
Youn S, Shin W (2020) Adolescents' responses to social media newsfeed advertising: the interplay of persuasion knowledge, benefit-risk assessment, and ad scepticism in explaining information disclosure. Int J Advert 39(2):213–231

Zagal JP, Björk S, Lewis C (2013) Dark patterns in the design of games. Proc Found Digit Games 2013:1–7

Zak PJ, Knack S (2001) Trust and growth. Econ J 111(470):295–321

Zardiashvili A, Sears AM (2023) Targeted advertising and consumer protection law in the EU. Vanderbilt J Transnatl Law 56(3):799–852

Zenith (2021) Digital advertising to exceed 60% of global adspend in 2022. Zenith. https://www.zenithmedia.com/digital-advertising-to-exceed-60-of-global-adspend-in-2022/

Zhang J, Wedel M (2009) The effectiveness of customized promotions in online and offline stores. J Mark Res 46(2):190–206

Zhang KZ, Zhao SJ, Cheung CM, Lee MK (2014) Examining the influence of online reviews on consumers' decision-making: a heuristic–systematic model. Decis Support Syst 67:78–89

Zhang Y, Li B, Luo X, Wang X (2019) Personalized mobile targeting with user engagement stages: combining a structural hidden markov model and field experiment. Inf Syst Res 30(3):787–804

Zuboff S (2019) The age of surveillance capitalism: the fight for a human future at the new frontier of power. Profile Books, London

Zuiderveen Borgesius FJ (2020) Strengthening legal protection against discrimination by algorithms and artificial intelligence. Int J Hum Rights 24(10):1572–1593

Zuiderveen Borgesius FJ, Poort J (2017) Online price discrimination and EU data privacy law. J Consum Policy 40(3):347–366

Chapter 4
Algorithmic Pricing: A Law and Economics Analysis

Abstract The advent of algorithmic pricing has transformed perfect price discrimination from a theoretical construct into a practical reality. This chapter analyzes algorithmic pricing through the lens of law and economics, focusing on its efficiency and equity implications. Particular attention is given to the efficiency-equity trade-off, exploring how these competing objectives influence the evaluation of algorithmic pricing practices. The discussion also assesses the extent to which current legal frameworks regulate algorithmic pricing, identifying potential gaps and challenges in addressing its impact on consumer markets.

4.1 Introduction

The *New Consumer Agenda* of the European Commission (EC) for the period 2020–2025 explicitly mentions the digital transformation as one of its five key areas of interest. More specifically, the EC aims to ensure that consumers are as protected online as offline, whereby protecting consumer rights in relation to AI is one of its specific objectives.[1] The digital age poses new challenges to consumer protection laws for which concrete action needs to be taken. Innovative data-processing techniques have enabled the development of state-of-the-art marketing strategies that are specifically focused on personalization. One of these strategies is *personalized pricing*. Collecting data about consumers and creating individualized consumer profiles make it possible to offer different people different prices for the same good

[1] Document 52020DC0696. Communication from the Commission to the European Parliament and the Council: New Consumer Agenda Strengthening Consumer Resilience for Sustainable Recovery. COM/2020/696 final. https://eur-lex.europa.eu/legal-content/EN/TXT/?uri=CELEX%3A52020DC0696.

A. J. van Heusden, *The Law and Economics of Personalization*, Economic Analysis of Law in European Legal Scholarship 20,
https://doi.org/10.1007/978-3-032-01468-9_4

or service.[2] This makes it a refined form of *price discrimination*, a well-known business practice of adapting prices based on *consumer heterogeneity*.[3]

The emergence of AI technologies has facilitated the use of AI-driven pricing techniques, which are extraordinarily effective and efficient at setting, monitoring, and correcting prices in the face of continuous market changes. Algorithms are becoming increasingly prevalent in online markets, and their precision is continuously evolving.[4] Personalized pricing that is enabled by algorithms is more popularly called *algorithmic pricing*.[5]

Consequently, consumer concerns are arising, and numerous consumer organizations are issuing reports analyzing the potential dangers of personalized prices.[6] The lack of transparency concerning the working of these AI-driven pricing techniques exacerbates consumer concerns.[7] The provision of information by firms to consumers regarding pricing mechanisms is far from being transparent.[8]

In this chapter, algorithmic pricing is analyzed from a law and economics perspective to determine its merits. To broaden the analysis, equity, fairness, and ethical considerations are taken into account.

The structure of the chapter is as follows. First, an introduction to algorithmic pricing is given to understand its workings and applications. Next, the role of marketing is highlighted, and the economic analysis of algorithmic pricing is conducted. In addition, the equity aspect of algorithmic pricing is investigated with a specific focus on fairness-based and ethical arguments. After that, the current legal framework will be reviewed. Consequently, the current state of affairs is discussed, and the corresponding conclusions are presented.

4.2 Algorithmic Pricing: An Exploration

Algorithms have been subject to numerous studies, and a multiplicity of definitions for AI technologies have been given in the existing literature.[9] This section briefly introduces the concept of algorithmic pricing and subsequently focuses on its

---

[2] European Commission (2016).

[3] Office of Fair Trading (2013a).

[4] Graef (2018), pp. 541–542.

[5] The concept of algorithmic pricing will be further discussed in Sect. 4.2.

[6] See, for example, Consumers International and Mozilla Foundation (2022). The report states that: "97% of surveyed consumers registered some level of concern about personalised pricing, with a lack of transparency and potential for unfairness identified as greatest risks." The Dutch Authority for Consumers and Markets also conducted an official study on personalized pricing, see ACM (2020).

[7] See Chap. 3.

[8] ACM (2020); Consumers International and Mozilla Foundation (2022).

[9] McCarthy et al. (2006); Nilsson (2009); Aghion et al. (2019); Cockburn et al. (2019).

applications and effects. This allows for an in-depth analysis rather than a recompilation of the existing literature on AI.

4.2.1 *Concept and Definitions*

Algorithmic pricing is receiving notable attention in the economic and legal literature, and large organizations, such as the OECD, have issued extensive reports on the subject.[10] The practice is defined as follows: "Algorithmic personalized pricing, as a specific form of discriminatory pricing, comprises any commercial practice setting prices according to consumers' personal characteristics to target as closely as possible their willingness to pay."[11] The seller's goal is to discover the maximum amount of money a consumer is willing to pay for a specific product or service. This is also called the *reservation price*, which indicates the subjective value that an individual attaches to a good.[12] The reservation price is also the benchmark with which consumer surplus is measured. Consumer surplus is "the difference between the market price for a good and the maximum price consumers would be willing to pay for that good."[13]

Through algorithmic pricing, the seller aims to ask for a price that accurately reflects consumers' reservation prices. If the market price equals the consumer's reservation price, the seller captures the entire consumer surplus. To determine the consumer's reservation price, considerable amounts of data must be collected and processed. Algorithms form the basis of this pricing technique, which explains the use of the term algorithmic pricing. Under algorithmic pricing, charging consumers different prices for the same good or service would become possible, whereby the production costs do not justify the difference. For this reason, algorithmic pricing has been deemed a form of *discriminatory pricing*.[14]

4.2.2 *Conditions*

To realize algorithmic pricing strategies, three conditions need to be fulfilled.[15] If one of the conditions does not hold, the ability to discriminate prices is severely limited. First, consumers differ in their levels of demand. If consumers have identical demands, their willingness to pay (WTP) and the quantity demanded will be the

---

[10] See, for example, OECD (2018).

[11] Chapdelaine (2020), p. 3.

[12] Parisi (2013), p. 256.

[13] Parisi (2013), p. 60.

[14] Parisi (2013), p. 229.

[15] Pigou (1920); McAfee (2008).

same, which impedes any form of price discrimination. Second, the firm has market power, meaning it can set prices above marginal costs. Price discrimination arises in accordance with the theory of monopoly and oligopoly. If the firm is a price-taker, the feasibility of charging different prices is limited since consumers would switch to competitors under perfect competition. This is in line with the *law of one price* under perfect competition. Nonetheless, the rigidity of this condition is debatable since, in practice, firms do have the ability to set prices rather than take them in the absence of market power.[16] Third, the firm can limit *arbitrage*. If consumers can resale the goods and arbitrage price differences, charging higher prices is largely restricted since the prices will converge to one price.

An extension of the arbitrage condition is related to *fairness*.[17] If consumers can discover, without incurring significant transaction costs, that they are paying more for a specific good than others, this will likely cause consumer outrage, which can be detrimental to the firm's reputation.[18] Hence, the seller needs to be active in a market or adopt a specific pricing strategy whereby it becomes too costly for consumers to directly observe the prices other consumers pay for the same product.[19] If price comparison can take place at a relatively low cost, consumers will switch to competitors, which could damage the firm's reputation and profitability. The firm should, therefore, be able to conceal the personalized prices to a certain extent. In theory, three conditions need to be fulfilled, but in practice, it seems that four requirements need to be met to make price discrimination possible.

4.2.3 Degrees of Price Discrimination

Price discrimination was first categorized by Pigou (1920).[20] There are three degrees of price discrimination. *First-degree price discrimination*, also called *perfect price discrimination*, occurs when a seller can charge each consumer a price equal to their maximum WTP, i.e., the reservation price. This can happen when a firm can observe all relevant heterogeneity among consumers related to their WTP and adapt prices accordingly.[21] This way, individual prices can be charged, and the seller can take all the consumer surplus.

Second-degree price discrimination takes place when a seller offers a menu of options with different versions (i.e., *versioning*) of a good or service, and consumers self-select which version they want to have according to their preferences.[22] The

---

[16] Motta (2004).

[17] Kahneman et al. (1986); Anderson and Simester (2010).

[18] Bar-Gill (2018).

[19] Bar-Gill (2018).

[20] Pigou (1920), part 2, chapter 14.

[21] Office of Fair Trading (2013a), p. 14.

[22] OECD (2018), p. 9.

variety of options can depend on various factors, such as the quantity demanded, product features, and quality levels.[23]

Third-degree price discrimination is also referred to as *group pricing*. The prices are set differently for different groups of consumers.[24] In contrast to first-degree pricing, the price depends on group rather than individual characteristics.[25] Third-degree price discrimination is seen as an imperfect form of price discrimination because it depends on observable group characteristics and in this case, it is practically not possible to perfectly observe the heterogeneity between individual consumers.[26]

Under the first degree of price discrimination, the seller has perfect information about the consumer, whereas under the third degree, the seller has imperfect information about the consumer. In both scenarios, the seller has some or complete ex-ante information about the consumer. Conversely, under second-degree price discrimination, the seller has no ex-ante information. By letting the consumer self-select, relevant information becomes available to the seller on an ex-post basis.[27]

The first and third degrees of price discrimination closely resemble each other since both methods depend on information about the characteristics of the consumer. Pursuant to the ex-ante information that the seller has, consumers can be charged different prices. For this reason, a modern alternative to the classification by Pigou (1920) is to call the first and third degrees of price discrimination *direct price discrimination*. The second degree falls under *indirect price discrimination* since all consumers are offered the same menu of options, regardless of their characteristics. Still, based on the consumer's choice, the seller can obtain information about the consumer and discriminate accordingly.[28]

Although the terms direct and indirect price discrimination are more commonly used in the economic literature, most consumer reports adhere to the original classification by Pigou (1920).[29] This chapter follows the classification of price discrimination in three degrees because the focus lies on the shifts between the degrees of price discrimination that algorithmic pricing causes.

---

[23] Miller (2014), p. 55.

[24] OECD (2018), p. 9.

[25] European Commission (2016), p. 34.

[26] Office of Fair Trading (2013a), p. 14.

[27] Townley et al. (2017), p. 689.

[28] McAfee (2008), pp. 468–469.

[29] OECD (2018); Office of Fair Trading (2013a); European Commission (2016); Consumers International and Mozilla Foundation (2022).

4.2.4 Price Discrimination in the Digital Age

In his description of the three types of price discrimination, Pigou (1920) states that all forms are theoretically possible but not equally important.[30] Third-degree price discrimination is most likely to be found in practice. In contrast, first-degree price discrimination is regarded as an unattainable ideal[31] or a theoretical benchmark in models of discriminatory pricing.[32] This line of thought has been followed for a considerable time in modern economic theory.[33]

The rationale behind dismissing first-degree price discrimination as a real-life possibility has been reasonable to accept in the last decades. In traditional brick-and-mortar shops, obtaining all relevant information about consumers to match their reservation price was practically impossible. There was a situation of information asymmetry between the seller and the buyer; therefore, third-degree price discrimination was a more feasible pricing strategy. By obtaining sufficient information about the common characteristics concerning the group to which the consumer belongs (e.g., gender, age, employment), an estimation of the consumer's WTP can be made.

Nevertheless, big data has caused significant shifts in discriminatory pricing. Townley et al. (2017) state: "The technological capacities of Big Data substantially enhance the ability of digital retailers to engage in much more precise, targeted, and dynamic forms of price discrimination that were not previously possible."[34]

By virtue of large-scale data extraction, firms can improve the predictability of consumer behavior.[35] Increasing amounts of data about consumers are collected, processed, and used. Not only data about the characteristics of consumers can be obtained, but also about their behavior. Accordingly, the firm can segment the population optimally for pricing purposes.[36]

The ability of firms to predict consumer behavior has been quickly improving due to the developments in ML. Algorithms are self-improving and self-updating through the continuous collection of new data. Based on incoming data regarding consumers' preferences, profiles, and choices, it becomes possible to enhance the personalization of transactions constantly.[37] A clear ramification of the use of algorithms is that the theoretical first-degree type of price discrimination is closer to becoming reality than one might think.

---

[30] Pigou (1920), p. 201.

[31] Odlyzko (2003).

[32] European Commission (2016), p. 34.

[33] See, for example, Varian (2009). This is confirmed by OECD (2018), p. 5; European Commission (2016), p. 34.

[34] Townley et al. (2017), p. 684.

[35] Zuboff (2019).

[36] Acquisti et al. (2016), p. 460.

[37] Golobardes (2022), p. 21.

As Acquisti, Taylor, and Wagman (2016) confirm: "Tracking and measurability, in addition to websites' ability to dynamically update and personalize prices for each visitor, are bringing online markets closer to the theoretical scenario of first-degree price discrimination."[38]

4.2.5 *The Role of Standard Forms*

To perform algorithmic pricing strategies, firms require vast amounts of personal data. Based on this data, consumer profiles can be made, and more accurate targeting can occur. When a firm can accurately predict consumers' WTP, the way to perfect price discrimination has been opened. Nonetheless, the collection and processing of data in the EU are regulated by the GDPR. One of the rules is that under the GDPR, firms are only permitted to gather data for profiling purposes if it is necessary for business activities, authorized by law, or based on explicit consent.[39] It is the latter part that seems to be the Achilles heel of the system. Due to the signing-without-reading problem with standardized consent notices, firms can quickly obtain the consent of consumers to collect and process personal and behavioral data.[40] In addition, companies can also obtain data from third-party data providers, such as marketing companies and data aggregators, which help them optimize their marketing strategies.[41]

Consequently, there is a discrepancy between consumers' expectations regarding the processing of their data and the actual practice. In essence, there is a lack of control on the side of consumers regarding their personal data, which is maintained, perhaps exacerbated, by using consent notices that provide firms with the necessary consent to collect and process the data. The consent provided by consumers could be a valid instrument if it would be given freely, genuinely, and in an informed manner.[42] Since this is currently not the case, consumers are providing consent during a transaction while being unaware of the consequences that processing their data will have on their future position in digital markets.[43]

---

[38] Acquisti et al. (2016), p. 466.

[39] See Sect. 3.6.2.1 for an elaborate analysis on the GDPR.

[40] Zuboff (2019).

[41] Bujlow et al. (2015); Christl et al. (2017).

[42] Gil González and De Hert (2019).

[43] Golobardes (2022), p. 41.

4.2.6 Algorithmic Pricing in Practice

Hitherto, algorithmic pricing has been discussed as a theoretical phenomenon, yet there is substantial evidence that algorithmic pricing is also taking place in practice. The first time the general public became acquainted with more sophisticated price discrimination was in 2000 when it was discovered that Amazon was charging regular returning customers a higher price for the same DVDs. By deleting the cookie history, the price would drop significantly. This caused public outrage, and Amazon reacted by apologizing and explaining that it was part of a price experiment; however, the apology was not well-received. Since then, the media, scholars, and consumers have been particularly skeptical of personalized pricing.[44] In the existing literature, there is widespread consensus that price discrimination is becoming increasingly pervasive in digital markets, and the underlying technologies rely increasingly on consumers' personal information.[45]

Nonetheless, the empirical evidence is not unequivocal when it comes to identifying the effects of price discrimination in practice. There are two principal reasons for this. First, as the Amazon case demonstrated, a real danger exists for businesses to suffer reputational damage by engaging in price discrimination techniques. Therefore, it could be less risky for companies to engage in alternative marketing strategies, such as targeted advertising, which evoke less public backlash. Second, it is highly likely that because of this potential threat of negative publicity, firms make the pricing strategies intentionally non-transparent. Through sophisticated pricing strategies, firms could reap the benefits of personalized pricing while minimizing the probability of getting exposed by the public.[46]

Finding empirical evidence for the practice is, therefore, particularly onerous. Table 4.1 presents a non-exhaustive list of studies on personalized pricing (the term is used interchangeably with algorithmic pricing). The studies were focused on the effects of algorithmic/personalized pricing from a consumer perspective. Research that analyzes the effects of algorithmic pricing on competition has been excluded from the list because it falls outside the scope of this study.[47] It must be noted, however, that in competition research, there is evidence that indicates that algorithmic pricing is taking place and that it could potentially have significant effects on competition through (tacit) collusion, reinforced dominant positions, and supracompetitive profits.[48]

Based on Table 4.1, it can be concluded that not all empirical evidence conclusively indicates that algorithmic pricing strategies consistently cause significant

[44] See for a further discussion of the Amazon case Miller (2014), p. 48.

[45] Dewan et al. (2003); Taylor (2004); Acquisti and Varian (2005); Turow et al. (2005).

[46] European Commission (2016), p. 43.

[47] See Sect. 1.5.

[48] Stucke and Ezrachi (2018); Calvano et al. (2020a and b); Musolff (2021); Sanchez-Cartas and Katsamakas (2022); Assad et al. (2024).

Table 4.1 Personalized pricing in practice

Study	Focus	Results	Overall
Hannak et al. (2014)	Personalized pricing on e-commerce websites	9 out of 16 e-commerce websites employed personalization	Significant evidence of price discrimination
Chen et al. (2016)	Algorithmic pricing on the Amazon marketplace	More than 500 sellers have been detected that employ AI-based price discrimination	Evidence of AI-based price discrimination
Mikians et al. (2012)	Price and search discrimination on the internet	Evidence of geographical price discrimination, but not of personal price discrimination	No evidence of algorithmic price discrimination based on consumer data
Mikians et al. (2013)	Price discrimination on the internet—Based on a crowdsourced dataset	10%—30% of price variations could neither be attributed to operating costs nor personal information	Inconclusive, further research is needed
Hogan (2018)	AI implementation for personalized consumer experience	40% of surveyed companies use AI for personalized pricing and advertising	Evidence for the use of AI-based price discrimination
Schleusener and Hosell (2016)	Personalized pricing in online markets	Personalized pricing in the tourism sector based on user-related features	Evidence for AI-based pricing
Newcomer (2017) and Mahdawi (2018)	Case study Uber	Uber publicly admits third-degree price discrimination, serious allegations of first-degree price discrimination	Anecdotal evidence of personalized pricing
Valentino-DeVries et al. (2012)	Varying prices based on consumer information	Real-life examples of personalized pricing in retail, financial, and educational industries	Anecdotal evidence of personalized pricing based on consumer information
Clifford (2012)	Personalized pricing in supermarkets	Higher prices for loyal customers than switching customers	Anecdotal evidence of personalized pricing

price differences. However, the overall tendency that can be identified is that companies effectively employ algorithmic pricing in practice.

In addition, research has been conducted on consumers' attitudes toward personalized pricing. It has been found that, overall, consumer awareness of personalized pricing has a significant negative impact on purchase intentions.[49] After experiencing personalized pricing, consumers also express less trust in the seller, which notably holds for consumers who lost and benefitted from the pricing strategy.[50] The EC (2016) found that 12% to 20% of consumers have had negative experiences with

[49] Pavlou et al. (2007).

[50] Garbarino and Lee (2003).

regard to personalized pricing.[51] In the US, a survey among American households found that between 64% and 91% of respondents registered an aversion to price discrimination.[52]

4.3 The Role of Marketing

Pricing is an integral part of marketing.[53] In the field of marketing, the pricing strategy constitutes one of the major critical tasks that needs to be faced.[54] A marketing plan is incomplete without an appropriate pricing strategy.[55] For this reason, the topic of pricing received and still keeps receiving (i.e., constantly growing literature) substantial attention in the area of marketing research.[56] Pricing is also deeply interconnected with other elements of the marketing mix, in particular advertising (i.e., promotion). Strategically coordinating the pricing and advertising strategy can raise profits significantly compared to a separated view of the two key factors for sales.[57] Accordingly, when discussing pricing strategies, among which algorithmic pricing, the role of marketing cannot be dismissed.

Traditionally, *pricing strategy research* (PSR) from a marketing perspective has been more consumer-oriented, whereas it has been more market-oriented in economics.[58] Nonetheless, over the course of the years, the two perspectives have become more intertwined, whereby there is a persistent focus on consumer markets and economic theories and an increasing consideration for the demand side (i.e., consumers). It must be noted that this has been, to a certain extent, at the expense of less research on the supply side.[59]

An integrated view of the economic and marketing literature on PSR is instrumental in explaining the advent of new pricing strategies, such as personalized and dynamic pricing. The emergence of these strategies poses challenges that, under conventional economic theory, could only be regarded as theoretical. One of these challenges is, for example, the possibility that algorithmic pricing enables firms to extract all consumer surplus. Through algorithmic pricing, prices can be discriminated dynamically over time and personally depending on individual consumer

[51] European Commission (2016), p. 169.

[52] Turow et al. (2005), p. 24.

[53] Borden (1964).

[54] Morris (1987).

[55] Gijsbrechts (1993).

[56] Kienzler and Kowalkowski (2017).

[57] Esteves and Resende (2019).

[58] Skouras et al. (2005).

[59] Kienzler and Kowalkowski (2017).

information.[60] In other words, AI is opening the way for perfect price discrimination.

Through sophisticated marketing techniques, firms can make consumers pay higher prices than they could charge in a perfectly competitive market. In existing economic literature, pricing is regarded to be a market-based outcome that is mainly driven by production costs.[61] If a firm decides to charge prices that are higher than the equilibrium price, consumers will switch to firms that offer the same good for a lower price. This theory assumes that consumers have perfect knowledge. In other words, they know how much the price of a certain good should be. Marketers have found, however, that if firms create *fog* regarding the price, consumers will be hampered in determining the correct price.[62] This fog can be created in numerous ways, among which the subtle concealment of prices and making products incomparable.

As a consequence, firms are in a position to apply differential pricing to extract the majority of the consumer surplus or overprice all consumers for a substantial aggregate gain.[63] In addition, prices can be framed in such a way that negative consumer perceptions are transformed into positive perceptions. This can, for example, be done by highlighting higher external prices, which make the stated price more attractive after price comparison,[64] by providing product-specific discount codes,[65] or by offering cashbacks.[66]

An example of a marketing strategy that creates synergy effects with algorithmic pricing concerns *hidden prices*.[67] Through hidden prices, the costs of knowing the real price of a good or service become significantly higher. This can be done by revealing the true price of a good after a consumer has arrived at the final stage of the buying process. They also exist in the form of *hidden fees*, which are mandatory surcharges that are tacked on the final price when the time comes to check out and purchase the goods. Notably, this marketing technique circumvents the benefits of search engine machines.[68]

[60] Graef (2018).

[61] Skouras et al. (2005).

[62] De Geest (2018), p. 23.

[63] De Geest (2018), p. 146.

[64] Lee and Monroe (2008).

[65] Weisstein et al. (2013).

[66] Ho et al. (2017).

[67] De Geest (2018), p. 127.

[68] It must be noted that according to the European Commission (2021), the adding of hidden fees during the purchase process, also called *drip pricing*, can be regarded as a practice that may amount to a misleading action or omission in breach of the UCPD.

4.3.1 Marketing and the Conditions for Price Discrimination

A closer inspection of the three conditions that need to be fulfilled to perform price discrimination demonstrates that AI-driven marketing strategies can easily satisfy or circumvent them. First, as described above, access to vast amounts of data enables firms to improve their predictive power and come closer to identifying the WTP of each consumer individually. The different levels of demand can, therefore, be targeted accurately. The second condition describes that the firm must have some level of market power. In perfectly competitive markets, prices will go down to marginal cost for all companies, and if a firm with a lack of market power raises prices, it will price itself out of the market.[69] Nonetheless, through a wide variety of marketing strategies, firms can substitute market power in the form of monopolies or oligopolies with market power in the form of customer retention.[70] For example, through fidelity programs, customer relationship management, and trust-building, firms can retain consumers by increasing switching costs. In addition, through *network effects,* consumers can be captured, and substantial influence can be exercised even though the firm has not formally reached a dominant position yet.[71] Accordingly, price discrimination can also occur in competitive markets where a firm does not have monopoly power.[72]

The third condition emphasizes that arbitrage should be limited for price discrimination to work. This means that consumers need to have limited resell possibilities. If consumers can detect the difference in prices, arbitrage possibilities emerge. Through sophisticated algorithms, firms can make it excessively onerous for consumers to compare prices. Besides, the uniform price can be concealed so that consumers only see their individual prices. This can be done by altering the price offerings and presenting them in a more complex manner.

Consequently, with the help of data-driven pricing strategies that monitor prices in real-time, arbitrage becomes practically unfeasible, making the condition less burdensome for companies.[73]

The ability of a firm to conceal the personalized pricing strategy is relevant to consumers' *fairness considerations*. Consumers should have the feeling that they are paying a fair price. If some consumers find out that they are spending more than others, this could cause outrage, which could damage the firm's reputation. For this reason, the firm needs to be sure that it can conceal the difference in prices, or else it risks losing part of its clientele, which could be more costly than the increase in revenue from personalized pricing.[74] Analogous to the case of arbitrage,

[69] Varian (2009).

[70] Townley et al. (2017).

[71] Chapdelaine (2020), p. 17.

[72] Levine (2002); Klein and Wiley Jr. (2003); Guttentag (2019).

[73] Chapdelaine (2020), p. 16.

[74] Odlyzko (2003).

complex-designed pricing schemes can minimize the chance of exposure.[75] If the discriminatory pricing scheme cannot be fully concealed, the firm can use marketing techniques to frame the difference in an alternative, more positive manner (i.e., *framing effect*). For example, a price difference can be described as a limited offer or a personalized discount.[76]

4.3.2 Value-Based Pricing

Data-driven marketing strategies have enabled firms to improve the identification of consumers' valuation of goods and services. The ability to identify consumers' valuation of goods and services is of particular relevance to marketing research. A multiplicity of marketing studies describes the most effective methods to charge higher prices without consumers knowing it.[77] It falls under the umbrella of *value-based pricing* that replaces the *cost-plus pricing* method typically found in economic literature. Under value-based pricing, prices are based on consumers' perceived value of a product rather than the product's cost price with an included markup. In practice, a shift from cost-based pricing to value-based pricing is visible.[78]

In the marketing literature, the profitability of several pricing strategies has been extensively analyzed. These include cost-based, markup, gross-margin, and competition-based pricing.[79] Each provides a useful starting point for developing a pricing strategy, yet consumer-based pricing is considered the better alternative.[80] This pricing type depends on the valuation of consumers (i.e., value-based pricing), which is affected by the other elements of the marketing strategy, such as the product, the distribution, and the promotion.[81] Accordingly, the price-setting element cannot be seen separately from the marketing strategy.[82]

The approaches to determining customer value are highly dependent on customer data and a comprehensive system of analysis. The measurement can be improved through more sophisticated technologies to collect and analyze the data.[83]

---

[75] See, for example, Zhang and Bell (2012).

[76] Ezrachi and Stucke (2016).

[77] See, for example, Gabaix and Laibson (2006); Ellison and Ellison (2009); Adaval and Wyer Jr. (2011).

[78] Gale and Swire (2006).

[79] See for an extensive analysis Schindler (2011).

[80] Ingenbleek et al. (2003).

[81] Schindler (2011), chapter 2.

[82] Foxall (1972); Schindler (2011), chapter 16.

[83] Gale and Swire (2006).

AI developments are, therefore, of significant value to the development of pricing strategies.[84]

4.3.3 Dynamic pricing: The More Accepted Alternative

Algorithmic pricing is the focus of this chapter; however, another data-driven pricing strategy is frequently utilized and has become increasingly feasible with the growth of online marketing,[85] namely *dynamic pricing*. The EC (2021) describes it as: "Dynamic pricing (also called real-time pricing) means changing the price for a product in a highly flexible and quick manner in response to market demands."[86] Traders can, in principle, freely engage in dynamic pricing and set their prices as they see fit as long as they adequately inform consumers about the costs of the products or services and how they are calculated.[87]

The definition of dynamic pricing has been further elaborated by the OFT (2013b):

> Online retailers use fluctuations in demand to change the prices of their products depending on availability. Products which are likely to be priced dynamically are those which may be perishable, time-sensitive (airline or travel tickets), those with a depreciating value (technology-based goods), or if they are scarce (event tickets).[88]

As can be deduced from this definition, it is more likely that dynamic pricing will be prevalent in the service sectors, which is also the case in practice.[89] A prominent example of dynamic pricing has been found in France. In the travel sector, significant price variations were found that were caused by the number of places that were left in the concerned means of transport and the time of day when the tickets were purchased.[90] Dynamic pricing is seen in an increasing number of markets, even those traditionally regulated by listed prices, such as electronics and apparel.[91] Marketers are more frequently resorting to dynamic pricing due to the lower costs of changing prices online. Yet, despite the benefits of dynamic pricing, there is also a threat to sellers. Dynamic pricing leads to reduced levels of trust among consumers. To maintain a trusting relationship between the seller and the consumer, adopting this strategy should be carefully considered.[92]

---

[84] Huang and Rust (2018); Davenport et al. (2020); Hagen et al. (2020).

[85] Haws and Bearden (2006).

[86] European Commission (2021), section 4.2.8.

[87] In accordance with Articles 6(1)(d) and 7(4)(c) of the UCPD.

[88] Office of Fair Trading (2013b).

[89] European Commission (2016), pp. 197, 260.

[90] Commission Nationale de l'Informatique et des Libertés (CNIL) et la Direction Générale de la Concurrence, de la Consommation et de la Répression des Fraudes (DG CCRF) (2014).

[91] Kannan and Kopalle (2001).

[92] Garbarino and Lee (2003); Haws and Bearden (2006).

Nonetheless, dynamic pricing is more accepted by consumers overall than personalized pricing. The reason for this is that dynamic pricing is based on market demands instead of personal characteristics. This leads to fewer concerns of discrimination among consumers.[93] However, the non-discriminatory nature of dynamic pricing is debatable. Varian (1980) demonstrates that dynamic pricing remains a form of price discrimination because it allows firms to differentiate between informed and uninformed buyers.[94] Consequently, firms can strategically price the products in such a way that uninformed consumers are exploited, and profits are increased.

All in all, dynamic pricing poses less of a threat to consumer welfare because it is non-personalized and leads to crude forms of price discrimination.[95] In contrast, algorithmic pricing has the potential to achieve a state of perfect price discrimination (i.e., first-degree price discrimination), which poses significant challenges to consumer welfare.

4.4 Economic Analysis of Algorithmic Pricing

In the existing literature, the practice of algorithmic pricing is regarded as a trade-off problem between efficiency and equity.[96] In this section, a traditional law and economics analysis focused on efficiency-based effects will be conducted first complemented with insights from behavioral law and economics. After that, an equity-based analysis will be conducted, whereby ethical and fairness-based arguments will also be considered. Lastly, the trade-off that regulators must face if they want to regulate algorithmic pricing will be discussed. In this way, this chapter strives to provide a comprehensive picture of algorithmic pricing and its implications.

4.4.1 Traditional Law and Economics: An Efficiency Perspective

The first step of the efficiency analysis is to recall the concept of efficiency.[97] In this study, efficiency refers to the maximization of the sum of wealth of all relevant parties. In this regard, it follows the *wealth maximization paradigm* when speaking of efficiency.[98] Social welfare is then defined as the sum of consumer and producer

---

[93] OECD (2018), p. 9.

[94] Varian (1980).

[95] OECD (2018), p. 9.

[96] See, for example, Weiss and Mehrotra (2001).

[97] See Sect. 2.2.1.

[98] Posner (1979); Posner (1981); Posner (1985).

surplus.[99] To analyze the desirability of algorithmic pricing in terms of efficiency, the effects need to be placed in the context of changes in the size of the total surplus, which equals social welfare.

4.4.1.1 Positive Efficiency Effects

In terms of *static efficiency* (i.e., allocative efficiency), algorithmic price discrimination could lead to an increase in social welfare. The reason for this is that in contrast to uniform pricing, whereby part of the consumer population is excluded from the market since the price of the good is higher than the WTP, firms would be able to lower prices under algorithmic pricing for the low-end consumers, while preserving high prices for high-end consumers, thereby safeguarding profitability.[100] An important consideration is that there is a lack of empirical evidence that supports the static efficiency of algorithmic pricing due to its novelty and secrecy. Yet, substantial evidence supports the static efficiency of traditional price discrimination.[101] Algorithmic pricing should, therefore, in theory, improve static efficiency even further since it is an enhanced form of price discrimination whereby the output is maximized.

It must be noted, however, that further empirical evidence is needed to corroborate that firms are offering their products to the lower end of the market in practice.

Furthermore, algorithmic pricing can have a positive effect on *dynamic efficiency*. This means that the pricing mechanism allows firms to raise revenues without sacrificing sales, which enables them to invest in innovation and differentiation.[102] Subsequently, innovation and differentiation can lead to product and service improvements and cost savings, which could benefit the consumer. To specify, through personalized prices, the innovating firm can recuperate its investments more effectively, which enlarges the incentive to innovate. Consequently, an increase in product quality or enhanced personalized services can be expected.[103]

If the market is sufficiently competitive, the innovation will not lead to a monopoly and the pricing practice could benefit consumer welfare.[104] In fact, algorithmic pricing could lead to an *intensified competition effect,*[105] also known as the *customer poaching effect.*[106] In essence, this means that if a seller knows that a consumer has a higher WTP for a competitor's product, then it will be able to offer the consumer a personalized price that is lower than the competitor's price, which will attract the

---

[99] Parisi (2013), p. 278.

[100] OECD (2018), p. 18.

[101] See OECD (2018), p. 19 for an extensive description of the relevant literature.

[102] OECD (2016).

[103] Choe and Wu (2015); Rayna et al. (2015).

[104] OECD (2018), p. 22.

[105] Office of Fair Trading (2013a), p. 25.

[106] Armstrong and Vickers (2001).

consumer. If more competitors do this to attract clientele, this could lead to intensified competition, which is beneficial for the consumer.[107]

Moreover, algorithmic pricing can lead to the growth of certain industries that face high fixed costs. This argument is best explained by using the airline industry as an example.[108] Airlines operate on high fixed costs and relatively low variable costs.[109] In the late 70s and early 80s, the airline industry was characterized by heavy regulation and limited competition. Since this hindered the growth of the industry, deregulation was advocated. Nonetheless, the boom in competition sparked price wars, which forced airlines to price themselves into bankruptcy.[110] The main problem was that with uniform pricing, the demand for flights was limited, and there was cross-subsidization. Business travelers paid relatively little in relation to their WTP, and part of the price-sensitive consumer market was not served (prices were too high for this group). The advent of Internet technologies allowed the industry to experiment with segmentation and dynamic pricing. This proved to be a highly successful strategy to optimize profits, which continuously improved over the years.[111] With this example in mind, it is straightforward to envisage the benefits that algorithmic pricing could bring to other ailing industries with high fixed and relatively low variable costs.

Lastly, in the economic literature, it has been found that (algorithmic) price discrimination leads to increased output.[112] This result holds for different markets since, on the whole, price discrimination allows firms to serve a greater part of the market.[113] Higher output levels enable the firm to increase production and optimize production capacity.[114] In addition, inventory management can be improved, which leads to substantial savings.[115] In short, increased output means more access, extra choices, cost-efficiencies, and more demand satisfied. As a result, it will lead to overall increased welfare.[116]

---

[107] Office of Fair Trading (2013a), pp. 25–28.

[108] See, for an extensive analysis of price discrimination in the airline industry, Weiss and Mehrotra (2001).

[109] Weiss and Mehrotra (2001), p. 4.

[110] Gesell and Farris (1992).

[111] McGill and Van Ryzin (1999).

[112] Schmalensee (1981); Varian (1985); Tirole (1988); Schwartz (1990).

[113] Hausman and MacKie-Mason (1988); Weisman and Kulick (2010).

[114] Ezrachi and Stucke (2016).

[115] Li et al. (2015); Tan et al. (2017).

[116] Varian (1985); Hausman and MacKie-Mason (1988); Weisman and Kulick (2010).

4.4.1.2 Negative Efficiency Effects

There are, however, also several adverse efficiency effects. First, the practice of algorithmic pricing is costly. Although BDA has significantly reduced the costs of segmentation for a firm, the cost is not zero. Whether the firm collects the consumer data or buys it from a data broker, costs must be incurred. As a result, operating costs (i.e., fixed costs) and marginal costs (i.e., variable costs) will increase.[117] These costs need to be offset against the additional revenues that algorithmic pricing brings. Rather than investing in additional product or service improvements, the firm is compelled to invest in data analytics and AI.

Second, inefficient competition can emerge that wastes resources and is disadvantageous for the firm.[118] It could lead to an arms race between the seller and the consumer, whereby both invest valuable resources to finance technologies and counter-technologies that, respectively, pierce the veil of consumer anonymity or warrant it.[119] Consumers will incur additional costs to circumvent the algorithmic pricing mechanism. A parallel can be drawn to consumer behavior concerning cookie tracking. If consumers know that their cookies are being tracked and they will be targeted based on the cookies, they can take anonymizing measures, such as deleting the cooking history or opening the same website in incognito mode. This will increase transaction costs for consumers, leading to efficiency losses.[120] Even though transaction costs rise, consumers will be incentivized to engage in anonymizing practices as long as the marginal benefit of doing so is greater than the marginal cost. Firms, however, can counteract these practices by means of sophisticated tracking techniques.[121]

Third, an essential mechanism to keep markets competitive is that consumers can compare prices and decide accordingly. Algorithmic pricing inhibits price comparison by making comparison tools less effective through personalized offers, constantly changing prices, opaque pricing schemes, and the avoidance of publicly listed prices.[122] This also increases switching costs because it becomes more demanding for consumers to decide if a change of seller is profitable. Accordingly, consumers can be locked-in, and the threat is present that loyal customers will be exploited since price differences that normally would induce a switch are more challenging to detect.[123]

Fourth, algorithmic pricing could lead to collusion. The algorithmic pricing mechanism learns autonomously through experimentation. By observing competitors' prices, it can choose the optimizing pricing strategy. It is not likely that the

[117] Office of Fair Trading (2013a), pp. 74–78.

[118] Pasquale (2007).

[119] Miller (2014), p. 67.

[120] Acquisti and Varian (2005), pp. 367–369.

[121] Conitzer et al. (2012).

[122] Kannan and Kopalle (2001), pp. 63–68.

[123] Seele et al. (2021), pp. 705–707.

algorithm will select a strategy that causes a price war that dissipates profits. Conversely, it will tend to keep prices high to generate high-profit margins. It is more likely that AI systems will explore profit-enhancing collusive pricing possibilities.[124] Besides, algorithms can check competitors' actions in real-time and react instantly. Thus, cheating the collusive agreement can be punished immediately, removing the incentive to defect. The emergence and the continuance of higher prices through collusive practices can be assisted by the instantaneous monitoring of competitors' prices.[125] There is experimental[126] and empirical[127] evidence showcasing collusive behavior by algorithmic pricing mechanisms.

Finally, since algorithmic pricing can lead to the transferal of consumer surplus, there is an incentive for firms to invest in improved rent extraction. This could lead to wasteful rent-seeking activities. Incurring costs for the sake of rent extraction does not increase productive output but decreases social welfare.[128] An example of these rent-seeking activities could be lobbying. Through political actions, firms can pressure legislators to introduce regulations that will shield incumbents' position in the market or oppose regulations that negatively affect their position, which leads to regulatory incumbency.[129] This would be positive for the incumbents yet detrimental to consumers. With respect to algorithmic pricing, it is conceivable that it could be highly beneficial for companies that profitably employ the strategy to lobby against further regulation.

The extent to which the positive effects outweigh the negative effects, or vice versa, depends on the magnitude of the effects. This is, however, the problematic part of the analysis. There is scarce empirical evidence on the static and dynamic efficiency effects. Still, there is even less about the overall impact (i.e., taking all efficiency effects into account) due to the difficulty of measuring the net effect of algorithmic price discrimination. Nevertheless, it is argued that the impact of algorithmic pricing on consumer welfare will ultimately depend on the market structure and the degree of competition in the market. It is expected that in monopolistic markets with little price competition, the dominant position will likely be exploited, with the help of algorithmic pricing, to the consumer's detriment. Conversely, algorithmic pricing could lead to more intense competition in more competitive markets, incentivizing firms to lower prices, thereby benefitting consumers.[130] In imperfectly competitive markets, the effects on aggregate welfare are estimated to be ambiguous, dependent on how the pricing techniques are employed, the type of

[124] Calvano et al. (2020a).

[125] Calvano et al. (2020a).

[126] Calvano et al. (2020b).

[127] Assad et al. (2024).

[128] Ezrachi and Stucke (2016).

[129] OECD (2018), p. 22.

[130] Office of Fair Trading (2013a), pp. 8–11; OECD (2018), p. 20; Chen et al. (2020).

price discrimination, and the market conditions. In such markets, a case-by-case assessment is required.[131]

In summary, algorithmic price discrimination will most likely reduce consumer welfare under a monopoly compared to uniform pricing. In imperfectly competitive markets, the net effect is expected to be ambiguous, whereas in competitive markets, algorithmic pricing will not necessarily be detrimental to consumer welfare. In the presence of competitive market conditions, algorithmic pricing could be welcomed from an efficiency perspective.

4.4.2 *Insights from Behavioral Law and Economics*

The notion of efficiency as a determinative normative paradigm to evaluate legal changes has been predominant in the law and economics literature. Wealth-maximization was advocated to be the goal since a focus on fairness could lead to adverse effects on welfare.[132] However, several prominent law and economics scholars have stated that efficiency cannot be the only relevant factor in the social welfare function. In other words, a change is only a social improvement if additional social goals such as equality or justice are also furthered.[133] The tendency to care about the equitableness or fairness of a policy, which diverges from the self-interest assumption in RCT has, among others, been explored by behavioral (law and) economics scholars. For example, Fehr and Schmidt (1999) demonstrated that individuals can be predominantly concerned with cooperation and vehemently oppose inequity.[134] The role of fairness can, therefore, not be underestimated.[135]

Algorithmic pricing could lead to *pricing unfairness*.[136] This refers to the feeling of consumers that they received an unfair price compared to other buyers, even though they are in a similar situation. In other words, the degree of similarity is essential for price fairness judgments.[137] The negative feelings concerning the price can damage trust in the market, cause consumer dissatisfaction, and lead to bad publicity.[138] Poort and Zuiderveen Borgesius (2019) found that consumers have a generally unfavorable attitude toward personalized prices, favoring a prohibition. In a study on the Dutch population, more than 80% of respondents considered online price discrimination to be unacceptable and unfair.[139]

---

131 Townley et al. (2017), p. 702.

132 Kaplow and Shavell (2001).

133 Calabresi (1980); Sen (1985); Nussbaum and Sen (1993).

134 Fehr and Schmidt (1999).

135 Rabin (1993).

136 This refers specifically to the perception of fairness from a consumer standpoint.

137 Xia et al. (2004), pp. 2–3.

138 Xia et al. (2004), pp. 6–8.

139 Poort and Zuiderveen Borgesius (2019).

Bar-Gill (2018) makes a compelling case that algorithmic pricing is not solely based on preferences but also misperceptions. Price discrimination targeting demand-inflating misperceptions could decrease efficiency and lead to more consumer harm.[140] The basic notion of an individual's WTP is based on the idea that optimal consumption levels are determined by preferences and budget constraints.[141] Bar-Gill (2018) argues that this view of WTP is too limited since it is also influenced by misperceptions, defined as mistakes that affect consumers' WTP.[142] The rationale behind the efficiency loss of algorithmic pricing is based on the overestimation bias. To specify, overestimation can induce consumers to buy a certain product because the perceived benefit exceeds the product cost; however, in reality, the cost of the product exceeds the actual benefit to the consumer.[143]

The role of misperceptions can be seen across multiple consumer markets. For example, consumers tend to overestimate the benefits they will gain from getting a gym subscription (i.e., the amount of visits is grossly overestimated) and underestimate the costs associated with credit cards, mortgages, and cell phone plans.[144] Accordingly, there can be cases in which consumers buy products based on misperceptions, which leads to efficiency losses that substantially harm consumers because they will have to bear the entire loss.[145] This is particularly relevant to algorithmic pricing since the price-setting mechanism is unclear to consumers and price comparison is made exceptionally onerous. Consumers need to base their decisions on perceived benefits and costs, thereby opening the way for decisions based on misperceptions.

Increased consumption based on misperceptions can make supracompetitive priced goods look like reasonably priced goods, which induces consumption that otherwise should not have taken place. If this consistently occurs, the disposable income of consumers is predominantly spent on consumer goods, whereas it decreases for other purposes that would increase their well-being. This raises wealth inequality concerns, particularly if low-income consumer groups suffer more from misperception-based overconsumption than high-income groups.[146]

4.4.3 Broadening the Analysis: An Equity Perspective

Weiss and Mehrotra (2001) state:

> Price discrimination may not be all bad. Indeed, economic theory suggests price discrimination may promote efficient use of a society's resources. In many cases, however,

---

140 Bar-Gill (2018).

141 Mas-Colell et al. (1995), pp. 6–9, 45–65.

142 Bar-Gill (2018), p. 2.

143 Bar-Gill (2018), p. 3.

144 Bar-Gill (2012).

145 Bar-Gill (2018), p. 11.

146 Ezrachi and Stucke (2016).

> efficiency must be balanced against the need to achieve equitable treatment of individual consumers. In such cases, government regulation, either through existing laws or new ones, may be necessary to ensure that the logic of efficiency does not overwhelm the need for fairness.[147]

This statement demonstrates that the analysis cannot stop at the assessment of the efficiency effects. To obtain a comprehensive picture of the effects of algorithmic pricing, further attention needs to be devoted to the equity side of the practice.

4.4.3.1 Positive Effects on Equity

Algorithmic pricing would primarily lead to greater access for consumers. Certain groups of consumers, mainly consumers with a low WTP, are excluded from the market under uniform pricing. Through algorithmic pricing, special discount prices could be offered to these groups, making certain products and services available that would otherwise not be available.[148] Rather than increasing prices to target consumers with a higher WTP, firms could selectively vary prices and offer consumers with a low reservation price a special, timely coupon.[149] Cross-subsidization under uniform pricing can be counteracted by making high-value consumers pay more, which opens the market for low-value consumers.

In addition, it has been found that, in some instances, personalized pricing can lead to an increase in consumer surplus.[150] Firms can decide to share the efficiency gains with consumers through lower prices, which benefits total consumer welfare. Tailored prices can also be used to generate positive consumer feedback.[151] Companies would then share part of the revenue increases (e.g., in the form of customer benefits) to build a good reputation and prevent public outrage.

On a macro level, algorithmic pricing can help solve other social problems, ultimately benefiting consumers and society. For example, it has been found that personalized pricing can remedy over- and underconsumption issues by more accurately responding to changes in demand.[152] Other examples are the ability of pricing algorithms to reduce food waste and improve water conservation while increasing revenue.[153]

If the firms' efficiency gains obtained through algorithmic pricing are used for socially beneficial goals, then consumers would ultimately benefit. Seele et al.

[147] Weiss and Mehrotra (2001), p. 2.

[148] Strahilevitz (2008).

[149] Ezrachi and Stucke (2016).

[150] Chen and Gallego (2019).

[151] Faruqui and Palmer (2011).

[152] Faruqui and Sergici (2010).

[153] Seele et al. (2021), p. 711.

(2021) go as far as saying that the efficiency gains can be utilized to reduce carbon footprints, which will benefit both the environment and society as a whole.[154]

4.4.3.2 Negative Effects on Equity

First and foremost, algorithmic pricing can fully transfer consumer surplus to the seller. If consumers are charged their reservation price, no consumer welfare remains. This evokes concerns among competition and consumer protection authorities because safeguarding consumer welfare is one of their primary goals.[155] One of the biggest problems these authorities face regarding intervention is that the current body of empirical literature cannot unequivocally demonstrate the effects of algorithmic pricing on consumer welfare. It has been found that personalized pricing in its current form leads to ambiguous effects that are dependent on the market structure.[156] The practice of algorithmic pricing, however, is constantly being perfected. It is predicted that it will likely approximate perfect price discrimination in the near future, enabling the complete capture of consumer surplus thereby causing substantial negative consumer welfare effects.[157]

Second, algorithmic pricing has the potential to decrease consumer trust in online markets.[158] As a consequence, demand can be significantly reduced. This would amount to a loss of consumer surplus compared to a situation without price discrimination. The rationale is that if consumers lose trust, demand goes down, reducing output levels and leading to a lower level of welfare.[159]

Third, price discrimination will most likely be more harmful to naïve than sophisticated consumers.[160] The rationale is that sophisticated consumers will be more effective in anticipating the effects of price discrimination and adapting accordingly. Consequently, naïve consumers will end up paying higher prices, making them lose a more substantial part of their welfare.[161] To the extent naïve consumers reflect poorer, less educated, and more vulnerable consumers in practice, it is highly questionable, in the light of distributive justice, if algorithmic pricing is desirable.[162]

---

[154] Seele et al. (2021), p. 711.

[155] OECD (1993), p. 28.

[156] Nevo and Wolfram (2002); Shiller and Waldfogel (2011); Grennan (2013); Beckert et al. (2015).

[157] Shiller (2014).

[158] Office of Fair Trading (2013a), pp. 84–87.

[159] Office of Fair Trading (2013a), pp. 84–87.

[160] Heidhues and Kőszegi (2017).

[161] Salop and Stiglitz (1977); Varian (1985); Armstrong (2006).

[162] See Helberger et al. (2022) for a further elaboration on the importance of considering consumer vulnerability in the digital economy.

4.4.3.3 Ethical Concerns

Apart from the distributive concerns, several ethical considerations that are relevant to the fairness assessment of algorithmic pricing should be discussed. Principally, algorithmic price discrimination can transcend the price dimension and lead to *algorithmic discrimination*. To work accurately, the algorithm is fed with consumer data that allows companies to target specific consumers or consumer groups with tailored prices.[163] The price directly or indirectly reflects consumer demographics since these are essential elements that constitute an individual's WTP.[164] Consequently, it is conceivable that the algorithm will have a discriminatory element toward certain groups of consumers. Although anti-discrimination laws are in place to guide the programming of algorithms, the ML element can (unintentionally) circumvent them and lead to practically the same result, namely algorithmic discrimination.[165] In other words, AI-applications can still discriminate against groups of people that are legally protected by anti-discrimination laws.[166]

Also, the desirability of algorithmic pricing will likely be determined by what it does for overall social welfare.[167] The danger that lures, in this case, is that the practice of algorithmic pricing will benefit some parts of society. In contrast, other parts will lose, albeit the consumer population as a whole (potentially) benefits.

If certain groups of consumers, for example, low-value consumers, are consistently harmed (i.e., they are always on the losing side), there is a case of perpetuated injustice. This phenomenon is also called social sorting,[168] whereby consumers are divided into a strong market (high-value consumers) and a weak market (low-value consumers). Subsequently, the latter market will experience different treatment from the former. It is feared that this will exacerbate existing vulnerabilities, reflect power disparities, and lead to more divided markets.[169]

Furthermore, algorithmic pricing could debilitate the bargaining position of consumers vis-à-vis sellers as a result of the enlarged information asymmetry.[170] By accumulating and analyzing consumer data, detailed behavioral patterns can be predicted, and the power asymmetries between the consumer and the seller can be reinforced.[171] Accordingly, it is argued that algorithmic pricing further detracts the market from a level playing field. The competition for the surplus generated by the transaction is fair when both parties are on somewhat equal footing, but that is not the case. It is hard to bargain if one party already has all, or practically all, relevant

[163] Chen and Chen (2015).

[164] Huang (2010).

[165] Bock (2016).

[166] Hacker (2018).

[167] Edwards (2006).

[168] See Sect. 3.5.3.3.

[169] Turow (2008); Nissenbaum (2009); Miller (2014), pp. 92–96.

[170] Seele et al. (2021), p. 706.

[171] Martin and Murphy (2017).

information about the other party. There is no leverage on the side of consumers since the seller can adequately predict the consumer's reservation price, and the possibility of bargaining is virtually ruled out. In essence, the parties compete for the surplus based on unfair terms.[172] Sellers can build accurate consumer profiles and obtain *superior knowledge*.[173] This means that a situation is approximated wherein the seller, allegedly, is better able to understand consumer needs than the consumers themselves.[174]

Lastly, the role of privacy cannot be overlooked. The practice of algorithmic pricing is only possible through the collection and processing of copious amounts of consumer data. To a certain extent, firms need to intrude on consumers' personal integrity and intimacy to collect the data, which could be problematic in terms of privacy. Consumers have expectations regarding the treatment of their privacy, and social norms mold these expectations.[175] A considerable fairness problem could persist if consumers' privacy expectations are consistently transgressed.[176] The privacy problem is exacerbated by the lack of transparency that surrounds algorithmic pricing[177] and algorithms in general.[178]

In short, from an equity perspective, the practice of algorithmic pricing seems to be problematic. The discrepancy is that the practice can be desirable from an efficiency perspective (assuming competitive market conditions). This creates a trade-off that should be carefully considered.

4.4.4 Efficiency-Equity Trade-Off

With respect to algorithmic pricing, there is a continuous tension between equity and efficiency. The relevance of the trade-off and its inherent contrariety has made it a subject of extensive study.[179] Nonetheless, the apparent ambivalence associated with the trade-off depends on the relationship between the two goals of efficiency and justice.[180] Three types of relationships are possible: *goal harmony*, *neutrality*, and *conflict*.[181] In the first case, efficiency would also bring a just outcome, whereas in the third case, the opposite is true. In the second case, pursuing one goal does not detract from the other.

172 Moriarty (2021).

173 Xu and Dukes (2019).

174 Mik (2016), p. 13.

175 Nissenbaum (2009); Townley et al. (2017), p. 711.

176 Nissenbaum (2009); Townley et al. (2017), p. 711.

177 Townley et al. (2017), p. 712.

178 Pasquale (2015).

179 See, for example, Okun (1975).

180 The terms equity and justice are used interchangeably, see Mathis (2009), chapter 9.

181 Mathis (2009), p. 185.

The idea of regulating the equity-efficiency trade-off concerning algorithmic pricing would be to achieve a state of *Rawlsian justice*.[182] This state is achieved when a system is in place that leads to efficient and fair outcomes. According to Rawls (1971), this outcome can be achieved when individuals choose an arrangement of society under a *veil of ignorance*. This is a thought experiment, in which individuals must select the principles for the structure of society without knowing which position in the world they would take. In light of individuals' distaste for risk and uncertainty, they would most likely choose the allocation of rights and entitlements that would be efficient and fair. A relevant observation is that inequality could be accepted, but only to the degree that it creates necessary incentives that increase social welfare. This trade-off is often modeled in law and economics with the Nash social welfare function.[183]

In contrast to the proposition that efficiency and justice should be separated,[184] whereby private exchanges should be guided by the efficiency objective, and tax and social law should pursue distributive justice goals, this study advocates an integrated approach. In other words, the objective is to jointly optimize efficiency and justice in policymaking.

The concepts of allocative efficiency and distributive justice are inextricably linked.[185] In particular, regarding the political feasibility of proposals for legal reforms, it is inconceivable that a legal change would be accepted based on allocative efficiency while wholly disregarding distributive justice.

Furthermore, in some instances, low-cost and effective redistribution can take place equally well by virtue of private law as by means of taxation.[186] Accordingly, the possibility of redistribution through law should also be explored.[187] Besides, the desirability of regulation solely focused on efficiency is debatable. In civil litigation, for example, the notion of justice is of particular relevance to the parties and cannot be subordinated to the idea of efficiency.[188] Consequently, the separation between efficiency and justice as objectives should be abandoned.

---

[182] Rawls (1971).

[183] Parisi (2013), p. 248.

[184] Polinsky (1989); Posner (1990); Kaplow and Shavell (2001).

[185] Mathis (2009), p. 201.

[186] Mathis (2009), p. 201.

[187] It must be noted that taxation is normally preferred to combat distributional injustices. This theory has been formally developed by Kaplow and Shavell (1994). They argue that only taxation is a good remedy to combat wealth inequality since alternative methods will lead to a double distortion. Although the soundness of this argument is severely criticized in the existing literature, see, for example, Markovits (2005), it also underestimates the problem-solving power of the law. Van Loo (2023), p. 2049 states: "A growing literature has shown how market laws, such as bankruptcy and consumer law, can in some contexts address distributional issues more efficiently than tax law."

[188] Mathis (2009), p. 201.

As Mathis (2009) puts it:

> It is rather the role of the legislator, and the courts in their turn, to strike a subtle balance between conflicting rights in all areas of the law. In doing so, the multiple interdependencies between efficiency and justice must be borne in mind.[189]

In conclusion, the practice of algorithmic pricing could be defended on efficiency grounds, but distributional concerns have evoked a call for regulation.[190] Considering the efficiency-equity trade-off, it is valuable to see how the current legal framework addresses algorithmic pricing.

4.5 Legal Framework

Traditionally, the freedom of enterprise is held in high regard, meaning businesses should be able to conduct their activities as freely as possible. This includes the freedom to set prices and the autonomy to enter into contracts as they see fit. The fair market value of a good or service is determined by the subjective judgments of the parties. Regulation of prices will, therefore, interfere with supplier freedom, parties' autonomy, and market efficiency. The pricing mechanism is regarded to work best when it can operate freely. Thus, the free-market principle prevails unless substantive reasons exist to regulate it.[191]

The analysis of Sect. 4.4 demonstrates that the efficiency-equity trade-off permeates the practice of algorithmic pricing. In such a scenario, the need for legal intervention depends on the relative weights given to the concepts of efficiency and distributive justice in the social welfare function.[192] If the consumer welfare hypothesis is followed, it can be argued that the potential for consumer welfare losses justifies intervention. In addition, the equity and ethical concerns reinforce the argument that regulation should be considered.[193]

4.5.1 Market-Based Solutions

Self-regulatory actions can take away the need for legal intervention.[194] For example, businesses could develop standards and best practices compliant with the existing legal framework. This can, for instance, be achieved with the cooperation of high-level European e-commerce organizations and associations.[195]

---

189 Mathis (2009), p. 201.

190 Van Heusden (2023)

191 Hayek (1944).

192 Shavell (2009), p. 597.

193 Miller (2014), p. 69.

194 See Sect. 3.6.1.

195 European Commission (2016), pp. 270–271.

The assertiveness of consumers should also not be underestimated. Through public outrage, consumers can punish firms that treat them unfairly.[196] The deterrent effect of consumer backlash can provide an incentive for sellers to self-regulate. Consumers have a predominantly negative attitude toward algorithmic pricing.[197] Consequently, it is conceivable that this unfavorable perception limits the further spread of price-discriminating strategies. Firms will be incentivized to self-correct in the development of the algorithms to prevent unfair outcomes.[198]

Technological tools can assist consumers in their assertiveness by enabling the monitoring of pricing strategies in the market.[199] These can be tools for consumers to oversee firms and guard themselves against algorithmic pricing practices, for example, by anonymizing themselves through the incognito mode or using several profiles to compare prices.[200]

In a sense, consumers are involved in a *digital arms race* where algorithmic technologies are used not only as market devices but also as consumer protection tools.[201] To make the race more balanced, policymakers should foster the development of AI-based consumer empowering tools. This could be done, for instance, by encouraging cooperation between researchers, practitioners, and administrations. That is to say, a collaboration between the public and private sectors. This will, however, not fully remedy the imbalance, particularly with a view to the private sector's superior financial and technological abilities. Accordingly, further action is warranted.[202]

4.5.2 Competition Law

In traditional economic literature, it is argued that the ability to price discriminate is largely dependent upon a firm's market power.[203] Solely through a position of *market dominance* would it be possible to charge consumers different prices for the same product without losing a substantial part of the clientele to the competitors. It is asserted that the degree to which consumer welfare is impacted depends on the competition in the market.[204] In markets that have a monopoly structure, it is expected that algorithmic pricing will be employed to exploit consumers since no threat of switching to a competitor is present. In a competitive market, however,

---

196 Edwards (2006), pp. 583–585.

197 See Sect. 4.2.6.

198 Odlyzko (2003).

199 Mikians et al. (2012).

200 Acquisti and Varian (2005).

201 Grochowski et al. (2022).

202 Grochowski et al. (2022).

203 See, for example, Varian (2009).

204 Chen et al. (2020).

algorithmic pricing could lead to fierce price competition, which could be beneficial for consumers. Accordingly, the market structure is a determinative factor to assess the welfare effects of algorithmic pricing.

It must be noted, however, that through, for example, network effects, consumers can be captured, and substantial influence can be exercised even though the firm has not formally reached a dominant position yet.[205] Price discrimination can, therefore, also take place in competitive markets where a firm does not have monopoly power.[206]

If the practice is undertaken by a dominant firm, it can create exclusionary and exploitative effects. The former referring to practices that seek to harm competition, the latter to those that harm consumers directly.[207] An alternative wording is that there can be *primary line* and *secondary line injury*. Primary line injury "occurs where the supplier's conduct produces effects against competitors in the market in which it operates"[208] and secondary line injury concerns "discrimination exercised by a supplier against some of its customers compared to one or more of its customers."[209]

Article 102 TFEU regulates the abuse of a dominant position. To date, no case law in competition law has dealt explicitly with algorithmic pricing.[210] This is understandable since the technology emerged recently, and the empirical evidence of its ubiquity in business practice is still lacking. Nonetheless, it can already be theorized if algorithmic pricing would fall within the definition of abuse under Article 102 TFEU and if competition law can provide adequate remedies.

Article 102(c) TFEU states that there is an abuse when a dominant firm applies "dissimilar conditions to equivalent transactions with other trading parties, thereby placing them at a competitive disadvantage." Thus, for a successful recourse to Article 102(c) TFEU, four conditions need to be fulfilled: (1) Equivalent transactions; (2) dissimilar conditions; (3) competitive disadvantage; (4) no objective justifications for different treatment.[211] The third condition makes the application of Article 102 particularly onerous since the CJEU has not provided clear-cut answers on how to interpret the competitive disadvantage.[212] Regarding the scope of Article 102(c), it seems that the provision targets customers of a dominant firm who compete with one another on a downstream market, not the final consumers.[213] A broader

---

205 Chapdelaine (2020), p. 17.

206 Levine (2002); Miller (2014), p. 74; OECD (2018), p. 13.

207 Akman (2009), p. 4.

208 Graef (2018), p. 542.

209 Graef (2018), p. 543.

210 Townley et al. (2017), p. 723.

211 A full analysis with the corresponding case law is provided by Van den Bergh (2017), section 7.5.3.

212 O'Donoghue and Padilla (2013), p. 789; Van den Bergh (2017).

213 Graef (2018), p. 543.

interpretation is, therefore, a prerequisite for intervention based on competition law.[214]

Although there is no specific case law on algorithmic pricing, one case supports the idea that discrimination between final consumers also falls within the working sphere of Article 102(c) TFEU. In the *Deutsche Post – Interception of Cross-Border Mail* case,[215] the EC decided that:

> In any event, the Court of Justice has stated that the list of abuses mentioned in Article 82 itself is not exhaustive and thus only serves as examples of possible ways for a dominant firm to abuse its market power. Article 82 may be applied even in the absence of a direct effect on competition between undertakings on any given market. This provision may also be applied in situations where a dominant undertakings behaviour causes damage directly to consumers.[216]

Consequently, the EC concluded that such a practice could be classified as an abuse of Article 102(c) TFEU.[217] Nonetheless, this case never went to the CJEU, which keeps the interpretation of Article 102(c) in relation to price discrimination that harms final consumers unclear. Since there is no legal standard for exploitative pricing that harms final consumers, it is uncertain if invoking Article 102 will be successful for cases of algorithmic pricing. In practice, Article 102 is more commonly applied (93% of the cases) to enforce cases against exclusionary abuses rather than exploitative abuses (7% of the cases).[218] This makes it dubious if the remediation of exploitative abuses will be a priority of the EC. It is, therefore, argued that consumer protection law would be more suitable to tackle price discrimination practices.[219]

Moreover, the EC will scrutinize the abuse in the light of its competitive effects (i.e., effects-based approach), which means that on a case-by-case basis, it must be decided if algorithmic price discrimination is beneficial or detrimental to competition.[220] For this consideration, the precise objective of competition law becomes relevant. If competition law enforcement is concerned with total welfare, algorithmic pricing will most likely not be considered anti-competitive; however, if the goal is maintaining consumer welfare, it will most likely be regarded as anti-competitive.[221] Although the EC has not clearly defined and openly endorsed the consumer welfare standard,[222] there are various indications that modern EU

[214] Graef (2018).

[215] 2001/892/EC. Commission Decision of 25 July 2001 relating to a proceeding under Article 82 of the EC Treaty (COMP/C-1/36.915 — Deutsche Post AG — Interception of cross-border mail), O.J. 2001, L 331/40.

[216] Para 133.

[217] Para 134.

[218] OECD (2018), p. 27. Statistics are based on Dethmers and Blondeel (2017).

[219] O'Donoghue and Padilla (2013), pp. 846–849.

[220] OECD (2018), pp. 27–28.

[221] Maggiolino (2017), p. 22.

[222] Van den Bergh (2017), Chap. 3 provides an extensive analysis on the goals of EU competition law.

competition policy is focused on protecting consumer welfare.[223] It would then be possible to address algorithmic pricing based on EU competition policy.[224]

Lastly, it is worth mentioning that the concept of fairness is also becoming relevant in competition law. Several scholars argue that fairness should be part of the consumer welfare standard.[225] For instance, Townley et al. (2017) argue that if algorithmic pricing would undermine both fairness and consumer welfare, then it should be judged as unlawful under Article 102 TFEU.[226] They further state that if consumer welfare is advanced by algorithmic pricing, then fairness considerations should be a secondary goal. Still, fairness considerations should outweigh the efficiency benefits when consumer welfare is reduced.[227] In this way, fairness is also accounted for in the consumer welfare standard, which would give competition authorities greater authority to intervene.

4.5.3 Consumer Protection Law

Consumer protection law and competition law are inextricably linked. Both laws aim to promote consumer welfare and improve market economic performance by fostering competition.[228] Nonetheless, as the previous section demonstrated, it is unclear to what extent final customers can be protected from algorithmic pricing through competition law. In addition, the element of market power is irrelevant for the application of consumer law provisions. Consumer protection law can, therefore, be a valuable instrument to address algorithmic pricing on the points where competition law falls short.

The UCPD does not preclude traders from using algorithmic pricing based on tracking and profiling. In other words, there is no *per se* prohibition of algorithmic (personalized) pricing under the UCPD. In accordance with Articles 6(1)(d) and 7(4)(c) UCPD, an unfair price is not, by definition, an unfair commercial practice as long as the price or the manner in which the price is calculated is communicated to the consumer transparently and intelligibly. Personalized pricing is also not mentioned as one of the blacklisted practices of Annex 1 of the Directive.

Nevertheless, algorithmic pricing can be tackled under the UCPD in two alternative ways. First, personalized pricing could be classified as unfair due to a lack of transparency. The UCPD requires that the price or the calculation of it must be communicated transparently and intelligibly, which, in the case of algorithmic pricing,

---

[223] Albæk (2013).

[224] OECD (2018), p. 30.

[225] See, for example, Ezrachi (2017); Kalimo and Majcher (2017); Townley et al. (2017); Graef (2018).

[226] Townley et al. (2017), p. 731.

[227] Townley et al. (2017), p. 743.

[228] OECD (2018), p. 32.

is highly dubious.[229] Although Article 6(1)(ea) of the CRD, which the *Omnibus Directive* added, requires that consumers are informed that the price has been personalized on the basis of automated decision-making, it is still debatable to what extent the price and calculation have been communicated transparently and intelligibly. The obligation does not entail disclosing the parameters being used, potential benchmark prices, or any other information that could be relevant to consumers.[230] It is, therefore, questionable if this provision will effectively aid consumers in their decision-making process.

Second, personalized pricing can be combined with other personalization techniques, such as personalized advertising and contracting. If the joint use of personalization techniques leads to undue influence over consumers (Articles 8 and 9), algorithmic pricing can be conducted in a manner that constitutes an unfair commercial practice.[231] In this context, "consumer protection law could be used to tackle unfair practices that can have the effect of reinforcing the negative impact of personalised pricing, i.e. those practices that facilitate effective personalised pricing."[232]

Analogous to the UCPD, there is no *per se* prohibition of unfair prices under the UCTD. Article 4(2) explicitly excludes the fairness assessment of prices. Thus, while prices must be communicated in plain, intelligible language, they cannot be addressed based on the UCTD. Notably, in the *Caja de Ahorros* case,[233] the CJEU ruled that Articles 4(2) and 8 of the UCTD must be interpreted as not precluding national legislation that authorizes a judicial review regarding:

> the unfairness of contractual terms which relate to the definition of the main subject-matter of the contract or to the adequacy of the price and remuneration, on the one hand, as against the services or goods to be supplied in exchange, on the other hand, even in the case where those terms are drafted in plain, intelligible language.[234]

However, this does not mean that new legal obligations, such as additional disclosure duties or *per se* prohibitions, can be created that would complement existing consumer protection laws.[235] In addition, the scope of the exclusion remains uncertain, and the CJEU still needs to provide further guidance on its interpretation.[236] For this reason, a successful invocation of the UCTD to address algorithmic pricing is not straightforward.

---

[229] OECD (2018), p. 35.

[230] Grochowski et al. (2022), p. 42.

[231] European Commission (2021), section 4.2.8.

[232] OECD (2018), p. 36.

[233] Case C-484/08, Caja de Ahorros y Monte de Piedad de Madrid v Asociación de Usuarios de Servicios Bancarios (Ausbanc), ECLI:EU:C:2010:309. The Court of Justice of the European Union. https://curia.europa.eu/juris/liste.jsf?language=en&num=C-484/08.

[234] Para 44.

[235] Grochowski et al. (2022), p. 44.

[236] Stuyck (2010).

In sum, it can be argued that although consumer protection law offers various tools to address algorithmic pricing, it will likely not suffice to regulate the practice adequately without legal reforms.[237]

4.5.4 Data Protection Law

Personal data is an essential source of information for algorithmic pricing to work. The more consumers are active online, the more data the algorithms can observe, test, recalibrate, and refine. Thus, the more data the firm can collect, the better the algorithm will work.[238] In this sense, it is predictable that firms will push the boundaries of what data can be collected from individuals.

Although algorithmic pricing differs in its workings from personalized advertising, the data collection and processing process that takes place to drive the personalization mechanism is not different. For this reason, applying the GDPR to algorithmic pricing will largely resemble the analysis of Sect. 3.6.2.1. In essence, the crux of the matter will be the emphasis on consent. Even though pricing concerns a different service than advertising, it can be argued that based on the *Meta v Bundeskartellamt* case, companies will not be able to rely on the necessity for the performance of a contract or legitimate interest legal bases for algorithmic pricing. The service is not indispensable to the contract, and consumers cannot reasonably foresee that when they want to use a service, their data will be collected to personalize prices. It is improbable that price personalization will be part of the main subject matter of the contract or that consumers desire this specific personalization service. Accordingly, in the same way as under personalized advertising, obtaining consent will be essential for price personalization, which due to the signing-without-reading problem will not offer additional protection to consumers.[239]

It must be noted, however, the EDPB is putting a stronger emphasis on the importance of explicit informed consent.[240] As the EDPB puts it: "It is important to distinguish between accepting terms of service to conclude a contract and giving consent within the meaning of Article 6(1)(a), as these concepts have different requirements and legal consequences."[241] In practice, this means that obtaining consent based on the current signing-without-reading practice is increasingly contested.[242] Consequently, if this call for changing the consent mechanism continues, data protection law can be instrumental in tackling algorithmic pricing by increasing

[237] Galli (2022).

[238] Ezrachi and Stucke (2016), p. 490.

[239] See Helberger et al. (2021), pp. 27–40 for a further elaboration on why the consent mechanism in its current form fails to provide adequate protection to consumers in terms of data management.

[240] Luzak (2014).

[241] European Data Protection Board (EDPB) (2019), para 20.

[242] See, for example, the fine the French National Data Protection Commission imposed in the case Délibération SAN-2019-001 du 21 janvier 2019. Délibération de la formation restreinte n° SAN –

transparency and mitigating information asymmetries.[243] Of note is that the AI Act also supports the call for transparency (in the context of algorithms).[244]

4.5.5 Human Rights Law

Human rights law could address some of the ethical concerns that are related to the unequal treatment of individuals through algorithmic pricing.[245] Algorithmic pricing intersects with various fundamental rights, such as human dignity, privacy, and self-determination. A complete analysis of these relationships and other relevant human rights laws falls outside the scope of this chapter. Still, one human right will be further explored in this section, namely *the right to non-discrimination*.

Article 21(1) of the CFR states:

> Any discrimination based on any ground such as sex, race, colour, ethnic or social origin, genetic features, language, religion or belief, political or any other opinion, membership of a national minority, property, birth, disability, age or sexual orientation shall be prohibited.

This is in line with Recital 75 of the GDPR. Accordingly, algorithmic price discrimination could be problematic if the personalization of prices is based on one of the abovementioned criteria. Naturally, firms will ensure that algorithms will not be programmed based on these criteria in order to prevent direct discrimination. Yet, through ML, it is conceivable that based on indirect factors, the algorithm will lead to the same outcome.[246]

It is debatable to what extent anti-discrimination law can deal with algorithmic pricing. In short, there is no specific legal prohibition of price discrimination. As long as the algorithms behind the pricing mechanism do not vary or personalize prices based on the criteria expressly prohibited by human rights laws such as the CFR or the ECHR, there is no strong case for effective intervention based on anti-discrimination law. Concerning the EU non-discrimination law regime, Xenidis and Senden (2020) conclude that: "The legal framework seems to fall short in effectively tackling algorithmic discrimination on the consumption market because of its

2019-001 du 21 janvier 2019 prononçant une sanction pécuniaire à l'encontre de la société GOOGLE LLC. https://www.legifrance. gouv.fr/cnil/id/CNILTEXT000038032552/.

[243] Zuiderveen Borgesius and Poort (2017).

[244] Regulation (EU) 2024/1689 of the European Parliament and of the Council of 13 June 2024 laying down harmonised rules on artificial intelligence and amending Regulations (EC) No 300/2008, (EU) No 167/2013, (EU) No 168/2013, (EU) 2018/858, (EU) 2018/1139 and (EU) 2019/2144 and Directives 2014/90/EU, (EU) 2016/797 and (EU) 2020/1828 (Artificial Intelligence Act). https://eur-lex.europa.eu/legal-content/EN/TXT/?uri=CELEX:32024R1689. Referred to as "AI Act".

[245] Cfr. Section 3.6.2.4.

[246] Bock (2016).

limitation both in terms of protected grounds and areas that are excluded from its scope."[247]

It should be pointed out, however, that several regulations which prohibit some discriminatory elements of pricing, such as the Geo-Blocking Regulation[248] and Article 20 of the Services Directive[249] (i.e., discrimination based on nationality, place of residence, or place of establishment), have successfully been adopted by the EU. This demonstrates that there is room for development and that the scope of anti-discrimination law might be broadened in the future to eliminate unequal treatment on arbitrary bases.[250]

4.5.6 Contract Law

Contract law provides various ex-post remedies to address, *inter alia*, duress, fraud, undue influence,[251] misrepresentation, and unconscionable dealing. In particular, the latter case has been advocated as a useful remedy to tackle algorithmic pricing since the other doctrines do not seem to apply in the realm of price discrimination.[252] It is argued that *price unconscionability* should include price discrimination without a cost justification, whereby charging different prices to consumers based on their identity should be prohibited.[253] Nonetheless, this price unconscionability doctrine, which is also called the *theory of a just price* (*Iustum Pretium*), is regarded as a weak spot in the legal system.[254]

The legal doctrine of price unconscionability tries to counteract excessive forms of overpricing. A price is excessive when it is grossly disproportionate to the cost or value of the good or service received in exchange.[255] However, the practice of determining a just price has been abandoned because of its infeasibility.[256] Apart from the practical difficulties that come with deciding a just price, the doctrine requires that

---

[247] Xenidis and Senden (2020), p. 170.

[248] Regulation (EU) 2018/302 of the European Parliament and of the Council of 28 February 2018 on addressing unjustified geo-blocking and other forms of discrimination based on customers' nationality, place of residence, or place of establishment within the internal market and amending Regulations (EC) No 2006/2004 and (EU) 2017/2394 and Directive 2009/22/EC. https://eur-lex.europa.eu/legal-content/EN/TXT/?uri=celex% 3A32018R0302.

[249] Directive 2006/123/EC of the European Parliament and of the Council of 12 December 2006 on services in the internal market. https://eur-lex.europa.eu/eli/dir/2006/123/oj.

[250] Chapdelaine (2020), p. 32.

[251] The role of undue influence is analyzed in more depth in the context of the UCPD, see Sect. 3.6.2.2.

[252] Klock (2002); Miller (2014), p. 69.

[253] Klock (2002), p. 367.

[254] Klock (2002), p. 338.

[255] Darr (1994).

[256] Zimmermann (1996), pp. 255–270.

there must be a case of grossly disproportionate overcharging. Historically, the threshold that could be found in Roman law was the *laesio enormis*, whereby the buyer was overcharged for 100% of the price. This idea of gross discrepancies remained the guiding principle when determining the degree of unfairness in pricing.[257]

In the case of algorithmic pricing, this grossly disproportionate overcharging does not seem to be applicable, especially considering the sophistication and subtlety of the pricing mechanism. Regulating algorithmic pricing based on the price unconscionability doctrine would, therefore, be based on a fragile foundation.[258]

Instead of looking at substantive fairness (i.e., the price), the procedural notion of *contractual justice theory* could play a role by looking at how the price came about (i.e., procedural fairness).[259] However, procedural fairness in contract law is limited to contract formation and the outcome, which do not encompass the root cause of algorithmic pricing, that is, the collection and processing of personal data. This is part of data protection law and the doctrines of private law seem to be deficient in this context.[260] Contract law needs revisitation to safeguard consumers' autonomy, remedy inequality in the bargaining process, and encapsulate the notion of fairness, in the face of the challenges that algorithmic pricing brings.[261] However, in its current form, contract law fall short of providing a meaningful solution.

4.5.7 *Digital Regulation*

The DSA is mainly relevant to the advertising part of personalized marketing, and, therefore, it has been discussed in depth in Sect. 3.6.2.3 of Chap. 3. The term algorithmic pricing, or pricing in general, is not mentioned once in the DSA.[262] Nevertheless, one specific part of the DSA seems to be applicable to algorithmic pricing, namely the obligations for providers of online platforms to ensure recommender system transparency. According to Article 27, they need to "set out in their terms and conditions, in plain and intelligible language, the main parameters used in their recommender systems, as well as any options for the recipients of the service to modify or influence those main parameters." Due to the inextricable relationship between advertising and pricing, it is plausible to assume that the pricing

[257] Eidenmüller (2015).

[258] Wagner and Eidenmüller (2019), pp. 589–590.

[259] Alper (2022).

[260] Alper (2022).

[261] Alper (2022); Golobardes (2022).

[262] Recital 23 mentions the word "price", but in a different context (the interplay between liability and authority).

dimension will be reflected in the parameters that need to be disclosed. Especially since the ranking of recommendations is primarily revenue-driven. Although it is not evident that all vital information on pricing will be displayed, it does help to explain to consumers how information is prioritized and what roles profiling and their online behavior play.[263]

In addition to the requirements of Article 27, VLOPs and VLOSEs are required to offer at least one option in their recommender system that is not based on profiling pursuant to Article 38. This will allow consumers to choose non-personalized alternatives. Accordingly, consumers are provided with more information about the algorithmic mechanism behind the recommender system, allowing them to select and modify their preferred option at any time. This induces AI-system accountability.

Nonetheless, the fact that this information is placed in the general terms and conditions makes it dubious to what extent consumers will be effectively aided in their decision-making process. In particular, with the existing challenges of mandated disclosures in mind.[264] In addition, this provision only targets recommender systems and covers only a fraction of the occasions in which personalized prices will be displayed.

In the realm of algorithmic pricing, the DMA is also applicable.[265] The opt-in option discussed in the DMA[266] offers a safeguard against consumer profiling since consumers can choose a less personalized but comparable option. In this way, consumer exploitation through, *inter alia*, algorithmic pricing can be limited.[267] In addition, pricing transparency is promoted by allowing advertisers and publishers to request access to the gatekeepers' performance-measuring tools.,[268] which include the methods with which prices, fees, and remunerations are calculated.[269]

Furthermore, self-preferencing by the gatekeeper is counteracted by requiring it to apply transparent, fair, and non-discriminatory conditions to its activities, including the pricing conditions.[270] However, it must be noted that the provisions seem to be aimed at avoiding gatekeepers' self-preferencing on their core platform services through ranking and related indexing and crawling.[271]

In short, the DMA makes significant efforts to improve the position of consumers vis-à-vis gatekeepers. However, for the sake of addressing algorithmic pricing, its contribution is limited. Transparency and consumer choice are certainly

---

[263] Recital 70 DSA.

[264] See for an extensive analysis of the failure of mandated disclosure Ben-Shahar and Schneider (2014).

[265] For an elaborate analysis of the DMA, see Sect. 3.6.2.3.

[266] Recitals 36 and 37 DMA.

[267] Petit (2021), p. 536.

[268] Article 6(8) DMA.

[269] Recital 45 and Article 5(9) and (10).

[270] Recitals 61 and 62, and Article 6(5), (11), and (12).

[271] Bougette et al. (2022); Peitz (2022), pp. 6–13.

enhanced; however, the DMA is far from being a panacea for the harms identified with algorithmic pricing. Besides, non-gatekeepers can also undertake algorithmic pricing, which further limits the DMA's scope of application. Nevertheless, the DMA can work in a complementary manner to the UCPD, whereby UCPD provisions are applied concurrently by covering the types of platforms or practices not regulated by the DMA.[272]

Finally, since AI is the driving force behind algorithmic pricing, the AI Act needs to be discussed. As became clear from Chap. 3,[273] the AI Act will likely not provide significant additional safeguards against the identified harms of personalization, including algorithmic pricing. It can be a useful complement to the UCPD, which could benefit enforcement; however, the lack of guidance on cross-sectoral interpretation and case law results in legal uncertainty.[274]

It is noteworthy, however, that Article 5(1)(b) of the AI Act prohibits AI systems that exploit vulnerabilities which arise due to age, disability, and a specific social or economic situation. The latter part is of particular interest in the context of algorithmic pricing, because it would mean that exploitative AI-driven pricing techniques could be tackled. Nevertheless, as is the case with the UCPD, which is also meant to deal with multi-dimensional forms of vulnerability,[275] it is unclear to what extent the provision can address systematic digital vulnerability[276] that plagues the personalized marketing context, including algorithmic pricing.

As Goanta (2024) describes it:

> As a result, vulnerability ought to be freed from traditional legal classifications such as those used in the wording of the AI Act, to reflect a digital reality where any individual, of any age and in any circumstance can be vulnerable against a commercial surveillance system.[277]

Hence, although the AI Act does provide a useful starting point to combat the exploitation of consumers through AI-based technologies, further guidance and case law is needed to see to what extent it can improve the protection of consumers' interests.

[272] European Commission (2022), p. 83.

[273] See Sect. 3.6.2.3.

[274] Goanta (2024), p. 87.

[275] European Commission (2021), section 2.6.

[276] See Sect. 2.4.1.

[277] Goanta (2024), pp. 83–84.

4.5.8 Current State of Affairs

Data-driven technologies provide opportunities not only to sellers but also to consumers. Yet, the degree to which technological tools and market-based solutions can sufficiently assist consumers in protecting themselves against algorithmic pricing remains questionable.

Competition law necessitates a broad interpretation of Article 102(c) TFEU to tackle algorithmic pricing. Currently, relevant case law is missing, and the CJEU still needs to provide guidance. If the scope of Article 102(c) would be extended to exploitative harms to final consumers, competition law could be useful. In addition, if fairness considerations are also considered in the analysis, the case for effective intervention becomes stronger. In its current state, however, competition law does not seem to be the most suitable instrument to challenge algorithmic pricing.

Consumer protection law has the great advantage that the element of market power, which is necessary for competition law, is irrelevant for interventions. Consumer protection could, therefore, target all companies that employ algorithmic pricing. However, based on the UCPD, there is no *per se* prohibition on price discrimination and, thus, neither on algorithmic pricing. Algorithmic pricing could only be classified as unfair under the UCPD when there is (1) a lack of transparency regarding the communication of the price mechanism to consumers or (2) the pricing mechanism leads to an unfair commercial practice. The legal analysis shows that this will be difficult to prove, thereby reducing the rigor of the UCPD as a tool to address the practice of algorithmic pricing.

Data protection law is an essential complement to consumer protection law. Data protection law emphasizes the roles of transparency, legitimacy, and accountability. However, as long as consumers' consent can easily be obtained, algorithmic pricing can take place without hindrance.

Human rights law can regulate cases that deal with overt forms of discrimination against individuals based on categories protected by law. Its relevance to algorithmic price discrimination, which in principle is based on the profiling of consumer characteristics that are not subject to a specific prohibition, is severely limited.[278]

Contract law provides various ex-post remedies to address, *inter alia*, duress, fraud, undue influence, misrepresentation, and unconscionable dealing. It is asserted that price unconscionability doctrine could be used to tackle algorithmic pricing. Yet, the doctrine is only useful to combat excessive forms of overpricing. The same lack of aptness applies for an appeal to procedural unfairness. Therefore, contract law is likely unfit to address algorithmic pricing.

Digital regulations have a positive effect on increasing transparency and accountability; however, the extent to which they effective enhance consumer protection vis-à-vis companies that employ algorithmic pricing is limited.

Based on the current state of affairs, it can be concluded that the current legal framework is providing only a partially functional approach to address algorithmic

---

[278] Xenidis and Senden (2020), p. 170.

pricing.[279] Therefore, additional legal remedies are needed to protect consumers adequately and effectively against exploitation.

4.6 Conclusion

AI is transforming the theoretical case of perfect price discrimination into a reality. Personalized consumer profiles can be generated and subsequently prices that approximate consumers' maximum WTP with ever-improving accuracy can be offered. The conditions for successful price discrimination can be readily fulfilled under algorithmic pricing. Combined with other marketing techniques, such as personalized offers and targeted advertising, algorithmic pricing is expected to work even more effectively.

The economic analysis of algorithmic pricing demonstrated that from an efficiency perspective, under competitive market conditions, the practice can lead to efficiency benefits. From an equity perspective, however, algorithmic pricing will most likely cause adverse effects and be detrimental to consumer welfare. Moreover, several ethical concerns can be raised, such as risks of discrimination, social sorting, pricing unfairness, weakened bargaining power, and privacy intrusion. Accordingly, there is an equity-efficiency trade-off that pervades algorithmic pricing. Therefore, the need for legal intervention depends on the relative weights given to the concepts of efficiency and justice in the social welfare function.

Due to the various equity and ethical concerns accompanying algorithmic pricing, a cogent argument can be made that the regulatory avenue should be explored. The analysis of the current legal framework shows that it falls short of providing an adequate approach to tackle algorithmic pricing. Accordingly, additional appropriate remedies are needed to protect consumers' autonomy, equity, and welfare.[280]

References

Acquisti A, Varian HR (2005) Conditioning prices on purchase history. Mark Sci 24(3):367–381

Acquisti A, Taylor C, Wagman L (2016) The economics of privacy. J Econ Lit 54:442–492

Adaval R, Wyer RS Jr (2011) Conscious and nonconscious comparisons with price anchors: effects on willingness to pay for related and unrelated products. J Mark Res 48(2):355–365

Aghion P, Jones BF, Jones CI (2019) Artificial intelligence and economic growth. In: Agrawal A, Gans J, Goldfarb A (eds) The economics of artificial intelligence: an agenda. University of Chicago Press, Chicago, pp 237–282

---

[279] Van Heusden (2023).

[280] While the public choice dynamics that challenge the enactment of regulation for algorithmic pricing, or personalized marketing more broadly, fall outside the scope of this study, they represent an important area for future research. The relevance of regulation and proposals for its implementation are discussed further in Chap. 7.

Akman P (2009) Exploitative abuse in article 82EC: Back to basics? Camb Yearb Eur Leg Stud 11:1–37

Albæk S (2013) Consumer welfare in EU competition policy. In: Aims and Values in Competition Law. DJØF Publishing, pp 67–88

Alper G (2022) Contract law revisited: algorithmic pricing and the notion of contractual fairness. Comput Law Secur Rev 47:105741. https://doi.org/10.1016/j.clsr.2022.105741

Anderson ET, Simester DI (2010) Price stickiness and customer antagonism. Q J Econ 125:729–765

Armstrong M (2006) Recent developments in the economics of price discrimination. In: Blundell R, Newey WK, Persson T (eds) Advances in economics and econometrics: theory and applications, ninth world congress. Cambridge University Press, Cambridge, pp 97–141

Armstrong M, Vickers J (2001) Competitive price discrimination. RAND J Econ 32(4):579–605

Assad S, Clark R, Ershov D, Xu L (2024) Algorithmic pricing and competition: empirical evidence from the German retail gasoline market. J Polit Econ 132(3):1–49

Autoriteit Consument & Markt (ACM) (2020) Leidraad bescherming online consument. ACM. https://www.acm.nl/sites/default/files/documents/2020-02/acm-leidraad-bescherming-online-consument.pdf

Bar-Gill O (2012) Seduction by contract: law, economics and psychology in consumer markets. Oxford University Press, Oxford

Bar-Gill O (2018) Algorithmic price discrimination: when demand is a function of both preferences and (mis)perceptions. Univ Chicago Law Rev 86(2):1–30

Beckert W, Smith H, Takahashi Y (2015) Competitive price discrimination in a spatially differentiated intermediate goods market. Int J Ind Organ 25(5):884–907

Ben-Shahar O, Schneider CE (2014) More than you wanted to know: the failure of mandated disclosure. Princeton University Press, Princeton

Bock C (2016) Preserve personal freedom in networked societies. Nature 537(7618):9

Borden NH (1964) The concept of the marketing mix. J Advert Res 4(2):2–7

Bougette P, Budzinski O, Marty F (2022) Self-preferencing and competitive damages: a focus on exploitative abuses. Antitrust Bull 67(2):190–207

Bujlow T, Carela-Español V, Solé-Pareta J, Barlet-Ros P (2015) Web tracking: mechanisms, implications, and defenses. arXiv:1507.07872, 1–29

Calabresi G (1980) An exchange about law and economics: a letter to Dworkin. J Leg Stud 9(2):553–562

Calvano E, Calzolari G, Denicolò V, Harrington JE Jr, Pastorello S (2020a) Protecting consumers from collusive prices due to AI. Science 370(6520):1040–1042

Calvano E, Calzolari G, Denicolò V, Pastorello S (2020b) Artificial intelligence, algorithmic pricing, and collusion. Am Econ Rev 110(10):3267–3297

Chapdelaine P (2020) Algorithmic personalized pricing. New York Univ J Law Bus 17(1):1–48

Chen L, Mislove A, Wilson C (2016) An empirical analysis of algorithmic pricing on Amazon Marketplace. In: Proceedings of the 25th International Conference on World Wide Web, pp 1339–1349

Chen M, Chen ZL (2015) Recent developments in dynamic pricing research: multiple products, competition, and limited demand information. Prod Oper Manag 24(5):704–731

Chen N, Gallego G (2019) Welfare analysis of dynamic pricing. Manag Sci 65(1):139–151

Chen Z, Choe C, Matsushima N (2020) Competitive personalized pricing. Manag Sci 66(9):4003–4023

Choe P, Wu J (2015) Customer perceptions toward dynamic pricing for wireless data service. Int J Mob Commun 13(2):172–187

Christl W, Kopp K, Riechert PU (2017) Corporate surveillance in everyday life. Cracked Labs 6(1):1–93

Clifford S (2012) Shopper alert: Price may drop for you alone. New York Times. https://www.nytimes.com/2012/08/10/business/supermarkets-try-customizing-prices-for-shoppers.html

Cockburn IM, Henderson R, Stern S (2019) The impact of artificial intelligence on innovation. In: Agrawal A, Gans J, Goldfarb A (eds) The economics of artificial intelligence: an agenda. University Chicago Press, Chicago, pp 115–152

Commission Nationale de l'Informatique et des Libertés (CNIL), Direction Générale de la Concurrence, de la Consommation et de la Répression des Fraudes (DG CCRF) (2014) «IP Tracking» : conclusions de l'enquête conjointe menée par la CNIL and la DGCCRF. Ministère de l'Économie, des Finances et de la Souveraineté industrielle et numérique. https://www.economie.gouv.fr/files/files/directions_services/dgccrf/presse/communique/2014/cp_tracking_27012014.pdf

Conitzer V, Taylor CR, Wagman L (2012) Hide and seek: costly consumer privacy in a market with repeat purchases. Mark Sci 31(2):277–292

Consumers International & Mozilla Foundation (2022) A consumer investigation into personalised pricing. Consumers International. https://www.consumersinternational.org/media/369078/personalised_pricing_15_02_2022.pdf

Darr FP (1994) Unconscionability and price fairness. Hous Law Rev 30(5):1819–1862

Davenport T, Guha A, Grewal D, Bressgott T (2020) How artificial intelligence will change the future of marketing. J Acad Mark Sci 48(1):24–42

De Geest G (2018) Rents: how marketing causes inequality. Beccaria Books, Leuven

Dethmers F, Blondeel J (2017) EU enforcement policy on abuse of dominance: some statistics and facts. Eur Compet Law Rev 38(4):147–164

Dewan R, Jing B, Seidmann A (2003) Product customization and price competition on the Internet. Manag Sci 49(8):1055–1070

Edwards MA (2006) Price and prejudice: the case against consumer equality in the information age. Lewis Clark Law Rev 10(3):559–596

Eidenmüller H (2015) Justifying fair price rules in contract law. Eur Rev Contract Law 11(3):220–228

Ellison G, Ellison SF (2009) Search, obfuscation, and price elasticities on the internet. Econometrica 77(2):427–452

Esteves RB, Resende J (2019) Personalized pricing and advertising: who are the winners? Int J Ind Organ 63:239–282

European Commission (2016) Consumer market study on online market segmentation through personalised pricing/offers in the European Union (Report No. Request for specific services 2016 85 02 for the implementation of framework Contract EAHC/2013/CP/04, final report). Publications Office of the European Union. https://op.europa.eu/en/publication-detail/-/publication/ed9ce056-c2cf-11e8-9424-01aa75ed71a1/language-en

European Commission (2021) Commission Notice: Guidance on the Interpretation and Application of Directive 2005/29/EC of the European Parliament and of the Council Concerning Unfair Business-to-consumer Commercial Practices in the Internal Market. https://eur-lex.europa.eu/legal-content/EN/TXT/?uri=CELEX%3A52021XC1229%2805%29

European Commission (2022) Behavioural study on unfair commercial practices in the digital environment: Dark patterns and manipulative personalization (Final report). Publications Office of the European Union. https://op.europa.eu/en/publication-detail/-/publication/606365bc-d58b-11ec-a95f-01aa75ed71a1/language-en

European Data Protection Board (EDPB) (2019) Guidelines 2/2019 on the processing of personal data under Article 6(1)(b) GDPR in the context of the provision of online services to data subjects (Version 2.0). EDPB. https://www.edpb.europa.eu/sites/default/files/files/file1/edpb_guidelines-art_6-1-b-adopted_after_public_consultation_en.pdf

Ezrachi A (2017) Sponge. J Antitrust Enforc 5(1):49–75

Ezrachi A, Stucke ME (2016) The rise of behavioural discrimination. Eur Compet Law Rev 37(2):485–492

Faruqui A, Palmer J (2011) Dynamic pricing and its discontents. Regulation 34(3):16–23

Faruqui A, Sergici S (2010) Household response to dynamic pricing of electricity: a survey of 15 experiments. J Regul Econ 38(2):193–225

Fehr E, Schmidt KM (1999) A theory of fairness, competition, and cooperation. Q J Econ 114(3):817–868
Foxall G (1972) A descriptive theory of pricing for marketing. Eur J Mark 6(3):190–194
Gabaix X, Laibson D (2006) Shrouded attributes, consumer myopia, and information suppression in competitive markets. Q J Econ 121(2):505–540
Gale BT, Swire DJ (2006) Value-based marketing & pricing. J Prof Pricing 15(3):30–33
Galli F (2022) Algorithmic marketing and EU law on unfair commercial practices. Springer Nature, Cham
Garbarino E, Lee OF (2003) Dynamic pricing in internet retail: effects on consumer trust. Psychol Mark 20(6):495–513
Gesell LE, Farris MT (1992) Airline deregulation: an evaluation of goals and objectives. Transp Law J 21(1):105–128
Gijsbrechts E (1993) Prices and pricing research in consumer marketing: some recent developments. Int J Res Mark 10(2):115–151
Gil González E, De Hert P (2019) Understanding the legal provisions that allow processing and profiling of personal data: an analysis of GDPR provisions and principles. ERA Forum 2019(4):597–621
Goanta C (2024) Regulatory siblings: the unfair commercial practices directive roots of the AI act. In: Graef I, van der Sloot B (eds) The legal consistency of technology regulation in Europe. Hart Publishing, Oxford, pp 71–88
Golobardes MA (2022) Algorithmic personalization of consumer transactions and the limits of contract law. J Law Mark Innov 1(1):17–43
Graef I (2018) Algorithms and fairness: what role for competition law in targeting price discrimination towards end consumers. Colum J Eur Law 24(3):541–560
Grennan M (2013) Price discrimination and bargaining: empirical evidence from medical devices. Am Econ Rev 103(1):145–177
Grochowski M, Jabłonowska A, Lagioia F, Sartor G (2022) Algorithmic price discrimination and consumer protection: a digital arms race? Technol Regul:36–47
Guttentag MD (2019) Law and surplus: opportunities missed. Utah Law Rev 2019(3):607–660
Hacker P (2018) Teaching fairness to artificial intelligence: existing and novel strategies against algorithmic discrimination under EU law. Common Mark Law Rev 55(4):1143–1186
Hagen L, Uetake K, Yang N, Bollinger B, Chaney AJ, Dzyabura D, Zhu Y (2020) How can machine learning aid behavioral marketing research? Mark Lett 31(4):361–370
Hannak A, Soeller G, Lazer D, Mislove A, Wilson C (2014) Measuring price discrimination and steering on e-commerce websites. In: Proceedings of the 2014 Internet Measurement Conference, pp 305–318
Hausman JA, MacKie-Mason JK (1988) Price discrimination and patent policy. Rand J Econ 19(2):253–265
Haws KL, Bearden WO (2006) Dynamic pricing and consumer fairness perceptions. J Consum Res 33(3):304–311
Hayek FA (1944) Road to serfdom. University Chicago Press, Chicago
Heidhues P, Kőszegi B (2017) Naivete-based discrimination. Q J Econ 132(2):1019–1054
Helberger N, Lynskey O, Micklitz HW, Rott P, Sax M, Strycharz J (2021) EU consumer protection 2.0: structural asymmetries in digital consumer markets. Joint report from EUCP2.0 Project BEUC, pp 1–207
Helberger N, Sax M, Strycharz J, Micklitz HW (2022) Choice architectures in the digital economy: towards a new understanding of digital vulnerability. J Consum Policy 45(2):175–200
Ho YC, Ho YJ, Tan Y (2017) Online cash-back shopping: implications for consumers and e-businesses. Inf Syst Res 28(2):250–264
Hogan K (2018) Consumer experience in the retail renaissance: how leading brands build a bedrock with data. Deloitte Digital. https://www.deloittedigital.com/us/en/blog-list/2018/consumer-experience-in-the-retail-renaissance%2D%2Dhow-leading-brand.html

Huang KW (2010) Equilibrium market segmentation for targeted pricing based on customer characteristics. SSRN Electron J. https://doi.org/10.2139/ssrn.1292508
Huang MH, Rust RT (2018) Artificial intelligence in service. J Serv Res 21(2):155–172
Ingenbleek P, Debruyne M, Frambach R, Verhallen TM (2003) Successful new product pricing practices: a contingency approach. Mark Lett 14(4):289–305
Kahneman D, Knetsch JL, Thaler RH (1986) Fairness as a constraint on profit seeking: entitlements in the market. Am Econ Rev 76(4):728–741
Kalimo H, Majcher K (2017) The concept of fairness: linking EU competition and data protection law in the digital marketplace. Eur Law Rev 42(2):210–233
Kannan PK, Kopalle PK (2001) Dynamic pricing on the internet: importance and implications for consumer behavior. Int J Electron Commer 5(3):63–83
Kaplow L, Shavell S (1994) Why the legal system is less efficient than the income tax in redistributing income. J Leg Stud 23(2):667–681
Kaplow L, Shavell S (2001) Fairness versus welfare. Harv Law Rev 114(4):961–1389
Kienzler M, Kowalkowski C (2017) Pricing strategy: a review of 22 years of marketing research. J Bus Res 78(1):101–110
Klein B, Wiley JS Jr (2003) Competitive price discrimination as an antitrust justification for intellectual property refusals to deal. Antitrust Law J 70(3):599–642
Klock M (2002) Unconscionability and price discrimination. Tenn Law Rev 69(2):317–384
Lee F, Monroe KB (2008) Dynamic pricing on the internet: a price framing approach. In: Lee AY, Soman D (eds) Advances in consumer research, Duluth, pp 637–638
Levine ME (2002) Price discrimination without market power. Yale J Regul 19(1):1–36
Li T, Sethi SP, He X (2015) Dynamic pricing, production, and channel coordination with stochastic learning. Prod Oper Manag 24(6):857–882
Luzak JA (2014) Privacy notice for dummies? Towards European guidelines on how to give "clear and comprehensive information" on the cookies' use in order to protect the internet users' right to online privacy. J Consum Policy 37(4):547–559
Maggiolino M (2017) Personalized prices in European competition law. Bocconi Leg Stud Res Pap 2984840:1–24
Mahdawi A (2018) Is your friend getting a cheaper Uber fare than you are? The Guardian. https://www.theguardian.com/commentisfree/2018/apr/13/uber-lyft-prices-personalized-data
Markovits RS (2005) Why Kaplow and Shavell's double-distortion argument articles are wrong. Geo Mason Law Rev 13(3):511–620
Martin KD, Murphy PE (2017) The role of data privacy in marketing. J Acad Mark Sci 45(2):135–155
Mas-Colell A, Whinston MD, Green JR (1995) Microeconomic theory. Oxford University Press, New York
Mathis K (2009) Efficiency instead of justice? Searching for the philosophical foundations of the economic analysis of law. Springer, Dordrecht
McAfee RP (2008) Price discrimination. Issues Compet Law Policy 1:465–484
McCarthy J, Minsky ML, Rochester N, Shannon CE (2006) A proposal for the Dartmouth summer research project on artificial intelligence, August 31, 1955. AI Mag 27(4):12–14
McGill JI, Van Ryzin GJ (1999) Revenue management: research overview and prospects. Transp Sci 33(2):233–256
Mik E (2016) The erosion of autonomy in online consumer transactions. Law Innov Technol 8(1):1–38
Mikians J, Gyarmati L, Erramilli V, Laoutaris N (2012) Detecting price and search discrimination on the Internet. In: Proceedings of the 11th ACM Workshop on Hot Topics in Networks, pp 79–84
Mikians J, Gyarmati L, Erramilli V, Laoutaris N (2013) Crowd-assisted search for price discrimination in e-commerce: First results. In: Proceedings of the ninth ACM conference on Emerging networking experiments and technologies, pp 1–6

Miller AA (2014) What do we worry about when we worry about price discrimination the law and ethics of using personal information for pricing. J Technol Law Policy 19(1):41–104
Moriarty J (2021) Why online personalized pricing is unfair. Ethics Inf Technol 23(3):495–503
Morris MH (1987) Separate prices as a marketing tool. Ind Mark Manag 16(2):79–86
Motta M (2004) Competition policy: theory and practice. Cambridge University Press, Cambridge
Musolff L (2021) Algorithmic pricing facilitates tacit collusion: evidence from e-commerce. In: Proceedings of the 23rd ACM Conference on Economics and Computation, 2022 (EC '22):32–33
Nevo A, Wolfram C (2002) Why do manufacturers issue coupons? An empirical analysis of breakfast cereals. Rand J Econ 33(2):319–339
Newcomer E (2017) Uber starts charging what it thinks you're willing to pay. Bloomberg. https://www.bloomberg.com/news/articles/2017-05-19/uber-s-future-may-rely-on-predicting-how-much-you-re-willing-to-pay
Nilsson NJ (2009) The quest for artificial intelligence. Cambridge University Press, Cambridge
Nissenbaum H (2009) Privacy in context. Stanford University Press, Stanford
Nussbaum M, Sen A (1993) The quality of life. Clarendon Press, Oxford
O'Donoghue R, Padilla AJ (2013) The law and economics of Article 102 TFEU, 2nd edn. Hart, Oxford
Odlyzko A (2003) Privacy, economics, and price discrimination on the Internet. In: Proceedings of the 5th International Conference on Electron Commerce, pp 355–366
OECD (1993) Glossary of industrial organisation economics and competition law. Organisation for Economic Co-Operation and Development. https://www.oecd.org/regreform/sectors/2376087.pdf
OECD (2016) Price discrimination—Background note by the Secretariat. Org Econ Co-Oper Dev, Doc No. DAF/COMP(2016)15. https://one.oecd.org/document/DAF/COMP(2016)15/en/pdf
OECD (2018) Personalized pricing in the digital era—Background note by the Secretariat. Org Econ Co-Oper Dev, Doc No. DAF/COMP(2018)13. https://one.oecd.org/document/DAF/COMP(2018)13/en/pdf
Office of Fair Trading (OFT) (2013a) The economics of online personalized pricing. Crown, Doc No. OFT1488. https://docplayer.net/9529539-The-economics-of-online-personalised-pricing.html
Office of Fair Trading (OFT) (2013b) Personalized pricing: Increasing transparency to improve trust. OFT, Doc No. OFT1489. https://webarchive.nationalarchives.gov.uk/ukgwa/20140402165101/http:/oft.gov.uk/shared_oft/markets-work/personalised-pricing/oft1489.pdf
Okun AM (1975) Equality and efficiency: the big tradeoff. Brookings Inst, Washington, DC
Parisi F (2013) The language of law and economics. Cambridge Books, Cambridge
Pasquale F (2007) Technology, competition, and values. Minn J Law Sci Technol 8(1):607–622
Pasquale F (2015) The black box society. Harvard University Press, Cambridge
Pavlou PA, Liang H, Xue Y (2007) Understanding and mitigating uncertainty in online exchange relationships: a principal-agent perspective. MIS Q 31(1):105–136
Peitz M (2022) The prohibition of self-preferencing in the DMA. CERRE Issue Paper, 1–31
Petit N (2021) The proposed digital markets act (DMA): a legal and policy review. J Eur Compet Law Pract 12(7):529–541
Pigou A (1920) The economics of welfare. Macmillan, London
Polinsky AM (1989) An introduction to law and economics, 2nd edn. Little, Brown & Co, Boston
Poort J, Zuiderveen Borgesius FJ (2019) Does everyone have a price? Understanding people's attitude towards online and offline price discrimination. Internet Policy Rev 8(1):1–20
Posner RA (1979) Utilitarianism, economics, and legal theory. J Leg Stud 8(1):103–140
Posner RA (1981) The economics of justice. Harvard University Press, Cambridge, MA
Posner RA (1985) Wealth maximization revisited. Notre Dame J Law Ethics Public Policy 2(1):85–106
Posner RA (1990) The problems of jurisprudence. Harvard University Press, Cambridge

Rabin M (1993) Incorporating fairness into game theory and economics. Am Econ Rev 83(1):1281–1302
Rawls JB (1971) A theory of justice. Belknap Press, Cambridge
Rayna T, Darlington J, Striukova L (2015) Pricing music using personal data: mutually advantageous first-degree price discrimination. Electron Mark 25(2):139–154
Salop S, Stiglitz J (1977) Bargains and ripoffs: a model of monopolistically competitive price dispersion. Rev Econ Stud 44(3):493–510
Sanchez-Cartas JM, Katsamakas E (2022) Artificial intelligence, algorithmic competition, and market structures. IEEE Access 10:10575–10584
Schindler RM (2011) Pricing strategies: a marketing approach. Sage, Thousand Oaks
Schleusener M, Hosell S (2016) Expertise zum Thema "Personalisierte Preisdifferenzierung im Online-Handel." SVRV, Sachverständigenrat für Verbraucherfragen, pp 1–32
Schmalensee R (1981) Output and welfare implications of monopolistic third-degree price discrimination. Am Econ Rev 71(1):242–247
Schwartz M (1990) Third-degree price discrimination and output: generalizing a welfare result. Am Econ Rev 80(5):1259–1262
Seele P, Dierksmeier C, Hofstetter R, Schultz MD (2021) Mapping the ethicality of algorithmic pricing: a review of dynamic and personalized pricing. J Bus Ethics 170(4):697–719
Sen A (1985) Commodities and capabilities. Elsevier, Amsterdam
Shavell S (2009) Foundations of economic analysis of law. Harvard University Press, Cambridge, MA
Shiller B (2014) First degree price discrimination using big data. Brandeis University, Working Paper No. 58
Shiller B, Waldfogel J (2011) Music for a song: an empirical look at uniform pricing and its alternatives. J Ind Econ 59(4):630–660
Skouras T, Avlonitis GJ, Indounas KA (2005) Economics and marketing on pricing: how and why do they differ? J Prod Brand Manag 14(6):362–374
Strahilevitz L (2008) Reputation nation: law in an era of ubiquitous personal information. Northwest Univ Law Rev 102(4):1667–1738
Stucke ME, Ezrachi A (2018) Antitrust, algorithmic pricing, and tacit collusion. In: Barfield W, Pagallo U (eds) Research handbook on the law of artificial intelligence. Edward Elgar, Cheltenham, pp 1–24
Stuyck J (2010) Case C-484/08 Caja de Ahorros y Monte de Piedad de Madrid v Asociación de Usuarios de Servicios Bancarios (Ausbanc). Eur Rev Contract Law 6(4):449–459
Tan Y, Paul AA, Deng Q, Wei L (2017) Mitigating inventory overstocking: optimal order-up-to level to achieve a target fill rate over a finite horizon. Prod Oper Manag 26(11):1971–1988
Taylor CR (2004) Consumer privacy and the market for customer information. Rand J Econ 35(4):631–650
Tirole J (1988) The theory of industrial organization. MIT Press, Cambridge
Townley C, Morrison E, Yeung K (2017) Big data and personalized price discrimination in EU competition law. Yearb Eur Law 36(1):683–748
Turow J (2008) Niche envy: marketing discrimination in the digital age. MIT Press, Cambridge
Turow J, Feldman L, Meltzer K (2005) Open to exploitation: America's shoppers online and offline. Annenberg Public Policy Center, University Pennsylvania, pp 1–36
Valentino-DeVries J, Singer-Vine J, Soltani A (2012) Websites vary prices, deals based on users' information. Wall St J. https://www.wsj.com/articles/SB10001424127887323777204578189391813881534
Van den Bergh RJ (2017) Comparative competition law and economics. Edward Elgar, Cheltenham
Van Heusden A (2023) Algorithmic pricing: the current state of affairs from a law and economics perspective. InDret 2023(3):329–395
Van Loo R (2023) The public stakes of consumer law: the environment, the economy, health, disinformation, and beyond. Minn Law Rev 107(5):2039–2114
Varian HR (1980) A model of sales. Am Econ Rev 70(4):651–659

Varian HR (1985) Price discrimination and social welfare. Am Econ Rev 75(4):870–875

Varian HR (2009) Intermediate microeconomics: a modern approach, 8th edn. W. W. Norton & Company, New York

Wagner G, Eidenmüller H (2019) Down by algorithms: Siphoning rents, exploiting biases, and shaping preferences: Regulating the dark side of personalized transactions. Univ Chicago L Rev 86(2):581–610

Weisman DL, Kulick RB (2010) Price discrimination, two-sided markets, and net neutrality regulation. Tulane J Technol Intellect Prop 13(1):81–102

Weiss RM, Mehrotra AK (2001) Online dynamic pricing: efficiency, equity and the future of e-commerce. Va J Law Technol 6(2):1–12

Weisstein FL, Monroe KB, Kukar-Kinney M (2013) Effects of price framing on consumers' perceptions of online dynamic pricing practices. J Acad Mark Sci 41(5):501–514

Xenidis R, Senden L (2020) EU non-discrimination law in the era of artificial intelligence: mapping the challenges of algorithmic discrimination. In: Bernitz U, Groussot X, Paju J, De Vries SA (eds) General principles of EU law and the EU digital order. Kluwer Law International, Alphen aan den Rijn, pp 151–182

Xia L, Monroe KB, Cox JL (2004) The price is unfair! A conceptual framework of price fairness perceptions. J Mark 68(4):1–15

Xu Z, Dukes A (2019) Product line design under preference uncertainty using aggregate consumer data. Mark Sci 38(4):669–689

Zhang M, Bell P (2012) Price fencing in the practice of revenue management: an overview and taxonomy. J Revenue Pricing Manage 11(2):146–159

Zimmermann R (1996) The law of obligations: Roman foundations of the civilian tradition. Clarendon Press, Oxford

Zuboff S (2019) The age of surveillance capitalism: the fight for a human future at the new frontier of power. Profile Books, London

Zuiderveen Borgesius FJ, Poort J (2017) Online price discrimination and EU data privacy law. J Consum Policy 40(3):347–366

Chapter 5
Signing-Without-Reading Revisited: A Law and Economics Analysis of Personalized Contracting

Abstract The wave of personalization extends beyond pricing and advertising to encompass contractual terms, amplifying the unilateral imposition of terms on consumers. This chapter explores the phenomenon of personalized contracts, a novel aspect of algorithmic personalization in consumer transactions. The analysis evaluates the promises and perils of this practice, with particular attention to its exacerbation of the "signing-without-reading" problem inherent in standard-form contracts. The chapter further evaluates the adequacy of existing legal frameworks and assesses the necessity for additional regulatory measures.

5.1 Introduction

Contract law usually assumes that parties read contracts before signing them. In the real world, very few people do so.[1] This creates a strong incentive for self-interested contract drafters to insert one-sided terms. Apart from the fact that this leads to unfair outcomes, it also leads to economic inefficiencies and market distortions. This could clearly be seen in the financial markets during the financial crisis of 2007–2008. Consumer mortgages and loans were governed mainly by the terms imposed by financial firms. In the end, the terms turned out to be excessively onerous and unfair. After an extensive evaluation of the contracts, it was found that the financial industry was able to impose these one-sided terms because consumers were suffering from imbalances in bargaining power, information asymmetry, and a lack of resources vis-à-vis the financial institutions.[2]

Accepting standard forms has become a matter of seconds, and practically no one reads or understands the contents of the boilerplate when clicking "I agree". Accordingly, an incentive has been created for firms to impose one-sided terms

[1] De Geest (2016), p. 2.

[2] Melecky and Rutledge (2011), p. 2.

A. J. van Heusden, *The Law and Economics of Personalization*, Economic Analysis of Law in European Legal Scholarship 20,
https://doi.org/10.1007/978-3-032-01468-9_5

unilaterally and this phenomenon is widely acknowledged in existing literature.[3] However, the emergence of BDA has taken the unilateral imposition of terms to a higher level. By leveraging AI and ML, personalization of all phases of the market transaction has become possible, including the design of the contract terms. Personalization of contract terms is a new phenomenon that is part of the *algorithmic personalization of consumer transactions*.[4]

The wave of personalization covers the advertisement that a consumer sees,[5] the price that is subsequently presented,[6] and the transaction terms that govern the contractual relationship. In this sense, the complete consumer transaction cycle can be personalized.[7] Consequently, the contract terms can be modified by experimenting with the data collected concerning consumers' preferences, characteristics, behaviors, and relevant circumstances. This will allow for more precise tailoring of terms.

Through the personalization of contracts, consumers could be placed in a particularly vulnerable position without being aware of or understanding the consequences.[8] The vital difference with standard forms is that this time, it is not about signing standard forms that nobody reads with general consequences. It concerns signing contracts that have been specifically adapted to the individual and have personal consequences.[9]

In this chapter, a deeper look into personalized contracts will be taken. First, the concept of personalized contracts is further explored. Subsequently, the link will be made to standard-form contracts, and an economic analysis will be performed. This will provide more clarity concerning the merits of the practice. Thereafter, the legal framework will be investigated to see to what extent current EU law can provide safeguards against personalized contract terms. Finally, the conclusion of the analysis will be presented.

[3] See, for instance, the notable works by Marotta-Wurgler (2007); Marotta-Wurgler (2011); Marotta-Wurgler and Taylor (2013); Bakos et al. (2014); Marotta-Wurgler (2015).

[4] The term has been coined by Golobardes (2022).

[5] See Chap. 3.

[6] See Chap. 4.

[7] Golobardes (2022), pp. 20–21.

[8] Golobardes (2022), pp. 20–22.

[9] The concept of personalizing contracts is novel and upcoming. Examples of this practice are scarce, but for the sake of illustrating the latest developments, see Scholz (2018), Pitt (2019), Agarwal (2023).

5.2 Personalizing Contracts: A New Marketing Strategy

Personalization in marketing is taking place in a variety of ways. Two of the most prominent forms of personalization are AI-driven personalization of advertisements and prices.[10] First, the consumer's attention is caught by a specifically targeted ad that caters to the pre-existing needs of the consumer or stimulates the emergence of a need. In both cases, the ad takes into account the relevant context, the characteristics of the consumer, and past consumer behavior in order to successfully attract attention. After catching the eye of the consumer, a personalized price is offered that aims to approximate the reservation price of the consumer. Then, it is time to conclude the contract. Traditionally, a standardized contract would be presented to consumers, and a signature or simply clicking "I agree" would suffice to conclude the transaction. Standardization of contracts was an economically-efficient manner to serve large amounts of consumers within a short period of time. Drafting personalized contracts for each consumer would cost unreasonable amounts of time and be highly cost-ineffective. Nevertheless, big data has made this form of personalization less far-fetched. Not only can prices and advertisements be personalized, but it has also become possible to personalize contract terms on a large scale.[11]

It could be argued, however, that the personalization of contract terms is an archaic form of contract formation. As seen in street markets and high-end luxury stores, sellers personalize the offer depending on the person they are talking to. In this sense, one could say that personalized contracts in the digital age are not a new phenomenon. The crucial difference, however, is that the traditional style of personalization results from a negotiation between the seller and the buyer. AI-driven personalization of contracts, in contrast, is based on vast amounts of data collected about the consumer, which allows for highly sophisticated targeting. The terms that subsequently are incorporated into the contract are not the result of an interaction but of a unilateral effort. Essentially, the consumer concludes an *algorithmic contract*, which means that an algorithm determines the parties' obligations.[12] Personalized contracts are algorithmic because the algorithm chooses which terms to include and offer, bypassing the actual negotiation between the parties.[13]

Algorithmic personalization of contracts touches upon various "different phases of consumers participation in markets, including their choices, the standard terms included in their contracts, and the remedies they may be entitled to in case of a breach of contract".[14] The closest form of personalization that consumers are familiar with is personalized insurance contracts, in which the insurance premium

[10] See Chaps. 3 and 4 for an in-depth discussion on algorithmic pricing and advertisement personalization.

[11] Helberger (2016).

[12] Scholz (2017).

[13] Scholz (2017) explains that another form of algorithmic contracting entails using the algorithm as a gap-filler after the formation of the contract.

[14] Golobardes (2022), p. 27.

depends, *inter alia*, on where someone lives, personal characteristics, and information about the insured person's past behavior.[15]

Nevertheless, the digital age has opened the door for the development of more applications of personalization that are fueled by vast amounts of personal and behavioral data and performed by virtue of advanced AI-driven data analytics. It is, therefore, conceivable that in the coming years, further steps will be taken toward personalizing contract terms in contexts different from insurance. Crude forms of contract personalization are already visible in credit card, mortgage, and cell phone markets.[16] Additionally, sophisticated applications of algorithmic contracts have been found in high-speed trading, online pricing, and Ethereum smart contracting contexts.[17]

A practical example of personalizing terms in a consumer contract setting would be the implementation of different termination clauses for different consumers. That is to say, varying the dispute resolution instructions or limitation periods depending on the consumer's propensity to initiate a claim.[18]

It must be noted, however, that personalizing contract terms is an inherently different marketing strategy than personalizing prices, advertisements, or shopping experiences. For example, in the case of a personalized advertisement, one of the goals of personalization is to grab the consumer's attention, which is paramount in the attention economy of the digital age. However, based on the vast research on standard forms and the signing-without-reading problem, it is known that consumers do not pay attention to standard forms.[19] In this sense, the first question that pops up would be: Why would a marketer personalize contract terms?

At first glance, it could be argued that standard forms lower transaction costs by governing contract contingencies to which a consumer does not pay attention. Personalizing them would be costly and inefficient, thereby having little marketing value. Nonetheless, by taking a deeper look at the marketing strategy as a whole, it becomes clear why personalizing contract terms is attractive and could become more prevalent in the coming years. Accepting the contract and the corresponding terms is the last phase of consumers' shopping experience. From a marketing perspective, it could be argued that at this moment no further marketing efforts could be undertaken, apart from the aftersales services. This would, however, leave money on the table.

As has been extensively demonstrated by Bar-Gill (2012), it can be highly profitable for companies to vary the contents of a consumer contract.[20] This can be done

---

[15] Helberger (2016), p. 139.

[16] Bar-Gill (2012).

[17] Scholz (2017).

[18] Having the EU unfair terms regulation in mind, it could be argued that this is not possible since it would be to the detriment of the consumer. However, as this chapter will show, in particular Sect. 5.4.2, it is particularly onerous to prove that this personalization "service" is detrimental to the consumer without having a thorough understanding of the algorithms facilitating it.

[19] See, for example, Bakos et al. (2014).

[20] Bar-Gill (2012).

by adapting contract terms in a manner that offers short-term benefits to consumers while imposing significant long-term costs. By increasing perceived benefits and decreasing perceived costs, consumers can be seduced by contracts without providing actual benefits and lowering expenses. Bar-Gill (2012) showcases by virtue of three case studies—credit cards, mortgages, and cell phones—that incorporating behavioral insights and tailoring contracts to specific consumers can be a successful strategy to withstand competition and exploit consumer biases and misperceptions for financial gain.

To illustrate, financially myopic consumers can be attracted with teaser rates, whereby the long-term costs are hidden in the complex boilerplate.[21] It can be attractive for companies to invest in such contract innovations, which could be seen as *exploitative innovations* when *value-increasing innovations* (i.e., product improvement) do not offer a desirable return on investment.[22] For the sake of consumer protection, further attention is therefore warranted to explore the phenomenon of personalized contracts.

5.2.1 Personalized Contracts: An Exploration

The personalization of e-commerce is taking place at a fast pace, and it is extending beyond the standard marketing mix of product, price, place, and promotion.[23] Personalization techniques can be seen in recommender systems, shopping assistants, and information retrieval systems.[24] The personalization of contracts is a new extension that has received scant attention in existing literature.[25] The continuous increase in computing power and the developments in AI technologies have transformed the personalization of contracts from a theoretical scenario into a real-life possibility.[26] Although the personalization of contracts is far from common practice at the moment, it is expected that in the coming years, more companies will adopt this strategy, and a growing body of research will emerge.[27] A look into the potential consequences of this personalization strategy is therefore justified.

A personalized contract is:

> An agreement that is designed by the entrepreneur to match the individual characteristics, preferences, or situation of the consumer and gives, or is likely to give, him the impression that the relationship with the trader is based on trust and knowledge.[28]

---

[21] Bar-Gill (2012).

[22] Heidhues et al. (2016).

[23] Kaptein and Parvinen (2015), p. 8.

[24] Mik (2016), p. 19; Galli (2022).

[25] Exceptions are the works by Południak-Gierz (2019), Południak-Gierz (2020), Golobardes (2022).

[26] Południak-Gierz and Tereszkiewicz (2023).

[27] Kaptein and Parvinen (2015), p. 7.

[28] Południak-Gierz (2020).

The contract becomes personalized by selecting and adapting the terms or clauses based on the information that has been collected about a specific consumer. This means that consumers can be presented with different contracts for the same product and potentially the same price.[29]

In this chapter, the personalization of contracts refers to the personalization of the terms that would otherwise have been part of the standardized boilerplate.[30]

Although contractual safeguards exist, such as the UCTD,[31] that provide a minimum harmonized level of protection from which cannot be departed through differentiation, it cannot be ruled out that AI-driven personalization mechanisms can find compositions of terms that subtly fall through the cracks of the legal framework.[32] Such scenarios have also been demonstrated to be feasible in the realms of algorithmic pricing and personalized advertising.[33] In the context of personalized contracts, it is possible to think of experiments with language, cultural, and socioeconomic information that fall within the confines of the law but which will likely affect consumers. To illustrate, an agreeable and conflict-sensitive consumer could be deterred by the use of "hostile" language in the boilerplate, or the attention of a money-conscious consumer could be attracted by terms that highlight the financial benefits and downplay the non-financial aspects. The promise and peril of AI-driven contract personalization is that the possibilities to modify the contract are infinite.[34]

In the case of personalized contracts, the contractual relationship between the trader and the consumer is characterized by a deepened asymmetry of information. On the one hand, the trader disposes of vast amounts of information about the consumer and applies advanced BDA to process the data. In this way, an accurate consumer profile can be made, leading to a situation whereby traders have all the relevant information about consumers to conduct the transaction in a manner that will maximize their own utility.[35] On the other hand, personalization is marketed in a way that convinces consumers that personalized contracts are made to match their desires, needs, and personal characteristics perfectly. Since the mechanism behind personalization is too complex to understand without further in-depth investigation on the part of the consumer, trust becomes of pivotal importance. Consumers need to trust that the contract will match their preferences. If consumer preferences are

---

[29] Schulte-Nölke et al. (2013) show that discrimination by virtue of contractual term diversification has already been taking place for many years between national and international consumers. The developments in AI have opened the door for significantly more advanced forms of targeting and discrimination that are not constrained by borders.

[30] For an in-depth discussion of the personalization of the main contract terms (i.e., the price), see Chap. 4.

[31] Council Directive 93/13/EEC of 5 April 1993 on unfair terms in consumer contracts. https://eur-lex.europa.eu/legal-content/EN/TXT/?uri=celex%3A31993L0013. Referred to as the "UCTD".

[32] This will be further discussed in Sect. 5.4.

[33] See Chaps. 3 and 4.

[34] Południak-Gierz and Tereszkiewicz (2023).

[35] The practice of profiling has been discussed in more depth in Chaps. 3 and 4. For an extensive discussion of profiling as a practice, see Gunter (2016).

matched, there is no pertinent threat; however, in case of a systemic mismatch or preference shaping, the market failure of information asymmetry can be exploited by the contract provider.[36]

Personalized contracts can be distinguished based on three factors: (1) The ability to change terms that would otherwise have been standardized; (2) the presence of a deepened information asymmetry with a superior knowledge on the seller's side; (3) a vital role for trust on the side of consumers to compensate for the lack of information. Noteworthy, the distinctive features of personalized contracts do not make them a new type of contract. They are the result of data-driven technologies that allow for the individualization of otherwise standardized terms. Personalized contracts can, therefore, be regarded as a new contractual model of standardized contracts.[37]

5.2.2 *Exploitative Contracting*

Personalized contracts are a new manifestation of standard-form contracts. The question that subsequently arises is: What makes personalized contracts different in terms of their impact on consumers' welfare compared to standardized contracts? The challenge posed by personalized contracts lies in their power to exploit, which is far greater than in the case of standard-form contracts. Large amounts of personal and behavioral data need to be collected to personalize contracts. With the power of AI, it becomes possible to process and analyze the data in a manner that accurately profiles consumers and exposes their vulnerabilities. The strategic behavior that aims to exploit these vulnerabilities is called *exploitative contracting*.[38]

In economics, a contract is exploitative when "the economically central considerations driving it derive from trying to profit from the agent's mistake, and other considerations or constraints are nonexistent, not binding, or not central."[39] This corresponds to the legal definition, which states that contracts are exploitative when a party utilizes its strategic advantage vis-à-vis the counterparty to influence the formation of a contract.[40] Due to the increasing use of AI technologies, recognizing vulnerabilities and finding exploitative opportunities will become more feasible. The collection of vast amounts of data creates a considerable information asymmetry, reinforcing companies' strategic advantage vis-à-vis consumers. Several economic studies demonstrate, both theoretically and empirically, that companies can maximize their expected utility by tailoring their contracts in manners that exploit

[36] Południak-Gierz (2020), p. 1012.

[37] Południak-Gierz (2020), p. 1018.

[38] Hacker (2017).

[39] Kőszegi (2014), p. 1104.

[40] Bigwood (2003).

the biases and heuristics of their customers.[41] This does not mean, however, that all personalized contracts will be exploitative. A contract would only be exploitative when it specifically targets cognitive weaknesses and has a negative expected value for the consumer.[42] Examples of this type of contract can be seen in a variety of markets, including cell phone,[43] credit card,[44] mortgage,[45] lending,[46] retail banking,[47] and fitness club markets.[48] These contracts can be distinguished into two categories: contracts that capitalize on consumers' false beliefs about the contents (e.g., hidden fees in credit card contracts) or contracts that leverage consumers' false beliefs about their future behavior under the contract (e.g., gym memberships exploiting the overestimation bias).[49]

Companies have an economic incentive to set strategic rationality traps in their contracts.[50] Firms can then systematically exploit both the structural and idiosyncratic behavioral biases and vulnerabilities of consumers. This could, for example, be done by increasing the complexity of the contract, which impedes the correct assessment of the long-term effects, experimenting with saliency, or playing on the insufficient willpower of the consumer. This is particularly the threat in algorithmically personalized contracts where the vulnerability of consumers is greater "given that, in addition to the informational and bargaining imbalances inherent to consumer contracts, it is difficult if not impossible to assess the configuration, implications, and effects of these personalised contracts for consumer welfare."[51]

Consequently, it has become clear that personalized contracting is opening the door to exploitative contracting, which is "not merely a theoretical concern, but a practical peril arising in situations of data driven informational asymmetry about personal preferences or behaviour in many important consumer markets."[52]

[41] Kőszegi (2014); Grubb (2015); Akerlof and Shiller (2015); Heidhues et al. (2016).
[42] Hacker (2017), p. 270.
[43] Bar-Gill (2012).
[44] Shui and Ausubel (2004); Heidhues and Kőszegi (2010); Bar-Gill (2012).
[45] Shui and Ausubel (2004); Heidhues and Kőszegi (2010); Bar-Gill (2012).
[46] Hawkins (2016).
[47] Willis (2013).
[48] DellaVigna and Malmendier (2006).
[49] Kőszegi (2014), p. 1104.
[50] Wagner and Eidenmüller (2019).
[51] Golobardes (2022), pp. 28–29.
[52] Hacker (2017), p. 272.

5.2.3 *Marketing Personalized Contracts*

Another factor that will exacerbate the signing-without-reading problem of personalized contracts is marketing. Specifically, sellers with a strong brand reputation can make consumers more willing to click "I agree" to a personalized contract. A prominent example of the power of branding is Apple. Apple has one of the most one-sided and ingenious rights-deletion schemes of all companies.[53] Despite this, the brand's popularity is sky-high, and the brand's financial value has been continuously increasing. It is conceivable that a client who appreciates the brand will be more inclined to accept the personalized contract in comparison with a brand that is unknown. *Brand equity* plays, therefore, a vital role in consumer transactions.[54]

Apart from branding, the role of market power is essential. It turned out that in the software industry, firms can impose one-sided terms because there are no realistic alternatives for certain platforms or applications.[55] If consumers believe no alternative is available, they do not even read the standard terms and feel compelled to accept the boilerplate.[56]

In the same manner that advertisements are tailored to consumers with messages that reinforce the idea that the offer has been specifically personalized to fit the buyer's needs, contracts could be promoted by stating that the contract has been designed to include the terms most beneficial to the consumer. To illustrate, a contract could personalize the payment method to attract consumers. If, from consumer profiling, it becomes clear that a specific consumer has limited disposable income, payment by installments could be made the default, which is attractive to the consumer in the short term but detrimental in the long term since it could lead to further debt accumulation. The personalized contract could then be considered to be a double-edged sword. On the one hand, it attracts the consumer's attention by satisfying the short-term preferences. On the other hand, it eventually benefits the seller by imposing costs on consumers in the long term. In the context of consumer credits, it has been found that such tailoring is already taking place.[57]

Likewise, contracts could be marketed to privacy-sensitive consumers as being specifically pro-privacy and targeted to their needs, which could draw their attention. However, this benefit to the consumer could be offset, perhaps overcompensated, by personalizing the less-salient terms to the benefit of the seller. For example, if from the data it can be inferred that this consumer is prone to complain, dispute resolution terms could be introduced that make seeking redress particularly onerous. It is then questionable to what extent the contract has been personalized to the consumer's benefit or detriment. Therefore, the desirability of personalized contracts is debatable and will be the subject of analysis in the next section.

---

53 Radin (2012), p. 86.

54 Fahy and Jobber (2015), chapter 6.

55 Braucher (2007), p. 19.

56 Howells (2005), p. 358.

57 Bar-Gill (2012).

5.3 Economic Analysis of Standard-Form Contracts

Personalized contracts are a relatively new phenomenon, and scant research has been conducted to discuss their merits. Although several studies have partly touched upon the desirability of personalized contracts, an in-depth analysis is missing. In this chapter, it is argued that personalized contracts are, in their essence, a new variation of the standard-form contractual model, as is known in existing literature. An economic analysis of standard-form contracts can, therefore, be particularly insightful in discussing the desirability of personalized contracts.[58] In this section, standard forms will be analyzed by reviewing what the existing law and economics approaches to consumer law[59] postulate about unfair contract terms and the prevalence of one-sidedness in standard forms. Consequently, the findings from the economic analysis of standard forms can be extrapolated to the realm of personalized contracts.

5.3.1 *Traditional Law and Economics Perspective*

The term traditional law and economics encompasses the neoclassical economic paradigm complemented with insights from information economics.[60] According to the neoclassical view, the standardization of contracts is welcomed based on the efficiency benefits it generates. Neoclassical economics asserts that interfirm competition and reputation concerns will ensure that efficient terms will be offered in the market, that is to say, terms that maximize the mutual benefits of the buyer and the seller.[61] Besides, it postulates that the voluntary nature of the exchange guarantees that parties will negotiate efficient terms, resulting in larger potential profits for both parties.[62]

Nevertheless, the use of standard terms has attracted harsh criticism due to its lack of actual assent. The *take-it-or-leave-it* nature of standard terms indicates that the seller has an inequitable degree of control over the bargaining process. For this reason, standard-form contracts have been referred to as *contracts of adhesion* as early as the 1940s.[63] However, neoclassical economics has responded to this criticism by positing three primary economic defenses. First, the standardization of contracts has led to substantial cost savings. Rather than drafting up individual terms for each contract separately, one boilerplate can be created that applies to all transactions. As a result, there is a sizeable decrease in negotiation costs and contract

[58] Van Heusden (2020).

[59] Based on Chap. 2.

[60] See, for a full elaboration on the traditional approach, Sect. 2.2.1.

[61] Luth (2010), p. 133.

[62] Posner and Rosenfield (1977), p. 89.

[63] Kessler (1943).

drafting costs. Consequently, lower transaction costs lead to lower prices, ultimately benefiting the consumer.[64]

Second, it could be argued that the pricing mechanism will inform consumers about the degree of quality of contract terms since high-quality contracts will be offered for premium prices. In contrast, low-quality contracts will be offered for low prices.[65] This puts a strong emphasis on the pricing mechanism in the market for the sake of information provision.[66]

Third, due to competitive pressure, firms are induced to draft terms that correspond to consumers' preferences. In this way, through the dynamic competition process, entrepreneurial discovery contributes to a more efficient (not perfect) resource allocation.[67] Correspondingly, if most firms offer low-quality contract terms because they want to exploit consumers, the entrepreneurial profitability of doing the same diminishes. Instead, entrepreneurs could see an opportunity to offer high-quality contract terms to cater to another group of consumers in the market that does value higher-quality terms. If the contractual needs of the consumers are not met adequately, the firm will lose clientele to a competitor.[68] This will contribute to the stabilization of contract quality in the market.

It could be argued, however, that the firm will be able to exploit the customers who do not read standard terms and, therefore, stay loyal to the firm. Nonetheless, neoclassical economics affirms that an *informed minority* of consumers that does read standard forms can discipline the market, albeit most consumers do not read the standard forms. Due to intense competition, firms cannot afford to lose the marginal consumer and solely retain inframarginal consumers.[69] In other words, the firm cannot lose term-conscious consumers who are willing to shop elsewhere if better terms are offered. Accordingly, firms will adopt efficient terms to retain marginal term-conscious consumers, which will also benefit the inframarginal term-unconscious consumers.[70] Thus, the informed minority can discipline the market, which leads to more efficient standard-term contracts.[71]

The ability of an informed minority to discipline the market depends on an implicit *duty to read,* which does not necessarily contradict neoclassical thought. The neoclassical perspective strongly emphasizes the freedom of contract principle. This principle offers parties the freedom to decide whether or not to enter a contract as they see fit. It is assumed that parties will only enter into a contract when it is mutually beneficial.[72] Applying this principle to standard terms, it could be argued

---

[64] Epstein (2008), p. 816.
[65] Wonnell (1985), p. 533.
[66] Hayek (1945).
[67] Wandel (2012), p. 51.
[68] Priest (1981), p. 1347.
[69] Hylton (2003), p. 3.
[70] Schwartz and Wilde (1978), p. 639.
[71] Goldman (1992), p. 716.
[72] Trebilcock (1997), pp. 15–22.

that buyers would not enter into a contract if the terms would be detrimental to their welfare. To determine the benefits of the terms, buyers have the duty to read the contract terms. If buyers assent to the contract, it automatically implies that they have read the terms and that the contract has been validly concluded.[73]

5.3.2 *Signing-Without-Reading*

The duty to read is an artificial construct. In the real world, very few people read the standard terms.[74] Nevertheless, even though buyers do not comply with their duty to read, it will be without prejudice to the assent covering all terms in the contract. Buyers will be bound to the contract, regardless of their actual contentment with the terms in the contract.[75] Therefore, the question arises as to why buyers do not "simply" read the terms before concluding the contract.

The decision to not read is economically justifiable and rational. Consumers make a rational cost-benefit analysis when they decide to read the terms or not. Reading standard forms is time-consuming, and given the concept of opportunity costs, time is money.[76] Standard forms are highly complex and lengthy, which increases the costs associated with reading them.[77] Besides, the boilerplate is basically offered on a take-it-or-leave-it basis, directly indicating to the consumer that further negotiation or examination is without merit.

It can be concluded that the consumer gains very little from reading the boilerplate, whereas it can generate significant transaction and opportunity costs.[78] Especially in the world of e-commerce, where products and services can be bought in a couple of minutes and consent can be given in a fraction of a second (clicking "I agree"), reading lengthy and complex boilerplates is burdensome.[79] It has been estimated that consumers would need to spend on average 8 h a day for 76 days per year to read the privacy policies of the websites that they visit.[80] Hence, consumers remain rationally ignorant because the costs of reading standard terms outweigh its benefits.

Accordingly, if there is *rational apathy* on the side of consumers, there is room for sellers to abuse it. To specify, firms could be incentivized to insert one-sided terms into a contract if they realize that consumers do not read the terms.[81] If the

[73] Rakoff (1983), p. 1190.
[74] De Geest (2016), p. 2.
[75] Barnett (2002), p. 635.
[76] Vandenberghe (2010), p. 88.
[77] Ayres and Schwartz (2014), pp. 549–550.
[78] Ben-Shahar (2009), p. 18.
[79] Hillman (2005a), pp. 840–842.
[80] Cranor (2012).
[81] De Geest (2016), p. 2.

firm conducts a high number of transactions, the insertion of one-sided terms, which redistribute wealth from the consumer to the seller, can be highly profitable.[82] Besides, firms will know that consumer shopping for alternative terms will not take place because that would mean that consumers need to incur even more transaction costs for the sake of comparing boilerplates.[83] Consequently, the abuse of rational apathy can take place on a market level.

5.3.3 The Insights from Information Economics

The information economics paradigm has complemented the neoclassical paradigm by emphasizing the role of information asymmetries. Information asymmetry leads to adverse selection on the boilerplate market, which can explain the one-sidedness of standard forms. A direct consequence of the signing-without-reading problem is that consumers lack essential information about the contract, which leads to the same market failures as in the case of asymmetric information regarding the quality of goods.[84] For a seller, the benefits of examining a contract term significantly outweigh the benefits that a consumer can gain. Thus, the seller will be better informed about the contract terms than the consumer.[85]

Consumers are unaware of the quality of the contract terms because they sign without reading. Thus, consumers will consider alternative product attributes, with price being the most prominent. Similar to the market for lemons, the competition will focus on price rather than quality.[86] Consequently, based on the premise that terms remain unobserved by consumers, the sellers' incentive to draft high-quality and consumer-friendly terms will disappear.[87] On an industry-wide level, the overall quality of standard-form contracts will go down for the sake of low-price competition, leading to a so-called *flea market situation*. In such a situation, competition for contract quality disappears. Consumers will be offered low prices but will be allocated the absolute minimum amount of rights.[88]

---

[82] Armstrong (2008), p. 120.

[83] Luth (2010), p. 143.

[84] Vandenberghe (2010), p. 88.

[85] Gillette (2011), p. 118.

[86] Akerlof (1970).

[87] Goldberg (1974), pp. 486–487.

[88] Schäfer and Leyens (2010), p. 105.

5.3.4 Behavioral Law and Economics Perspective

Behavioral economics postulates that certain consumer biases and heuristics will further exacerbate the problems associated with the duty to read and consumers' ability to discipline the market. Behavioral economics argues that psychological phenomena can explain why consumers do not read terms, why they cannot evaluate contracts correctly, and how sellers can manipulate consumers.[89]

The behavioral economics literature has discovered numerous biases that influence consumer decision-making. In Chap. 2, an extensive account of the most common biases and heuristics has been presented. Therefore, in this chapter, only the three behavioral propositions that are most relevant to standard-form contracting will be highlighted. First is the information overload phenomenon. The consumer has cognitive limitations, and it cannot, therefore, process all relevant information.[90] Due to the overload of information in contracts, consumers are inclined to focus on a few components, namely, the most salient ones, such as price and other conspicuous product attributes.[91] As a result, firms will discover what product features are salient and which are non-salient based on consumer feedback. The firm will compete on the salient attributes, whereas the non-salient ones are disregarded at the expense of the consumer. Standard terms form precisely one of the product attributes that are non-salient in the consumer's buying decision.[92]

Second, consumers are limited in their ability to evaluate prospects of future risks and uncertainty.[93] The terms in the boilerplates cover unpleasant situations in which the contract is not respected by one of the two parties. In the majority of cases, these risks do not materialize; therefore, consumers regard these contingencies as having a low probability risk. Accordingly, consumers tend to neglect these terms, which is described as *low probability neglect*.[94]

Thirdly, the *self-commitment bias* compels consumers to accept the terms even though they are opposite to their preferences.[95] Standard terms are typically placed at the end of the shopping process, and this causes consumers to attach less importance to the terms and continue with the order. Two psychological phenomena can explain this. In the first place, the sunk cost effect induces consumers to continue with the order because they have already invested time and effort into the process. Consumers do not want to waste time and effort and wish to maintain their

---

[89] Becher (2007), p. 120.

[90] Becher and Zarsky (2007), p. 312.

[91] Korobkin (2003), pp. 1225–1226.

[92] Korobkin (2003), pp. 1206–1207.

[93] Becher and Zarsky (2007), p. 313.

[94] Eisenberg (1995), pp. 223–224.

[95] Becher (2007), p. 179 discusses in depth the various common psychological phenomena such as the sunk cost effect, cognitive dissonance, confirmation bias, and the low-ball technique that influence the perception of self-commitment.

self-esteem regarding previous actions.[96] In the second place, cognitive dissonance causes a feeling among consumers to commit to the contract because they want to avoid conflicting evidence or ideas. As a result, people will tend to devalue evidence that undermines their ex-ante choice, which persuades them to commit to their choice, albeit the consumer would have been persuaded not to sign if it would have received the information at the initial stage of the decision process.[97]

The result is that "to avoid paralysis (and the associated anxiety), most people resort to the simple heuristic of always consenting (unless the risk of serious harm is apparent) so as to have a seamless online experience."[98]

The prevalence of consumer biases and heuristics provides the opportunity for sellers to exploit them. Standard forms are strategically drafted with a high degree of complexity, substantial length, and a great deal of legal jargon. Due to the cognitive limitations of consumers, these boilerplates will be disregarded, which enables sellers to insert one-sided terms to their own benefit.[99]

5.3.5 The Need for Intervention

From an economic perspective, the degree to which intervention is necessary is debatable. The various paradigms offer different perspectives on the merits of standard forms. Likewise, the approaches have conflicting views on the need for intervention in the market. The neoclassical perspective is critical of government intervention. The neoclassicists promulgate that the allocation of risks between the buyer and the seller is more efficiently done by the market participants than by the government, courts or other institutions.[100] The market is apt to generate fair and efficient standard terms through competition and reputation building.[101]

In addition, neoclassicists argue that, in practice, sellers will be reluctant to abuse consumers through standard terms because more effective and less risky strategies can be created to yield profits, for example, by focusing on product attributes such as price and quality.[102] Moreover, if the standard in the market is that boilerplates are one-sided in favor of sellers, this still indicates efficiency, according to the neoclassicists. To clarify, one-sided terms deter buyers from acting opportunistically (i.e., exploiting consumer-friendly terms). Sellers, on the other hand, are less inclined to

---

[96] Korobkin and Ulen (2000), pp. 1124–1126.

[97] Whitford (1973), p. 426.

[98] Galli et al. (2022), p. 501.

[99] Eisenberg (1995), pp. 241–243.

[100] Rakoff (1983), p. 1204.

[101] Johnston (2006), pp. 858–859.

[102] Baird (2006), p. 937.

act opportunistically because of reputational constraints. Thus, the market allocates the risks more efficiently, even if imposing one-sided terms is the norm.[103]

Lastly, it is claimed that the freedom of contract will lead to an increasingly efficient economy, and it should, therefore, be warranted.[104] The continuous process of accumulating knowledge is vital, and consumers should, thus, be in a position to learn the value of their actions through effective feedback.[105] In practice, this means that by concluding transactions with different firms, consumers will learn which terms they regard as value-increasing and which ones as value-decreasing. In this sense, the market will be self-correcting, and consumers will choose the firms with the best terms.

The insights from information economics, however, demonstrate that the market failure of information asymmetry justifies government intervention.[106] The provision of information to consumers is regarded as being essential to increase social welfare.[107] From this perspective, three proposals for intervention are advocated. First, firms should be obligated to provide consumers with mandated disclosures before any particular transaction so that consumers can read and compare boilerplates before making a purchase. Second, default rules need to be set.[108] Default rules allow parties to depart, but they are likely to be followed rather than diverged from. The government can set customer-friendly default rules. In this way, transaction costs are reduced, and if the default turns out to be inefficient in a certain industry, parties can contract around it. Conversely, mandatory rules are likely inefficient because they disregard industry-specific circumstances and knowledge. Third, to prevent the flea market situation which results from adverse selection, a minimum level of quality for boilerplates should be set, which effectively amounts to mandatory substantive intervention.[109] This would enable courts to strike out terms based on the fairness of their content (i.e., how onerous they are for the consumer). Consumers would then no longer need to read boilerplates because they are assured that the unfair terms are not enforceable.

The behavioral approach advocates more extensive intervention than the traditional approach.[110] First, due to psychological phenomena such as information overload and sunk cost effects consumers fail to read and assess standard forms.[111] Disclosure without attention to the presentation will likely aggravate this problem.[112] Second, due to self-commitment bias and biased risk perceptions, behavior-

[103] Bebchuk and Posner (2006), p. 830.

[104] Wonnell (1985), p. 542.

[105] Sowell (1980), pp. 110–111.

[106] Luth (2010), p. 163.

[107] Luth (2010), p. 164.

[108] Ayres and Gertner (1989).

[109] The UCTD is an example of this.

[110] Faure and Luth (2011), p. 350.

[111] Faure and Luth (2011), pp. 346–348.

[112] Jolls et al. (1998), pp. 1533–1534.

alists argue that consumer vigilance will not be sufficient to discipline the market.[113] Consequently, the behavioral perspective emphasizes the importance of debiasing consumers' decision-making. For this reason, policy measures solely aimed at enabling consumers to read the boilerplates are deemed insufficient.[114]

Three proposals that behavioralists have proffered are noteworthy. First of all, consumers should be provided with less and clearer information rather than providing more information. Consumers' understanding of the terms will increase by highlighting the most important terms and presenting the boilerplate in plain intelligible language.[115] Moreover, the use of a credible signal of quality, such as ratings or labels, could stimulate sellers into drafting higher-quality contract terms to attract consumers.[116] The rationale is based on the economic concept of signaling, whereby sellers voluntarily convey information about themselves to inform the consumers about the quality of their product.[117] Finally, involving consumers or consumer organizations in the drafting process of standard forms could increase the quality of boilerplates and the mutual satisfaction of the buyer and the seller. Besides, the idiosyncrasies of each industry can be taken into account, and no general imposed rules are required.[118]

As can be seen from the economic analysis of the different perspectives, no unequivocal answer can be given regarding the desirability of standard terms and the need for intervention. Nonetheless, empirical research has been conducted to see to what extent the signing-without-reading problem is prevalent in consumer markets and to what extent it causes consumer harm.

Concerning consumers' ability to discipline the market, it has been found that less than 5% (4.4%[119] and 0.2%[120]) of all consumers read boilerplates. The most common reasons for not reading boilerplates are trust in the company,[121] the length of the form,[122] and impatience.[123] Accordingly, *the theory of the informed minority*, which states that a minority of readers would be able to discipline the market, does not seem to hold in practice. The minimum amount of readers to discipline the market, which is approximated at one-third of all consumers,[124] is not even remotely met. To specify, the one-third criterion is based on the theoretical model by Schwartz and Wilde (1978), who demonstrate that if one-third or more of the consumers do

[113] Luth (2010), pp. 172–173.

[114] Becher and Unger-Aviram (2009), p. 226.

[115] Loos (2015), p. 184.

[116] Ben-Shahar (2009).

[117] Connelly et al. (2011), p. 40.

[118] Braucher (2007), p. 16.

[119] Stark and Choplin (2009), p. 617.

[120] Bakos et al. (2014), p. 1.

[121] Bakos et al. (2014), p. 31.

[122] Stark and Choplin (2009), p. 657.

[123] Hillman (2005b), p. 2.

[124] Schwartz and Wilde (1978), p. 661; Goldman (1992), p. 719.

comparative shopping, the observed price distribution of the good clusters around the competitive price. Conversely, if less than one-third of the consumers do comparative shopping, the seller can impose monopolistic prices because of the lack of competition. Likewise, they find that the one-third criterion applies to contract terms. Namely, if less than one-third of the consumers read the terms, the seller can maintain a monopolistic term structure (i.e., one-sided in favor of the seller).[125]

Furthermore, it has been discovered that standard forms, in general, do contain terms that are specifically tilted in favor of the seller.[126] Over time, the average contract has become increasingly pro-seller, and the length of the contract has increased as well.[127] In addition, evidence has been found that sellers offer certain warranties on their websites, which are later disclaimed in the boilerplate.[128] Finally, sellers generally do not comply with disclosure duties imposed by regulatory authorities or courts, i.e., less than 6% of the sellers have legally enforceable standard forms on their websites.[129]

Based on the empirical evidence, it could be argued that a need for intervention could be justified in the realm of standard-form contracts. There is a significant signing-without-reading problem that poses challenges to consumer protection. The remarkable development, however, is that the digital age has brought the signing-without-reading problem to a whole new level. Consumers will not only be unaware of contract terms that apply to all, but they will be unaware of the terms that apply specifically to them.

5.3.6 *Broadening the Analysis: Implications for Consumer Policy*

The benefits and downsides of standard forms are magnified in the context of personalized contracts. Principally, the efficiency gains that standard forms generate are expected to be substantially larger for personalized contracts. Personalization will lead to an improved identification of consumer needs. Since consumers will only see relevant choices, utility maximization is more likely to happen at lower transaction costs. If personalization benefits both parties, then the contractual surpluses can be enlarged compared to a non-personalization context.[130]

Additionally, personalized contracts remedy the downsides of uniform standard-form contracts. Uniform contracts are unable to account for consumer

[125] Schwartz and Wilde (1978), pp. 652–653, 661.
[126] Marotta-Wurgler (2007); Marotta-Wurgler (2011).
[127] Marotta-Wurgler and Taylor (2013), p. 240.
[128] Hillman and Barakat (2008), p. 1.
[129] Mann and Siebneicher (2008), p. 998.
[130] Golobardes (2022), p. 36.

heterogeneity, which means that it has the potential to lead to cross-subsidization.[131] Consumers face a uniform distribution of risks with standard forms, although they may value the contract differently. This means that consumers who are better able to utilize the standard form to their benefit are subsidized by the consumers who pay for the same legal protection but do not exercise their rights.

Personalized contracts, in contrast, could more effectively satisfy the risk preferences of the consumers, leading to a more efficient allocation of risks. Consumers would only pay for the provisions they value. This way, deadweight losses are eliminated, cross-subsidies are remedied, and optimal contracting incentives are provided.[132]

Lastly, competition can be sparked between companies that promise consumers to offer contracts that fit their needs and preferences. The competition would create an upward spiral of consumer-preference matching. When sellers can charge different prices for different contracts, the consumer population can be differentiated, and a larger share of the market can be served.[133]

Nevertheless, this scenario of perfect contract personalization reflects an ideal rather than a conceivable reality. The dark implications that come along with personalized contracts are worrisome from a broadened consumer perspective.

First and foremost, to personalize contract terms, it is essential to collect vast amounts of data that help construct an adequate consumer profile. This consumer profile will not only demonstrate the preferences of the consumer but also the individual cognitive biases and vulnerabilities. In addition, the relevant circumstances are also taken into account, which include the consumers' current situation, informational deficits, and irrationalities.[134]

Accordingly, there is ample room for the exploitation of consumers, which offers sellers the opportunity to extract consumer surplus, shape consumer preferences, and steer consumption patterns.[135] This means that contract personalization could have considerable welfare effects, both in terms of efficiency and distribution.[136] By exploiting behavioral biases, contract terms can be inserted that prevent consumers from accurately assessing the merits of the contract.[137]

Second, it is unlikely that consumers will have the possibility to discipline the market of personalized contracts.[138] The contract presented to individuals can only

---

[131] Golobardes (2022), p. 22.

[132] Ben-Shahar and Posner (2011), pp. 127–128, 144–145; Porat and Strahilevitz (2014), pp. 1453–1454; Cfr. Ben-Shahar and Porat (2019), part II.D; Golobardes (2022), p. 37.

[133] Ben-Shahar and Posner (2011), pp. 127–128, 144–145; Porat and Strahilevitz (2014), pp. 1453–1454; Cfr. Ben-Shahar and Porat (2019), part II.D; Golobardes (2022), p. 37.

[134] Południak-Gierz (2021).

[135] Wagner and Eidenmüller (2019).

[136] Bar-Gill (2018) demonstrates the efficiency and distributional effects in the context of algorithmic pricing.

[137] DellaVigna and Malmendier (2004), Gabaix and Laibson (2006), Varian (2009), Shiller (2014), Grubb (2015).

[138] Cfr. Informed-minority hypothesis, see Schwartz and Wilde (1978); Goldman (1992).

be reviewed by the individuals themselves, which, with the no-reading problem in mind, is unlikely to occur. In addition, it is particularly onerous for consumer authorities to review personalized contracts since there is no uniformity. As a consequence, enforcement is significantly impaired. This gives sufficient leeway to sellers to introduce one-sided terms without the threat of facing severe repercussions.

Third, similar to the situation with personalized pricing and advertising, there is the expectation that the personalization of contracts could lead to algorithmic discrimination. In this case, it would not be a direct form of discrimination because that is prohibited, but an indirect form that would lead to the practically same result.[139] To the extent that particularly poorer, less educated, and more vulnerable consumers are discriminated against in practice, contract personalization could be highly problematic in the light of distributive justice.[140]

Finally, and perhaps most importantly, personalized contracting is only one part of the consumer shopping experience. On its own, the adverse effects of accepting personalized terms could potentially be moderate in practice. However, the real peril of personalized contracting is that it works together with other personalizing technologies. That is to say, the terms that consumers will receive result from a personalization process that has also impacted the advertisement they have seen, the environment in which they made the purchase, and the price they have paid. The combined and mutually-enforcing aspect of personalization poses a serious threat to consumer autonomy, equity, and welfare.[141] Personalizing contract terms is the last step of the different stages that consumers pass in their decision-making process. Accordingly, another avenue for manipulation, and potential exploitation, has been opened with personalized contracting.

In conclusion, the economic analysis of standard-form contracts has emphasized the dangers of the signing-without-reading problem that plagues consumers. This problem is expected to become significantly more impactful in the context of personalized contracts. Personalized contracts reinforce the issues with standard forms, while posing a bigger threat to consumer autonomy, equity and welfare. In other words, personalized contracting is another driver of marketing-induced market failures in consumer markets. Consequently, in accordance with the consumer welfare hypothesis and a broadened analysis perspective,[142] it is crucial to investigate the legal framework's ability to address these challenges.

[139] Harvey (2019).

[140] Several additional downsides of personalized contracts are reflected in the practices of algorithmic pricing and personalized advertising. See Chaps. 3 and 4 for an in-depth discussion of other relevant economic arguments.

[141] Mik (2016), pp. 6–7.

[142] See Sect. 2.4.4.

5.4 Legal Framework

Since the personalization of contracts is still in development and is not ubiquitous in practice, it is no surprise that there is no law (or case law) that deals explicitly with personalized contracts. Nevertheless, a multiplicity of piecemeal regulations partly address personalization, and there is a clear legal framework regarding standard forms. *Per analogiam*, the existing rules can be applied to personalized contracting. This section examines the extent to which the current legal framework can prevent or sanction exploitative personalized contracting. For the sake of conciseness, only the parts of the regulations that are explicitly applicable to personalized contracting will be discussed.[143] In this way, the current state of affairs can be determined.

5.4.1 Linking Personalized Contracts and Standard Forms

Standard-form contracts allowed for the replacement of individually negotiated contracts, or at least the parts of the contract that were less salient to the negotiations. In this way, negotiations could focus on the *essentialia negotii.*[144] The seller would then unilaterally impose the non-essential parts of the contract via the standard terms. A term can be regarded to be standard when it is not individually negotiated, it has been drafted in advance, and the consumer has not been able to influence its substance.[145] Assent to the standard form as a whole is sufficient to conclude the contract. From an economic point of view, this is highly efficient because transaction costs are lowered. Individualizing the terms of the contract would be prohibitively costly.

Nevertheless, personalization has enabled the re-individualization of the standard forms. By virtue of AI-driven technologies, the costs of personalizing contracts have decreased substantially, making it profitable for sellers to adjust contract terms for individualization.

Południak-Gierz (2019) states: "The possibility of concluding contracts on a massive scale is retained, but with added granularity and flexibility that mimic the individualisation of transactions."[146]

However, does this mean that from a legal perspective, a personalized contract differs from a standard-form contract? To answer this question, the first step should be to define a standard-form contract. In line with Articles 3 and 4(2) of the UCTD,

[143] A broader discussion of the interplay between the various European regulations and personalization can be found in Chaps. 3 and 4.

[144] In the common law tradition, this is embodied by the notion of dickered terms, see Llewellyn (2016).

[145] Article 3(2) UCTD.

[146] Południak-Gierz (2019), p. 161.

it can be asserted that standard-form contracts are recognized by three criteria: 1) A set of provisions that have been drafted in advance (pre-formulated); 2) the consumer cannot influence the substance of the terms (unilaterally imposed); and 3) the terms do not relate to the main subject matter of the contract, such as the price and remuneration (excluding the *essentialia negotii*).

Based on these criteria, it can be determined if personalized contracts could be placed under the umbrella of standard-form contracts. Although the words standardized and personalized are practically antonyms, it could be argued that from a legal perspective, personalized contracts should be seen as a new model of standard-form contracts rather than a different contract.[147]

At first glance, it seems questionable if personalized contract terms are preformulated within the meaning of Article 3(2) UCTD, which would mean that they do not fall under the scope of the UCTD.[148] Case law is missing, and further academic guidance is lacking.[149] For the sake of consumer protection, this would be detrimental since the UCTD would be inapplicable. Consumers would then need to resort to contract law, which effectively provides fewer safeguards for the B2C dynamic.[150]

Nevertheless, it can be argued that personalized contracts are formed based on data collected about the consumer prior to the conclusion of the contract. The contract terms are designed and adapted in accordance with the profile that has already been formed about the consumer. In other words, before the consumer sees the contract, the terms have been personalized. In the case of a standard-form contract, the seller drafts the terms in advance based on the data it has about the general population of consumers. In the case of a personalized contract, the seller also drafts the terms in advance yet based on the data of a specific consumer. This means the first criterion for classifying a contract as a standard-form contract is satisfied.

It must be noted, however, that in some legal systems, such as the Dutch and German ones, part of this criterion is that the standard form will be utilized in various contracts (i.e., more than one contract).[151] It could be contended that if every contract is personalized, the terms are not drafted for multiple uses, which would declassify them from being standard-form contracts. However, this argument overlooks the scale at which personalization is taking place. Personalization is possible by virtue of the collection of vast amounts of personal and behavioral data, and it can be applied to a substantial amount of transactions. The fact that the contract is personalized does not mean that, by definition, it is unique to the individual. As with personalized advertising and pricing, the individual price can be displayed to groups of people with similar characteristics and behaviors. In simple terms, many

[147] This is in line with Południak-Gierz (2020).

[148] Möslein (2023), p. 307.

[149] Möslein (2023).

[150] The contract law perspective will be further discussed in Sect. 5.4.4.

[151] Book 6, Article 231(a) Dutch Civil Code (DCC) and Section 305 of the German Civil Code.

consumers can be regarded as identical for the sake of targeting.[152] The ramifications of this are twofold: On the one hand, the trader can use the same personalized contracts for virtually identical consumers, satisfying the criterion. On the other hand, if perfect contract personalization takes place, which could be problematic in several national legal systems, the trader can scale back and go for a mix of personalization and cruder forms of segmentation, such as group targeting, to prevent legal consequences. In short, the additional requirement (i.e., the *multiple-contract purpose*) for standard forms found in some legal systems will likely not stand in the way of classifying personalized contracts as standard-form contracts.

Furthermore, to satisfy the second criterion, consumers should not be able to influence the substance of the terms. To personalize the contract terms, data needs to be collected, which means that if there is no consent, consumers can indirectly influence the terms they will see, namely non-personalized terms. Alternatively, consumers could manipulate the outcomes through strategic behavior if they consent, for example, by providing incomplete or incorrect information when filling out a form in order to manipulate the final contract that will be presented.[153] In this sense, it seems that the consumer can exert influence, to a certain degree, on the substance of the terms. However, this line of reasoning overlooks the essence of what is meant by exerting influence. It refers to the ability to negotiate in order to adjust the substance of the terms, as is the case in negotiating a price or a specific product attribute (e.g., the color).[154] In the case of personalized contract terms, there is no room for modification through negotiation. The role of consent or strategic behavior influences how the contract terms are designed. However, this does not mean that the terms can be qualified as individually negotiated. Południak-Gierz (2019) argues: "Unilaterality means there is a lack of negotiation, not of individual approach. Therefore, the premise of unilaterality should be understood strictly as the lack of dialogue between the parties, and personalized contracts can be considered unilaterally shaped by the entrepreneur".[155] Accordingly, the second criterion is also satisfied.

Lastly, the terms may not relate to the main subject matter of the contract. For this to hold, a distinction in the definition of personalized contracts must be made. Following a broad definition of a personalized contract, it could be argued that it also encompasses price and remuneration. A narrow definition of personalized contracts, on the contrary, excludes price as subject matter and covers the part of the contract that does not fall under the *essentialia negotii*. In this sense, personalized contracts refer to *the terms that would otherwise have been standardized*. In this chapter, the latter (narrow) definition is followed.

---

[152] Kant (2020).

[153] For example, by effectively providing incomplete or incorrect information to get a different personalized credit or insurance contract. It must be noted that, in some instances, this can be regarded as fraud.

[154] Południak-Gierz (2019), p. 166.

[155] Południak-Gierz (2019), p. 166.

The algorithmic personalization of prices is a phenomenon with a substantial impact on consumers' autonomy, equity, and welfare, which, therefore, merits a separate analysis from the personalization of contracts. For this reason, algorithmic pricing has been discussed in Chap. 4. This chapter focuses on the terms that would have been standardized in the absence of personalization. Since the narrow definition of personalized contracts is adopted, it can be concluded that personalized contracts satisfy all three criteria, making them fall under the umbrella of standard-form contracts. This allows for the *per analogiam* application of the legislations concerning adhesion contracts such as the UCTD, which provides consumers with a higher level of protection than national contract law provisions on individually negotiated terms.

5.4.2 Consumer Protection Law

The first legal instrument that comes to mind when discussing unfair contract terms in the digital age is the UCTD.[156] As described in the previous section, a cogent argument can be made that personalized contracts fall under the UCTD. The asymmetry of information, unequal bargaining power, and undue influence over contract terms and the corresponding distribution of the contract surplus have been the basis for controlling unfair terms in standard-form contracts.[157] The UCTD is the prominent instrument in consumer protection law to combat unfair terms. Since the information asymmetries are enlarged in the case of personalized contracts, the role of unfair terms control becomes of pivotal importance.

The UCTD applies to terms that have not been individually negotiated (Article 3). Although the contract terms have been personalized, taking away the standardized character does not mean they have been individually negotiated.[158] The CJEU explained in the *Ibercaja Banco SA* case[159] that consumers should obtain a genuine opportunity to influence the content of a term for it to be considered negotiated. It does not matter if the terms have been drafted for a specific contract.[160] Accordingly, if the terms have been drafted in advance, be they in standardized form or personalized based on personal consumer data, they should not be considered individually negotiated. Only if the consumer gets the chance to personalize the contents or modify the terms can they be seen as individually negotiated. Consequently, although not formally acknowledged by the UCTD framework, personalized terms

---

[156] Gardiner (2022).

[157] Golobardes (2022), p. 31.

[158] Loos and Luzak (2021), pp. 32–33.

[159] Case C-452/18, XZ v Ibercaja Banco, SA, ECLI:EU:C:2020:536. The Court of Justice of the European Union. https://curia.europa.eu/juris/liste.jsf?num=C-452/18&language=EN.

[160] Paras 33–38.

should be governed by the UCTD.[161] This would open the door for procedural and substantial controls to promote fairness and balance rights and obligations.[162]

The most relevant part of the UCTD regarding personalized contracts has been discussed in the *Mohammed Aziz* case.[163] Terms that deviate to the consumers' detriment from the otherwise applicable rules of national law are likely to be unfair in light of Article 3(1). In other words, to determine if there has been a significant imbalance, the court performs a comparative analysis with national law to evaluate to what extent "the contract places the consumer in a legal situation less favourable than that provided by the national law in force."[164]

The court needs to assess if the seller could reasonably assume that the consumer would have agreed to the terms in individual contract negotiations (i.e., good faith requirement).[165] In the context of personalized contracts, a case could be made that personalized terms that the consumer would most likely not have consented to in individual negotiations and that take away the protection provided by national contract law should be considered unfair. The challenge lies, however, in proving that the term is to the detriment of the consumer.

Companies could justify the contract by highlighting the personalized benefit while downplaying the non-salient costs.[166] The contract could be marketed as satisfying the consumer's overall needs and preferences. The unfairness of a term could be compensated by another advantage in the contract (e.g., a lower price), whereby the interrelationship is intricate to ascertain.[167] It would then be virtually insurmountable for consumers to demonstrate that the contract is to their detriment without having knowledge of the algorithmic personalization mechanism behind it. The court would also need to be able to accurately weigh the benefits and costs, which are highly complex, technical, and context-dependent in the case of algorithmic personalization.

An alternative solution would be to expand on the workings of the gray—and blacklists that can be found in the national legal systems of the Member States as a result of the indicative list of unfair terms in the Annex of the UCTD. The graylist indicates presumably unfair terms, and the blacklist shows the terms that are unfair by definition. To illustrate, under Dutch law, the gray—and blacklists can be found

---

[161] Loos and Luzak (2021), pp. 32–33.

[162] Helberger (2016), pp. 146–147.

[163] Case C-415/11, Mohamed Aziz v Caixa d'Estalvis de Catalunya, Tarragona i Manresa (Catalunyacaixa), ECLI:EU:C:2013:164. The Court of Justice of the European Union. https://eur-lex.europa.eu/legal-content/EN/TXT/?uri=CELEX%3A62011CJ0415.

[164] Para 68.

[165] Para 69.

[166] Matzner et al. (2016), p. 297.

[167] Case C-226/12, Constructora Principado SA v José Ignacio Menéndez Álvarez, ECLI:EU:C:2014:10. The Court of Justice of the European Union. https://eur-lex.europa.eu/legal-content/EN/TXT/?uri=CELEX%3A62012CJ0226. The CJEU expressed, in paragraph 29, that a term that simply states that it is compensated by a lower price does not equate to proof of that relation.

in Articles 236 and 237 of Book 6 of the Dutch Civil Code. In Belgian law, a blacklist can be found in Article VI. 83 of the Code of Economic Law, and in German law, the gray—and blacklists are mentioned in Sections 308 and 309 of the German Civil Code.

The striking part of the blacklists is that once the court finds that an unfair term in the contract is mentioned as a blacklisted term, then automatically, the term is regarded as being unfair, which means no further analysis or discussion is needed.[168] When a term is found to be unfair, it is no longer binding on the consumer. The court cannot amend or revise the term to make it fair, as this would undermine the UCTD's deterrent effect.[169] Instead, the application of that clause must be excluded in its entirety.[170] In such cases, the court can either substitute the term with the relevant provision of national law if necessary to preserve the contract's validity and balance between the parties,[171] or annul the contract in its entirety when the balance between the parties cannot be restored after the term's removal and the contract's validity cannot be upheld.[172] The latter, however, can only occur when the contract's annulment does not disproportionately harm the consumer.[173]

It is proffered that a gray—or blacklist could be adopted with personalized contract terms.[174] In the case of a graylist, a personalized contract term would be regarded as presumably unfair, and the trader would need to demonstrate why the term is not to the consumer's detriment. A more far-reaching alternative would be to blacklist personalized contract terms, which means that if a consumer or a representative organization would complain about the personalization of the contract, the terms would automatically be declared unbinding. Nevertheless, regardless of the alternative chosen, this option does not currently exist under the UCTD. Thus,

---

[168] Steennot (2015), p. 593.

[169] Case C-618/10, Banco Español de Crédito, SA v Joaquín Calderón Camino, ECLI:EU:C:2012:349. The Court of Justice of the European Union. https://eur-lex.europa.eu/legal-content/EN/TXT/?uri=CELEX%3A62010CJ0618.

[170] Case C-488/11, Dirk Frederik Asbeek Brusse and Katarina de Man Garabito v Jahani BV, ECLI:EU:C:2013:341. The Court of Justice of the European Union. https://curia.europa.eu/juris/liste.jsf?num=C-488/11&language=EN.

[171] Case C-26/13, Árpád Kásler and Hajnalka Káslerné Rábai v OTP Jelzálogbank Zrt, ECLI:EU:C:2014:282. The Court of Justice of the European Union. https://curia.europa.eu/juris/liste.jsf?num=C-26/13.

[172] Case C-397/11, Erika Jőrös v Aegon Magyarország Hitel Zrt, ECLI:EU:C:2013:340. The Court of Justice of the European Union. https://curia.europa.eu/juris/liste.jsf?num=C-397/11&language=EN; Case C-453/10, Pereničová and Perenič, ECLI:EU:C:2012:144. The Court of Justice of the European Union. https://curia.europa.eu/juris/liste.jsf?num=C-453/10&language=EN.

[173] Case C-482/13, Unicaja Banco, SA v José Hidalgo Rueda and Others and Caixabank SA v Manuel María Rueda Ledesma and Others, ECLI:EU:C:2015:21. The Court of Justice of the European Union. https://curia.europa.eu/juris/liste.jsf?num=C-482/13. Joined Cases (C-484/13, C-485/13 and C-487/13).

[174] Poncibò (2023).

legislative amendments or new regulations would be required to propose such a solution.[175]

Lastly, the difficulties currently experienced with enforcing "classic standard forms" will most likely be exacerbated in the context of personalized contracts. As long as the case does not lead to court proceedings, it is plausible to assume that companies can keep using unfair terms.[176] Although the courts are obliged to invoke the unfairness of a term *ex officio*,[177] proceedings are still needed. Considering that consumers are often unaware of the contract terms, collective action problems exist, and consumer protection organizations have limited financial means to initiate proceedings, it can be stated that private enforcement will not suffice to ensure consumer protection from unfair terms. Public enforcement is, therefore, necessary as a complement.[178]

In spite of the fact that there has been a surge in unfair terms litigation since the adoption of the UCTD,[179] there is an issue of underenforcement.[180] Potentially, the developments in collective actions can offer a solution. However, this does not take away from the fact that policing unfair terms will become even more difficult in the case of personalized contracts.

Consumer awareness of unfair terms is already low in the context of standard terms, and this will likely become lower when contracts involve dynamic and rapidly changing terms that can be updated in real-time and are not discussed with the consumer. Consumers will be unable to use other consumers' knowledge about a specific contract (i.e., the informed minority hypothesis).

In addition, the fairness assessments made by consumer associations will become more burdensome since personalization will make bundling similar claims a demanding task. The fact that one consumer got an unfair term in the personalized contract does not mean that other consumers have faced the same unfair term, which was the case before with uniform standard terms. Consumer organizations are bound by limited resources, which only makes it feasible to tackle the practice of personalized contracting as a whole rather than being able to deal with very specific

---

175 The regulation of personalized practices will be further discussed in Chap. 6.

176 Steennot (2015).

177 Case C-168/05, Elisa María Mostaza Claro v Centro Móvil Milenium SL, ECLI:EU:C:2006:675. The Court of Justice of the European Union. https://curia.europa.eu/juris/liste.jsf?num=C-168/05; Case C-240/98, Océano Grupo Editorial SA v Roció Murciano Quintero (C-240/98) and Salvat Editores SA v José M. Sánchez Alcón Prades (C-241/98), José Luis Copano Badillo (C-242/98), Mohammed Berroane (C-243/98) and Emilio Viñas Feliú (C-244/98), ECLI:EU:C:2000:346. The Court of Justice of the European Union. https://curia.europa.eu/juris/liste.jsf?num=C-240/98; Case C-243/08, Pannon GSM Zrt. v Erzsébet Sustikné Győrfi, ECLI:EU:C:2009:350. The Court of Justice of the European Union. https://eur-lex.europa.eu/legal-content/EN/TXT/?uri=CELEX%3A62008CJ0243; Case C-472/11, Banif Plus Bank Zrt v Csaba Csipai and Viktória Csipai, ECLI:EU:C:2013:88. The Court of Justice of the European Union. https://curia.europa.eu/juris/liste.jsf?num=C-472/11&language=EN.

178 Steennot (2015).

179 Reich and Micklitz (2014).

180 Steennot (2015).

and idiosyncratic cases. The same is to be expected from private enforcement. Collective actions can be a valuable tool when claims can be bundled and are sufficiently similar. This will likely be particularly difficult with personalized contracts, making private enforcement through collective actions less feasible. In short, although the UCTD does provide protection against unfair terms, it is questionable if it will be an effective instrument in addressing personalized contracts.

The second consumer law instrument that could be employed to address personalized contracts is the UCPD. The UCPD has been elaborately discussed in the contexts of personalized advertising and pricing. In this section, the relevant provisions of the UCPD will be directly applied to personalized contracting.[181]

The main challenge of addressing personalized contracts by virtue of the UCPD is delineating where contract personalization functions as a legitimate persuasive marketing strategy and where it transgresses into an unfair commercial practice.[182] Having detailed knowledge about an individual consumer, which includes data about preferences, biases, and vulnerabilities, is a powerful tool for effective persuasion, which can result in the material distortion of a consumer's economic behavior.[183] Suppose a contract is drafted in a manner that is most likely to persuade the consumers that are addressed. In that case, it needs to be proven that it leads to a situation in which the consumers make decisions they would otherwise not have made. The ways in which incentives can be used under contract personalization are plentiful, and their effect can vary strongly between consumers.

The average consumer benchmark is not instrumental in establishing that a particular consumer's behavior has materially been distorted as a result of the contract. Certain contract incentives (e.g., salient teaser rates and non-salient overdraft fees) can effectively incentivize short-term oriented consumers with limited financial resources but prove less effective in incentivizing long-term oriented consumers. Hence, with the current point of reference, the UCPD is limited in ability to tackle individualized practices.[184]

Nevertheless, there is a case to be made that exploitative contracting can be tackled pursuant to Articles 6 and 7 of the UCPD if the contract leads consumers to make transactional decisions they would not have made if they had been adequately informed. To illustrate, if a contract presents information that might be factually correct but is likely to deceive the consumer, it can be classified as unfair under Article 6. Similarly, if a contract omits material information to consumers, for example, by highlighting the rewards but burying the fees in the fine print, Article 7 can be invoked.

Moreover, in cases where contracts are personalized to exploit consumers' needs, misfortunes, or circumstances of such gravity that they impair consumer's

[181] For an explanation of the relevant concepts in the UCPD, see Sect. 3.6.2.2.

[182] Cfr. Helberger (2016), pp. 151–152.

[183] Helberger (2016), pp. 155–157.

[184] Południak-Gierz (2019), p. 172.

judgment, contract personalization can be regarded as an aggressive commercial practice (Articles 8 and 9).

However, the UCPD's shortcoming is that AI-driven personalization mechanisms are likely too subtle to be detected and labeled overtly unfair.[185] Establishing a personalization technique's misleading or aggressive character has proven to be onerous.[186] AI-induced bargaining advantages are objectionable but are not by definition prohibited by law. They are likely to fall into a *gray zone*.[187] The lack of transparency surrounding the practice could be tackled; however, this would require broad interpretations of the provisions, which to date is not clear-cut.[188] In the same vein, an argument could be made that personalized contracts that go against the fundamental rights of consumers (e.g., consumer autonomy) are infringing the notion of professional diligence as described in Article 5(2)(a) UCPD. However, this would also require further corroboration in case law.[189]

Finally, it is worth noting that the *Omnibus Directive* has introduced the obligation to inform consumers that prices have been personalized on the basis of automated decision-making.[190] This duty to inform does not cover contract terms that have been personalized on the basis of automated decision-making. Loos and Luzak (2021) argue that this should be updated to include all terms.[191] This would mean that if consumers get personalized contract terms, they should be informed accordingly. If a personalized term is not or inappropriately disclosed to the consumer, this would *prima facie* indicate unfairness. Nevertheless, this extension remains a recommendation and has not yet been formally introduced or developed in case law.[192]

---

[185] Galli (2022).

[186] See, for an in-depth analysis of the issues with applying the UCPD to personalization, Chaps. 3 and 4.

[187] Mik (2016), p. 36.

[188] Helberger et al. (2021), p. 143.

[189] Leiser and Caruana (2021).

[190] Recital 45 and the newly added Article 6(1)(ea) of the Consumer Rights Directive (added by Directive (EU) 2019/2161 of the European Parliament and of the Council of 27 November 2019 amending Council Directive 93/13/EEC and Directives 98/6/EC, 2005/29/EC and 2011/83/EU of the European Parliament and of the Council as regards the better enforcement and modernisation of Union consumer protection rules. https://eur-lex.europa.eu/eli/dir/2019/2161/oj. Referred to as "Omnibus Directive".

[191] Loos and Luzak (2021), pp. 32–33.

[192] Loos and Luzak (2021), pp. 32–33.

5.4.3 Data Protection Law

Contract personalization occurs by collecting extensive amounts of personal data about consumers. Chapters 3 and 4 thoroughly investigate the relationship between personalization and the GDPR.[193] This section will discuss only the parts of the GDPR that are pertinent to personalized contracting. Pursuant to the analysis of Sect. 3.6.2.1, the critical point with GDPR protection is that although companies may not rely on the legitimate bases of necessity for the performance of a contract or legitimate interest (Articles 6(1)(b) and (f)), they can still rely on the legal basis of consent.

In terms of contracting, it is conceivable that consent for personalized terms can straightforwardly be obtained by phrasing the purpose of personalization as providing better contracting services that will enhance customer experience. In combination with dark patterns, consent notices can work to the benefit of companies instead of consumers. Especially when marketing efforts inflate the perceived benefits of a personalized contract, the likelihood of acceptance increases.

Companies willing to employ personalized contracting services would be able to obtain consent from the user to comply with the requirements of the GDPR. As became clear from the economic analysis in Sect. 5.3, there is a significant signing-without-reading problem that impedes the proper functioning of the consent mechanism. This result is corroborated by studies analyzing privacy notices, which demonstrate that practically nobody reads them, and consent is almost always given.[194] Consequently, companies can quickly obtain consumers' consent, collect the necessary data, and implement contract personalization strategies.[195]

It could be argued that Article 22(3) GDPR provides a safeguard against automated decision-making for exploitative personalized contracting purposes. Although consumers give their explicit consent, data controllers are still obliged to:

> implement suitable measures to safeguard the data subject's rights and freedoms and legitimate interests, at least the right to obtain human intervention on the part of the controller, to express his or her point of view and to contest the decision.

However, it is questionable to what extent the personalization of contracts will be fully automated (i.e., without any human intervention) and to what extent personalized contracts significantly affect consumers' legal status, which restricts the provision's application.

Recital 71 provides a relevant consideration for the safeguards of Article 22 in the sense that it mentions that, for the sake of ensuring fair and transparent data processing, the controller should use appropriate mathematical or statistical procedures for profiling. In addition, technical and organizational measures need to be taken to make sure that profiling risks and errors are minimized, personal data is

---

193 See, in particular, Sect. 3.6.2.1.

194 Bakos et al. (2014); Ben-Shahar and Chilton (2016); Obar and Oeldorf-Hirsch (2020).

195 Galli et al. (2022).

secured, and discriminatory effects are prevented. This alludes to more protection for data subjects against profiling. Nevertheless, the suitable measures that need to be taken remain indeterminate, which in Recital 53 are left to further development in Union or Member State law. The provisions of Article 22(2)(b), (3), and (4) seem to be of rather procedural than substantial value, which makes Article 22 relatively ineffective in counteracting personalized exploitative contracting.[196]

A final possibility under the GDPR would be to invoke Article 5(1)(a) concerning the principle of fairness. The concept of personalized exploitative contracts seems to go directly against this principle.[197] However, as Hacker (2017) clarifies, "this vague principle is notoriously difficult to define and apply."[198] It is not evident that the principle of fairness will effectively lead to more than a call for transparency.[199] In short, although the GDPR does provide certain safeguards against exploitative personalized contracting, it is expected that the emphasis on consent, which requires an active attitude from consumers (i.e., objecting), will hinder the ability of the GDPR to address personalized contracting effectively. It merits, therefore, further attention to see what other potential remedies are provided by the legal framework.

5.4.4 Contract Law

Hacker (2017) argues that contract and tort law are best suited to combat exploitative contracting.[200] The rationale is that personalized contracts target vulnerabilities and exploiting them constitutes a breach of pre-contractual good faith. If one of the parties breaches its explicit or implicit contractual duties, the exploiting party may be liable for damages.[201] The difficulty lies, however, in establishing the point when the transaction has been compromised. The freedom of contract implicitly entails that parties can engage in their own bargaining tactics and that they are able to recognize and, to a certain degree, counter each other's bargaining strategies. One should, therefore, be wary of immediately invoking a breach of pre-contractual good faith.[202]

Alternatively, specific doctrines in contract law, such as mistake, deceit, and fraud, could be invoked when sellers breach their information duties, leading to a defect in consent. A complete analysis of these doctrines falls outside the scope of

[196] Hacker (2017), p. 275.

[197] Bigwood (2003); Fikentscher et al. (2013).

[198] Hacker (2017), p. 276.

[199] Brownsword (2009).

[200] Hacker (2017), pp. 279–280 demonstrates that exploitative contracting practices can focus on the pricing dimension of the contract, but they can also be extended to the less salient parts of the contract.

[201] Hacker (2017), p. 280.

[202] Mik (2016), p. 27.

this chapter.[203] However, the relevant observation is that the data-driven mechanisms behind personalization are designed to subtly fall through the cracks of the legal doctrines.[204] That is to say, it is far from evident that in the context of personalized contracts, the invocation of the doctrines on mistake, deceit, or fraud will be successful.[205]

Mik (2016) states: "Absent overt pressure, technological influences seem too subtle to be registered on the radar of traditional protective mechanisms - despite the fact that they affect (or: attack) one of the central values of contract law: autonomy."[206]

The actual threat of facing claims based on contract law will not be substantial. In contract law, the burden of proof lies on the plaintiff, who, in this case, is the buyer who will need to prove the exploitative nature of the contract. Considering the technical sophistication and complexity of the AI-driven personalization mechanisms, it is unlikely that buyers will be able to prove exploitation. In particular, since there is no full access to the data that has been used.

It could be argued, however, that pursuant to Article 15(1)(h) GDPR, the data subject has the right to access the data that is being used in automated decision-making, including profiling, and receive meaningful information about the logic involved, as well as the significance and the envisaged consequences of such processing for the data subject. Nevertheless, this would require from data subjects that, based on the data, they can establish that the company had a profile that included their vulnerabilities but also that the company specifically targeted the vulnerabilities identified in the profile. It is evident that this is a threshold that will be onerous to pass.[207]

As Golobardes (2022) concludes: "Contract law does not appear sufficient to ensure that the expected welfare consumers obtain from non-digital non-personalised contracts is equivalent to that obtained in the digital personalised realm."[208]

5.4.5 Digital Regulation

The change from standard forms to personalized contract terms is facilitated by the digital transformation. Since the mechanisms behind the personalization of contracts are data-driven and standard terms are effectively being digitized,[209] the latest developments concerning European digital regulation merit further attention. Although none of the latest digital regulations talk about personalized contracts, the

203 See for an in-depth discussion of the doctrines Lohsse (2016), Patti (2016), Schulze (2016).

204 De Geest (2018), p. 5.

205 Mik (2016).

206 Mik (2016), p. 31.

207 Galli (2021).

208 Golobardes (2022), p. 39.

209 Gardiner (2022).

practice of personalization is addressed, in particular when it comes to pricing and advertising. In the context of these provisions, this section theorizes what potential protection digital regulations could offer consumers against personalized contracts.[210]

Where the UCTD focuses on terms in all contexts, the DSA focuses specifically on the digital context, thereby taking into account the digitalization of consumer markets. The DSA can, therefore, complement the UCTD in the context of online transactions.

First, the DSA could be a valuable instrument for tackling digital-specific unfair terms. Recital 45 states:

> Whilst the freedom of contract of providers of intermediary services should in principle be respected, it is appropriate to set certain rules on the content, application and enforcement of the terms and conditions of those providers in the interests of transparency, the protection of recipients of the service and the avoidance of unfair or arbitrary outcomes.

The recital further elaborates that this duty to inform users encompasses content moderation, the right to termination, and unilateral (significant) amendment clauses. This touches upon the use of certain clauses often found to be unfair in digital consumer contracts, such as liability clauses concerning content moderation, unilateral terms modification, and termination procedures.[211] Recital 45 is closely connected to Article 14, which aims to enhance the transparency of the processes governing the restriction of the provision of intermediary services by creating information obligations that need to be set out in "clear, plain, intelligible, user-friendly and unambiguous language, and shall be publicly available in an easily accessible and machine-readable format."

Second, concerning VLOPs and VLOSEs, the DSA provides additional requirements regarding the transparency of the terms and conditions. Pursuant to Article 14(5) and (6), they are required to, respectively, provide recipients of the service with "a concise, easily-accessible and machine-readable summary of the terms and conditions, including the available remedies and redress mechanisms, in clear and unambiguous language," and they need to "publish their terms and conditions in the official languages of all the Member States in which they offer their services." Accordingly, this makes terms and conditions more accessible, intelligible, and actionable for consumers.

Third, the DSA aims to remedy the problem that consumers are often unaware of how automated systems make decisions on their behalf and the corresponding implications. The DSA seeks to answer the need for more transparency in this regard.

To prevent digital service intermediaries from making unilateral decisions that negatively impact users, users are empowered by notice and action mechanisms that allow them to receive more information about decisions made by hosting service

---

[210] This section will only touch upon the aspects that are relevant to personalized contracting. For a further discussion of the digital regulations in the contexts of personalized advertising and pricing, see Chaps. 3 and 4.

[211] Lagioia et al. (2022).

providers and enable them to contest the decisions (Articles 16 and 17). In addition, the DSA requires service providers to disclose the use and impact of automated means (Article 15). This disclosure not only enhances transparency but also encourages service providers to self-audit their algorithms to ensure that they comply with the principles of transparency and accountability. In this way, the DSA provides an additional layer of consumer protection.[212]

Nevertheless, it is doubtful that the DSA can effectively limit the practice of personalized contracting. Although it increases transparency and touches upon specific aspects of unfair contract terms, the DSA is a more adequate tool to address personalized advertising instead of contracting. Although increasing transparency can remedy information asymmetries, it will likely be insufficient to deal with the more problematic parts of personalized contracting, such as the coercive nature of the contract, the targeting of vulnerabilities, or the exploitation of biases and heuristics, which compromise consumers' autonomy, equity, and welfare.

The DMA is also relevant to personalized contracting since gatekeepers employ terms and conditions to dictate what is happening on their platform. The terms to which the parties agree profoundly impact the individual transactions on the platform. The default rules of contract law are replaced by the private rules through the standard terms and conditions, thereby transforming platforms into lawmakers that develop their own normative order in the platform environment.[213] Accordingly, the DMA can be a valuable instrument for guiding platforms' behavior. In Chap. 3, the DMA is elaborately discussed in the context of personalized advertising.[214] It became clear that the DMA is particularly valuable as an instrument to unlock consumer choice, counteract self-preferencing, and promote transparency.

In the context of personalized contracting, it is noteworthy that the DMA aims to limit the ability of gatekeepers to avail themselves of their obligations through their terms and conditions (i.e., anti-circumvention rule). In addition, the DMA also allows the consumer to reject personalization by obliging gatekeepers to offer a less personalized but equivalent alternative. Accordingly, this would mean that the DMA provides consumers with a tool to reject personalized contracts offered by gatekeepers. Nonetheless, this is with the caveats in mind that the scope of the DMA is limited to gatekeepers, and the consent mechanism still plays a key role, which has been found to be of limited effectiveness for consumer protection. Thus, it is likely that there will still be ample room for personalized contracting to take place in consumer markets.

The AI Act provides a valuable starting point for combating the exploitation of consumers through AI-based technologies. Similar to the context of personalized advertising and pricing, Article 5 of the AI Act will be of limited added value to combat the identified harms of personalized contracting.[215] It must be noted, how-

[212] Poncibò (2023), p. 335.

[213] Grundmann and Hacker (2017); Möslein (2023).

[214] See Sect. 3.6.2.3.

[215] See Sect. 3.6.2.3 for an elaborate analysis of the AI Act.

ever, that Article 5(1)(c) of the AI Act can be helpful in tackling contract personalization by means of the classification of individuals based on their social behavior or personal characteristics. Social scoring that leads to detrimental or unfavorable treatment of specific individuals or groups is prohibited. In this sense, the potentially discriminating character of personalized contracting could be addressed.

Overall, digital regulations offer novel tools to address personalized contracting. However, on a more critical note, it is unlikely that they will be sufficient to adequately tackle personalized contracts.

5.4.6 Current State of Affairs

The personalization of contract terms takes place by virtue of the collection of large amounts of personal data from consumers. This creates a knowledge advantage on the seller's side, exacerbating the information asymmetry problem in consumer markets. As a result, consumers are placed in a situation where they are more vulnerable than they usually are in consumer markets.[216]

The first step was to analyze the consumer protection tools, specifically focusing on the UCPD and the UCTD. With respect to the UCPD, the personalization mechanisms will likely be too subtle to be caught and labeled unfair. It will be arduous to prove a personalized contract's misleading or aggressive nature. Broader interpretations of the UCPD, which are currently missing, that put contract personalization under the scope of Article 7 (omitting material information) or Article 5(2)(a) (professional diligence), are needed.[217] The analysis of the UCTD as an instrument has led to two conclusions. First, there is a cogent argument to be made that personalized contract terms fall under the scope of the UCTD. Second, the UCTD does not ensure adequate protection of consumers. The main challenge will be to demonstrate that personalized contract terms have a detrimental effect on consumers. The absence of provisions on personalized unfair terms hinders the assessment of unfairness under the UCTD.

Next, the GDPR was analyzed, and it was found that although the GDPR's provisions do strengthen the consumer's position, they can be undermined due to their emphasis on consent. Therefore, the GDPR's ability to effectively address personalized contracting is limited.

Subsequently, a contract law perspective was taken. Although traditional contract law doctrines provide tools to combat exploitative contracting, it will prove hard to invoke doctrines, such as mistake, deceit, and fraud, in the absence of overt pressure. In addition, the actual threat of facing claims based on contract law is expected to be trivial.[218] Contract law will, therefore, most likely not be enough to

---

[216] Golobardes (2022), p. 40.

[217] Galli (2022).

[218] Mik (2016), p. 37.

adequately protect consumers' autonomy, equity, and welfare from algorithmically personalized contracts.

The new digital regulations, the DSA, DMA, and the AI Act, seem to provide further safeguards against exploitative personalized contracting. The DSA contributes to increasing transparency on online platforms, which also benefits the contracting element; however, it is only a partially suitable tool to tackle the identified harms of personalized contracting.

The DMA prevents gatekeepers from availing themselves of their obligations through their terms and conditions. However, the key role of consent and the limited scope of the DMA are reasons to believe that there is still considerable room for personalized contracting to take place.

The AI Act complements the previous regulations by addressing the social sorting aspect of personalized contracting. Nevertheless, this only concerns one of the various facets of personalization. When it comes to tackling the harms that pervade personalized contracting, the AI Act does not offer significant improvements over the safeguards that are provided by the UCPD.

In short, each of the digital regulations comes short of effectively limiting the practice of personalized contracting. The emphasis on transparency will not solve the problem.[219] As long as consumers do not read the terms, do not understand the implications of the contract, and sign without knowing what is happening, the information paradigm is doomed to fail.[220] There is no full meeting of minds under the current notice and choice mechanism, whether standardized or personalized. There is ample opportunity for sellers to introduce one-sided contract terms to the consumer's detriment.[221] The current EU instruments, which include pre-contractual information duties, contractual transparency control, and ex-post remedies for breach, are limited in providing relief to consumers in personalized transaction settings.[222] There is a role for regulation to play in safeguarding consumer expectations.[223] New strategies are needed that improve understanding on the side of the consumer, increase accountability, and warrant consumer autonomy.[224]

A comprehensive approach that reaches beyond the current legal framework is, thus, needed.[225] As Golobardes (2022) summarizes: "The approaches adopted to date do not protect consumer welfare and they call into question the overall effectiveness of the European consumer protection regime when it comes to algorithmically personalised consumer contracts."[226]

[219] Desai and Kroll (2017).

[220] Hondius (2016), p. 461.

[221] Ben-Shahar and Porat (2019).

[222] Ben-Shahar and Bar-Gill (2013); Golobardes (2022), p. 38.

[223] Garello (2003).

[224] Hacker (2017).

[225] Golobardes (2022), p. 42.

[226] Golobardes (2022), pp. 42–43.

5.5 Conclusion

AI-driven technologies have taken the unilateral imposition of terms to a whole new level. Contract personalization is expected to deepen the information asymmetries that already exist in the realm of standard forms. The pervasive signing-without-reading problem will likely be exacerbated; however, in contrast to the standard-form context, consumers will face their own tailored consequences. The personalization of contract terms has opened the door for exploitative contracting practices.

The economic analysis demonstrated that the merits of standard forms are disputable depending on the perspective taken. Traditional law and economics emphasizes the economic benefits of standard-form contracts, downplaying the need for intervention. Behavioral law and economics points out the prevalence of consumer biases and heuristics that impede rational decision-making and, therefore, refutes the utility of standard forms (in their current form).

Although the two perspectives provide contradictory answers regarding the desirability of standard forms, numerous empirical studies have demonstrated that, in reality, consumers do not read standard forms, do not understand them, and are unable to discipline the market. One-sided terms are, therefore, prevalent in the market, which leads to substantial consumer harm. Accordingly, the need for intervention could be empirically justified.

The problems identified in the economic analysis are expected to become significantly more impactful in the context of personalized contracts. Personalized contracting aggravates the issues with standard forms while presenting new challenges in terms of consumer exploitation, discrimination, and welfare reduction.

Consequently, the legal framework was analyzed to see to what extent it can address the challenges posed by personalized contracting. Based on the current state of affairs, it is possible to conclude that the current legal framework falls short of adequately protecting consumers. Novel protection strategies are needed that are able to tackle the signing-without-reading problem, counteract the insertion of one-sided terms, and safeguard consumer expectations.

References

Agarwal K (2023) The future of legal documents: What's an AI contract generator? Spotdraft. https://www.spotdraft.com/blog/ai-contract-generator

Akerlof GA (1970) The market for "lemons": quality uncertainty and the market mechanism. Q J Econ 84(3):488–500

Akerlof GA, Shiller RJ (2015) Phishing for phools: the economics of manipulation and deception. Princeton University Press, Princeton

Armstrong M (2008) Interactions between competition and consumer policy. Compet Policy Int 4(1):97–147

Ayres I, Gertner R (1989) Filling gaps in incomplete contracts: an economic theory of default rules. Yale Law J 99(1):87–130

Ayres I, Schwartz A (2014) The no-reading problem in consumer contract law. Stanford Law Rev 66(3):545–610

Baird DG (2006) The boilerplate puzzle. Mich Law Rev 104(5):933–952

Bakos Y, Marotta-Wurgler F, Trossen DR (2014) Does anyone read the fine print? Consumer attention to standard-form contracts. J Leg Stud 43(1):1–35

Bar-Gill O (2012) Seduction by contract: law, economics and psychology in consumer markets. Oxford University Press, Oxford

Bar-Gill O (2018) Algorithmic price discrimination: when demand is a function of both preferences and (mis)perceptions. Univ Chicago Law Rev 86(2):1–30

Barnett RE (2002) Consenting to form contracts. Fordham Law Rev 71(3):627–646

Bebchuk LA, Posner RA (2006) One-sided contracts in competitive consumer markets. Mich Law Rev 104(5):827–836

Becher SI (2007) Behavioral science and consumer standard form contracts. La Law Rev 68(1):117–180

Becher SI, Unger-Aviram E (2009) The law of standard form contracts: misguided intuitions and suggestions for reconstruction. DePaul Bus Commer Law J 8(3):199–228

Becher SI, Zarsky TZ (2007) E-contract doctrine 2.0: standard form contracting in the age of online user participation. Mich Telecommun Technol Law Rev 14(1):303–366

Ben-Shahar O (2009) The myth of the ‘opportunity to read’ in contract law. Eur Rev Contract Law 5(1):1–28

Ben-Shahar O, Bar-Gill O (2013) Regulatory techniques in consumer protection: a critique of European consumer contract law. Common Mark Law Rev 50:109–126

Ben-Shahar O, Chilton A (2016) Simplification of privacy disclosures: an experimental test. J Leg Stud 45(S2):S41–S67

Ben-Shahar O, Porat A (2019) Personalizing mandatory rules in contract law. Univ Chicago Law Rev 86(2):255–282

Ben-Shahar O, Posner EA (2011) The right to withdraw in contract law. J Leg Stud 40(1):115–148

Bigwood R (2003) Exploitative contracts. Oxford University Press, Oxford

Braucher J (2007) US influence with a twist: lessons about unfair contract terms from US software customers. Aust Compet Consum Law J 15(1):1–20

Brownsword R (2009) Consent in data protection law: privacy, fair processing and confidentiality. In: Gutwirth S, Poullet Y, De Hert P, De Terwangne C, Nouwt S (eds) Reinventing data protection? Springer, Dordrecht, pp 83–110

Connelly BL, Certo ST, Ireland RD, Reutzel CR (2011) Signaling theory: a review and assessment. J Manag 37(1):39–67

Cranor LF (2012) Can users control online behavioral advertising effectively? IEEE Secur Priv 10(2):93–96

De Geest G (2016) Signing without Reading. In: Marciano A, Ramello GB (eds) Encyclopedia of law and economics. Springer, Cham, pp 1–8

De Geest G (2018) Rents: how marketing causes inequality. Beccaria Books, Leuven

DellaVigna S, Malmendier U (2004) Contract design and self-control: theory and evidence. Q J Econ 119(2):353–402

DellaVigna S, Malmendier U (2006) Paying not to go to the gym. Am Econ Rev 96(3):694–719

Desai DR, Kroll JA (2017) Trust but verify: guide to algorithms and the law. Harv J Law Technol 31(1):1–64

Eisenberg MA (1995) The limits of cognition and the limits of contract. Stan Law Rev 47(2):211–259

Epstein RA (2008) The neoclassical economics of consumer contracts. Minn Law Rev 92(3):803–835

Fahy J, Jobber D (2015) Foundations of marketing. McGraw-Hill Education, London

Faure MG, Luth HA (2011) Behavioural economics in unfair contract terms. J Consum Policy 34(3):337–358

Fikentscher W, Hacker P, Podszun R (2013) FairEconomy: crises, culture, competition and the role of law. MPI Studies Intellect Prop Compet Law 19:1–22
Gabaix X, Laibson D (2006) Shrouded attributes, consumer myopia, and information suppression in competitive markets. Q J Econ 121(2):505–540
Galli F (2021) Online behavioural advertising and unfair manipulation between the GDPR and the UCPD. In: Ebers M, Gamito MC (eds) Algorithmic governance and governance of algorithms: legal and ethical challenges. Springer Nature, Cham, pp 109–135
Galli F (2022) Algorithmic marketing and EU law on unfair commercial practices. Springer Nature, Cham
Galli F, Lagioia F, Sartor G (2022) Consent to targeted advertising. Eur Bus Law Rev 33(4):485–512
Gardiner C (2022) Unfair contract terms in the digital age: the challenge of protecting European consumers in the online marketplace. Edward Elgar Publishing, Cheltenham
Garello P (2003) The breach of contract in French law: between safety of expectations and efficiency. Int Rev Law Econ 22(4):407–420
Gillette CP (2011) Standard form contracts. In: De Geest G (ed) Contract law and economics. Edward Elgar Publishing, Cheltenham, pp 115–124
Goldberg VP (1974) Institutional change and the quasi-invisible hand. J Law Econ 17(2):461–492
Goldman L (1992) My way and the highway: the law and economics of choice of forum clauses in consumer form contracts. Nw Univ Law Rev 86(3):700–741
Golobardes MA (2022) Algorithmic personalization of consumer transactions and the limits of contract law. J Law Mark Innov 1(1):17–43
Grubb MD (2015) Overconfident consumers in the marketplace. J Econ Perspect 29(4):9–36
Grundmann S, Hacker P (2017) Digital technology as a challenge to European contract law: from the existing to the future architecture. Eur Rev Contract Law 13(3):255–293
Gunter B (2016) The psychology of consumer profiling in a digital age. Routledge, Abingdon
Hacker P (2017) Personal data, exploitative contracts, and algorithmic fairness: autonomous vehicles meet the internet of things. Int Data Privacy Law 7(4):266–286
Harvey HH (2019) Justifying the efficacy of contract discrimination. J Law Innov 2:47–70
Hawkins J (2016) Using advertisements to diagnose behavioral market failure in the payday lending market. Wake Forest Law Rev 51(1):57–102
Hayek FA (1945) The use of knowledge in society. Am Econ Rev 35(4):519–530
Heidhues P, Kőszegi B (2010) Exploiting naivete about self-control in the credit market. Am Econ Rev 100(5):2279–2303
Heidhues P, Kőszegi B, Murooka T (2016) Exploitative innovation. Am Econ J Microecon 8(1):1–23
Helberger N (2016) Profiling and targeting consumers in the internet of things—a new challenge for consumer law. In: Schulze R, Staudenayer D (eds) Digital revolution: challenges for contract law in practice. Nomos, Baden-Baden, pp 135–164
Helberger N, Lynskey O, Micklitz HW, Rott P, Sax M, Strycharz J (2021) EU consumer protection 2.0: structural asymmetries in digital consumer markets. Joint report from EUCP2.0 Project BEUC, pp 1–207
Hillman RA (2005a) Online boilerplate: would mandatory website disclosure of e-standard terms backfire. Mich Law Rev 104(5):837–856
Hillman RA (2005b) Online consumer standard-form contracting practices: a survey and discussion of legal implications. Cornell Leg Stud Res Pap 05-012:1–30
Hillman RA, Barakat I (2008) Warranties and disclaimers in the electronic age. Yale J Law Technol 11(1):1–69
Hondius EH (2016) Unfair contract terms and the consumer: ECJ case law, foreign literature, and their impact on Dutch law. Eur Rev Priv Law 24(3/4):457–472
Howells G (2005) The potential and limits of consumer empowerment by information. J Law Soc 32(3):349–370
Hylton KN (2003) Antitrust law: economic theory and common law evolution. Cambridge University Press, Cambridge

Johnston J (2006) The return of bargain: an economic theory of how standard-form contracts enable cooperative negotiation between businesses and consumers. Mich Law Rev 104(5):857–898
Jolls C, Sunstein CR, Thaler RH (1998) A behavioral approach to law and economics. Stan Law Rev 50(5):1471–1550
Kant T (2020) Making it personal: algorithmic personalization, identity, and everyday life. Oxford Univ Press, Oxford
Kaptein M, Parvinen P (2015) Advancing e-commerce personalization: process framework and case study. Int J Electron Commer 19(3):7–33
Kessler F (1943) Contracts of adhesion—some thoughts about freedom of contract. Colum Law Rev 43(5):629–642
Korobkin R (2003) Bounded rationality, standard form contracts, and unconscionability. Univ Chicago Law Rev 70(4):1203–1296
Korobkin RB, Ulen TS (2000) Law and behavioral science: removing the rationality assumption from law and economics. Calif Law Rev 88(4):1051–1144
Kőszegi B (2014) Behavioral contract theory. J Econ Lit 52(4):1075–1118
Lagioia F, Jabłonowska A, Liepina R, Drazewski K (2022) AI in search of unfairness in consumer contracts: the terms of service landscape. J Consum Policy 45(3):481–536
Leiser MR, Caruana M (2021) Dark patterns: light to be found in Europe's consumer protection regime. J Eur Consum Mark Law 10(6):237–251
Llewellyn KN (2016) The common law tradition: deciding appeals. Quid Pro Books, New Orleans
Lohsse S (2016) Information duties and defects in consent. In: Schulze R, Viscasillas PP (eds) The formation of contract: new features and developments in contracting. Nomos Verlag, Baden-Baden, pp 73–88
Loos M (2015) Transparency of standard terms under the unfair contract terms directive and the proposal for a common European sales law. Eur Rev Priv Law 23(2):179–194
Loos M, Luzak J (2021) Update the unfair contract terms directive for digital services. European Parliament Think Tank, Report No. PE 676.006. https://www.europarl.europa.eu/thinktank/en/document/IPOL_STU(2021)676006
Luth HA (2010) Behavioural economics in consumer policy: the economic analysis of standard terms in consumer contracts revisited. Erasmus Univ Rotterdam, Rotterdam
Mann RJ, Siebneicher T (2008) Just one click: the reality of internet retail contracting. Colum Law Rev 108(4):984–1012
Marotta-Wurgler F (2007) What's in a standard form contract? An empirical analysis of software license agreements. J Empir Leg Stud 4(4):677–713
Marotta-Wurgler F (2011) Some realities of online contracting. Supreme Court Econ Rev 19(1):11–23
Marotta-Wurgler F (2015) Even more than you wanted to know about the failures of disclosure. Jerusalem Rev Leg Stud 11(1):63–74
Marotta-Wurgler F, Taylor R (2013) Set in stone: change and innovation in consumer standard-form contracts. New York Univ Law Rev 88(1):240–285
Matzner T, Masur PK, Ochs C, Pape TV (2016) Do-it-yourself data protection—empowerment or burden? In: Gutwirth S, Leenes R, De Hert P (eds) Data protection on the move: current developments in ICT and privacy/data protection. Springer, Dordrecht, pp 277–305
Melecky M, Rutledge S (2011) Financial consumer protection and the global financial crisis. MPRA Pap No. 28201:1–21
Mik E (2016) The erosion of autonomy in online consumer transactions. Law Innov Technol 8(1):1–38
Möslein F (2023) Digitized terms: the regulation of standard contract terms in the digital age. Eur Rev Contract Law 19(4):300–320
Obar JA, Oeldorf-Hirsch A (2020) The biggest lie on the internet: ignoring the privacy policies and terms of service policies of social networking services. Inf Commun Soc 23(1):128–147
Patti FP (2016) Fraud and misleading commercial practices: modernizing the law of defects in consent. Eur Rev Contract Law 12(4):307–334

Pitt W (2019) Fighting legalese with digital, personalized contracts. Harv Bus Rev https://hbr.org/2019/02/fighting-legalese-with-digital-personalized-contracts
Południak-Gierz K (2019) Consequences of the use of personalization algorithms in shaping an offer: a private law perspective. Masaryk Univ J Law Technol 13(2):161–188
Południak-Gierz K (2020) Personalized agreement—a new contractual model. Vestn Sankt-Petersburg Univ Prav 11(4):1009–1021
Południak-Gierz K (2021) Personalization of consumer contracts—should we personalize interpretation rules? In: Rodriguez AML, Green MD, Kubica ML (eds) Legal challenges in the new digital age. Brill Nijhoff, Leiden, pp 264–280
Południak-Gierz K, Tereszkiewicz P (2023) Digitalization's big promise and peril: the personalization of insurance contracts and its legal consequences. In: Mathis K, Tor A (eds) Law and economics of the digital transformation. Springer, Cham, pp 33–49
Poncibò C (2023) The UCTD 30 years later: identifying and blacklisting unfair terms in digital markets. Eur Rev Contract Law 19(4):321–345
Porat A, Strahilevitz LJ (2014) Personalizing default rules and disclosure with big data. Mich Law Rev 112(8):1417–1478
Posner RA, Rosenfield AM (1977) Impossibility and related doctrines in contract law: an economic analysis. J Leg Stud 6(1):83–118
Priest GL (1981) A theory of the consumer product warranty. Yale Law J 90(6):1297–1352
Radin MJ (2012) Boilerplate: the fine print, vanishing rights, and the rule of law. Princeton University Press, Princeton
Rakoff TD (1983) Contracts of adhesion: an essay in reconstruction. Harv Law Rev 96(6):1173–1284
Reich N, Micklitz HW (2014) The court and sleeping beauty: the revival of the unfair contract terms directive (UCTD). Common Mark Law Rev 51(3):771–808
Schäfer HB, Leyens PC (2010) Judicial control of standard terms and European private law. In: Larouche P, Chirico F (eds) Economic analysis of the DCFR. Sellier, Munich, pp 97–122
Scholz LH (2017) Algorithmic contracts. Stanford Technol Law Rev 20:128–169
Scholz LH (2018) Law and autonomous systems series: toward a consumer contract law for an algorithmic age. Oxford Bus Law Blog. https://blogs.law.ox.ac.uk/business-law-blog/blog/2018/04/law-and-autonomous-systems-series-toward-consumer-contract-law
Schulte-Nölke H, Zoll F, Macierzyńska-Franaszczyk E, Sebastian S, Charlton S, Barmscheid M, Kubela M (2013) Discrimination of consumers in the digital single market. Directorate General for Internal Policies, Policy Department A: Economic and Scientific Policy, pp 1–52. https://www.europarl.europa.eu/RegData/etudes/STUD/2013/507456/IPOLIMCO_ET(2013)507456_EN.pdf
Schulze R (2016) Pre-contractual duties: a brief introduction. In: Schulze R, Viscasillas PP (eds) The formation of contract. Nomos Verlag, Baden-Baden, pp 25–28
Schwartz A, Wilde LL (1978) Intervening in markets on the basis of imperfect information: a legal and economic analysis. Univ Pa Law Rev 127(3):630–682
Shiller B (2014) First degree price discrimination using big data. Brandeis University, Working Paper No. 58
Shui H, Ausubel LM (2004) Time inconsistency in the credit card market. SSRN Working Paper No. 586622
Sowell T (1980) Knowledge and decisions. Basic Books, New York
Stark DP, Choplin JM (2009) A license to deceive: enforcing contractual myths despite consumer psychological realities. New York Univ J Law Bus 5(2):617–744
Steennot R (2015) Public and private enforcement in the field of unfair contract terms. Eur Rev Priv Law 23(4):589–620
Trebilcock MJ (1997) The limits of freedom of contract. Harvard University Press, Cambridge
Van Heusden A (2020) The impact of branding on boilerplates: a law and economics analysis of standard-form contracting. EMLE. https://emle.org/wp-content/uploads/2020/11/EMLE-Thesis-Van-Heusden-Adrianus.pdf

Vandenberghe AS (2010) The role of information deficiencies in contract enforcement. Erasmus Law Rev 3(1):71–92

Varian HR (2009) Intermediate microeconomics: a modern approach, 8th edn. W. W. Norton & Company, New York

Wagner G, Eidenmüller H (2019) Down by algorithms: siphoning rents, exploiting biases, and shaping preferences: regulating the dark side of personalized transactions. Univ Chicago Law Rev 86(2):581–610

Wandel J (2012) Competition and antitrust policy: an Austrian economics perspective. In: Tavidze A (ed) Progress in economics research, vol 30. Nova, Hauppauge, pp 47–60

Whitford WC (1973) The functions of disclosure regulation in consumer transactions. Wisconsin Law Rev 1973(2):400–470

Willis LE (2013) When nudges fail: slippery defaults. Univ Chicago Law Rev 80(3):1155–1230

Wonnell CT (1985) Contract law and the Austrian school of economics. Fordham Law Rev 54(4):507–543

Chapter 6
Regulating Personalized Marketing: A Policy Perspective

Abstract Building on the preceding analyses, this chapter explores pathways for regulatory reform to address the challenges posed by personalized marketing in the digital age. A law and economics analysis of innovative regulatory approaches is undertaken, culminating in a series of policy proposals. These proposals aim to safeguard consumer autonomy, equity, and welfare, thereby enhancing the effectiveness of consumer protection laws in an increasingly digital marketplace.

6.1 Introduction

In the previous chapters, the practice of personalized marketing, in its different forms, has been analyzed, and it was found that the existing EU regulatory framework insufficiently addresses the concerns identified. Therefore, new strategies to enhance consumer protection are needed, which allow consumers to reap the benefits of personalization while avoiding the drawbacks of prohibitions. More specifically, this means enabling consumers to benefit from, for example, more relevant and better-timed ads, while limiting the exploitation of consumers' autonomy, equity, and welfare. In this chapter, a novel regulatory approach will be presented, which complements the current legal framework and aims to address the concerns identified.

The challenge in tackling personalized marketing lies in its subtlety. By means of sophisticated AI-driven technologies, it has become possible for firms to exploit the wiggle room in the current regulatory framework and thereby "meet the letter but not the spirit of the rules".[1]

Data-driven marketing strategies have paved the way for new methods of online manipulation that are not covered by existing regulations. Online manipulation refers to the "particular class of manipulative practices enabled by a broad range of

[1] Willis (2015), p. 1327.

A. J. van Heusden, *The Law and Economics of Personalization*, Economic Analysis of Law in European Legal Scholarship 20,
https://doi.org/10.1007/978-3-032-01468-9_6

information technologies."[2] This comes into effect when marketing practices become more complex, hidden, and targeted. Since the success of these strategies lies in their sophistication, it becomes immediately apparent that cases of manipulation or exploitation will be more challenging to identify.

In the age of personalized marketing, vulnerabilities can be exploited on an individual level without the individual being aware of it due to a profoundly complex mechanism concealing the true intentions of the manipulator. Marketers have found legal gaps and can use the gray area between lawful persuasion and unlawful manipulation to their benefit.[3] As a consequence, personalized marketing strategies are utilized on a massive scale,[4] whereas adequate regulation is lacking.

6.2 Personalized Marketing: A Review of Its Challenges

Before discussing the proposed legal interventions, a review of the justifications for intervention will be given.[5] Personalized marketing poses a new challenge to the consumer protection framework in the digital age. Through large-scale data collection, it has now become possible to target consumers on a micro level. Three personalization techniques have been investigated, which have been found to impact consumer decision-making negatively.

The first technique concerned personalized advertising.[6] This form of personalization has opened the door for effective behavior modification in order to extract value. From a consumer welfare hypothesis perspective, the practice is problematic since it negatively impacts consumer welfare overall. Although personalized advertising can lead to higher ad relevance, it will most likely lead to welfare losses by steering consumers toward products or services that do not optimally match their needs or by aiming to extract the maximum amount of consumer surplus.

Personalized advertising becomes more troublesome from a broader consumer policy perspective, which considers equity, consumer perceptions, and ethical considerations. In terms of equity, the practice causes regressive effects through the exploitation of biases and the modification of preferences. Especially for vulnerable and less sophisticated consumers this form of exploitation seems to have a profound impact. The use of dark patterns exacerbates these effects. Serious privacy concerns override consumers' positive perceptions of personalized advertising. In addition, consumer autonomy, non-discrimination, and human dignity are at risk. Accordingly, further legal intervention has been advocated on the topic of personalized advertising.

[2] Susser et al. (2019), pp. 2–3.

[3] De Geest (2018b), p. 5.

[4] Statista (2023).

[5] Cfr. Bar-Gill (2008) provides a four-step framework to assess if intervention in consumer markets can be justified.

[6] See Chap. 3.

Personalized advertising becomes more powerful when it is combined with algorithmic pricing.[7] Algorithmically-determined prices have the potential to approximate consumers' reservation prices with every-improving accuracy. As a consequence, the total amount of consumer surplus can be captured and transferred to the seller. Although under competitive market conditions it can be argued that algorithmic pricing leads to efficiency benefits for the market as a whole (i.e., inducing fiercer competition), consumer welfare will in all likelihood be negatively affected. Moreover, from an equity perspective, algorithmic pricing will most likely cause regressive effects. Additionally, several ethical concerns can be raised, such as risks of discrimination, social sorting, unfair pricing, unequal distributions of power, and privacy intrusion.

The third and final technique is the personalization of contract terms.[8] Through algorithmic personalization of contracts, it becomes possible to transform traditional standard terms into personalized terms that target consumers' individual preferences, characteristics, behaviors, and circumstances, but also biases and vulnerabilities. As a result, the existing signing-without-reading problem encountered in the context of standard terms will have even greater implications for consumers. Although personalized contracting can enhance transactional efficiency, it has the potential to lead to exploitation, discrimination, and consumer welfare-reduction.

The common denominator of these three personalization techniques is that they create marketing-induced market failures,[9] which the seller can exploit strategically.[10] The legal analyses of each practice have demonstrated that the current legal framework falls short of providing adequate protection to consumers.[11] Consequently, it is argued that further legal interventions should be implemented to address personalized marketing adequately. Where in the past, consumer issues could be classified as information asymmetry problems, there are serious reasons to believe that personalized marketing in the digital age supersedes this market failure.

In this study, it is asserted that personalization techniques facilitate the emergence of marketing-induced market failures, which are reinforced by the presence of high transaction costs and unequal bargaining positions. Accordingly, the traditional information paradigm,[12] followed in consumer law, will not suffice to tackle the problem. After all, marketing-induced market failures are more than an information problem. Providing more information to consumers will not help them better satisfy their preferences and protect them from welfare-reducing transactions.[13]

---

[7] See Chap. 4.

[8] See Chap. 5.

[9] See Sect. 2.4.1.

[10] Chapters 3–5 demonstrated how personalized advertising, pricing, and contracting lead to the extraction of rents, the exploitation of biases and vulnerabilities, and the shaping of preferences to the detriment of consumers' autonomy, equity, and welfare.

[11] See Sects. 3.6, 4.5, and 5.4.

[12] Busch (2019).

[13] Oehler and Wendt (2017).

Marketing personalization opens the way for optimal extraction of rents, bias exploitation, and preference shaping. It allows persuasive appeals to be matched to individuals' psychological characteristics, causing a significant alteration in online behavior.[14] It has become technically possible to successfully micro-target individuals,[15] and thereby effectively manipulate consumers on a large scale. The current legal framework is deficient; therefore, it can be argued that legal intervention is warranted.[16] However, this raises the question of what these interventions should look like. This will be further elaborated in the next sections.

6.3 Liability Versus Regulation

The law and economics literature has demonstrated that before delving into the question of regulation, it is relevant to see what liability rules can do. A full law and economics analysis of the liability versus regulation debate falls outside the scope of this section.[17] However, the necessary steps will be taken to indicate to what extent liability and regulation can complement each other in the realm of personalized marketing.

The starting point of the analysis is the *Coase Theorem*.[18] Pursuant to the Coase Theorem, "if one assumes rationality, no transaction costs, and no legal impediments to bargaining, *all* misallocations of resources would be fully cured in the market by bargains."[19] In that regard, it could be asserted that legal interventions would not be needed when consumers and marketers can bargain an efficient allocation of resources. In a zero-cost transaction setting, introducing liability rules, for example, would not affect the market's levels of care and output.[20] If the pricing-mechanism works smoothly, the well-informed consumer will be able to deduce all relevant information from the product's price. That is to say, the price adequately indicates the costs and the risks.[21] To illustrate, introducing a strict liability rule to protect consumers would be counterproductive in a Coasian setting because the pricing system will pass on the additional liability costs to the consumers.[22]

The *internalization rule* dictates that the liable party will fully internalize the costs of the risk (i.e., prevention and compensation) and reflect this in the final

[14] Matz et al. (2017).

[15] Faizullabhoy and Korolova (2018). See Sect. 2.4.1 for the concept of micro-targeting.

[16] See Chaps. 3–5, for an elaborate discussion of the applicable frameworks.

[17] See for an in-depth analysis, for instance, Shavell (1984); Kolstad et al. (1990).

[18] Coase (1960). See also Sect. 2.2.3.

[19] Calabresi (1968), p. 68.

[20] Oi (1973).

[21] Polinsky (1989), pp. 97–99.

[22] Faure (2016b), p. 637.

price.[23] Likewise, when there is no liability, consumers will take the risks into account and expect them to be reflected in the (lower) price as well. If both parties are fully informed and liability is freely transferable, there is no necessity to designate a liable party.[24] The parties can allocate the liability according to their preferences, corresponding to the Coase Theorem.[25] As long as the conditions of the Coase Theorem are met, an optimal level of care and output will ensue. This is the case regardless of the legal rule applied, meaning that legal intervention is unnecessary.[26]

Nevertheless, when there are positive transaction costs, the final allocation of resources depends on the choice of legal rules and remedies (i.e., the *normative Coase Theorem*).[27] As has been demonstrated in the cases of personalized advertising,[28] algorithmic pricing,[29] and personalized contracting,[30] the context of personalized marketing is characterized by positive transaction costs, unequal bargaining power, and information asymmetries. Consumers are not well-informed, perhaps even fully unaware, about the implemented personalization practices, and negotiating with the seller is prohibitively costly due to the highly complex nature of the practices and the lack of consumer bargaining power.[31] It can, therefore, be argued that Coasian negotiations are not likely to take place.

Although legislative efforts are in place to provide consumers with more information to improve their knowledge (i.e., mandated disclosure), it can be stated that, ultimately, they fail to improve consumers' decision-making process.[32] There are built-in transaction costs that hamper the application of the Coase Theorem to personalized marketing.[33] Consequently, since consumers are not and cannot become fully informed by means of the price mechanism, the implementation of further regulation and/or liability rules can be considered.[34]

The insights of Shavell (1984)[35] offer a valuable framework to determine the necessity of liability, regulation, or both. Shavell's framework discusses the four general determinants of the relative desirability of liability and regulation. He demonstrates that administrative costs and differential knowledge favor liability in gen-

---

[23] Fiore (2009), p. 419.

[24] Faure (2016a), p. 631.

[25] Faure (2016a), p. 631.

[26] Faure (2016b), p. 636.

[27] Parisi (2013), pp. 202–204.

[28] See Chap. 3.

[29] See Chap. 4.

[30] See Chap. 5.

[31] Cfr. Gilead (1985) demonstrates that in the context of product liability, the ability to freely negotiate in a competitive market with no transaction costs is also lacking.

[32] Ben-Shahar and Schneider (2014).

[33] Gilead (1985), pp. 41–42.

[34] Gilead (1985), pp. 41–42.

[35] Shavell (1984).

eral. In contrast, incapacity to pay for inflicted harm and the chance of escaping suit for harm done favor regulation. As a result, in some instances, the joint use of liability and regulation can be advocated.[36] By applying this framework to personalized marketing, it can be assessed whether it is justified to use both liability and regulation.

The first determinant, the difference in knowledge about risky activities between regulators and private parties relates to the benefits of the activities, the costs of reducing risks, and the probability or severity of the risks.[37] Shavell (1984) states that "private parties should generally enjoy an inherent advantage in knowledge".[38] With personalized marketing, it can be argued that this is currently the case considering the complexity and opacity of the techniques underlying the personalization mechanisms. The developers of the marketing techniques are aware of the benefits and costs of the implemented techniques since this is essential to determine their effectiveness. The regulator, in contrast, would need to invest significant resources to study the underlying techniques, understand their complexity, and act accordingly. Therefore, it is safe to say that marketers possess more specific knowledge about the practices than regulators, which favors the use of liability rules.

The second determinant concerns the capacity of private parties to pay for the harm done.[39] In principle, liability rules would not provide adequate incentives since a private party "will treat liability that exceeds his assets as imposing an effective financial penalty only equal to his assets".[40] This means that the expected penalties might be less than the expected losses for which the private party is liable because it cannot pay the full amount for which it has been found liable, thereby making the party *judgment proof*.[41] This provides a *prima facie* justification for the use of regulation. Under regulation, the ability to pay for harm is peripheral since private parties need to comply with pre-set requirements to engage in the activity.

In the realm of marketing, it is conceivable that effectively addressing personalized marketing practices on a large scale could cause companies substantial financial difficulties, given the significant share of personalized marketing in their total budgets.[42] In addition, marketing firms are often organized as limited liability companies, meaning their liability is capped. This has three consequences: it might lead to insufficient levels of care to prevent the damage, victims (i.e., the consumers) will not be fully compensated, and not all costs from the activity will be internalized.[43] As a consequence of the latter, the costs will be externalized to society. For these

[36] Shavell (1984), p. 365.

[37] Shavell (1984), p. 359.

[38] Shavell (1984), p. 360.

[39] Shavell (1984), p. 360.

[40] Shavell (1986), p. 45.

[41] Shavell (1986), p. 45.

[42] Statista (2023) indicates that "many companies are already spending more than half of their budgets on personalization efforts today."

[43] Fiore (2009), pp. 418–419.

reasons, it can be asserted that marketers' incapacity to pay for the harm done favors the use of regulation.

The third determinant relates to the threat of suit for the harm inflicted.[44] Similar to the capacity to pay, the threat of suit generally favors regulation since liability rules will likely fail to provide adequate incentives to reduce the risk of harm. With respect to personalized marketing in consumer markets, it can be stated that the threat of suits is low. First, the harms to consumers are widespread. Each consumer is micro-targeted, and the corresponding harms will be subtle and difficult to identify. The private costs of bringing suit will be higher than the projected private benefits, resulting in rational apathy.[45] The rational apathy of consumers is evidenced by the insufficient private enforcement of consumer law, especially in the absence of effective collective action mechanisms.[46] Second, due to the complexity of the personalization mechanism, it is particularly difficult to prove causation between the technique and the harm done. Third, even if specific parties can be held liable through collective actions, it is unlikely that large-scale changes will be implemented, given the immense size of the marketing industry. Consequently, it can be stated that the threat of suits that firms face is small, favoring regulation.

The last determinant is the magnitude of the administrative costs associated with the use of liability rules or regulations.[47] By and large, liability rules have lower administrative costs because they are only incurred when harm occurs, whereas under regulation, the costs are incurred even though no harm has been done.[48] Besides, liability rules provide incentives specifically to the sub-groups of injurers that are most likely to cause harm since they will be facing the threat of suit. In contrast, under regulation, there is no differentiation between the parties. Administrative costs are incurred, even though the risk might have been removed from the market.[49]

However, the scale on which personalized marketing is taking place (i.e., fastest growing marketing strategy worldwide) and the size of the potential harm that can be inflicted on consumers do make a compelling argument in favor of regulation. It can be asserted that the administrative costs of regulation will be outweighed by the benefits that will accrue to consumers when exploitative marketing practices are regulated. Due to the ubiquity of personalized marketing techniques, a wave of liability-based litigation would need to take place to adequately protect consumers, which, based on the current state of affairs, is not likely to occur. Although it is inevitable that administrative costs will be incurred in order to regulate personalized marketing, it can be argued that the administrative costs of regulation will not be

[44] Shavell (1984), p. 363.

[45] Van den Bergh and Visscher (2008).

[46] Van den Bergh and Visscher (2008). It must be noted that the collective action problem is ameliorating by the trends in civil litigation financing, see, for instance, Tuil and Visscher (2010).

[47] Shavell (1984), p. 363.

[48] Shavell (1984), p. 363.

[49] Shavell (1984), p. 364.

disproportionate in comparison to the use of liability. Moreover, there is a lack of information due to latency (i.e., *long-tail damage*), it is hard to establish causality or gather proof, and insolvency problems are present, all of which support the use of regulation.[50]

All in all, based on the assessment of Shavell's (1984) criteria, it can be concluded that in the context of personalized marketing, regulation should be used as the primary instrument and liability should have a supplementary role. The analysis of the four determinants demonstrated that the joint use of liability rules and regulation is warranted.

6.4 Policy Recommendations

The challenge that consumer policy is facing in the digital age is that, in its current state, it is not fit to address the threats that personalized marketing poses to consumer autonomy, equity, and welfare.[51] The purpose of legislative intervention is to tackle personalized marketing in a manner that enhances consumer protection in the market. This study identified five goals that legal intervention should achieve: (1) Update the archaic mandated disclosure mechanism to aid consumers in their decision-making process. (2) Monitor marketing activities in order to prevent the development and execution of consumer welfare-decreasing personalization practices. (3) Provide consumers with a genuine opt-out option to stay away from personalization services. (4) Discourage exploitative practices through liability rules. (5) Offer a policy approach that explicitly takes the equity-efficiency trade-off into account.

In law and economics, the law is not seen as an end but as a means to achieve a socially desirable outcome.[52] In light of this credo, a stepwise discussion of all policy proposals will take place in the following sections.

6.4.1 Tackling the Boilerplate and Updating Disclosure

Based on the information paradigm,[53] mandated disclosures play a key role in consumer protection law. The rationale is that by providing information to consumers, they will be aided in their decision-making process, which will increase transparency and help them to act upon their preferences.[54] This has resulted in the ubiquity

[50] Faure (2014).

[51] Based on the current state of affairs that results from the analyses in Chaps. 3–5.

[52] Faure and Visscher (2018).

[53] Oehler and Wendt (2017).

[54] Oehler and Wendt (2017).

of the boilerplate, which allows companies to meet information requirements through a standardized document. If additional information needs to be disclosed, this can automatically be added to the boilerplate. Therefore, it should come as no surprise that boilerplates have become longer and more complex over the years.[55] More information, however, does not equal greater awareness and better understanding. As thoroughly substantiated by Ben-Shahar and Schneider (2014), mandated disclosure has failed to be a helpful instrument for consumers.[56] It could be argued that mandated disclosures are ineffective because they have not been simplified enough. However, in the realm of privacy disclosures, it has been found that simplifying disclosures does not significantly alter consumers' understanding of the disclosure, their expectations about their rights, or their willingness to share personal information.[57]

To revive the usefulness of mandated disclosure, it has been advocated that behaviorally- informed disclosures could significantly improve the instrument's effectiveness by taking consumer biases and heuristics into account and designing the requirements accordingly.[58] This may involve giving more attention to the visual elements of disclosure, the amount of information, and the frame in which the information is presented. Another contribution is the use of a multidisciplinary perspective to design transparent online disclosures.[59]

Nonetheless, the advent of big data has brought about new technologies that could prove to be more effective in satisfying consumers' personal preferences and informational needs. Information technology offers the possibility to design disclosures that account for consumer heterogeneity. In the same way marketers can personalize marketing messages to consumers, it is also possible to personalize disclosures. This gives rise to the concept of *personalized disclosure*; disclosure that is tailored to the individual.[60]

6.4.1.1 Personalized Disclosure

The advancements in digital technologies can aid the development of consumer protection tools in the same way they aid marketing strategies. In essence, this alludes to the use of AI to improve the disclosure mechanism.

Under the existing consumer protection laws, traders have the obligation to disclose a variety of snippets of information to consumers. To illustrate, in the realm of algorithmic pricing, traders must inform consumers about the fact that the offered

[55] Marotta-Wurgler (2015).

[56] Ben-Shahar and Schneider (2014).

[57] Ben-Shahar and Chilton (2016).

[58] Barr et al. (2009); Reisch and Thøgersen (2017); Reisch and Zhao (2017).

[59] Seizov et al. (2019).

[60] Porat and Strahilevitz (2014).

price has been personalized based on automated decision-making.[61] Effectively, this consists of a notification that the price has been personalized, similar to an ad notification alongside an advertisement. In essence, with such a notification, the trader complies with the duty to inform consumers. However, disclosure does not equal an improved understanding of the price. More specifically, it remains a mystery to what extent the price is fully individualized or derived from group characteristics, and how much it differs from the uniform price.

Simply put, the disclosure does not provide sufficient information to effectively contribute to consumers' decision-making process. The seller utilizing the personalized pricing mechanism has access to all of this information but does not wish to disclose it. Under personalized disclosure, these key pieces of information would have to be disclosed to the consumer.[62]

However, an economically inefficient way of implementing personalized disclosures would be to require the government to collect all relevant information and provide consumers individually with the necessary information. This would lead to wasteful duplication of efforts. The value of the mechanism lies in creating an additional purpose for data that has already been collected.

Originally, the purpose of these data is, by definition, commercial since they are collected to be monetized by firms. The additional purpose, however, would be to inform consumers of the data that has been collected. Instead of making the government responsible, responsibility could be placed on the businesses themselves. In other words, the efforts already undertaken by companies could be utilized for the sake of informing consumers instead of collecting the data twice (once by the firm and once by the regulator). The regulator would then only require the companies to disclose the metrics used for personalization and decide what is authorized. That way, the regulator does not need to assess or determine all individual metric scores, which can be delegated to the companies. Still, the regulator will know what categories have been used and if they comply with the existing legal framework.[63]

Accordingly, the question arises: How would personalized disclosure look in practice? For the sake of clarity, the setting of algorithmic pricing will be used to explain the concept. Under personalized price disclosures, consumers would, *inter alia*, see a brief and clear calculation of the price, the difference with the uniform price, and the personal information on which the price has been based. In this way, consumers receive information that can effectively assist them in their decision-making process.

An essential part of the disclosure is that consumers can compare the personalized price with the prices offered to other consumers in, for example, brick-and-mortar stores. To illustrate, when a consumer goes to a supermarket, the prices displayed are uniform for all consumers. If consumers would do online shopping at

[61] European Commission (2021).

[62] See, for example, the work on personalized law by Porat and Strahilevitz (2014); Ben-Shahar and Porat (2021).

[63] For an elaborate discussion of the mechanics behind this system, see Hacker (2017b).

the same supermarket, they could, in theory, compare the online personalized price with the offline standardized price in the store. Personalized price disclosures would offer this opportunity while eliminating the transaction costs of going to the store.

Of note is that this mechanism is not impeded by the absence of a physical store. Online firms can in such cases display a randomized sample of prices (approximating the average uniform price) that have been offered to other consumers in the same period, so consumers can compare the offers and decide if the price is acceptable to them.[64] This does not only benefit consumers by making them more aware of the personalization mechanism, but it also fosters competition since comparison shopping comes into play again. In this way, the consumer is presented with information that can effectively aid the decision-making process.[65] Transposing this mechanism to personalized advertising would mean that the consumer gets a clear and simplified report that indicates based on which information the ad has been personalized. An extension could be to show, if desired by the consumer, a random sorting of ads shown to consumers that used the same query or ads that have been generated based on the search history of other consumers with different characteristics and preferences, thereby allowing for comparison.[66] This report should be immediately available (e.g., via an information button) when the ad is displayed to the consumer.

Of note is that Meta has undertaken several steps to provide consumers with more specific information about its advertising. When receiving a personalized ad, the user can click on an information button to see based on what information the ad has been personalized.[67] Nonetheless, this disclosure differs fundamentally from personalized disclosure as described in this section. First, the information provided by Meta relates to broad categories to which a user has been assigned (for example, interests, age, and location). This makes it arduous for users to identify the individualized aspect of the ad. Second, for more information about which factors influence the ads that users see, Meta refers to its general page, thereby keeping consumers in the dark. Third, Meta does not disclose for what purpose the ad has been personalized. At first glance, the ad seems to have been based on consumers' interests. However, further study would reveal that a specific product is being presented to consumers because they have recently exhibited signs of vulnerability in their online behavior, such as stress, anxiety, or insecurity.[68] The capitalization on consumer vulnerabilities is skillfully swept under the rug. In short, the current degree of granularity of disclosures by Meta can be significantly improved.

More abstractly, personalized disclosures can be valuable in a variety of situations where currently standard forms are used. When entering a transaction, a

[64] Davola et al. (2023), p. 20.

[65] Davola et al. (2023), p. 1.

[66] Davola et al. (2023), p. 20.

[67] Clicking on "Why am I seeing this ad?" next to the advertisement will reveal this information. Kim et al. (2019) show that this requires an additional active effort from the consumer, which eventually does not lead to an increased level of understanding.

[68] Davidson (2017).

consumer is provided with general information that is not presented in a way that is convenient for and adapted to the specific consumer. To illustrate, when concluding a credit card contract, it could be the case that one consumer is particularly privacy-sensitive and is mainly preoccupied with the risk of data leaks of payment information. In contrast, another consumer could be specifically worried about the financial consequences of the agreement, such as the magnitude of the overdraft fee. Regardless of their situation, the same disclosure is used, leading to information overload, as it provides details about all contractual stipulations, preventing consumers from finding the information that is most relevant to them.

Personalized disclosures can improve consumer understanding by altering the way in which information is presented, namely by reducing total information and underlining vital pieces of information that have wide-ranging consequences for the specific consumer. Even if an opt-in mechanism for personalized marketing would be established,[69] the personalized disclosures would remain the same since the consumer's attention always needs to be steered to the parts of the consent form that significantly influence the consumer's position vis-à-vis the seller. In contrast to standardized disclosures, personalized disclosure is able to account for the heterogeneity of the consumer population, thereby taking into account the variance in consumer preferences,[70] perceptions of risk,[71] and vulnerabilities.[72] Hence, personalized disclosures highlight the information relevant to consumers, effectively aiding their decision-making.[73]

Two potential ways to personalize contractual information are through a *pre-selection mechanism* or *use-pattern information*.[74] In the former case, consumers can tick the boxes (e.g., through an online tool) of the contract terms that are of interest to them. This could mean, for instance, that the attention of privacy-sensitive consumers will be drawn to the privacy-related parts of the disclosure, which will be displayed in a conspicuous and simplified manner. In the latter case, information about consumers' past behavior is used to help consumers become aware of the aspects that are most important to them, as reflected by their actions.[75] Although the technological mechanism underlying personalized disclosure can vary, the outcome is that consumers will get the information they need to make an informed decision.

It is worth noting that personalized disclosures should allow consumers to change their preferences. It is imaginable that pre-selection or use-pattern mechanisms reflect preferences that might have changed over time. To illustrate, a consumer who

---

[69] As argued by Max Schrems in NOYB (2023).

[70] Wisniewski et al. (2017).

[71] Bhatia and Breaux (2018).

[72] Busch (2019), p. 321.

[73] Of note, while rational apathy may persist, personalized disclosures mitigate this by presenting tailored and salient information that directly aids decision-making. Busch (2019) propounds that consumers are more likely to engage with concise and relevant content, making personalized disclosures a pragmatic improvement over standard boilerplates.

[74] Bar-Gill and Ferrari (2010).

[75] Hacker (2017b).

has always been very financially oriented can become more interested in the privacy aspects of personalized services over the years. If the personalized disclosure highlights information that does not meet the consumer's needs, its effectiveness will be limited. A potential solution for this could be to build an online tool, for example, an AI-driven chatbox, with which consumers can request and look up different parts of the disclosure. This also includes requests about contract terms that have been updated or deleted but are of specific interest to the consumer. For instance, a consumer who has always traveled by plane is now interested in driving to Spain for a vacation. It could be the case that the personalized disclosure will show information on air travel coverage under the travel insurance. The consumer should then be able to request, via the tool, a change in the personalized disclosure, whereby critical information concerning the coverage of road trips will be displayed, and simultaneously, all information on air travel will be filtered out.

The effect of such a system is twofold. On the one hand, consumers can get the information they are most interested in when making a specific decision, thereby helping them make more informed decisions. On the other hand, it allows for the development of a learning system based on consumer feedback. This learning system has the potential to continuously improve the relevance of personalized disclosures, reinforcing the adequacy of the information provided.[76]

6.4.1.2 AI-Driven Detection of Unfair Terms

The personalized disclosure mechanism can be complemented with AI and *natural language processing* (NLP) techniques that flag digital-specific unfair terms. This would build upon the automated process that Micklitz et al. (2017) proposed to check the fairness of clauses in online consumer contracts.[77] In essence, they designed a software program[78] that automates the work of consumer-protection organizations, which currently exceeds the capabilities of these organizations because they have to manually conduct an abstract control of each and every clause. In this way, it contributes to preventing the continued use of unfair terms in consumer contracts.[79]

The idea has been further developed by Lagioia et al. (2022), who refined the process of controlling for unfair terms using an AI system.[80] The system is called *Claudette*, which is an automated unfairness detection tool.[81] The program can assess language complexity, detect ambiguity, and identify unfair and unlawful

[76] Busch (2019), pp. 325–326.

[77] Micklitz et al. (2017).

[78] The software is called uTerms and can be accessed via http://uterms.software/.

[79] Objective of the UCTD as it is set out in Article 7(1) UCTD.

[80] Lagioia et al. (2022).

[81] Lagioia et al. (2022), p. 489. It is part of the Claudette project, which focuses on machine learning-powered analysis of consumer contracts and privacy policies. The project can be found via http://claudette.eui.eu/.

clauses often incorporated in consumer contracts that relate to, for example, the limitation of liability, unilateral changes, unilateral terminations of contracts, content removal, and arbitration.

The AI system can offer valuable insights into consumer contracts and help in their legal qualification.[82] Concerning the latter, Ruggeri et al. (2022)[83] further developed mechanisms to detect and explain unfairness in consumer contracts through memory networks. These improve the explainability of classifier outcomes (i.e., indicating unfairness) by including legal rationales. More specifically, the *Memory-Augmented Neural Network* (MANN) uses legal justifications to explain the identification of an unfair clause. This helps to improve the system's accuracy and offer meaningful explanations of the identifiers.

An additional benefit of these systems is that the flagging of unfair terms allows for the creation of a database of known unfair terms, which aids investigations and enforcement. Although the tools are still in the developmental stage, that is to say, the analyzing power and accuracy can be strongly enhanced,[84] they demonstrate AI-driven technologies' potential to improve consumer protection against unfair terms. In that regard, the AI-driven control of personalized contracts can be a highly valuable complement to the personalized disclosure mechanism.

Overall, the development of personalized disclosure seems to be a promising regulatory avenue. It can effectively aid consumer decision-making, and it is capable of tackling the issues that are encountered with standard mandated disclosures. In addition, in combination with AI-driven controls, it offers a valuable tool to address personalized contracts. The regulatory avenue, however, does not end at disclosure.

Considering the marketing perspective, it would be beneficial if a trader would cease potential harmful behavior before one needs to go down the enforcement path. This is where the second prong of the policy proposal comes into play.

6.4.2 Monitoring the Marketer

The ex-ante solution of personalized disclosure gives companies considerable freedom in designing the disclosure, albeit governmental guidelines could indicate the metrics companies are allowed to use for personalization. Compliance monitoring and algorithmic auditing are of pivotal importance to ensure that companies fulfill their duties in the consumer's interest.[85] Public enforcement agencies could perform random audits of the technologies used and monitor the big companies in the market

[82] Lagioia et al. (2022), p. 489.

[83] Ruggeri et al. (2022).

[84] Poncibò (2023), p. 330.

[85] Busch (2019), p. 328.

to set a precedent.[86] However, to conduct audits, criteria need to be in place to assess the companies against.

Willis (2015) introduced the concept of *performance-based consumer law.*[87] Performance-based consumer law "moves regulators' focus from firms' actions to the effects of those actions on consumers."[88] This approach is based on two pillars. First, the establishment of performance standards, for example, consumer comprehension or suitable product use, which firms are free to meet in their own creative manner. Second, the institutionalization of a monitoring system that provides feedback to firms regarding consumer comprehension and product use. The benefit of this approach is that it aims "to make the law as agile as firms are".[89] This is an objective that the present approach to regulating personalized marketing shares.

Willis (2015) focuses on *consumer comprehension* (i.e., do consumers understand what the firm is offering them?) and *suitability requirements* (i.e., are consumers using the product suitably for their purposes?). The regulator (e.g., a specific public authority) would then set these requirements and monitor if companies comply with them. Performance-based regulations differ from prescriptive regulations because, under the former, regulated entities are free to determine how to meet the set standard, whereas under the latter, the conduct of the regulated entity is formally dictated.[90]

Under performance-based regulation, companies can be incentivized to find the least-cost means of reaching the regulatory goal, which makes it more market-reliant and appreciative of the knowledge that companies possess.[91] The danger lurks, however, in regulatory capture due to lobbying efforts for lenient standards by the industries that are being regulated.[92]

A dual solution to this problem can be provided in a consumer setting. First, the performance could be assessed by a third party, such as a consumer organization with no ties to the industry, which can prevent the watering down of standards. Second, rather than measuring performance before or after, compliance must be measured at regular but random intervals. In this way, it can be prevented that on an ex-post basis, it becomes clear that there has been underenforcement, which has led to unnecessary harm to consumers.[93]

[86] Busch (2019), p. 330.

[87] Willis (2015).

[88] Willis (2015), p. 1314.

[89] Willis (2015), p. 1309.

[90] Willis (2015), p. 1330.

[91] Willis (2015), p. 1335.

[92] See, for instance, in the context of environmental regulation, Faure and Partain (2019), p. 9.

[93] Willis (2015), p. 1332.

6.4.2.1 Manipulation Standards

Applying the concept of performance-based consumer law to the marketing realm would translate into establishing so-called *manipulation standards*. The legislator would then determine a threshold for what counts as a manipulative marketing practice. A marketing tactic is manipulative if:

> it is intended to motivate by undermining what the marketer believes is his/her audience's normal decision-making process either by deception or by playing on a vulnerability that the marketer believes exists in his/her audience's normal decision-making process.[94]

This differs from lawful rational persuasion, whereby individuals are presented with information (e.g., arguments) that allows them to reflect on it and make a conscious choice.[95] It becomes unlawful manipulation when an attempt is made to interfere with individuals' capacity to consciously make their decisions (i.e., competence) and self-authorship to endorse decisions as their own (i.e., authenticity).[96]

To measure the degree of manipulation, empirical research could be conducted to determine the likelihood that a consumer will be misled by a market practice. This can be done in two ways. At first, the test can focus on the design of the mechanism, whereby the hypothetical harm is ascertained though surveys and experiments. This would put a larger emphasis on the potential to harm consumers. This would be in correspondence with the principles of fairness and privacy by design as they are discussed in the realms of data protection and AI. The downside, however, is that such experiments on hypothetical harm could be seen as overreaching, because there is no evidence on the actual harm in practice. Therefore, an alternative could be to conduct empirical studies that identify how many consumers have been influenced by a marketing strategy into making a decision that is welfare-decreasing for themselves but beneficial to the seller. In other words, measuring the actual effect of marketing strategies over a specific period of time. The drawback here is that actual effects can be difficult to determine due to the subtlety of the personalization mechanisms. It is, therefore, likely that a combination of both methods (experiments on likelihood to harm and actual impact) will be needed to determine if a marketing practice transgresses the manipulation standards.

If the legislator's manipulation standard states that no more than a specific percentage of consumers might be misled, it can be determined if there is a case of online manipulation (i.e., exceeding the threshold). The reason for setting a threshold rather than aiming for 0% manipulation is that an economic trade-off needs to be made. Imposing rigorous manipulation standards might excessively burden businesses and consequently detract from market efficiency, which is also harmful to consumers. This effectively amounts to a *limiting principle* on intervention.[97] From

[94] Sher (2011), p. 97.
[95] Susser et al. (2019), p. 14.
[96] Susser et al. (2019), p. 38.
[97] Hoffman (2006); Calo (2014), pp. 1022–1023.

an economic perspective, "we should accept some degrees of consumer deception for the greater good (efficient markets)."[98]

Moreover, the standards should be adjusted over time commensurate with state-of-the-art marketing and information technologies.[99] This aligns with the principles of *adaptive management* or *smart governance*, whereby "regulators have the responsibility and authority to routinely review the performance of regulation and to make continuous adjustments to steer regulation closer to its goals."[100]

Utilizing empirical methods allows consumer law to depart from the standardized concepts of the average and vulnerable consumer and look at what the "actual" consumer does in practice.[101] However, two objections are made in the literature against the use of empirical evidence. In the first place, in Recital 18 of the UCPD, it is stated that the average consumer test is not a statistical test, which would mean that the use of empirical evidence is not feasible.[102] Nevertheless, in the *Gut Springenheide* case,[103] regarding the MCAD, the CJEU asserted with respect to the average consumer test that national courts are allowed, in some instances, to request an expert opinion or commission a consumer research poll to determine if a promotional description or statement is misleading or not.[104] The reference to expert opinions or consumer surveys effectively opens the door for the use of statistical evidence,[105] which in this study would relate to the use of manipulation standards.

In the second place, it is argued that due to hyper-personalization, it will be particularly onerous to collect empirical evidence.[106] However, this overlooks the fact that firms are already implementing sophisticated tests, such as A/B testing, to see how effective their strategies are at changing consumer behavior.[107] The information on the manipulative character is, thus, readily available. The next step is to make this information accessible to enforcement authorities. In this regard, the DSA is of particular interest. The ad repository requirements can elucidate a valuable part of the obscurity surrounding personalized marketing. Authorities can obtain relevant information to see to what extent the targeting of a firm is manipulative. This also

---

[98] Trzaskowski (2011), pp. 375–376.

[99] Willis (2015), p. 1364.

[100] Willis (2015), p. 1406.

[101] Willis (2015), p. 1407.

[102] Trzaskowski (2011), p. 384.

[103] Case C-210/96, Gut Springenheide and Rudolf Tusky v. Oberkreisdirektor des Kreises Steinfurt, ECLI:EU:C:1998:369. The Court of Justice of the European Union. https://eur-lex.europa.eu/legal-content/EN/TXT/?uri=CELEX%3A61996CJ0210.

[104] Paras 35–37.

[105] Trzaskowski (2011: 384); See also Case C-220/98, Estée Lauder Cosmetics GmbH and Co. OHG v. Lancaster Group GmbH, ECLI:EU:C:2000:8. The Court of Justice of the European Union. https://curia.europa.eu/juris/liste.jsf?language=en&num=c-220/98.

[106] Galli (2022).

[107] Luguri and Strahilevitz (2021), p. 99.

facilitates the use of behavioral insights to determine the manipulative character, as an alternative or supplement to empirical proof.[108]

The manipulation standards also reveal information regarding the ubiquity of the marketing practice and the corresponding size of the harm. As regards the harm, it can be established that when a substantial amount of consumers is found to be misled by a marketing practice, by definition, the size of the harm will be significant.[109] Likewise, if the marketing industry fails as a whole to meet the standards, it will divulge valuable information regarding the prevalence of manipulative marketing practices in consumer markets.

Finally, manipulation standards also provide the opportunity to make blacklists, as is the case under the UCTD. If specific commercial practices consistently lead to the manipulation of consumers, they could be put on a list of practices deemed unfair. These can then be indicative, as the Annex of the UCTD, or they can be listed as *per se* prohibited. In either case, the list will contribute to legal certainty because it will make clear to both marketers and consumers which practices are, by definition, deemed unfair and give rise to the opportunity to prevent the continued use of such practices.

In short, manipulation standards can be a useful tool for consumer authorities to monitor the practices of marketers and hold them accountable. It will undoubtedly be an arduous task to develop accurate manipulation standards, facilitate effective monitoring, and preserve compliance. However, the developments in AI make it a promising avenue to explore.[110]

6.4.2.2 Internal Supervision

Monitoring does not only have to take place externally. There could also be a form of internal monitoring. For instance, improved identification of exploitation by means of an internal supervisory board that focuses on marketing and consumer interests.[111] More specifically, an internal committee of relevant stakeholders that monitors ethics, consumer interests, and technological developments. Although the board is internal, the stakeholders could be both internal and external members. Potential valuable external members could be consumer rights advocates, scholars in consumer law (and economics), and ethics compliance specialists. In this way, a balance between the business and consumer interests is safeguarded.[112]

The idea stems from the institutional review boards in academic research, whereby researchers need to demonstrate that their (behavioral) experiments are in

---

[108] Laux et al. (2021), p. 743.

[109] Luguri and Strahilevitz (2021), p. 99.

[110] See, for instance, Smith (2014) for the developments in the field of product liability.

[111] Calo (2014).

[112] This idea of internal and external supervision seems to also be embraced by the DSA, see, for example, Recitals 88 and 98.

accordance with the rules and guidelines provided by, for example, a university. It is, to say the least, remarkable that marketers can perform state-of-the-art behavioral research and numerous neuromarketing-based experiments without facing the degree of control that academic researchers face. In practice, the control of marketing research methods is meager and remains largely unregulated territory.[113]

Protecting consumers from intrusive and potentially harmful marketing strategies is a task that mainly lies in the hands of ex-post enforcement by consumer authorities and individuals. However, there should be a step before that: a review mechanism that ensures adequate reporting, communication to the public, and safeguards ethical marketing research.

The *stewardship model* can work as an inspiration for the internal supervision approach. The stewardship model is based on three pillars: iterative review, layered accountability, and institutionalized opposition.[114] More specifically, iterative review "sets benchmarks through adjudication and requires improvement over time", layered accountability "requires broad input from stakeholders, including consumers, advocates, and experts", and institutionalized opposition "sets up a constant counterweight to established narratives in government and the private sector. It thus reduces the risk of capture of regulators by algorithmic entities."[115]

Notably, Hacker (2020) argues that this internal supervision could be required from a professional diligence point of view (in accordance with the UCPD).[116] More specifically, he points out that traders should audit their algorithmic models (mechanism behind personalized marketing) for manipulative features. The traders can use in-house, but also external experts for these auditing services. The obligation to audit for manipulative tendencies stems from the duty to act in good faith. Intentionality should not play a role, which means that even though the mechanism leads to unintentional manipulation, this risk should be borne by the trader (denoting the balance between risk and reward). Failure to successfully audit should be considered a breach of professional diligence.[117]

From a consumer perspective, internal supervision (i.e., between company and marketer) is desirable since it will ensure that marketers' activities are somewhat restrained and consumer interests are taken into account. At the same time, the company can demonstrate that it values consumer trust, research integrity, and transparency, which will aid reputation building and its defense in potential investigation cases initiated by consumer authorities.

The internal monitoring mechanism could be strengthened through self-regulatory actions.[118] Two possible courses of action could be the development of

---

[113] Main (2012), pp. 625–627.

[114] Margulies (2023).

[115] Margulies (2023), p. 41.

[116] Hacker (2023).

[117] Hacker (2023), p. 159.

[118] See for a discussion of the benefits of self-regulation Miller (1985). The value of self-regulatory actions is also acknowledged in the DSA, see Articles 45 and 46, and Recitals 102 and 103.

best practices and the adoption of industry-wide standards, which are in line with EU regulations and consumer preferences. Especially dominant firms (e.g., Amazon, Apple, and Google) could set a consumer-friendly standard for the entire industry. The benefit of incentivizing self-regulatory actions is that the marketing industry itself has the greatest knowledge and expertise regarding personalization. The industry can then, to a great extent, impose standards that fit the technicalities of the marketing techniques. Consequently, the administrative and information costs of regulation can be reduced.[119] It must be noted, however, that self-regulation can also lead to regulatory capture or the creation of entry barriers.[120] Accordingly, some measure of external constraint is needed to mitigate the dangers of self-regulation and find an optimal mix between public and private regulation.[121]

6.4.2.3 Facilitating the Monitoring

The current EU legal framework falls short of effectively protecting consumers against personalized marketing.[122] An essential aspect of this is that the legal provisions do not sufficiently provide the necessary tools to enforcement agencies to tackle personalized marketing practices. Monitoring could be facilitated when the EU consumer *acquis* would be updated with a *new consumer benchmark*, the introduction of a *marketing-specific clause*, and *improved transparency* for enforcers.[123] Each of these aspects will be discussed separately against the background of the UCPD, the UCTD, and the DSA.

First, the UCPD uses standard consumer benchmarks to assess the fairness of a commercial practice. This can be the average consumer, a member of the target group, or the vulnerable consumer. The average consumer benchmark can be used for mass-marketed media communications. However, it comes up short when assessing personalized marketing communications tailored to the individual's specific characteristics (i.e., the opposite of the average). The UCPD also looks at commercial practices specifically targeted at a group of consumers, whereby the average member of that group is used as the benchmark.[124] The same problem persists, however. Personalized marketing uses the individual's personal and behavioral data to tailor the content to that individual. There is not always a clearly identifiable group,

---

[119] Ogus (1995).

[120] Kay (1988).

[121] Faure (2014), p. 696.

[122] See the analyses of the current legal framework in Chaps. 3, 4, and 5.

[123] The proposals will be focused on substantive changes. The discussion of the procedural aspects of enforcement falls outside the scope of this study. For an elaborate discussion on how to improve consumer law enforcement and consumers' access to justice, see, for instance, Wrbka (2014); Weber (2016).

[124] Article 5(2)(b) UCPD.

and when personalization approximates perfection, one cannot speak of a group at all.[125]

A counterargument is that the Guidance on the UCPD[126] states that the target group can also consist of one individual, making the UCPD benchmarks sufficient for the assessment.[127] Nevertheless, Strycharz and Duivenvoorde (2021) demonstrate that the text of the UCPD excludes this interpretation by explicitly mentioning an actual group for the target group benchmark to be applicable.[128]

An alternative benchmark in the UCPD is the vulnerable consumer.[129] Nevertheless, in this context, vulnerability has been narrowly interpreted as only referring to vulnerability due to age, mental or physical infirmity, or credulity (i.e., group-based vulnerabilities), which does not seem to encompass the exploitation of individual and contextual vulnerabilities,[130] as is the case under personalized marketing. Accordingly, there is a need to redesign the consumer benchmark.

Duivenvoorde (2023) makes a compelling case for using the notion of the *benchmark consumer*.[131] In essence, the benchmark varies along the degree of targeting. Thus, if a marketing technique targets the general public, the average consumer can be taken as the benchmark. The target benchmark applies if it is directed at a specific group. When the individual is the target, the reasonably acting targeted individual will be used as the benchmark. Then, the individual consumer is not required to belong to a specific subgroup, which contrasts with the current reading of the UCPD.[132] The benchmark consumer is expected to act reasonably, which highlights the responsibility of the individual to take adequate measures to get informed and emphasizes what can reasonably be expected from a consumer. This will prevent the benchmark consumer test from becoming too tolerant, justifying all behaviors of individual consumers. Reasonability acts as a normative correction to the actual behavior.[133]

To illustrate, a personalization technique that targets the specific vulnerabilities of a consumer and leads to an unwanted transactional decision can be classified as an unfair commercial practice. The criterion of reasonable acting cannot be held against consumers in such instances of exploitation. In contrast, when a personalized communication is clearly and intelligibly presented to the consumer, whereby

[125] Strycharz and Duivenvoorde (2021).

[126] European Commission (2021), Section 4.2.7.

[127] European Commission (2021). Section 4.2.7 states: "For the purposes of this assessment, the benchmark of an average or vulnerable consumer can be modulated to the target group and, if the practice is highly personalised, even formulated from the perspective of a single person who was subject to the specific personalization."

[128] Strycharz and Duivenvoorde (2021), p. 12.

[129] Article 5(3) UCPD.

[130] Helberger et al. (2021), p. 179.

[131] Duivenvoorde (2023).

[132] Strycharz and Duivenvoorde (2021), p. 12.

[133] Duivenvoorde (2023) states that the actual behavior should not necessarily be decisive for the assessment.

material information is prominently displayed, and the consumer decides to disregard all of this and not take time for the decision-making process, the reasonability criterion serves as a safeguard against consumers' lack of incentive to protect themselves from risks that the provision aims to mitigate (i.e., moral hazard). The aim of instituting the benchmark consumer is that all types of targeting can be covered, individual circumstances can be reasonably considered, and the way can be cleared for enforcement against personalized marketing.

Second, introducing marketing-specific clauses in, for example, the UCPD could assist in effective monitoring. Many consumer protection laws focus on the provision of sufficient information and the promotion of transparency.[134] The UCPD does this through its prohibitions of misleading actions and omissions, which corresponds to the idea that by providing information, consumers can be aided in their decision-making without drastically intervening in the market.[135] There is substantive regulation for cases in which the provision of information does not suffice. The UCPD, for instance, prohibits aggressive commercial practices in Article 8. However, fundamentally, this relates to cases of blatant unfairness that ultimately lead to the erosion of consumer autonomy.[136] In its multiformity, personalized marketing is too subtle and sophisticated to be captured by those provisions.

For this reason, it can be argued that marketing techniques causing marketing-induced market failures, which ultimately harm consumers, need to be addressed separately. In correspondence with the manipulation standards of Sect. 6.4.2.1, it is asserted that marketing manipulation should be incorporated as a separate clause in the UCPD. The clause should specifically tackle the issues identified within the marketing-induced market failure framework.[137] More specifically, all marketing practices, intentional or non-intentional, automated or not, personalized or generic, aimed at extracting rents, exploiting biases and vulnerabilities, and/or shaping preferences to the detriment of consumers' autonomy, equity, and welfare, should be prohibited.[138] It must be noted that it is claimed that the term manipulation requires intent on the side of the marketer.[139] For this reason, the proposed clause explicitly states that intentional and non-intentional techniques are covered. The same applies for the automated part, which prevents further discussions regarding what is automated and what is not.[140]

Further complementary action could be taken by extending the Annex of the UCTD and allowing for the expansion of the blacklists in the laws of the Member States.[141] This would practically consist of explicitly flagging certain terms that have

---

[134] Oehler and Wendt (2017).

[135] Oehler and Wendt (2017).

[136] Laux et al. (2021); Strycharz and Duivenvoorde (2021); Hacker (2023).

[137] See Sect. 2.4.1.

[138] An alternative is provided by Duivenvoorde (2023), p. 182.

[139] Helberger et al. (2021), pp. 195–196.

[140] Helberger et al. (2021), p. 187.

[141] See Sect. 5.4.2 for a further discussion of this idea.

been personalized as unfair. This would allow for the creation of a database of blacklisted unfair terms, which helps companies to self-regulate and effectively simplify enforcement for regulatory authorities.[142]

Additionally, in combination with the personalized disclosure system, consumers can be adequately informed about pre-defined sets of unfair practices and terms, thereby allowing them to actually make informed decisions.

Lastly, inspired by Article 39 of the DSA, monitoring could be aided by increasing transparency regarding personalized marketing practices. Pursuant to Article 39 DSA, VLOPs and VLOSEs are required to maintain a repository with essential information about advertisements concerning their nature, target group, and the parameters used for targeting. Such public databases effectively aid enforcement because they offer a look behind the scenes of the marketing industry.[143] However, where the DSA provision is limited to VLOPs and VLOSEs, it is argued that this should be extended to all companies that employ personalized marketing techniques.[144]

Notably, the repository contains information that can elucidate the personalization process. In other words, it makes conspicuous why a consumer has been targeted and on what grounds. Only then will it be feasible for enforcers to identify if consumers have been manipulated or specific vulnerabilities have been exploited.[145] If maintaining such a repository would be too costly for smaller and medium enterprises, these companies could be exempted from the obligation.[146] However, they should be obliged to give full transparency regarding their personalization practices when asked to do so by regulatory agencies.

Consequently, revisiting some existing regulations would be necessary to implement these changes. However, the reforms align with the EU strategy to make consumer protection fit for the digital age.[147] To facilitate monitoring, it is necessary to clear the haze around the practice of personalized marketing.

[142] Poncibò (2023), pp. 341–343.

[143] See Leerssen et al. (2018) for an elaborate discussion of the intricacies of platform ad archives and the corresponding promises and perils.

[144] Strycharz and Duivenvoorde (2021), p. 21.

[145] Cfr. Cobbe and Singh (2019) propose that service providers should be required to keep logs of recommended content in order to facilitate review by users and oversight bodies.

[146] Cfr. Article 91 and Recital 150 DSA.

[147] European Commission (2023).

6.4.3 A Genuine Opt-out

By providing personalized disclosures, consumers can decide on an ex-ante basis what is beneficial to them and stick with their choice. This assumes that the preferences of the consumer remain stable.[148] However, it is more than possible that consumers will change their mind about the practice over time. For example, after deliberate evaluation, it can be the case that consumers feel like they were taken by surprise and consented to a specific practice, which ultimately they found detrimental to their interests. In the consumer law framework, a response to this possibility has been the introduction of cooling-off periods that provide consumers with a specific period of time to evaluate their decisions.[149] An essential aspect of cooling-off periods is that they are only assigned to situations where the right to withdraw concerns products that require after-sale inspection and do not depreciate rapidly or in a way for which compensation can be measured and given.[150]

This is problematic in terms of personalized marketing. It is not possible to unsee and erase the impact of a personalized ad or price. In a sense, it cannot be returned to the seller.[151] However, there is an insight that can be taken from the use of withdrawal rights and can be applied to the context of personalized marketing. It relates to the concept of *regret contingency*.[152] The regret contingency refers to situations where "one of the parties might wish to exit the contract based on changes that occurred in the external environment rendering the transaction no longer profitable."[153] In other words, after the conclusion of the contract, the consumer finds that the transaction is no longer in her interest, which can depend on various financial, psychological, and social factors.[154]

In the context of personalized marketing, it is conceivable that after experiencing the world of personalization, a consumer wants to opt out and go back to a state of anonymity. That is to say, receiving non-personalized offers in a non-personalized setting. Accordingly, the consumer should be granted a choice to become anonymous and withdraw from personalized marketing.[155] This effectively means instituting an *opt-out regime* aimed at giving consumers the possibility to take back control

---

148 Based on the rational choice model in economics, see, for instance, Mas-Colell et al. (1995), chapter 1.

149 See Chap. 2 for an analysis of the cooling-off period as a consumer protection device.

150 Ben-Shahar and Posner (2011).

151 It must be noted that products or services that have been sold through personalized offerings can be returned by means of the legally established cooling-off periods (In EU law, 14 days—for any reason). In this case, the return of the product and the exposure to a personalized ad or price should not be conflated. It concerns the effect of seeing a personalized ad or price and the influence this has on consumers' behavior.

152 Goetz and Scott (1980).

153 Rekaiti and Van den Bergh (2000), p. 376.

154 Sparks et al. (2014).

155 Cfr. Gal (2018).

at the lowest possible cost, thus, in layman's terms, giving consumers a genuine possibility to *shut it off*.

At the moment, achieving a state of anonymity is hard to manage. Pursuant to Article 21(2) GPDR, consumers have a right to object at any time to the processing of personal data for direct marketing purposes. In this regard, it can be stated that a formal opt-out regime already exists. In practice, however, it has been made particularly difficult to opt out, effectively undermining the opt-out regime envisioned by the GDPR.[156] Opting out currently requires high levels of technical sophistication, significant transaction costs, and the overcoming of various decision biases.[157] Accordingly, to make the opting-out regime effective, it is pivotal to make the opt-out option available with any personalized marketing message. It should be maximally conspicuous to the consumer how to withdraw from the practice, and the user interface should be designed to make opting out as accessible and easy as possible.[158] Simply put, opting out should be made as easy as liking or sharing a message on social media. Only then would the opt-out regime transform itself into a functional instrument for consumer protection.[159]

A key aspect of the genuine opt-out is that consumers should be able to receive the same services if they decide to opt out and go for non-personalized content. If the functionality of the services is decreased in case of an opt out, a limit will still be placed on consumers' free choice. Accordingly, the same services would need to be accessible, but then with non-personalized advertisements, which can subsidize the use of the services (as was the case before the era of personalization).[160]

A valuable benefit of this approach is that it prevents far-reaching paternalism. If consumers enjoy receiving personalized prices, advertisements, and other marketing messages, they should not be protected against their will. If personalization effectively serves consumers and they reap the benefits without regret, as many marketers advocate,[161] there should be no need to take away these welfare-enhancing tools. However, if consumers feel that they are harmed by the personalization practices,[162] then it should be made as easy and clear as possible to withdraw. In this

[156] See, for instance, Leon et al. (2012); Habib et al. (2019); Kuntsman et al. (2019); Habib et al. (2020).

[157] Willis (2013).

[158] See, for instance, Bannihatti Kumar et al. (2020). They introduce the *Opt-Out Easy*, a web browser extension designed to present available opt-out choices to users as they browse the web.

[159] Wagner and Eidenmüller (2019), p. 591.

[160] Helberger et al. (2021), p. 207. It is of note that such a development is visible in the context of platform services, see the Meta Platforms v. Bundeskartellamt case, and the DMA (Recitals 36 and 37).

[161] See, for instance, Constantinides (2006); Kwon and Kim (2012); Dantas and Carrillat (2013); Dawn (2014); Satish and Yusof (2017).

[162] This is based on the assumption that they are aware of the harm. If the assumption does not hold, the opt-out mechanism is supported by the other regulatory recommendations. The different elements of the policy proposal are mutually reinforcing.

way, the opt-out mechanism functions as an effective counterbalance to personalization.

Of note is that this opt-out mechanism works in harmony with the use of privacy-preserving defaults. It could be argued that the default should be an opt-in for the sake of privacy protection. This line of reasoning seems to come forward in the *Meta v Bundeskartellamt* case. The CJEU emphasizes that personalized marketing does not fall under the legal bases of Article 6 GDPR, and that specific consent is needed. Although the CJEU states that the processing of personal data for direct marketing purposes can still be carried out for a legitimate interest,[163] it can be argued that this decision implicitly amounts to an opt-in regime for personalized advertising.[164] However, it remains to be seen how this implication will develop in the future, both in practice and in case law.[165]

In any case, deciding if the default should be an opt-in or an opt-out remains a highly normative question since it remains unclear as to what weights should be given to efficiency or fairness considerations. As soon as consensus has been reached that personalized marketing leads to excessive privacy intrusions that should be remedied, the default could be set on non-personalization. In contrast, if the benefits of personalization seem economically desirable, the default could remain personalization. This requires a debate on a broader societal level.[166]

The opt-out mechanism, however, works either way. If the default is non-personalization, and the consumer decides to opt in, then the opt-out should always be readily available. If the default is personalization, the opt-out mechanism should work likewise. In short, it provides a robust tool to safeguard consumers' autonomy and choice.

Finally, the use of the opt-out mechanism indirectly provides legislators and sellers with valuable information, thereby creating an automatic feedback loop. To specify, if the advocates of personalized marketing are correct and personalization mainly leads to the promotion of consumers' interests, the opt-out mechanism will be scarcely used. In the context of algorithmic pricing, this would mean that personalized prices will not deter consumers with a high willingness to pay, and consumers with a low willingness to pay will benefit from the personalized price, resulting in a low opt-out rate. In the context of personalized advertising, consumers might prefer personalized ads instead of generalized ads. However, if the opposite is true and most consumers opt out, it will signal to the legislators that the practice mainly serves the sellers rather than the consumers.

[163] Meta Platforms v. Bundeskartellamt, para 47.

[164] NOYB (2023); Schechner and Dolby (2023).

[165] Notable developments have been Meta's announcement that they will ask for users' consent to show personalized advertisements and the Norwegian Data Protection Authority's decision to order Meta to stop showing users personalized ads in Norway. See IAPP (2023); Meta (2023); Politico (2023); Reuters (2023).

[166] Tene and Polonetsky (2013).

A practical example of market feedback on a legal intervention is the failure of cookie banners. European regulations[167] were adopted to provide consumers with some degree of control over the tracking of their data by requiring prior consent. In practice, however, the legal requirements resulted in the widespread use of cookie banners, pop-ups, and cookie walls, which caused user annoyance rather than improved understanding or control. The majority of users simply click "accept" in order to continue using the website.[168] In addition, the cookie banners were also frequently violating applicable laws, infringing purpose specificity obligations, and informed consent requirements.[169]

Apart from the frustration among consumers, it also resulted in substantial backlash from the advertising industry and web publishers. The cookie regulation is, therefore, seen as a case of regulatory failure.[170] The lesson drawn from this example is that the market can provide valuable feedback to legal interventions. In the context of the opt-out mechanism for personalized marketing, consumer opt-out behavior can provide meaningful insights into the workings of the intervention. If it works effectively, it could force sellers to react accordingly, which could pre-empt further regulatory interventions such as prohibitions.[171] To illustrate, if consumers massively opt out of personalized marketing services, sellers will understand that the practices are ineffective, and they will have to scale back on personalization. In this sense, the market can respond to personalization instead of having predetermined *per se* prohibitions.

Finally, to work effectively, the opt-out mechanism must be monitored. As explained above, the opt-out mechanism described by the GDPR is, generally, implemented by companies to benefit themselves rather than consumers. That is to say, opting out is made as onerous as possible. An example of how consumer

---

[167] Directive 95/46/EC of the European Parliament and of the Council of 24 October 1995 on the protection of individuals with regard to the processing of personal data and on the free movement of such data. https://eur-lex.europa.eu/legal-content/EN/TXT/?uri=CELEX%3A31995L0046; Directive 2002/58/EC of the European Parliament and of the Council of 12 July 2002 concerning the processing of personal data and the protection of privacy in the electronic communications sector (Directive on privacy and electronic communications). https://eur-lex.europa.eu/legal-content/EN/TXT/?uri =celex%3A32002L0058. Referred to as the "ePrivacy Directive"; Directive 2009/136/EC of the European Parliament and of the Council of 25 November 2009 amending Directive 2002/22/EC on universal service and users' rights relating to electronic communications networks and services, Directive 2002/58/EC concerning the processing of personal data and the protection of privacy in the electronic communications sector and Regulation 2006/2004 on cooperation between national authorities responsible for the enforcement of consumer protection laws. https://eur-lex.europa.eu/legal-content/EN/TXT/?uri=celex%3A32009L0136.

[168] Ogut (2023). The study states: "90% of the participants said they accepted or closed it just to continue their task and remove the consent notice from the interface."

[169] Trevisan et al. (2019); Santos et al. (2021).

[170] Leenes and Kosta (2015).

[171] This is based on the assumption that the market will not be plagued by consumer opportunism, which is likely to hold in practice, see, for example, Block-Lieb and Janger (2006). In addition, firms can manage opportunism strategically by designing incentives that promote longer-term engagement, allowing them to recoup the short-term benefits provided to consumers.

protection provisions can be sabotaged can be seen in the degree of compliance with privacy notices. It has been found that firms undermine privacy disclosures by, for example, determining in which situations consumers are most unlikely to utilize the disclosed information, framing the disclosure in such a way that comprehension is complicated, and pushing consumers in a direction that sets aside the examination of the disclosure for convenience purposes.[172] To illustrate the latter, adding a delay (e.g., 15 s) between the privacy disclosure and the loading of the screen in which the consumer makes a privacy choice reduces the privacy-protective effect of the disclosure significantly.[173] Thus, to make sure that the opt-out mechanism is not undermined, monitoring of the system by consumer authorities as well as private parties would be required.[174] Accordingly, the mechanism must be effectively enforced to provide consumers with a genuine opt-out.[175]

6.4.4 *Liability as a Last Resort*

The liability versus regulation analysis demonstrated that liability could complement the proposed regulatory framework. Personalized marketing poses new challenges to the liability-regulation interplay, which requires a more elaborate examination. As stated before, personalized marketing is characterized by its subtle nature. With respect to the subtlety, "any particular attempt to prevent or to counteract it will often lead to new and unanticipated forms of manipulation."[176]

Regulation can be quickly outdated, prohibitively costly, and heavily dependent on enforcement. In addition, the regulatory standards might be distorted by private interest lobbying.[177] Accordingly, liability and regulation can play complementary roles in remedying each other's weak spots and effectively controlling risks.[178] As emphasized by Shavell (1984),[179] Kolstad et al. (1990),[180] Burrows (1999),[181] Faure

---

[172] Willis (2015), p. 1322.

[173] Adjerid et al. (2013).

[174] Proposals for effective monitoring have been made by, for instance, Utz et al. (2019); Nouwens et al. (2020); Papadogiannakis et al. (2021); Bollinger et al. (2022).

[175] A full analysis on the enforcement of consumer law falls outside the scope of this chapter. See Chap. 1 concerning the focus of the present study. For a comprehensive study on the optimal enforcement of consumer law, see, for instance, Weber (2016).

[176] Hanson and Kysar (1999a), p. 1555.

[177] Hanson and Kysar (1999a), p. 1555.

[178] Hanson and Kysar (1999a), p. 1555.

[179] Shavell (1984).

[180] Kolstad et al. (1990).

[181] Burrows (1999).

et al. (2016),[182] and Li et al. (2022),[183] the joint use of liability and regulation merits further attention.

The increased capacity of the legal system to deal with complex situations should not be underestimated. Over time, the legal framework has expanded exponentially, thereby attacking more and more types of harmful behavior. Consequently, it is warranted to explore how the law can be reformed in innovative ways to combat new undesirable market behaviors.[184]

6.4.4.1 Providing the Right Incentives

It can be argued that personalized marketing does not lend itself to be solely regulated by command-and-control regulatory approaches. A more fruitful approach would be to incentivize marketers to refrain from using exploitative marketing practices. From a law and economics perspective, considering the law's incentivizing effect is of pivotal importance. The economic analysis of tort law has demonstrated that the precedent-setting effect of the law should not be underestimated, and that careful attention needs to be devoted to the effect of incentives on the future behavior of potential injurers and victims.[185] The proposed regulatory approach puts the incentivizing role of the law at the center and embodies the credo expressed by Levitt and Dubner (2006): "An incentive is a bullet, a lever, a key: an often tiny object with astonishing power to change a situation."[186] If the proper incentives are not given, a market-efficient outcome will not be achieved, and social costs will be created that would otherwise have been managed.[187]

Hanson and Kysar (1999a) argue in favor of changing the underlying incentives of the parties to remedy manipulation in consumer markets.[188] The importance of providing the right incentives is emphasized by the economic rationale that competition will not solve perverse incentives but exacerbate them. Hanson and Kysar (1999b) assert that firms will have to continue to manipulate consumers to survive the competitiveness of the market.[189] In other words, firms will be pressured to respond to market incentives in order to maximize profits, even though this might lead to consumer manipulation.[190]

---

[182] In the context of unknown risks, see Faure et al. (2016).

[183] Li et al. (2022).

[184] De Geest (2018a).

[185] Mathis (2009), p. 69.

[186] Levitt and Dubner (2006), p. 2.

[187] Hanson and Kysar (1999a), p. 1557.

[188] Hanson and Kysar (1999a), pp. 1553–1557.

[189] Hanson and Kysar (1999b), p. 726.

[190] This is also a challenge to competition law, however, an analysis from this perspective falls outside the scope of the chapter. See, for instance, Ezrachi (2016).

Providing the right incentives requires the consideration of not only business insights but also consumer marketing insights. For this reason, a so-called marketing perspective is advocated, which employs the insights from marketing scholarship to the benefit of consumers.[191] Accordingly, insights from marketing are used to understand the sophistication behind marketing strategies and their corresponding goals. A marketer understands how a certain marketing strategy will impact consumers. They construct *laboratories of consumerism,*[192] in which they can see how consumer behavior can be incentivized, and anomalies can be captured. If the mechanism behind the strategy can be identified, it becomes more feasible to understand the underlying goal and, thereby, detect whether there is evidence of marketing manipulation.

The rise in AI-driven technologies has made marketing techniques significantly more puzzling. Maintaining high levels of ambiguity is profitable because it enables the exploitation of consumers with a low probability of being detected or facing consumer backlash.[193] The new targeting techniques "prevent consumers from relying on the market to push quality up and prices down. Instead, each consumer must navigate the market alone."[194] Consequently, a novel strategy is needed to incentivize marketers to refrain from consumer exploitation.[195]

6.4.4.2 Introducing Marketer Liability

When it comes to the incentivizing function of the law, invaluable insights have been provided by the law and economics literature on product liability.[196] In short, although liability rules are not perfectly deterrent, they can offer crucial incentives to manufacturers to increase product safety.[197] Given the role that liability rules play in regulating a manufacturer's behavior (in combination with regulation), a proposal is made to introduce so-called *marketer liability*.[198] Marketer liability can be defined as *using liability rules to hold marketers liable for the costs of all marketing-related harms inflicted on consumers*.

---

[191] See Sect. 2.4.2.

[192] Hanson and Kysar (1999b), p. 744.

[193] See, for instance, Gabaix and Laibson (2006); Bar-Gill (2012); De Geest (2018b).

[194] Willis (2015), p. 1321.

[195] Cfr. Laffont and Martimort (2002).

[196] See Faure (2016b) for a summary of the economic approach to product liability.

[197] Faure (2016b).

[198] The term marketer liability has been used before in the existing literature, however, always in the context of product liability—manufacturer and marketer are assumed to be the same. In contrast, the application of marketer liability in this study singularizes the role of the marketer. See for previous discussions of marketer liability, for instance, Morgan et al. (1995); Morgan and Stoltman (1997); O'Reilly and Dalal (2003).

Under the existing EU framework, the UCPD and the MCAD can remedy marketing efforts that could be seen as unfair or harmful.[199] There is, however, no specific liability imposed on marketers for their harmful behaviors. In practice, harmful marketing communications are remedied by injunctions initiated by consumer authorities or private parties that target the companies selling the product or service, which sometimes also give rise to compensatory damages.[200] In addition, Article 11a of the *Omnibus Directive* grants individual remedies to consumers who have been harmed by unfair commercial practices. The remedies under the UCPD are ancillary to the general remedies under national law.[201] More specifically, consumers can employ the legal remedies provided by national tort and contract law.[202]

Nevertheless, marketer liability complements the current liability framework in three ways. First, under the UCPD framework, the focus lies primarily on remedying the adverse effects of the unfair commercial practice and sanctioning the trader.[203] However, the marketer behind the exploitative practice remains practically untouched. Marketer liability advocates a more rigorous application of liability rules to incentivize the relevant party, the marketers, to reduce social costs in the form of consumer-related harm.[204] This would result in joint liability for both the marketer and the seller.

Second, the proposal for a marketing-specific clause in the UCPD[205] works in tandem with marketer liability. The marketing clause specifically deals with the issues identified within the marketing-induced market failure framework. Accordingly, if a marketing technique aims to extract rents, exploit biases and vulnerabilities, and/or shape preferences at the expense of consumers' autonomy, equity, and welfare, a case for marketer liability can be made. This allows for a better targeting of the harms that are inflicted by marketing in the digital age compared to the national provisions on contract and tort law, which would otherwise require creative interpretations.[206]

---

199 It must be noted that the MCAD deals with B2B relationships. In B2C relationships the UCPD applies. However, the European Commission (2021) states that the rules of the MCAD continue to provide a general test, based on fully harmonized criteria, for assessing whether comparative advertising is lawful in B2C transactions. The MCAD is, therefore, also relevant to B2C relationships. The Commission specifically refers to Case C-562/15, Carrefour Hypermarchés SAS v ITM Alimentaire International SASU, ECLI:EU:C:2017:95. The Court of Justice of the European Union. https://curia.europa.eu/juris/liste.jsf?num=C-562/15 for its justification.

200 See the general design of the enforcement mechanism in consumer law as described by Micklitz and Saumier (2018).

201 Chatzipanagiotis (2024), p. 125.

202 Cseres (2014), p. 24.

203 Chatzipanagiotis (2024), p. 115.

204 The concept of liability that comes closest to marketer liability has been proposed by Brenkert (1998). He advocates the use of *targeted consumer liability*, whereby marketers are held to a moral liability standard for the manner in which they market to consumers, with special attention to vulnerable consumers.

205 See Sect. 6.4.2.3.

206 Golobardes (2022).

Third, marketer liability is specifically designed to address the subtlety of the personalized marketing strategies, which causes them to slip through the cracks of the current EU legal framework.[207] In this respect, marketer liability works as a gap-filler in the current liability regime and aims to complement the broader enforcement framework, which also comprises public enforcement, collective redress and alternative dispute resolution (ADR).[208]

In the US, the *doctrine of negligent marketing* exists, which refers to marketing that involves the creation of unreasonable risks of harm.[209] Negligent marketing efforts can result in claims based on product design, advertising, promotional activities, or distribution practices.[210] Although several cases have been brought before a court, they all relate to egregious conducts of marketers such as: (1) Marketing a product that presents an unusually high risk of harm and negligible utility for legitimate purposes; (2) implementing a strategy that deliberately, recklessly, or negligently targets criminal consumers; or (3) failing to take reasonable steps to minimize the risk that the products will be purchased by persons likely to misuse them.[211] This has amounted to cases against firearm manufacturers and prescription drug manufacturers, to name a few.[212]

Therefore, the doctrine of negligent marketing is not of great use for the subtle practice of personalized marketing. Hence, an alternative application of liability rules is necessary to deter marketers from implementing harmful personalized marketing strategies.

The concept of marketer liability is inspired by the work of Li et al. (2022), in which they proffer the idea that liability rules can be used to regulate developers and operators of AI systems, frontend and backend, to combat AI-inflicted harm.[213] By imposing a mix of fault-based and strict liability regimes, incentives can be generated that induce operators to take "both optimal care and optimal activity levels as well as facilitating the effective spreading of risk."[214] The liability of an operator should then be determined by the severity of risk, the heterogeneity of operators, and the automation level of the AI system. Li et al. (2022) argue that to remedy the harms, it is vital that not only one appropriate party bears the risk, but also, from an economic perspective, all relevant actors that influence the risk of harm should be incentivized to take preventative measures.[215]

---

207 This has become clear from the legal analyses in Chaps. 3–5.

208 Chatzipanagiotis (2024), p. 113.

209 McClurg (1995), p. 799.

210 Ausness (2002a).

211 McClurg (1995), p. 799.

212 Ausness (2002b).

213 Li et al. (2022).

214 Li et al. (2022), p. 16.

215 Li et al. (2022).

A factor that could be considered in the analysis, which is increasingly investigated in computer science, is *algorithmic fairness*.[216] This term refers to the techniques being developed to prevent algorithms from learning bias (i.e., discriminatory behavior in society), make them fairness-aware, and let them detect and correct unfair and discriminatory results.[217] The goal is to measure whether factors that should not be influential had a significant impact on the algorithmic process, resulting in undue differentiation between groups or individuals.[218] Companies could then be held strictly liable for unfair procedures since they significantly influence the use of the technology.[219] This would contribute to solving the discriminatory and unfairness components of AI-driven marketing techniques.

Marketer liability works by virtue of incentives given on an ex-ante basis. The liability will foster the internalization of the social costs inflicted on consumers, and, through the competitive process, companies will be encouraged to find the least-cost methods to decrease their exposure to liability claims.[220]

It is then the question what the optimal liability rules should look like. The desirability of a liability rule is determined based on the social welfare criterion.[221] Social welfare is determined by the deterrent effect of liability rules and the risk-shifting effect.[222]

The deterrence factor is influenced by the level of care and the activity level. A desirable liability rule in terms of social welfare provides both parties with incentives to take optimal care, which is where the marginal cost of taking precautionary measures intersects with the marginal benefit (i.e., reduction of expected harm) of doing so.[223] Subsequently, the level of activity needs to be considered, which refers to the frequency in which an individual engages in the activity for which care needs to be exercised.[224] Social welfare can be further enhanced when all parties also optimize their activity levels. To optimize activity levels, the corresponding costs need to be internalized. However, under the existing liability rules, it is not possible to incentivize both parties (injurer and victim) to optimize their activity levels because residual liability, when both parties have exercised optimal care, needs to be allocated to one of the parties.[225]

Accordingly, a question that first needs to be answered is: What is the desirable level of care and activity that we would like marketers to exert in the context of

---

[216] Dwork et al. (2012); Zemel et al. (2013); Friedler et al. (2021).

[217] Hacker (2017a); Friedler et al. (2021).

[218] See Friedler et al. (2021) for an in-depth technical discussion of the mechanism.

[219] Hacker (2017a), p. 285.

[220] Hanson and Kysar (1999a), p. 1556.

[221] Shavell (1987), p. 7 notes that the social welfare criterion in the context of accidents means the minimization of total social costs.

[222] Shavell (1987).

[223] Shavell (1980); Shavell (1987), pp. 9–21.

[224] Shavell (1987), p. 21.

[225] Dari-Mattiacci and Parisi (2015).

personalized marketing? The challenge, however, lies in the fact that it is particularly difficult to establish an optimal level, in other words, to assign a value to the activity and care levels. It is more feasible to define the boundaries of personalized marketing and set procedural conditions that the marketers must meet. This corresponds to the concept of manipulation standards that has been discussed in the context of monitoring the marketer.[226]

Without going into the specifics of all potential liability rules,[227] it becomes clear from the framework proposed by Shavell (1987)[228] that if the goal is to let injurers behave in such a way that maximizes social welfare, which means choosing the optimal level of care and activity, strict liability should be the applicable regime. Strict liability gives the injurer the proper incentives to exercise due care and control their activities. It must be noted, however, that if the activities are valuable and desirable, levels of precaution can significantly reduce total social costs, and less strict liability rules, such as fault-based rules, would be desirable. Consequently, the desirability of strict liability depends on the societal need to control the activity levels of the injurer more than that of the victim.[229]

The optimal liability rule is, however, determined not only by its deterrent effect (i.e., levels of care and activity) but also by its risk-shifting effect.[230] To understand the latter, it is necessary to refer to Calabresi's (1970)[231] classification of costs and subgoals of accident cost reduction. Accident costs are classified into *primary costs* (the direct costs of accidents, determined by their number and severity), *secondary costs* (societal costs arising from inefficient risk distribution), and *tertiary costs* (the administrative expenses incurred in establishing and enforcing liability).[232] Liability rules must minimize the total costs of accidents to enhance social welfare.[233] This is achieved by pursuing three subgoals: reducing accidents (to minimize primary costs), ensuring efficient risk-spreading (to minimize secondary costs), and lowering administrative burdens (to minimize tertiary costs).[234] The deterrent effect of liability rules focuses on reducing primary costs by preventing accidents, while the risk-shifting effect addresses secondary costs by reallocating risks to parties better able to bear or spread them efficiently. The design of liability rules also reduces tertiary costs by ensuring efficient processes for assigning and enforcing liability, thus minimizing administrative burdens. Social welfare increases when risks are shifted to the less risk-averse party or the party that can spread losses more

[226] See Sect. 6.4.2.1.

[227] See, for instance, Shavell (1980).

[228] Shavell (1987).

[229] Shavell (1987), p. 31.

[230] Shavell (2009), pp. 267–269.

[231] Calabresi (1970).

[232] Van den Bergh (2008).

[233] Calabresi (1970) also devotes special attention to the concepts of justice and fairness.

[234] Faure (2008).

efficiently, thereby minimizing secondary costs. However, achieving this requires an assessment of the parties' risk attitudes.[235]

Nevertheless, when additional factors, such as insurance, influence the allocation of risks, the deterrent effect of liability rules typically takes precedence over the risk-shifting effect in determining the optimal liability rule, as effective deterrence is crucial for preventing the incurrence of costs.[236]

To determine the optimal liability regime for personalized marketing, insights can be drawn from the implementation of the *Product Liability Directive* (PLD),[237] which established a strict liability regime for defective products across the EU. Manufacturers create a substantial risk by bringing products to the market, which could result in significant losses from damage caused by defects. Consequently, it is necessary to provide manufacturers with the right incentives to take optimal care and choose optimal activity levels. This would contribute to the deterrence of wrongful conduct and enable victims to claim compensation.[238]

The choice for strict liability can be economically justified. It will induce the manufacturer to take efficient care, but it will also lead to optimal output. In cases of information asymmetries leading to the underestimation of risk, strict liability is an appropriate remedy. Furthermore, it is justified to impose liability on manufacturers since they are better able to bear the risk of losses than consumers. Manufacturers are less risk averse and can spread losses among consumers via the pricing mechanism. Strict liability is then the desirable liability rule because it leads to a higher level of social welfare.[239] Accordingly, the PLD seems to provide broad protection to victims of losses of harm caused by defective products.

Per analogiam, it could be argued that the PLD regime should be applied to the marketing industry. The PLD was, however, adopted with traditional mass-production sectors in mind. New technologies have emerged, and it is argued that the PLD is lagging behind the developments of the digital age.[240] For this reason, an EU proposal has been made for a *Revised PLD*,[241] which modernizes the provisions to make the product liability regime fit for the digital age.[242] Against this back-

---

[235] Li et al. (2022), p. 624.

[236] Shavell (2009), pp. 210–215.

[237] Council Directive 85/374/EEC of 25 July 1985 on the approximation of the laws, regulations and administrative provisions of the Member States concerning liability for defective products. https://eur-lex.europa.eu/legal-content/EN/TXT/?uri=celex%3A31985L0374.

[238] Goldberg and Zipursky (2010).

[239] Faure (2016b) explains that there are sound economic reasons for a differential regime (including strict and fault-based liability), however, the legislator decided to have generalized strict liability.

[240] De Luca (2023).

[241] European Parliament legislative resolution of 12 March 2024 on the proposal for a directive of the European Parliament and of the Council on liability for defective products (COM(2022)0495 – C9-0322/2022 – 2022/0302(COD)). https://www.europarl.europa.eu/doceo/document/TA-9-2024-0132_EN.html. Referred to as "Revised PLD".

[242] Of note is that the European Commission also proposed the AI Liability Directive (see Document 52022PC0496. Proposal for a Directive of the European Parliament and of the Council on adapting

ground, the purpose of introducing marketer liability would be to deal specifically with the challenges posed by personalized marketing.

Marketer liability would focus on four specific parts of personalized marketing: the economic operators, the techniques, the damage, and the burden of proof. First, concerning the economic operators, two parties can be distinguished, which, in certain cases, are the same. The developers of the personalized marketing technique and the sellers employing it. As became clear from the analysis of Shavell (1987),[243] when the goal is to make the injurers take optimal levels of care and activity instead of the victims, the strict liability regime should be applicable. Analogous to the case of product liability, it could be argued that in order to prevent the development and use of exploitative marketing techniques, strict liability should be imposed on the developers. The developers have more relevant information about the marketing techniques (i.e., a better understanding of the complexity), making them more apt to avoid the risk at a lower cost than consumers.[244] Strict liability would cause marketers to internalize all harms to consumers and invest in the prevention of exploitative marketing techniques. Second, the strict liability regime would optimize marketers' activity levels since they have to bear all the costs of potential damage, which means that the market price will reflect the full price of the product, enabling consumers to make an informed decision.[245]

Nevertheless, the economic analyses of the personalized marketing techniques have demonstrated that there are not only downsides, but also benefits associated with personalization.[246] Establishing a strict liability regime could be too intrusive and hamper marketing innovation. To specify, strict liability could work as an over-deterrent, resulting in a chilling effect in the marketing industry.[247] To prevent that consumers' welfare will be diminished because certain personalized services cannot be provided anymore, or they become costly (e.g., recommendations on Spotify or Netflix would become a service against a fee), a less strict liability regime would be preferred. In other words, since it is desirable that the benefits that marketing personalization offers to consumers are retained, a fault-based regime would need

non-contractual civil liability rules to artificial intelligence (AI Liability Directive). https://eur-lex.europa.eu/legal-content/EN/TXT/?uri=CELEX%3A52022PC0496), which, pursuant to Article 1(1), lays down common rules on: (a) the disclosure of evidence on high-risk artificial intelligence (AI) systems to enable a claimant to substantiate a non-contractual fault-based civil law claim for damages; (b) the burden of proof in the case of non-contractual fault-based civil law claims brought before national courts for damages caused by an AI system. Accordingly, both proposals aim to adapt liability rules to the developments spurred on by the digital transformation.

[243] Shavell (1987).

[244] Cfr. Carbonara et al. (2016).

[245] Li and Faure (2024), p. 145.

[246] See Sects. 3.5, 4.4, and 5.3.

[247] Li and Faure (2024), p. 156.

to be chosen.[248] Under this regime, both the marketers and the consumers would be incentivized to take optimal care levels.[249]

Accordingly, an approach is favored that sets a duty for marketers to comply with (e.g., manipulation standard), and will only result in liability when failing to do so (e.g., negligence). In essence, this amounts to a fault-based liability regime for marketing.[250] The notion of a marketing-induced market failure could be the relevant mechanism to set the appropriate duty for marketers. That is to say, the manipulative character of a marketing technique would be assessed by looking at the degree to which it has the potential to extract rents, exploit biases and vulnerabilities, and/or shape preferences to the detriment of consumers' autonomy, equity and welfare. This opens up the possibility to look at the techniques behind personalization and encourage changes in their design and development. The policy proposals concerning personalized disclosure, the monitoring of marketers, and the offering of a genuine-opt out can provide the necessary framework to set out the desired due care level for marketers.

To avert the risk that optimal care levels are underestimated (e.g., by courts) because of the complexity behind the personalization mechanisms, which fails to provide marketers with the incentives to increase their levels of care, the framework of Sects. 6.1 to 6.3 can provide a valuable starting point to determine the optimal due care levels.[251] The framework can be complemented by efforts from self-regulatory and supervisory bodies that actively fill the gaps in the determination of the due care level.[252] Consequently, legal uncertainty and the risk of errors concerning the due care level under the fault-based liability regime can be reduced.[253]

Notably, there should be a possibility for the injured party to hold the seller liable when the developer of the marketing technique cannot be identified, or the developer is established outside the EU.[254] The goal of marketer liability would be to provide marketers with an extra incentive to control their activity and exercise additional care beyond the precautional measures defined in the current consumer law framework, particularly the UCPD.

---

[248] Cfr. Li and Faure (2024).

[249] Cooter and Ulen (2016), p. 218.

[250] Cfr. Li et al. (2022), pp. 620–621.

[251] For example, failure to provide personalized disclosures, not meeting the manipulation standards, and/or not offering consumers a genuine-opt option could be sufficient evidence that the due care level has not been met.

[252] Li and Faure (2014) refer to the EU New Legislative Framework, which consists of sector-specific regulations that established the safety requirements that a specific product must meet before it can be placed on the market.

[253] Li and Faure (2024), p. 146.

[254] This is similar to Article 8(3) of the Revised PLD, which offers the opportunity to hold the distributor of a product liable when the manufacturer cannot be identified or when she is located outside the EU. Pursuant to Article 8(4) Revised PLD, this provision also extends to providers of online platforms that allow consumers to conclude distance contracts with traders and that are not manufacturers, importers, or distributors.

Second, the scope of the liability regime. Marketer liability would exclusively focus on exploitative marketing techniques. As became clear from Chaps. 3–5, these techniques are aimed at creating marketing-induced market failures, which are detrimental to consumers' autonomy, equity, and welfare. The benefit of having a marketing-induced market failure as the criterion, rather than listing specific marketing practices, is that it keeps the criterion flexible enough to deal with newer and more advanced marketing techniques that might be developed in the coming years.

Third, with regard to the damage, apart from the material damages that have been described in the Revised PLD, that is, material losses resulting from death or personal injury, including medically recognized harm to psychological health, damage to property, or loss or corruption of data,[255] the definition of damage under marketer liability could be extended to include damages arising from a loss of consumer welfare, which can be calculated by means of economic tools.[256] A potential addition would be to include losses due to the decay of consumer autonomy.[257]

Lastly, the burden of proof under marketer liability should be eased to make it more feasible for consumers and the relevant authorities to file claims for losses as a result of exploitative personalized marketing techniques.[258] Drawing upon the provisions of the Revised PLD (in particular Articles 8 and 9), the developers of the marketing techniques could be forced to disclose relevant information that helps the injured party support the plausibility of the compensation claim. This would aid the claimants to penetrate the opacity of the marketing techniques. Moreover, there should be a *presumption of exploitativeness,* which means that exploitation is presumed when it concerns personalized marketing techniques, and a *prima facie* causal link can be established. The latter part could be subject to conditions as they have been defined by the UCPD concerning misleading and aggressive commercial practices.[259]

The supplier of the personalized marketing technique would then need to demonstrate that it complies with the law, pre-set standards (e.g., manipulation standards) or that necessary safeguard measures have been taken to avoid infringements of the law.[260]

The presumption of a causal link helps combat the technical complexity of personalized marketing techniques, which makes it difficult to prove liability.[261]

---

[255] The exact description of these damages can be found in Article 6 Revised PLD.

[256] New calculation techniques driven by big data allow for precise estimations of consumer surplus. See, for instance, Cohen et al. (2016).

[257] Several scholars have made substantial advances in formalizing and measuring the loss of consumer autonomy, see, for instance, André et al. (2018); Bjørlo et al. (2021); Hyman et al. (2023).

[258] De Meeus (2019) argues that the complexity of the emerging technologies might hamper consumers from claiming their rights before court; Galli (2022).

[259] Articles 5–9 UCPD.

[260] Helberger et al. (2021).

[261] Cfr. De Bruin (2016), p. 495 argues that a complete reversal of the burden of proof might be justified, however, this could foster a claim culture and have a negative impact on innovation; see also Dheu et al. (2022).

Naturally, the developers of the marketing techniques would retain the right to rebut the presumption and invoke defenses. Similar to Article 10 of the Revised PLD, these could include the following: they did not put the technique into circulation, the exploitative character was not present when introducing the technique to the market, or the so-called *development risk defense* applies.[262] Risk predictability should be considered based on the state of the art in technology. This prevents the liability regime from resulting in overdeterrence, which will hamper beneficial innovation activities.[263]

It must be noted, however, that Faure (2016b)[264] demonstrates that *development risk liability* can be economically justified. Holding marketers liable ex post for behavior that causes harm (i.e., liability for behavior that was not previously deemed harmful) incentivizes them to obtain as much information as possible about the risks associated with their behavior and invest in preventing or minimizing those risks.[265] Failure to apply this liability regime might lead to inefficiencies and suboptimal regulation because it reduces the incentives for marketers to care beyond the existing standard.[266] However, the fear of new standards being applied retrospectively, which might hamper innovation, detracts from the desirability of the liability rule.[267] To remedy this risk, *prospective overruling* might be considered, whereby new standards are not applied retrospectively, but the standards of liability can be made stricter over time to deal with new risks posed by technological developments in order to incentivize marketers to minimize risks continuously.[268] Hence, incorporating development risk liability combined with prospective overruling might provide a valuable complement to the marketer liability framework for optimizing the incentives given to marketers. In this way, marketer liability would incentivize marketers to take precautionary measures to prevent consumer harm while still offering the opportunity for the development of novel welfare-enhancing marketing strategies.

Of note is that, in many cases, the marketer and the company fall under the same umbrella. Yet, the aim of marketer liability is not to impose additional liability on the same parties; instead, its objective is to give enforcers (private and public) an extra tool to go directly after the developers of exploitative marketing practices and, if necessary, summon the external marketing companies that designed the marketing strategy.

Especially in the context of marketing in the digital age, consumers are more disadvantaged in making their case under the existing liability regime. The complexity behind personalization, the lack of access to relevant information and the

---

[262] Refers to the objective state of scientific and technical knowledge at the time when the product was placed on the market, which was not sufficient to discover the defectiveness.

[263] Faure et al. (2016).

[264] Faure (2016b).

[265] Faure and Grimeaud (2003).

[266] Shavell (1992).

[267] Faure (2016b).

[268] Faure (2016b).

lack of technical sophistication require complementation of the liability regime. The need to remedy this situation can be seen from the attempts in the Revised PLD to facilitate victims' access to justice.[269]

Per analogiam, it can be argued that the need for more disclosure of relevant evidence, an eased burden of proof, and the presumption of a causal link could be beneficial to consumer protection. Marketer liability would aim to provide the proper incentives to marketers and facilitate consumers' ability to claim damages, while preventing overdeterrence that leads to less innovative marketing activities.

In addition, employing the concept of marketer liability will incentivize marketers to self-monitor in order to prevent exposure to increased liability costs. This means that action can be undertaken against marketing practices that the regulator has not yet recognized. Marketers who know that they will bear the costs when the marketing strategy harms consumers will be disincentivized to continue its use because the practice's profitability will be significantly less. Of course, it could be the case that the benefits still exceed the costs, yet in such cases, regulation plays a key role.[270]

In conclusion, liability can be a helpful complement when regulation falls short. It can function as a last resort in remedying the harms of personalized marketing.

6.5 Analyzing the Policy Approach

Section 6.4 introduced a new approach to dealing with personalized marketing. In short, the policy approach is based on four pillars: (1) personalized disclosure, (2) monitoring, (3) a genuine opt-out mechanism, and (4) marketer liability.

The goal is to remedy marketing-induced market failures by presenting a mix of novel strategies aimed at: (a) informing consumers adequately, (b) supervising marketing techniques, (c) giving consumers a real way out of personalization, and (d) providing the proper incentives to marketers.

In Chaps. 3–5, law and economics analyses were conducted on the existing legal frameworks concerning, respectively, personalized advertising, pricing, and contracting. In this way, the functionality of the legal framework in addressing the issue at hand could be determined. In the same fashion, the presented policy approach will be scrutinized. Consequently, the merits of the proposed approach can be advocated while accounting for the potential limitations.

[269] Li and Faure (2014), p. 167; Article 10 Revised PLD.

[270] Shavell (1984).

6.5.1 Scope of the Policy

In this study, personalized marketing has been analyzed by looking at three specific marketing practices: personalized advertising, pricing, and contracting. The proposed four-pillar approach, based on disclosure, monitoring, opt-out, and marketer liability, has been formulated to deal with personalized marketing as a whole. This means that the regulatory approach amalgamates the findings from the different chapters and provides general guidelines that can be applied to all forms of personalization. In addition, the pillars of the proposals are mutually reinforcing, which means that the approach is most effective when all four features are implemented. Solely opting for disclosure or monitoring changes, for example, will not suffice.

The rationale is that the framework can be used to address the current marketing techniques analyzed in the study, but also future personalization techniques. Regulating the existing marketing practices individually leads to a situation in which the law is always lagging behind the developments in marketing.[271] For instance, creating a regulatory framework for solely algorithmic pricing might be useful when tackling the pricing dimension of personalized marketing is the only goal. However, as has been demonstrated in this study, personalized marketing has many guises, which are mutually reinforcing, and will be continuously developed. The progress made in the realm of algorithmic contract personalization is an example of this. Regulating personalized marketing must for that reason take account of current and future challenges, which means being cognizant of and accommodating innovation.

The current EU legal framework is not future-proof for the challenges that personalized marketing will bring. Quick fixes are not at hand and, thus, a regulatory change is necessary to adequately protect consumers, both in the present as in the future.[272] The regulatory proposal aims, therefore, to provide a starting point for further regulation and, most importantly, make EU consumer law future-proof.[273]

The regulatory framework will be applied to each of the personalization practices to demonstrate its working. To start with, its implementation in the context of personalized advertising will be illustrated. Updating the disclosure mechanism and personalizing the information to the benefit of the consumer (pillar one) will ensure that when a consumer sees an ad, the consumer will understand why it is shown, based on what parameters, and what the objective of the ad is, instead of seeing a simple notification that an ad is personalized on the basis of crude criteria as is currently the case. In combination with the personalized disclosure, the consumer would get the option for a genuine opt-out (pillar three), which would depersonalize the ads shown.

Monitoring (pillar two) plays a key role in tackling personalized advertising. The monitoring can take place by virtue of the manipulation standards. If the mechanism

[271] De Geest (2018b).

[272] Duivenvoorde (2023).

[273] Cfr. Ranchordás and Van't Schip (2020).

behind an ad is capable of inciting a number of consumers, which exceeds the predefined threshold, to take an action that they would not otherwise have taken, enforcement can proceed on the basis of the UCPD. To establish the manipulative nature of the ad, empirical evidence or behavioral insights can be used for the analysis. The ad repository requirement of the DSA can make sure that authorities can access relevant information, thereby facilitating monitoring. Additionally, internal supervision can make sure that ads are not put into circulation before they are checked for manipulativeness. Finally, in case a specific advertising technique is able to fall through the cracks of the proposed regulatory framework, marketing liability (pillar four) can play a complementary role by facilitating litigation against individual companies that employ the technique in question.

With respect to algorithmically-determined personalized prices, personalized disclosure is of pivotal importance. Consumers can then, *inter alia*, see a brief and clear calculation of the price, the difference with the uniform price or the price offered to other consumers, and the basis on which the price has been formed. In terms of monitoring, enforcement on the basis of the UCPD can be facilitated by establishing that a consumer would not have a bought a product if all relevant information regarding the price would have been provided by the seller. Failure to disclose this information would amount to an unfair commercial practice. Furthermore, the genuine opt-out is paramount to tackle algorithmic pricing. If consumers want to receive uniform prices, as in a regular brick-and-mortar shops, this option should be made as accessible and conspicuous as possible. Lastly, in case, it can be established that certain algorithmic pricing techniques have led to the large-scale overcharging of consumers, the way can be paved for collective action on the basis of the marketer liability regime.

Concerning personalization of contract terms, personalized disclosure and monitoring play a vital role. Updating the archaic boilerplates is essential to tackle the signing-without-reading problem and the one-sidedness of contract terms. By means of personalized disclosures, the attention of consumers can be directed to the terms that are most pertinent to their situations, have the most impact on their welfare, and negatively affect their autonomy and equity.

Monitoring materializes through the revisitation of the UCTD, whereby the blacklist can be extended to cover terms that consistently lead to the manipulation or exploitation of consumers. This way, consumers can be certain that excessively one-sided marketing terms will not be binding on them, which also facilitates enforcement. The genuine-opt out is helpful to maintain the option for consumers to get standardized contracts and thereby not be bound to algorithmically-personalized contract terms. At last, marketer liability can provide a final recourse to take action against algorithmic contracts that are particularly one-sided to the detriment of the consumer but are still able to circumvent the contractual safeguards of the UCTD.

In the same way, the four-pillar framework can be applied to novel forms of personalization. Although the different pillars are synergetic, they can be tailored to fit the context of a specific personalization technique. The proposed framework allows for these adjustments. It is argued that the policy proposals are adequate to cover all three personalization practices discussed, while being broad enough in scope to cover future forms of marketing personalization.

6.5.2 Efficiency-Equity Analysis

The proposed regulatory approach aims to strike a balance between efficiency and equity, which could be regarded as the fifth and last pillar.[274] The approach has departed from prohibition recommendations to safeguard the positive efficiency effects of personalized marketing. Although there are voices that propose prohibitions of personalized marketing practices,[275] it has been a deliberate choice to diverge from these *per se* prohibitions. The rationale behind this is that the various economic benefits that personalized marketing would bring would be lost entirely, which does not only harm sellers but also consumers. By virtue of the presented policy approach, the aim is to put consumers in a situation where they can independently decide if they want to proceed with receiving personalized services or not.

Accordingly, it is asserted that the benefits of the policy proposals will outweigh the costs. The proposals aim to actively thwart the exploitation of consumer vulnerabilities and the large-scale extraction of consumer surplus. It can be argued that although, from an efficiency perspective, the intervention will need to prove itself to be welfare-enhancing for all parties, it is more than plausible to expect consumer welfare to be improved. Accordingly, from a consumer perspective, the presented approach can be considered promising for safeguarding distributive justice.

Moreover, at the moment, consumers' general attitude toward personalization is unfavorable.[276] Providing consumers with tools that assist them in protecting their autonomy, equity, and welfare could create the possibility for them to enjoy the benefits of personalization without the fear of exploitation. In this way, the generally negative attitude toward personalization could be partially remedied, which should be welcomed from the marketing side.

Yet, it could be asserted that the policy approach will demand more from small and medium enterprises (SMEs) in terms of costs than from big firms, thereby creating a competitive disadvantage. This is a valid concern, and to counteract this effect, a solution could be the introduction of a type of *de minimis rule* whereby only larger sellers will fall under the scrutiny of consumer authorities.[277] However, the focus on big firms will set a precedent for the entire industry and strengthen the effect on SMEs to comply. In addition, SMEs could be notified through public announce-

---

[274] See the introduction of Sect. 6.5.

[275] See, for instance, Chapdelaine (2020) who proposes a ban on certain aspects of personalized pricing and Claxton (2021) who advocates a ban on targeted advertising in the context of private offerings.

[276] European Commission (2016); Leszczynska and Baltag (2024).

[277] Cfr. Ayres and Schwartz (2014). A similar line of thought can be found in the DSA, see Article 91 and Recital 150.

ments that specific marketing practices are formally considered manipulative. The clarity regarding manipulative marketing practices will make collective redress more accessible, which could limit the potential for abuse among SMEs.[278]

Furthermore, the cost side of the intervention may not be overlooked. The regulatory changes will demand more efforts on the seller's side to enhance consumer protection. Personalization is a highly profitable marketing strategy for companies, and it has increased the profitably of direct marketing efforts to record levels.[279] The personalized disclosure requirements will require firms to invest in technologies that display relevant, individualized information to the consumer. It must be noted, however, that the personalized disclosure approach accounts explicitly for the fact that companies already have this information.

Despite this, the monitoring mechanism will impose additional costs on companies. In addition, the opt-out mechanisms will likely enlarge the foregone revenues in comparison with the scenario in which personalization could freely take place.

Although these are valid concerns from a business perspective, it could be argued that from a consumer perspective, the additional consumer benefits will outweigh these costs. The exploitation of consumers will be actively counteracted, whereas companies are still given the possibility to offer personalization services that can generate sizeable profits.[280] Rather than proposing an outright ban on personalized marketing, which could lead to substantial economic losses, the goal is to set safeguards that prevent the abatement of consumer autonomy, equity, and welfare. In this way, personalized marketing will still be possible, however, within a robust consumer protection framework.

6.5.3 Societal Analysis

Apart from the efficiency-equity analysis, there are societal values that the public expects to be honored in the market, which are, *inter alia*, the preservation of autonomy, non-discrimination, privacy, and good faith.[281] In terms of autonomy, the policy approach can be seen as having a two-fold effect. On the one hand, it preserves the autonomy of consumers (and businesses) by not taking away any of the marketing tools through prohibitions. A consumer who benefits from personalized marketing communications can continue to do so. On the other hand, the policy reforms will ensure that the liberty of marketers to engage in exploitative marketing practices will be limited, ultimately fortifying consumer autonomy. In this sense, consumer autonomy regains its value in the digital age.

---

[278] Ayres and Schwartz (2014), pp. 589–590.

[279] Rossi et al. (1996); Zhang and Wedel (2009); Johnson (2013); Statista (2023).

[280] Wagner and Eidenmüller (2019), p. 606 state: "Hence, the core business model of internet giants is not in danger – they would just be less profitable than they are today."

[281] Helveston (2016).

Although anti-discrimination laws are in place that prohibit disparate treatment, there are serious concerns that personalization practices will lead to a *disparate impact*.[282] This means that regardless of intent, members of certain protected groups are still disadvantaged because the underlying mechanism (e.g., the algorithm) discriminates among consumers based on characteristics that are not part of the protected classes but that are highly correlated to the ones that are, thereby leading to practically the same result.[283] This problem must be remedied to a large extent at the design level of algorithms. However, the presented policy approach takes heed of the non-discrimination norms by providing consumers a way out of personalized marketing. Ex ante, through personalized disclosure, consumers can identify the constituting factors of a personalized price or ad and decide accordingly. The marketing monitoring that is advocated will provide an internal and external layer of supervision that can prevent, detect, and correct discriminatory outcomes. Ex post, consumers can withdraw from the personalized services if they experience regret based on discrimination grounds. This will immediately give an incentive to marketers to cease potential discriminatory practices. Besides, consumer backlash can be a powerful deterrent to control for potential discrimination.[284]

The embrace of BDA also encompasses a degree of data surveillance that poses a significant threat to consumers' privacy interests. The rationale is that companies can obtain monetary benefits by collecting more and more personal and behavioral data.[285] This will continue until the marginal benefit of doing so meets the marginal cost,[286] whereby their intersection can lie far beyond the threshold of what consumers find acceptable. Accordingly, the proposed policies consider these privacy concerns by tackling the boilerplate system, which allows companies to collect vast amounts of data based on uninformed consent, and by providing an opt-out to consumers to preserve their right to anonymity. In this way, an attempt can be made to curtail the rapid increase in consumer surveillance.[287]

Finally, by changing the incentives for the marketer to prevent exploitation, the mutual relationship can be revived after the breach of trust created by personalization.[288] It is of utmost importance that the lion's share of consumer transactions will and can be governed by the principle of good faith. The obligation of both parties to uphold their end of the bargain is a vital aspect of a contractual relationship.[289] It is, therefore, necessary that marketers have the incentives to serve consumers' best

[282] Rutherglen (2006).

[283] Crawford and Schultz (2014).

[284] See for the role of consumer backlash in algorithmic pricing, for instance, Odlyzko (2009); Grochowski et al. (2022); Van der Rest et al. (2022).

[285] Helveston (2016), p. 899.

[286] Based on microeconomic theory. See, for instance, Cooter and Ulen (2016), chapter 2.

[287] Zuboff (2019).

[288] Hemker et al. (2021).

[289] Houh (2003).

interests and that consumers will subsequently be able to trust, to a large degree, the marketing efforts of the seller.[290]

The societal analysis shows that various fundamental values are interdependent and must be jointly considered. However, the problem lies in coming to a final evaluation of a system that is expected to pursue incommensurable values.[291] The legislator and the courts are expected to strike a subtle balance between conflicting rights in all areas of the law, including the efficiency-equity trade-off.[292] Accordingly, the aim to achieve optimal efficiency needs to be balanced against the desire to achieve equitable treatment of individuals. This requires regulation that encourages efficiency but does not suppress the need for fairness.[293] The approach advocated in this chapter proposes policy changes that can be justified from an economic perspective while accounting for autonomy and equity concerns. In this way, a balance of societal interests can be obtained, which can be regarded as desirable from a consumer policy perspective.

6.5.4 General Objections and Replies

Several general objections can be raised to the proposal that do not necessarily fall within the law and economics analysis. Although this subsection does not aim to be exhaustive, it endeavors to demonstrate that many concerns that could be expressed regarding specific aspects of the proposal can be managed.

First, an immediate objection that could be raised against adopting a marketing perspective to consumer law is that special attention is already given to marketing. The UCPD and MCAD are examples of legislations that explicitly deal with marketing. Besides, newer regulations, such as the GDPR, expressly refer to marketing efforts. Accordingly, it could be argued that there is nothing new under the sun. There is, however, a common tendency to be seen in the approach taken to address marketing efforts. Marketing laws include broad prohibitions on unfair, abusive, and deceptive practices. These laws include targeted prohibitions but also prohibitions that require the interpretation of courts.[294] This allows courts to address new marketing challenges as they appear, but this also means that marketing harms are remedied once they have already occurred. Therefore, the system is complaint-driven, whereby the initiative lies with public enforcement agencies, business competitors, and consumer plaintiffs to prove unfair business conduct in court. In other words, the framework is strongly reactionary.

[290] Marketing efforts can also be directed to promote social goals. For example, reducing drunk driving and aiding financial decision-making among the poor. See, respectively, Elder et al. (2004) and Bertrand et al. (2006).

[291] Helveston (2016), p. 901.

[292] Mathis (2009), p. 201.

[293] Weiss and Mehrotra (2001), p. 2.

[294] Willis (2020), p. 151.

The sophistication of digital marketing techniques makes claims more difficult to prove, thereby "leaving digital deception increasingly immunized from the law".[295] The contribution of the marketing perspective is that the ex-post enforcement is complemented by ex-ante incentive-based regulation. In this way, an approach can be presented that anticipates marketing developments instead of lagging behind them, as is currently the case.

Second, an argument could be made that, for example, personalized disclosures substantially increase the *complexity costs* of the legal system.[296] An alternative way of putting it is that the proposals will lead to prohibitively high *administrative costs*.[297] However, this argument can be relativized on two points. The (economic) feasibility of providing personalized disclosures has greatly improved with the rise of big data and the associated costs of personalization technology are expected to go down.[298] This will also lead to a reduction in regulatory *error costs* by "minimizing false positive and false negative attributions of subjects to categories",[299] which can offset part of the administrative costs.[300]

In addition, the degree of granularity of the personalized disclosures can be determined based on the costs. Regulators could experiment with the required degree of granularity of the disclosures, the intensity of enforcement, and the specificity of the permitted categories.[301] More specifically, if it turns out that personalized disclosure is relatively costly, cruder forms of personalization can take place, such as providing information based on the categorization of consumers into sophisticated, average, and vulnerable consumer groups. Personalization can be further developed if the costs go down over time, thereby making the disclosure more tailored to the individual. Accordingly, the administrative costs do not necessarily have to be an unsurmountable obstacle for personalized disclosure. The same rationale holds for the establishment of an opt-out regime.

Third, monitoring marketers is costly. It can be argued that monitoring marketers' compliance with manipulation standards will impose an additional financial burden on consumer authorities. As a consequence, the new regulations will detract from the enforcement of other regulations. In principle, this refers to a *crowding-out effect* of regulation.[302] However, the incentive-based structure of the policy approach is more likely to supplement rather than supplant other regulatory approaches.[303]

---

[295] Willis (2020), p. 152.

[296] Kaplow (1995) explains: "The complexity of legal rules refers to the number and difficulty of distinctions the rules make." This means that the more difficult it is to determine the applicable category to which the rules apply, the greater the complexity. The more precise tailoring of rules implies, therefore, greater complexity costs.

[297] See, for an analysis of the role of administrative costs in enforcement, Faure et al. (2009).

[298] Faure et al. (2009).

[299] Hacker (2017b), p. 676.

[300] Faure et al. (2009).

[301] Busch and De Franceschi (2018).

[302] Willis (2015), p. 1402.

[303] Willis (2015), p. 1403.

The rationale is that the goal of the new approach is to provide marketers with different incentives that will prevent the emergence of exploitation problems. This will clear part of the regulatory opportunity costs.[304] The incentive structure will save consumers organization some of the financial resources they need to spend to remedy consumer harms on an ex-post basis. In this sense, the policy approach is expected to lead to regulatory synergies, which will counteract the crowding-out effect.

6.5.5 An Overall Assessment

The law and economics analysis has provided insights into the proposal's merits from an efficiency, equity, and societal perspective. In addition, special consideration has been given to general objections that could potentially be raised. The purpose of the policy proposal is twofold. On the one hand, the proposal aims to protect consumers adequately from the harms that could be inflicted on them through exploitative personalized marketing practices. On the other hand, it has tried to do so without impairing consumers' ability to reap the benefits that personalization might bring. In other words, enhancing the level of consumer protection with as little market disruption as possible.[305]

The reasoning behind this balancing of regulatory goals stems from the law and economics analyses of the marketing practices.[306] It has become clear that personalized marketing offers considerable efficiency benefits in comparison with traditional marketing but that it concomitantly poses significant threats to consumers' autonomy, equity, and welfare. From a broadened consumer policy perspective, the practice is problematic in its unregulated form.

Precisely because the merits of personalization are debatable and dependent on the perspective taken, the extreme solutions on either part of the regulatory spectrum have not been taken. More specifically, *per se* prohibitions have been discouraged in the same way that complete inaction has been dissuaded. Failure to regulate would exacerbate the harm caused by personalized marketing strategies. Strict regulation by virtue of prohibitions, on the other hand, is highly likely to cause more adverse effects than benefits.[307]

The tension between the efficiency considerations and the fairness-based considerations has made clear that there is no room for across-the-board optimization.[308]

---

[304] Agarwal et al. (2015) provide a practical example relating to the credit card market, in which it is shown that the incentivizing effect of a regulation can offset its implementation costs and benefit consumers.

[305] Helveston (2016), p. 905.

[306] See Sects. 3.5, 4.4, and 5.3.

[307] Bamberger and Mulligan (2011); Laux et al. (2021).

[308] Helveston (2016), p. 912.

Accordingly, the approach taken was to balance the values at stake and propose regulatory reforms that materialize this balance.

Naturally, as with any balancing exercise in regulation, there can be a debate regarding the relative importance of the values that have been taken into consideration, thereby questioning the desirability of the policy proposal. Nevertheless, the law and economics analysis has offered the opportunity to see if the proposed policy could be justified both from an economic and a legal perspective. To improve the validity of the analysis, the scope of examination has been broadened to include the fundamental values of autonomy and equity. As a consequence, a more comprehensive picture of the regulatory problem could be painted. Although, in a normative sense, the approach can be disputed based on ideological preferences, in this research, the approach has been taken whereby the promotion and protection of consumer interests are put at the heart of consumer policy.[309]

All in all, the presented policy approach has positioned itself between an overly restrictive and market-intrusive regulatory system that would discard the efficiency benefits of personalization and an overly permissive system that keeps facilitating the exploitation of consumers.[310] In this way, it is expected that, overall, consumers and in particular the most vulnerable groups, will likely benefit more than they lose from the proposed policy approach.

6.6 Conclusion

In the digital age, every consumer can be rendered vulnerable. Personalized marketing has the potential to lead to large-scale exploitations of consumers' autonomy, equity, and welfare. The analysis of the current legal framework has demonstrated that it falls short when it concerns personalized marketing. Consequently, a policy approach has been presented that aims to fill the identified gaps in order to contribute to the protection of consumer interests in the digital age.

From an ex-ante perspective, the archaic boilerplate needs to be updated. This can be accomplished through personalized disclosures. Personalized disclosures can work hand in hand with the AI-driven detection of unfair terms. The information relevant to consumers would be highlighted and shown depending on their individual needs and preferences. At the same time, changed preferences and interests will be easily accommodated by presenting an AI-driven tool in which an individual can request information on different topics.

Furthermore, monitoring marketers is of pivotal importance. This can be achieved by establishing manipulation standards, encouraging internal supervision, and facilitating the monitoring process with a new consumer benchmark, a marketing-specific clause, and increased transparency. The marketing-induced market failure

[309] Helveston (2016), p. 912.

[310] Cfr. Helveston (2016), p. 916.

framework can serve as a flexible criterion to tackle the manipulative nature of personalized marketing techniques.

Moreover, providing consumers with an easily accessible and conspicuous opt-out mechanism is essential. Consumers should maintain their autonomy and should be given the opportunity to opt out of personalized marketing strategies as they see fit.

Finally, marketer liability can work as a last resort to provide marketers with the proper incentives and address the exploitation practices that circumvent the regulatory safeguards.

The analysis of the policy approach has demonstrated that the proposals can be justified from a law and economics perspective. Tackling the new challenges posed by marketing in the digital age requires the adoption of a broader perspective that also incorporates autonomy and equity considerations. This research supports the notion that consumers should be put at the center of consumer law[311]; however, marketers cannot be left out of the equation to do so.

It is time to take marketing seriously.

References

Adjerid I, Acquisti A, Brandimarte L, Loewenstein G (2013) Sleights of privacy: framing, disclosures, and the limits of transparency. Symp Usable Priv Secur (SOUPS):1–17

Agarwal S, Chomsisengphet S, Mahoney N, Stroebel J (2015) Regulating consumer financial products: evidence from credit cards. Q J Econ 130(1):111–164

André Q, Carmon Z, Wertenbroch K, Crum A, Frank D, Goldstein W et al (2018) Consumer choice and autonomy in the age of artificial intelligence and big data. Cust Needs Solut 5:28–37

Ausness RC (2002a) Tort liability for the sale of non-defective products: an analysis and critique of the concept of negligent marketing. South Carolina Law Rev 53(4):907–966

Ausness RC (2002b) Will more aggressive marketing practices lead to greater tort liability for prescription drug manufacturers. Wake Forest Law Rev 37(1):97–140

Ayres I, Schwartz A (2014) The no-reading problem in consumer contract law. Stanford Law Rev 66(3):545–610

Bamberger KA, Mulligan DK (2011) Privacy on the books and on the ground. Stanford Law Rev 63(2):247–315

Bannihatti Kumar V, Iyengar R, Nisal N, Feng Y, Habib H, Story P et al. (2020) Finding a choice in a haystack: automatic extraction of opt-out statements from privacy policy text. In: Proceedings of the Web Conference 2020, pp 1943–1954

Bar-Gill O (2008) The behavioral economics of consumer contracts. Minn Law Rev 92(3):749–802

Bar-Gill O (2012) Seduction by contract: law, economics and psychology in consumer markets. Oxford University Press, Oxford

Bar-Gill O, Ferrari F (2010) Informing consumers about themselves. Erasmus Law Rev 3(2):93–120

Barr MS, Mullainathan S, Shafir E (2009) The case for behaviorally informed regulation. In: Moss D, Cisternino J (eds) New perspectives on regulation. The Tobin Project, Cambridge, pp 25–61

Ben-Shahar O, Chilton A (2016) Simplification of privacy disclosures: an experimental test. J Leg Stud 45(S2):S41–S67

[311] Willis (2015), p. 1407.

Ben-Shahar O, Porat A (2021) Personalized law: different rules for different people. Oxford University Press, Oxford
Ben-Shahar O, Posner EA (2011) The right to withdraw in contract law. J Leg Stud 40(1):115–148
Ben-Shahar O, Schneider CE (2014) More than you wanted to know: the failure of mandated disclosure. Princeton University Press, Princeton
Bertrand M, Mullainathan S, Shafir E (2006) Behavioral economics and marketing in aid of decision making among the poor. J Public Policy Mark 25(1):8–23
Bhatia J, Breaux TD (2018) Empirical measurement of perceived privacy risk. ACM Trans Comput-Hum Interact 25(6):1–47
Bjørlo L, Moen Ø, Pasquine M (2021) The role of consumer autonomy in developing sustainable AI: a conceptual framework. Sustainability 13(4):1–18
Block-Lieb S, Janger EJ (2006) The myth of the rational borrower: rationality, behavioralism, and the misguided reform of bankruptcy law. Tex Law Rev 84(6):1481–1566
Bollinger D, Kubicek K, Cotrini C, Basin D (2022) Automating cookie consent and GDPR violation detection. In: Proceedings of the 31st USENIX Security Symposium, pp 2893–2910
Brenkert GG (1998) Marketing and the vulnerable. Bus Ethics Q 8(S1):7–20
Burrows P (1999) Combining regulation and legal liability for the control of external costs. Int Rev Law Econ 19(2):227–244
Busch C (2019) Implementing personalized law. Univ Chicago Law Rev 86(2):309–332
Busch C, De Franceschi A (2018) Granular legal norms: big data and the personalization of private law. In: Mak V, Tjong Tjin Tai E, Berlee A (eds) Research handbook in data science and law. Edward Elgar, Cheltenham, pp 408–424
Calabresi G (1968) Transaction costs, resource allocation and liability rules: a comment. J Law Econ 11(1):67–73
Calabresi G (1970) The cost of accidents: a legal and economic analysis. Yale University Press, New Haven
Calo R (2014) Digital market manipulation. Geo Wash Law Rev 82(4):995–1051
Carbonara E, Guerra A, Parisi F (2016) Sharing residual liability: the cheapest cost avoider revisited. J Leg Stud 45(1):173–201
Chapdelaine P (2020) Algorithmic personalized pricing. New York Univ J Law Bus 17(1):1–48
Chatzipanagiotis M (2024) Trying to fit a square peg into a round hole: individual remedies for unfair commercial practices under Art. 11a UCPD. J Eur Consum Market Law 13(3):113–125
Claxton CM (2021) Private offerings in the age of surveillance capitalism and targeted advertising. Vanderbilt Law Rev 74(4):1187–1229
Coase RH (1960) The problem of social cost. J Law Econ 3(1):1–44
Cobbe J, Singh J (2019) Regulating recommending: motivations, considerations, and principles. Eur J Law Technol 10(3):1–37
Cohen P, Hahn R, Hall J, Levitt S, Metcalfe R (2016) Using big data to estimate consumer surplus: the case of Uber. Natl Bur Econ Res Work Pap No w22627, pp 1–42
Constantinides E (2006) The marketing mix revisited: towards the 21st century marketing. J Mark Manag 22(3–4):407–438
Cooter R, Ulen T (2016) Law and economics, 6th edn. Berkeley Law Books, Berkeley
Crawford K, Schultz J (2014) Big data and due process: toward framework to redress predictive privacy harms. Boston Coll Law Rev 55(1):93–128
Cseres KJ (2014) Enforcing the unfair commercial practices directive: the enforcement model of The Netherlands. In: Tóth T (ed) Unfair commercial practices: the long road to harmonized law enforcement. Pázmány Press, Budapest, pp 19–36
Dantas DC, Carrillat F (2013) The relational benefits of personalized communications in an online environment. Can J Adm Sci/Revue Canadienne des Sci l'Administration 30(3):189–202
Dari-Mattiacci G, Parisi F (2015) Liability rules: an economic taxonomy. In: Bussani M, Sebok AJ (eds) Comparative tort law: global perspectives. Edward Elgar Publ, Cheltenham, pp 122–143

Davidson D (2017) Facebook targets 'insecure' young people to sell ads. The Australian. https://www.theaustralian.com.au/business/media/facebook-targets-insecure-young-people-to-sell-ads/news-story/a89949ad016eee7d7a61c3c30c909fa6
Davola A, Querci I, Romani S (2023) No consumer is an Island—relational disclosure as a regulatory strategy to advance consumer protection against microtargeting. J Consum Policy 46(1):1–25
Dawn SK (2014) Personalised marketing: concepts and framework. Productivity 54(4):370–377
De Bruin R (2016) Autonomous intelligent cars on the European intersection of liability and privacy: regulatory challenges and the road ahead. Eur J Risk Regul 7(3):485–501
De Geest G (2018a) Old law is cheap law. In: Faure M, Schreuders W, Visscher LT (eds) Don't take it seriously: essays in law and economics in honour of Roger Van den Bergh. Intersentia, Cambridge, pp 505–522
De Geest G (2018b) Rents: how marketing causes inequality. Beccaria Books, Leuven
De Luca S (2023) New product liability directive. EPRS | European Parliamentary Research Service. https://www.europarl.europa.eu/RegData/etudes/BRIE/2023/739341/EPRS_BRI(2023)739341_EN.pdf
De Meeus C (2019) The product liability directive at the age of the digital industrial revolution: fit for innovation? J Eur Consum Mark Law 8(4):149–154
Dheu O, De Bruyne J, Ducuing C (2022) The European commission's approach to extra-contractual liability and AI–A first analysis and evaluation of the two proposals. SSRN. https://ssrn.com/abstract=4239792
Duivenvoorde B (2023) Redesigning the UCPD for the age of personalised marketing. J Eur Consum Mark Law 12(5):177–184
Dwork C, Hardt M, Pitassi T, Reingold O, Zemel R (2012) Fairness through awareness. In: Proceedings of the 3rd Innovations in Theoretical Computer Science Conference, pp 214–226
Elder RW, Shults RA, Sleet DA, Nichols JL, Thompson RS, Rajab W, Task Force on Community Preventive Services (2004) Effectiveness of mass media campaigns for reducing drinking and driving and alcohol-involved crashes: a systematic review. Am J Prev Med 27(1):57–65
European Commission (2016) Consumer market study on online market segmentation through personalised pricing/offers in the European Union (Report No. Request for specific services 2016 85 02 for the implementation of framework Contract EAHC/2013/CP/04, final report). Publications Office of the European Union. https://op.europa.eu/en/publication-detail/-/publication/ed9ce056-c2cf-11e8-9424-01aa75ed71a1/language-en
European Commission (2021) Commission Notice: Guidance on the Interpretation and Application of Directive 2005/29/EC of the European Parliament and of the Council Concerning Unfair Business-to-consumer Commercial Practices in the Internal Market. https://eur-lex.europa.eu/legal-content/EN/TXT/?uri=CELEX%3A52021XC1229%2805%29
European Commission (2023) Digital fairness—fitness check on EU consumer law. European Commission. https://ec.europa.eu/info/law/better-regulation/have-your-say/initiatives/13413-Digital-fairness-fitness-check-on-EU-consumer-law_en
Ezrachi A (2016) Virtual competition: the promise and perils of the algorithm-driven economy. Harvard University Press, Cambridge
Faizullabhoy I, Korolova A (2018) Facebook's advertising platform: new attack vectors and the need for interventions. arXiv preprint arXiv:1803.10099:1–6
Faure MG (2008) Calabresi and behavioural tort law and economics. Erasmus Law Rev 1(4):75–102
Faure MG (2014) The complementary roles of liability, regulation and insurance in safety management: theory and practice. J Risk Res 17(6):689–707
Faure MG (2016a) Attribution of liability: an economic analysis of various cases. Chi-Kent Law Rev 91(2):603–636
Faure MG (2016b) Economic analysis of product liability. In: Machnikowski P (ed) European product liability: an analysis of the state of the art in the era of new technologies. Intersentia, Cambridge, pp 619–665

Faure MG, Grimeaud DJ (2003) Financial assurance issues of environmental liability. In: Faure MG (ed) Deterrence, insurability and compensation in environmental liability—future developments in the European Union. Springer, Dordrecht, pp 7–255

Faure MG, Partain R (2019) Environmental law and economics: theory and practice. Cambridge University Press, Cambridge

Faure MG, Visscher LT (2018) Rechtseconomie en privaatrecht in de Lage Landen. In: Dirix E, Falconis J (eds) Interdisciplinariteit in het recht: Law and…-bewegingen in het privaatrecht. Intersentia, Antwerp, pp 15–39

Faure MG, Ogus A, Philipsen N (2009) Curbing consumer financial losses: the economics of regulatory enforcement. Law Policy 31(2):161–191

Faure MG, Visscher LT, Weber F (2016) Liability for unknown risks: a law and economics perspective. J Eur Tort Law 7(2):198–227

Fiore K (2009) No-fault compensation systems. In: Faure M (ed) Tort law and economics, vol 1. Edward Elgar Publishing, Cheltenham, pp 406–432

Friedler SA, Scheidegger C, Venkatasubramanian S (2021) The (im)possibility of fairness: different value systems require different mechanisms for fair decision making. Commun ACM 64(4):136–143

Gabaix X, Laibson D (2006) Shrouded attributes, consumer myopia, and information suppression in competitive markets. Q J Econ 121(2):505–540

Gal MS (2018) Algorithmic challenges to autonomous choice. Mich Technol Law Rev 25(1):59–104

Galli F (2022) Algorithmic marketing and EU law on unfair commercial practices. Springer Nature, Cham

Gilead I (1985) Coase theorem, competitive market and products liability law. Isr Law Rev 20(1):39–48

Goetz CJ, Scott RE (1980) Enforcing promises: an examination of the basis of contract. Yale Law J 89(7):1261–1322

Goldberg JC, Zipursky BC (2010) The easy case for products liability law: a response to professors Polinsky and Shavell. Harv Law Rev 123(8):1919–1948

Golobardes MA (2022) Algorithmic personalization of consumer transactions and the limits of contract law. J Law Market Innov 1(1):17–43

Grochowski M, Jabłonowska A, Lagioia F, Sartor G (2022) Algorithmic price discrimination and consumer protection: a digital arms race? Technol Regul 2022:36–47

Habib H, Zou Y, Jannu A, Sridhar N, Swoopes C, Acquisti A, Schaub F (2019) An empirical analysis of data deletion and opt-out choices on 150 websites. In: Fifteenth Symposium on Usable Privacy and Security (SOUPS 2019), pp 387–406

Habib H, Pearman S, Wang J, Zou Y, Acquisti A, Cranor LF, Schaub F (2020) "It's a scavenger hunt": Usability of websites' opt-out and data deletion choices. In: Proceedings of the SIGCHI conference on human factors in computing systems, pp 1–12

Hacker P (2017a) Personal data, exploitative contracts, and algorithmic fairness: autonomous vehicles meet the internet of things. Int Data Privacy Law 7(4):266–286

Hacker P (2017b) Personalizing EU private law: from disclosures to nudges and mandates. Eur Rev Priv Law 25(3):651–678

Hacker P (2023) Manipulation by algorithms: exploring the triangle of unfair commercial practice, data protection, and privacy law. Eur Law J 29(1–2, 142):–175

Hanson JD, Kysar DA (1999a) Taking behavioralism seriously: some evidence of market manipulation. Harv Law Rev 112(7):1420–1573

Hanson JD, Kysar DA (1999b) Taking behavioralism seriously: the problem of market manipulation. New York Univ Law Rev 74(3):630–749

Helberger N, Lynskey O, Micklitz HW, Rott P, Sax M, Strycharz J (2021) EU consumer protection 2.0: structural asymmetries in digital consumer markets. Joint report from EUCP2.0 Project BEUC, pp 1–207

Helveston MN (2016) Consumer protection in the age of big data. Wash Univ Law Rev 93(4):859–918

Hemker S, Herrando C, Constantinides E (2021) The transformation of data marketing: how an ethical lens on consumer data collection shapes the future of marketing. Sustainability 13(20):1–13

Hoffman DA (2006) The best puffery article ever. Iowa Law Rev 91(5):1395–1448

Houh EM (2003) Critical interventions: toward an expansive equality approach to the doctrine of good faith in contract law. Cornell Law Rev 88(4):1025–1096

Hyman MR, Kostyk A, Trafimow D (2023) True consumer autonomy: a formalization and implications. J Bus Ethics 183(3):841–863

IAPP (2023) Norway's DPA bans behavioral advertising by Instagram, Meta. IAPP. https://iapp.org/news/a/norways-dpa-bans-behavioral-advertising-by-instagram-meta

Johnson JP (2013) Targeted advertising and advertising avoidance. Rand J Econ 44(1):128–144

Kaplow L (1995) A model of the optimal complexity of legal rules. J Law Econ Organ 11(1):150–163

Kay JA (1988) The forms of regulation. In: Seldon A (ed) Financial regulation - or over-regulation. Inst Econ Aff, pp 33–42

Kim T, Barasz K, John LK (2019) Why am I seeing this ad? The effect of ad transparency on ad effectiveness. J Consum Res 45(5):906–932

Kolstad CD, Ulen TS, Johnson GV (1990) Ex post liability for harm vs. ex ante safety regulation: substitutes or complements? Am Econ Rev 80(4):888–901

Kuntsman A, Miyake E, Martin S (2019) Re-thinking digital health: data, appisation and the (im) possibility of 'opting out'. Digital Health 5:1–16

Kwon K, Kim C (2012) How to design personalization in a context of customer retention: who personalizes what and to what extent? Electron Commer Res Appl 11(2):101–116

Laffont JJ, Martimort D (2002) The theory of incentives. Princeton University Press, Princeton

Lagioia F, Jabłonowska A, Liepina R, Drazewski K (2022) AI in search of unfairness in consumer contracts: the terms of service landscape. J Consum Policy 45(3):481–536

Laux J, Wachter S, Mittelstadt B (2021) Neutralizing online behavioural advertising: algorithmic targeting with market power as an unfair commercial practice. Common Mark Law Rev 58(3):719–750

Leenes R, Kosta E (2015) Taming the cookie monster with Dutch law–a tale of regulatory failure. Comput Law Secur Rev 31(3):317–335

Leerssen P, Ausloos J, Zarouali B, Helberger N, De Vreese CH (2018) Platform ad archives: promises and pitfalls. Internet Policy Rev 8(4):1–21

Leon P, Ur B, Shay R, Wang Y, Balebako R, Cranor L (2012) Why Johnny can't opt out: a usability evaluation of tools to limit online behavioral advertising. Proc SIGCHI Conf Hum Factors Comput Syst:589–598

Leszczynska M, Baltag D (2024) "Can I have it non-personalised?" an empirical investigation of consumer willingness to share data for personalized services and ads. J Consum Policy 47:345–372

Levitt S, Dubner S (2006) Freakonomics: a rogue economist explores the hidden side of everything. HarperCollins Publ, New York

Li S, Faure M (2024) The revised product liability directive: a law and economics analysis. J Eur Tort Law 15(2):140–171

Li S, Faure M, Havu K (2022) Liability rules for AI-related harm: law and economics lessons for a European approach. Eur J Risk Regul 13(4):618–634

Luguri J, Strahilevitz LJ (2021) Shining a light on dark patterns. J Leg Anal 13(1):43–109

Main ME (2012) Simply irresistible: neuromarketing and the commercial speech doctrine. Duq Law Rev 50(3):605–658

Margulies P (2023) Adjudicating algorithms: accountability in regulation of surveillance, privacy, and discrimination. Roger Williams Univ Leg Stud Pap (216):1–41

Marotta-Wurgler F (2015) Even more than you wanted to know about the failures of disclosure. Jerusalem Rev Leg Stud 11(1):63–74

Mas-Colell A, Whinston MD, Green JR (1995) Microeconomic theory. Oxford Univ Press, New York

Mathis K (2009) Efficiency instead of justice? In Searching for the philosophical foundations of the economic analysis of law. Springer, Dordrecht

Matz SC, Kosinski M, Nave G, Stillwell DJ (2017) Psychological targeting as an effective approach to digital mass persuasion. Proc Natl Acad Sci USA 114(48):12714–12719

McClurg AJ (1995) The tortious marketing of handguns: strict liability is dead, long live negligence. Seton Hall Legis J 19(3):777–820

Meta (2023) How meta uses legal bases for processing ads in the EU. Meta. https://about.fb.com/news/2023/01/how-meta-uses-legal-bases-for-processing-ads-in-the-eu

Micklitz HW, Saumier G (2018) Enforcement and effectiveness of consumer law. In: Micklitz HW, Saumier G (eds) Enforcement and effectiveness of consumer law. Springer, Cham, pp 3–45

Micklitz HW, Pałka P, Panagis Y (2017) The empire strikes back: digital control of unfair terms of online services. J Consum Policy 40:367–388

Miller J (1985) The FTC and voluntary standards: maximizing the net benefits of self-regulation. Cato J 4(3):897–904

Morgan FW, Stoltman JJ (1997) Vicarious franchisor liability: marketing and public policy implications. J Bus Ind Mark 12(5):297–314

Morgan FW, Schuler DK, Stoltman JJ (1995) A framework for examining the legal status of vulnerable consumers. J Public Policy Mark 14(2):267–277

Nouwens M, Liccardi I, Veale M, Karger D, Kagal L (2020) Dark patterns after the GDPR: Scraping consent pop-ups and demonstrating their influence. Proc 2020 CHI Conf Hum Factors Comput Syst:1–13

NOYB (2023) Breaking: meta prohibited from use of personal data for advertising. NOYB. https://noyb.eu/en/breaking-meta-prohibited-use-personal-data-advertising

O'Reilly J, Dalal A (2003) Off-label or out-of-bounds prescriber and marketer liability for unapproved uses of FDA-approved drugs. Ann Health Law 12(2):295–324

Odlyzko A (2009) Network neutrality, search neutrality, and the never-ending conflict between efficiency and fairness in markets. Rev Netw Econ 8(1):40–60

Oehler A, Wendt S (2017) Good consumer information: the information paradigm at its (dead) end? J Consum Policy 40(2):179–191

Ogus AI (1995) Rethinking self-regulation. Oxford. J Leg Stud 15(1):97–108

Ogut A (2023) "Stay out of my way!": the impact of cookie consent notice design on young users' decision. In: Proceedings of the XXIII International Conference on Human Computer Interaction, pp 529–541

Oi WY (1973) The economics of product safety. Bell J Econ Manag Sci 4(1):3–28

Papadogiannakis E, Papadopoulos P, Kourtellis N, Markatos EP (2021) User tracking in the post-cookie era: how websites bypass GDPR consent to track users. Proc Web Conf 2021:2130–2141

Parisi F (2013) The language of law and economics. Cambridge Books, Cambridge

Polinsky AM (1989) An introduction to law and economics, 2nd edn. Little, Brown & Co, Boston

Politico (2023) Facebook, Instagram face Norwegian ban from tracking users for ads. Politico. https://www.politico.eu/article/facebook-instagram-norway-ban-track-users-ads/

Poncibò C (2023) The UCTD 30 years later: identifying and blacklisting unfair terms in digital markets. Eur Rev Contract Law 19(4):321–345

Porat A, Strahilevitz LJ (2014) Personalizing default rules and disclosure with big data. Mich Law Rev 112(8):1417–1478

Ranchordás S, Van't Schip M (2020) Future-proofing legislation for the digital age. In: Ranchordás S, Roznai Y (eds) Time, law, and change: an interdisciplinary study. Hart, Oxford, pp 347–366

Reisch LA, Thøgersen JB (2017) Behaviorally informed consumer policy: Research and policy for "humans." In: Keller M, Halkier B, Wilska TA, Truniger M (eds) Routledge handbook on consumption. Routledge, London, pp. 242–253

Reisch LA, Zhao MIN (2017) Behavioural economics, consumer behaviour and consumer policy: state of the art. Behav Public Policy 1(2):190–206

Rekaiti P, Van den Bergh R (2000) Cooling-off periods in the consumer laws of the EC Member States: a comparative law and economics approach. J Consum Policy 23(4):371–408
Reuters (2023) Meta to seek user consent for targeted ads in the EU. Reuters. https://www.reuters.com/technology/meta-seek-user-consent-targeted-ads-eu-2023-08-01/
Rossi PE, McCulloch RE, Allenby GM (1996) The value of purchase history data in target marketing. Mark Sci 15(4):321–340
Ruggeri F, Lagioia F, Lippi M, Torroni P (2022) Detecting and explaining unfairness in consumer contracts through memory networks. Artif Intell Law 30(1):59–92
Rutherglen G (2006) Disparate impact, discrimination, and the essentially contested concept of equality. Fordham Law Rev 74(4):2313–2338
Santos C, Rossi A, Sanchez Chamorro L, Bongard-Blanchy K, Abu-Salma R (2021) Cookie banners, what's the purpose? Analyzing cookie banner text through a legal lens. In: Proceedings of the 20th Workshop on Workshop on Privacy in the Electronic Society, WPES'21, Association for Computing Machinery, pp 187–194
Satish L, Yusof N (2017) A review: big data analytics for enhanced customer experiences with crowd sourcing. Proc Comput Sci 116:274–283
Schechner S, Dolby N (2023) Meta's Facebook faces fresh threat to sending personalized ads in EU. Wall Street J. https://www.wsj.com/articles/metas-facebook-needs-consent-to-personalize-ads-eu-court-rules-6c705f18
Seizov O, Wulf AJ, Luzak J (2019) The transparent trap: a multidisciplinary perspective on the design of transparent online disclosures in the EU. J Consum Policy 42:149–173
Shavell S (1980) Strict liability versus negligence. J Leg Stud 9(1):1–26
Shavell S (1984) Liability for harm versus regulation of safety. J Leg Stud 13(2):357–374
Shavell S (1986) The judgment proof problem. Int Rev Law Econ 6(1):45–58
Shavell S (1987) Economic analysis of accident law. Harvard University Press, Cambridge
Shavell S (1992) Liability and the incentive to obtain information about risk. J Leg Stud 21(2):259–270
Shavell S (2009) Foundations of economic analysis of law. Harvard University Press, Cambridge
Sher S (2011) A framework for assessing immorally manipulative marketing tactics. J Bus Ethics 102:97–118
Smith B (2014) Proximity-driven liability. Geo Law J 102(6):1777–1820
Sparks BA, Bradley GL, Jennings GR, Johnston NR (2014) Cooling off and backing out: understanding consumer decisions to rescind a product purchase. J Bus Res 67(1):2903–2910
Statista (2023) Marketing personalization worldwide—statistics & facts. Statista. https://www.statista.com/topics/4481/personalized-marketing/
Strycharz J, Duivenvoorde BB (2021) The exploitation of vulnerability through personalized marketing communication: are consumers protected? Internet Policy Rev 10(4):1–27
Susser D, Roessler B, Nissenbaum H (2019) Online manipulation: hidden influences in digital world. Georgetown Law Technol Rev 4(1):1–46
Tene O, Polonetsky J (2013) Big data for all: privacy and user control in the age of analytics. Nw J Technol Intellect Prop 11(5):239–273
Trevisan M, Stefano T, Bassi E, Marco M (2019) 4 years of EU cookie law: results and lessons learned. Proc Priv Enhancing Technol 2019(2):126–145
Trzaskowski J (2011) Behavioural economics, neuroscience, and the unfair commercial practices directive. J Consum Policy 34(3):377–392
Tuil M, Visscher LT (2010) New trends in financing civil litigation in Europe: a legal, empirical, and economic analysis. Edward Elgar Publ, Cheltenham
Utz C, Degeling M, Fahl S, Schaub F, Holz T (2019) (Un)informed consent: studying GDPR consent notices in the field. In: Proceedings of the 2019 ACM SIGSAC Conference on Computer and Communications Security, pp 973–990
Van den Bergh RJ (2008) Introduction: the impact of Guido Calabresi on law and economics scholarship. Erasmus Law Rev 1(4):1–6

Van den Bergh RJ, Visscher LT (2008) The preventive function of collective actions for damages in consumer law. Erasmus Law Rev 1(2):5–30

Van der Rest JP, Sears AM, Kuokkanen H, Heidary K (2022) Algorithmic pricing in hospitality and tourism: call for research on ethics, consumer backlash, and CSR. J Hosp Tour Insights 5(4):771–781

Wagner G, Eidenmüller H (2019) Down by algorithms: siphoning rents, exploiting biases, and shaping preferences: regulating the dark side of personalized transactions. Univ Chicago Law Rev 86(2):581–610

Weber F (2016) The law and economics of enforcing European consumer law: a comparative analysis of package travel and misleading advertising. Routledge, London

Weiss RM, Mehrotra AK (2001) Online dynamic pricing: efficiency, equity and the future of e-commerce. Va J Law Technol 6(2):1–12

Willis LE (2013) When nudges fail: slippery defaults. Univ Chicago Law Rev 80(3):1155–1230

Willis LE (2015) Performance-based consumer law. Univ Chicago Law Rev 82(3):1309–1409

Willis LE (2020) Deception by design. Harv J Law Technol 34(1):115–190

Wisniewski PJ, Knijnenburg BP, Lipford HR (2017) Making privacy personal: profiling social network users to inform privacy education and nudging. Int J Hum-Comput Stud 98:95–108

Wrbka S (2014) European consumer access to justice revisited. Cambridge University Press, Cambridge

Zemel R, Wu Y, Swersky K, Pitassi T, Dwork C (2013) Learning fair representations. Int Conf Mach Learn:325–333

Zhang J, Wedel M (2009) The effectiveness of customized promotions in online and offline stores. J Mark Res 46(2):190–206

Zuboff S (2019) The age of surveillance capitalism: the fight for a human future at the new frontier of power. Profile Books, London

Chapter 7
Conclusions and Recommendations

Abstract The concluding chapter synthesizes the findings from previous chapters to address the research questions posed in the study. It evaluates the extent to which personalized marketing constitutes a novel challenge to consumer policy, its implications for consumer welfare, equity, and autonomy, and the potential for legal reforms to enhance consumer policy. The chapter also outlines recommendations for future research, encouraging further inquiry into the intersection of personalized marketing and consumer protection policy to address emerging challenges in the digital economy.

7.1 Conclusions

Marketing is constantly evolving. The developments in AI-driven marketing have paved the way for a new marketing technique called personalized marketing. This technique has advanced considerably over the last few years and is expected to undergo further development in the coming years. This has caused enthusiasm among marketers, who see personalized marketing as an up-and-coming marketing strategy, yet it has simultaneously caused concerns regarding the protection of consumers.

Although the practice of personalized marketing has grabbed the attention of scholars, consumer protection authorities, and policymakers, an in-depth law and economics analysis of its promises and perils was missing. This study aimed to fill this gap by addressing personalized marketing in the digital age from a law and economics perspective.

To provide a comprehensive assessment, the deliberate choice was made to incorporate autonomy and equity considerations. By doing so, it enabled a broadened analysis of the multifaceted nature of personalized marketing, the identification of the potential benefits and harms to consumers, the ascertainment of the degree to which consumers are protected by the legal framework, and the determination of the extent to which consumer policy could be improved.

A. J. van Heusden, *The Law and Economics of Personalization*, Economic Analysis of Law in European Legal Scholarship 20,
https://doi.org/10.1007/978-3-032-01468-9_7

In this way, the study aimed to answer the four research questions that were posed in Chap. 1, namely:

1. *How is marketing in the digital age different from traditional marketing from a consumer policy perspective?*
2. *To what extent does personalized marketing pose a threat to consumer welfare? Moreover, to what degree is it problematic in terms of equity and consumer autonomy?*
3. *To what extent is personalized marketing addressed under the current EU legal framework?*
4. *To what extent can consumer policy regarding personalized marketing be improved by virtue of legal reforms?*

These questions were tackled in different chapters, and a summary of the results will be presented in the following sections.

7.1.1 Marketing in the Digital Age

Traditionally, consumer law and economics focused on remedying information asymmetries, which were the leading cause of inefficiencies in consumer markets. Consumer policy that extended beyond the remediation of information asymmetries was regarded as overreaching and could potentially lead to the implementation of rules whereof the social costs would exceed the benefits. The traditional information paradigm has, therefore, been leading in both consumers law and economics and consumer policy.

Nevertheless, Chap. 2 demonstrates that, over time, challenges have emerged that have called for additional legal devices that transcend the provision of information. Most prominently, these included the introduction of cooling-off periods, mandatory legal warranties, default rules, and unfair term regulation. These devices were implemented to tackle the information asymmetry market failure and concomitantly address inefficiencies arising from unequal bargaining power and transaction costs.

However, the economic analysis of these existing legal devices identified their shortcomings. Although traditional legal instruments can improve the consumer's position vis-à-vis the seller, they cannot fully remedy the harm to consumer welfare in the market. The economic analysis of consumer law has thereby greatly benefitted from the insights stemming from behavioral science. Through empirical behavioral research, it has been found that irrational behavior, as result of a myriad of biases and heuristics, detracts from the effectiveness of the traditional devices. This does not automatically mean that consumers are not protected in their dealings with sellers. Private provision of information, insurance, reputation, ratings, relational contracts, consumer learning, and consumer-based innovations are market-based solutions created to remedy the inefficiencies in consumer markets. However, an extensive body of empirical research demonstrates that the market fails to lead to self-correction by sellers, highlighting the need for measures to protect consumers.

In case a market failure persists, it is asserted that a *prima facie* argument for market intervention can be made. The economic analysis of consumer law shows that an ex-ante cost-benefit analysis of the proposed regulation is indispensable before its implementation. Failing to assess a regulation's economic impact can lead to adverse effects and regulatory failures. An accurate assessment of consumer policies should thereby consider all relevant economic effects, including distributional and welfare effects. In this way, a complete and economically sound analysis of the effects of the proposed regulation can be provided.

The law and economics approach emphasizes that one must be wary of intervening in the market because of the adverse effects of regulation. However, not providing consumers with adequate protection might lead to equally undesired or worse outcomes. This requires a careful balancing act, which is facilitated by the ability to pinpoint the presence of a market failure. Regulation can be considered if there is a demonstrable market failure in the consumer market. If no market failure can be detected, intervention should be discouraged to ward off overregulation.

The digital age, however, challenges the classic economic justifications for regulatory intervention in consumer markets. The advent of big data and AI-driven technologies calls into question the degree to which traditional rationales for consumer policy will suffice to address the emerging challenges consumers will face. One of these challenges has been the primary subject matter of this study, namely, the rise of personalized marketing.

Personalized marketing differentiates itself through its combination of subtlety and sophistication. Personalized marketing is a new form of marketing that has marked a significant break between traditional forms of marketing, which were mass-oriented, and marketing in the digital age, which is individual-oriented. The developments in AI have paved the way for the approximation of perfect personalization. It is argued that due to these personalized marketing strategies, which include personalized advertising, pricing, and contracting, the consumer experience can be fully tailored, and individuals' biases, heuristics, and vulnerabilities can be targeted. Consequently, the challenges consumers face cannot only be ascribed to information asymmetries anymore. In this study, the proposition is made that personalized marketing facilitates the extraction of rents, the exploitation of biases and vulnerabilities, and the shaping of preferences to the detriment of consumers' autonomy, equity, and welfare, leading to marketing-induced market failures.[1]

This terminology is justified because traditional market manipulation cannot cover the workings and consequences of personalized marketing. Due to the critical role of AI-driven technologies, marketing in the digital age has transcended the concept of marketing as it was known before. From a law and economics perspective, a cogent argument is made that marketing deserves special attention in consumer policy. The realization that marketing in the digital age has the potential to

[1] See Sect. 2.4.1.

create market failures, which cannot be resolved by traditional legal devices and can threaten consumer autonomy, equity, and welfare, provides a valuable starting point for consumer policymaking. The examination of marketing in the digital age can significantly benefit from the insights developed in marketing scholarship. To identify a marketing-induced market failure, it does not suffice to look at the consumer's perspective only; carefully assessing it from the marketer's perspective is of pivotal importance as well.

7.1.2 *Personalized Advertising*

The advent of targeted advertising has spurred on the wave of marketing personalization. Due to the developments in AI, many possibilities have been created to tailor ads to individuals in a manner that has not been seen before. Personalized advertising is the fastest-growing and most effective form of online advertising.[2]

Targeted advertising is nowadays a ubiquitous practice. However, the mechanism underlying the tailoring of ads is continuously being improved, thereby approximating perfect personalization. This has made advertising significantly more relevant to consumers, yet it has also opened the way for exploiting individual biases, heuristics, and vulnerabilities. The effects of targeting are intensified by the sophisticated use of dark patterns, which essentially shape the online environment in which consumers see ads and make purchase decisions. Dark patterns can capitalize on consumers' biases and heuristics to obtain consumers' consent to collect and process all data of interest and design ads in a way that can lead to effective behavior modification. The implication is that dark patterns go hand in hand with personalized advertising. Consequently, the far-reaching personalization of advertisements sparks the debate as to what extent marketing has gone from lawful persuasion to unlawful manipulation.[3]

The economic analysis of personalized advertising assessed its benefits, drawbacks, perceptions, and concerns. With respect to the benefits it brings to consumers, it can be argued that personalized advertising leads to improved tailoring of ads, increased relevance, and more accurate matching of consumer preferences. Ad timing can be improved and transaction costs can be reduced. Due to the effectiveness of personalized advertising, higher advertising revenues can be earned, which facilitates an increase in the provision of "free" services.

In addition, from a business perspective, it is a highly profitable practice. The click-through rates of personalized marketing are significantly higher compared to traditional marketing, and substantial costs can be saved by only showing ads to the right audience instead of investing money in advertising to consumers who perceive

[2] See Sect. 3.1.

[3] See Sect. 3.2.3.

it as irrelevant. In this way, it can create a competitive advantage for firms that invest in personalized advertising.[4]

At the same time, however, the door has been opened for the exploitation of consumers. The sophisticated profiling of consumers not only enables the identification of consumer preferences but also allows for the targeting of individual biases and vulnerabilities. By means of persuasion profiling, marketing strategies can be continuously tested and further individualized to modify the consumer's behavior most effectively. A significant information asymmetry exists between the consumer and the seller, which deteriorates the already weaker bargaining position of the former. Tech-savvy consumers can employ tools to try to protect themselves, leading to more transaction costs and an arms race between the marketer and the consumer. However, less sophisticated consumers are left at the mercy of marketers.[5]

Personalized advertising can potentially cause privacy harm, which can be both subjective, namely the unwanted feeling of being surveilled, and objective, which occurs when all the information about the consumers is used to extract the largest amount of consumer surplus. Personalized ads might trigger unpleasant feelings in consumers, detracting from their appeal and reducing trust in the market. It can also result in consumer welfare losses by steering them toward products or services that do not optimally match their needs or clearly aim to extract rents. It is, therefore, no surprise that the general consumer perception of personalized advertising is negative.[6]

Privacy concerns and lack of trust override the potential benefits and emphasize consumers' call for protection. In addition, the threats of jeopardizing consumer autonomy, the circumvention of anti-discrimination laws, and the endangering of human dignity reinforce the need for regulation.[7]

From a total welfare perspective, it can be argued that the benefits might, in some cases, outweigh the drawbacks, however, from a consumer policy perspective, it is clear that the practice is welfare-decreasing and problematic in terms of equity, autonomy, and fundamental rights.

7.1.3 Algorithmic Personalized Pricing

Price discrimination in the digital age has reached new heights. Where third-degree price discrimination (i.e., group price discrimination) would be the most attainable goal in the past, first-degree price discrimination, also called perfect price discrimination, has become a reality.[8] With AI, a strategy can be developed that

[4] See Sect. 3.5.1.

[5] See Sect. 3.5.3.

[6] See Sect. 3.5.3.1.

[7] See Sect. 3.5.3.3.

[8] See Sect. 4.2.3.

approximates consumers' reservation prices with ever-improving accuracy. This has ushered in the next personalization stage, which is currently increasingly prevalent in online consumer markets. The critical role of algorithms in developing perfect price-discriminating techniques has led to the term algorithmically personalized prices (i.e., charging hyper-personalized prices to extract the maximum amount of consumer surplus).

The economic analysis of algorithmic pricing demonstrated that an efficiency-equity trade-off permeates the practice.[9] In terms of efficiency, several benefits are created by algorithmic pricing. Static efficiency is enhanced because a more significant part of the market can be served. Similarly, dynamic efficiency is improved because prices can be differentiated better, leading to more revenues being invested in innovation. Competition can also be intensified since sellers are pressured to compete for consumers based on who has the best knowledge about their willingness to pay. Furthermore, the ability to price discriminate more accurately will help ailing industries with high fixed costs and remedy cross-subsidization that occurs under uniform pricing schemes. Lastly, output management can be ameliorated by serving a more significant part of the market, increasing overall output, and optimizing production capacity.

There are, however, also negative efficiency effects. Companies are investing considerable amounts of resources in developing algorithmic pricing mechanisms to extract rents, amounting to substantial opportunity costs of not investing in process, product, or service improvements. In addition, transaction costs have increased in the market because consumers will invest more time and effort in circumventing far-reaching personalization. To counteract these efforts, firms invest in sophisticated tracking techniques. In essence, companies are displaying rent-seeking behavior in a consumer context.

Price comparison will also be impeded due to price personalization, which can make quality estimations for consumers more difficult and be problematic from a competition perspective. Opportunities for collusion are, therefore, expected to emerge. Finally, the role of marketing in inflating consumers' willingness to pay can be worrisome, especially since more consumption based on misperceptions can make supracompetitive priced goods look like reasonably priced goods.

In terms of equity, algorithmic pricing proves to be more troublesome. Although it can lead to greater access to the market for consumers, the division of efficiency gains, and the resolution of social problems due to its more precise targeting (e.g., counteracting under- and overconsumption), the negative equity effects appear to outweigh these benefits. The idea of transferring all consumer surplus from the consumer to the seller is undesirable from a consumer welfare hypothesis perspective. This hypothesis states that maximizing consumer welfare should be the economic goal in competition and consumer law. If this hypothesis is followed, it can be argued that algorithmic pricing runs counter to this goal.

[9] See Sect. 4.4.

Furthermore, algorithmic pricing is likely to decrease consumer trust in the market. Especially less sophisticated consumers are expected to be negatively impacted compared to sophisticated consumers. It has been found that wealthier and more educated consumers are better able to avoid overcharge, which causes great inequality concerns.[10] Lower-income and less educated consumers are more likely to be overcharged because they are exposed to more markets in which they have a weaker bargaining position, for example, credit markets, and they spend a greater share of their income in comparison with higher-earning consumers on consumer goods. Ethical concerns complement these equity issues. There is a likelihood that algorithmic pricing will also lead to algorithmic discrimination, social sorting, pricing unfairness, a deterioration of consumers' bargaining power, and the intrusion of privacy.[11]

All things considered, from a total welfare perspective, algorithmic pricing can be defended under competitive market conditions. However, this does not hold from a consumer welfare perspective. In addition, equity and ethical concerns reinforce the call for regulation in terms of consumer policy.

7.1.4 Personalized Contracting

The algorithmic personalization of consumer transactions is an ongoing process. Personalized contracting is a novel phenomenon that is expected to be further developed in the near future. The advances in AI-driven technologies allow for the personalization of the traditional uniform contracts that are unilaterally offered to consumers (i.e., the boilerplates). This means that standard contract terms can be tailored to an individual, which brings the well-known signing-without-reading problem to the next level. Consumers' individual preferences, characteristics, behaviors, circumstances, biases, and vulnerabilities can be targeted while being practically assured that consumers will accept the contract terms. For the sake of consumer protection, this is a daunting outlook.

The economic analysis of standard-form contracts provided valuable insights into the desirability of personalized contracts.[12] From a traditional law and economics perspective, it can be argued that standard forms are efficiency-enhancing because they reduce transaction costs. The insights from information economics complement the analysis by emphasizing the presence of information asymmetries in consumer markets due to the signing-without-reading problem. Behavioral law and economics alludes to the need for intervention by highlighting consumers' biases and heuristics, which impede the reading and monitoring of standard-form contracts. Empirical studies demonstrate that, in practice, this is actually the case;

[10] See Sect. 4.4.3.

[11] See Sect. 4.4.3.

[12] See Sect. 5.3.

less than 1% of consumers read standard forms, implying that consumers are unable to discipline the market.[13] One-sided terms are, therefore, found to be ubiquitous in consumer markets.

By extrapolating these insights to personalized contracts, the negative implications for consumers are expected to be exacerbated. Employing personalized contracts enables firms to capitalize on the signing-without-reading problem in a way that allows for maximal rent extraction. The issues encountered with regard to standard forms will be intensified in a personalized setting, thereby posing a threat to consumer autonomy, equity, and welfare.[14] Consumers are already experiencing significant difficulties in understanding the consequences of a standardized contract (e.g., credit card contracts). These problems will become considerably larger when they concern terms that apply specifically to consumers' individual situations because, in that case, all terms matter.

7.1.5 The Existing EU Legal Framework

The analysis of the current legal framework shows that personalized marketing is addressed by a patchwork of different directives, which can only provide partial protection to consumers. In the EU *acquis*, a *per se* prohibition of personalized marketing in any shape or form does not exist, which results in lacunas permeating the consumer protection framework.

Data protection laws, particularly the GDPR and the ePrivacy Directive, limit unbridled personalization to a certain extent. These legislations require transparency, legitimacy, and accountability, which safeguard the unlawful processing of consumers' personal data. However, the emphasis on consent gives companies enough leeway to continue with personalized marketing. Due to the signing-without-reading problem, obtaining consent will not be difficult. Accordingly, the right to withdrawal, in its current form, will most likely not be of great value since it requires a certain level of awareness and activity from consumers, which cannot be found in the realm of standard-form contracting and will, therefore, probably not be found in personalized contracting.

The consumer protection law framework does prevent blatantly unfair commercial practices; however, it is found to be unfit to deal with the subtleties of personalized marketing. Using the tools provided by the UCPD and UCTD would require broad interpretations of the provisions to address personalized marketing adequately, but those are still missing in CJEU case law. To effectively protect consumers against personalized marketing, the UCPD and UCTD would need to be redesigned. Changes in the UCPD regarding consumer benchmarks and substantive

[13] See Sect. 5.3.5.

[14] See Sect. 5.3.6.

clauses are needed because currently employed marketing techniques will likely fall through the cracks of the UCPD provisions.

Similarly, terms can be drafted in a manner that circumvents the unfairness test of the UCTD or the list of the Annex while remaining particularly effective in targeting consumers. For example, it cannot be prohibited based on the UCTD that personalized contracts will use different language, levels of complexity, or triggers for agreeable and conflict-sensitive consumers than for more disagreeable and complaining consumers. In addition, salience can play a significant role in differentiating consumers. Short-term financial benefits can be highlighted, whereas long-term consequences can be made non-salient. With this, the peril lies in the fact that the number of possibilities for modifying an ad, price, or contract is infinite.

In principle, contract law provides tools to tackle algorithmic pricing and personalized contracting. The price unconscionability doctrine could tackle overcharges; however, for a successful invocation of this doctrine, there must be cases of gross overcharges that can be proven with a just price as the benchmark. This is highly unlikely to work for algorithmic pricing practices that are known for their subtlety. Concerning personalized contracting, it is likely that, again, the subtlety of the personalization mechanism will impede a successful invocation of the traditional doctrines of mistake, deceit, or fraud. Freedom of contract and the parties' leeway when negotiating will also be problematic when proving a breach of pre-contractual good faith. Of note is that even though such a claim would be made, it is difficult to enforce it before court since the burden of proof lies on the claimant. Consumers would then need to prove the exploitative character of the contract, which will be a significant obstacle to overcome because of the technical sophistication driving the personalization mechanism.

Competition law could be relevant to tackle algorithmic pricing by adopting a broad interpretation of Article 102(c) TFEU, which is relevant when a firm with market power price differentiates. However, it is still unclear whether the provision can be extended to cover exploitative harms to final customers. If fairness considerations were considered in the analysis, the case for effective intervention becomes stronger. Further guidance by the CJEU in this regard is deemed necessary. It must be noted, however, that this provision is only helpful to tackle firms with market power. It has been demonstrated that firms can also perform algorithmic pricing without having a dominant market position, so consumer policy seems better suited.

Nevertheless, the primary instrument, the UCPD, does not prohibit algorithmic pricing *per se*. The practice can only be categorized as unfair when there is a lack of transparency in communicating the price or if it amounts to an unfair commercial practice. Sellers can easily circumvent the first requirement by simply stating that the price has been personalized, which also complies with the new transparency requirement of the CRD.

Human rights law can be a valuable instrument to address overt forms of discrimination. However, its scope of application is too limited to deal with sophisticated profiling that is not based on prohibited categories but eventually leads to the same discriminatory outcomes.

The digital regulations provide promising tools, particularly the DSA, DMA, and AI Act. These regulations are more tailored to the technological developments driving the personalization mechanisms and effectively contribute to more transparency, yet none specifically address personalized marketing.

The DSA clears the fog surrounding the personalization mechanisms, which allow for individualized targeting. Although the DSA does not encompass a ban on personalized marketing, it does limit advertising based on sensitive personal data. In addition, the DSA imposes several transparency requirements that can provide the consumer with more relevant information and induce platforms to self-audit their algorithms.

The DMA fosters fair behavior by gatekeepers and makes significant steps to create more transparency in the realm of online advertising. The combination of personal data is tackled, more insights are provided to advertisers and publishers, and a higher level of transparency concerning consumer profiling is created. In particular, the DMA's anti-circumvention rule seems promising due to its complementary working to the UCPD provisions, which will be applied to cover the platforms that the DMA does not regulate.

In the realm of personalized marketing, the AI Act can be regarded as a regulatory sibling of the UCPD. It can complement the UCPD and result into better enforcement against AI practices that manipulate or exploit consumers. However, at this stage, further developments in case law and further guidance need to be awaited to see to what extent the AI Act leads to regulatory synergy that effectively enhances consumer protection. There is reason to be skeptical of its added value to tackle consumer harm, but the AI Act can be helpful in combating the social sorting element of personalized marketing.

Notably, the digital regulations seem auspicious in combating dark patterns in online interfaces. Significant steps have been made to remediate the harms of dark patterns. Nevertheless, this degree of protection is still lacking for personalized marketing. The digital regulations do improve transparency; however, a lack of awareness, a lack of choice, and an overall lack of protection persists.

Considering everything, it can be concluded that the current legal framework is not sufficiently equipped to deal with personalized marketing. A cogent argument is, therefore, made to complement the legal framework with legal reforms that effectively enhance consumer protection.

7.1.6 The Current State of Affairs

The law and economics analysis of personalized marketing demonstrated that its perils outweigh the promises. Personalized marketing has the potential to target individual biases and heuristics and exploit vulnerabilities, which is a threat to consumers' autonomy, equity, and welfare. The subtlety of the personalization mechanisms creates an opportunity for the marketing techniques to fall through the cracks of the current legal framework. For that reason, the EU *acquis* is not future-proof and cannot effectively protect consumers against the threats of personalized marketing.

Consequently, consumer policy would benefit from legal reforms. However, the law and economics analysis shows that authorities should be wary of eliminating the potential welfare gains from personalized marketing by implementing new interventions. The use of prohibitions, or other consumer choice limitations, is, therefore, dissuaded.[15] The legal reforms should be based on making consumers well-informed, limiting the possibility of exploitation, and preserving consumer autonomy.

7.1.7 *Policy Proposals*

The current state of affairs concerning personalized marketing calls for legal reform. In this study, several policy proposals are presented to improve consumer policy in a manner that effectively protects consumers and leaves room to preserve the benefits of marketing innovation. The goal is thereby to tackle the current threats of personalized marketing while offering sufficiently flexible tools that can handle future refinements.

7.1.7.1 Updating Disclosure

From an ex-ante perspective, it is essential to tackle the archaic boilerplate. Disclosure needs to be updated to allow consumers to make an informed choice. This can be achieved through personalized disclosures. A personalized disclosure considers consumers' characteristics, preferences, and needs, and informs them about relevant information intelligibly and conspicuously. The aim is to empower consumers in exercising their autonomy by effectively making their consent informed. To prevent abuse by companies, third-party auditing of the personalized disclosures should take place.

A valuable complement is using AI to facilitate the detection of unfair terms (e.g., Claudette). This could work in tandem with personalized disclosures and clear the way for effective enforcement.

[15] This corresponds to the political consensus in the European Parliament, in which no majority was found for an overall prohibition of targeted advertising (one of the prominent pillars of personalized marketing) in the proposal for the DSA. See European Parliament (2021).

7.1.7.2 Monitoring the Marketer

More information, however, does not equal better protection *per se*. Therefore, monitoring the marketer is essential. The monitoring consists of three parts. First, setting manipulation standards. These standards indicate the threshold the legislator can set to determine whether a practice is manipulative or not. In practice, this would require empirical studies to determine the likelihood that a personalization strategy incites consumers to take transactional decisions they would otherwise not have taken. For perfect personalization, individual complaints can be taken into account to see if a specific company is particularly active in exploitative marketing. Personalization strategies that are considered manipulative (i.e., exceeding the threshold) could be blacklisted. This requires external monitoring by, for example, consumer authorities or watchdogs.

The monitoring should not only take place externally; there must also be internal supervision. Stemming from institutional review boards in academia or supervisory boards in businesses, it would be recommended to let an internal supervisory board oversee marketing practices. Relevant stakeholders could monitor the ethical aspects, consumer interests, and technological developments. The desirable outcome would be that the marketing industry would further develop best practices, and a more substantial degree of self-regulation would take place.

Third, monitoring needs to be facilitated. To a certain extent, this requires the redesign of consumer protection instruments. It is recommended that the traditional consumer benchmarks (i.e., the average and vulnerable consumer) are changed and replaced with the so-called benchmark consumer. In essence, this refers to a benchmark that varies along with the degree of targeting. On the one side of the spectrum, the average consumer suffices if a marketing communication is aimed at the general public. On the other hand, for highly personalized communications, the targeted consumer should be taken as the benchmark. This remedies the problem that the individually targeted vulnerabilities cannot be placed under the generic categories of average or vulnerable consumers, as described in the UCPD. Such an interpretation of the consumer benchmark corresponds with the contemporary view on vulnerability in digital markets.

Moreover, it is recommended that a marketing-specific clause is introduced in the UCPD. Rather than trying to fit all marketing communications under the current provisions, the marketing-specific clause could assist the monitoring of the issues identified within the marketing-induced market failure framework.

The final step that can be proposed to aid monitoring would be to build on the ad repository requirement constituted by the DSA and extend it to all users of personalized marketing strategies. This allows the consumer and consumer authorities to obtain relevant information regarding the personalization mechanism and identify why a consumer has been targeted and on what grounds. Only then can effective action be taken when biases have been exploited or vulnerabilities have been targeted to the consumer's detriment.

7.1.7.3 A Genuine Opt-Out

To preserve consumer autonomy, consumers should be provided with a genuine opt-out. At the moment, it is particularly onerous to opt out of personalization services, whereas it is straightforward to opt in. Moreover, consumers should be empowered to decide whether to receive a personalized offer in a personalized setting or not. This decision should be facilitated instead of hampered. Consequently, regulatory steps must be undertaken to create an opt-out regime allowing consumers to take back control at the lowest possible cost. Also, opting out should be made as easy and accessible as possible; only then will consumer choice and autonomy be kept intact.

7.1.7.4 Providing Marketers with the Proper Incentives

Regulation is, however, not the panacea for all the harms that have been identified in this study. Liability can play an essential complementary role. Law and economics has demonstrated that the law can have an incentivizing effect on legal actors. As long as the law does not provide sufficient incentives to marketers to refrain from conducting personalized marketing in a manner that targets consumers' biases, heuristics, and vulnerabilities, exploitative practices will remain in use. The analysis has shown that a combination of liability and regulation would provide the optimal incentives.

To begin with, marketers should be held liable for the harm inflicted on consumers through their marketing strategies. This refers to the introduction of marketer liability. Under the current liability regime, sellers can be held liable for products that do not correspond to the marketing communication (i.e., non-conformity), which allows consumers to seek redress.

However, the marketer behind the marketing strategy remains practically untouched. Fostering a more scrupulous application of liability rules to hold marketers accountable for their practices would be more meaningful. Marketer liability can work closely together with the proposal of a marketing-specific clause in the UCPD. Harms that are the result of marketing-induced market failures can then be directly tackled, thereby complementing the current liability regime.[16]

Second, it is asserted that a fault-based liability regime is most appropriate to address personalized marketing. The law and economics analyses of the practices have shown that personalized marketing also brings considerable benefits that should not be discarded. A less strict regime is needed to balance marketing innovation and consumer protection. Accordingly, a fault-based regime is favored that will be based on the concept of a marketing-induced market failure. The capability of a marketing technique to extract rents, exploit biases and vulnerabilities, and/or shape preferences to the detriment of consumers' autonomy, equity, and welfare shall be decisive. This criterion keeps the regime flexible and future-proof for marketing

[16] See Sect. 6.4.4.2.

techniques that are still in development. The determination of the optimal level of due care can be complemented through efforts from self-regulatory and supervisory bodies. Consequently, legal uncertainty and the risk of errors regarding the level of due care under the fault-based liability regime can be diminished.

Third, liability must be limited to economic harm, which is the loss of consumer welfare.[17] This keeps the assessment of damages feasible and does not impede marketing innovation. Nevertheless, the argument can be made that the assessment of losses due to the decay of consumer autonomy should be considered, yet this requires further development.

Lastly, the burden of proof should be eased for consumers and the relevant authorities to warrant effective enforcement. This can be done by introducing a presumption of exploitativeness on the sellers' side when considering personalized marketing techniques. Marketers would then need to demonstrate that personalization benefits consumers, and they would need to disclose all relevant information for the proceedings. Marketers would be subject to development risk liability in combination with prospective overruling to ensure that marketers are incentivized to take the necessary precautionary measures while still having the possibility to innovate.

7.1.7.5 Observe the Equity-Efficiency Trade-Off

The assessment of the policy approach showed that by implementing the proposed changes, consumer protection can be enhanced while maintaining the possibility for consumers to reap the benefits from personalized marketing. The economic analyses of personalized marketing practices demonstrated that the threats outweighed the benefits. However, there is no justification for a general ban. There is a delicate efficiency-equity trade-off that permeates the practice. The developments in marketing offer efficiency benefits, yet they also threaten consumers' autonomy, equity, and welfare. The goal was to find a balance between economic benefits and the protection of consumers. Special attention has also been given in this debate to fairness considerations.

This study does not state that the proposed approach achieves an across-the-board optimal outcome. It is asserted, however, that this study presents proposals that aim to take into account the tension between the inherent efficiency and fairness-based aspects of the practice. Without a doubt, there is room for debate regarding the relative importance of the respective values, yet this study aims to base itself on economic and legal rationales. These rationales are influenced by the normative criterion taken. In this study, the guiding principle has been the protection of consumer interests. In line with the consumer welfare hypothesis, it is argued that the maximization of consumer welfare should be the goal of consumer policy.

[17] See Sect. 6.4.4.

In addition, the fundamental values of consumer autonomy and equity should be considered.

Consequently, the presented policy approach distances itself from intrusive prohibitions that would forsake the efficiency aspect of personalized marketing, but it also opposes a laissez-faire policy. Legal reforms that attempt to counter the exploitation of marketing-induced market failures that harm consumers in terms of autonomy, equity, and welfare are highly encouraged. This study aimed to offer a policy approach that sets out the necessary steps that could be taken to improve consumer protection and make consumer policy fit for personalized marketing in the digital age.

7.2 Recommendations for Future Research

Although this study intended to address the various aspects of personalized marketing in the digital age in a comprehensive manner, further research is needed. The call for future research stems from the limitations of this study, on the one hand, and the necessity for a more extensive exploration of personalized marketing, on the other hand. Therefore, future research concerning personalized marketing is highly encouraged, and several recommendations and research directions can be presented.

7.2.1 The Multiformity of Personalized Marketing

Marketing is an extensive and multifaceted field of study. There is a multiplicity of marketing techniques that are constantly evolving. One of these techniques is personalized marketing, which comes in many forms. This study focuses on personalized advertising, pricing, and contracting. However, more personalized marketing techniques exist that merit further attention. It was unfeasible to discuss all existing techniques in this study, yet to get a complete picture of personalized marketing; future research is advocated. Some techniques that are currently being used and further explored are personalized email communications, website content, product recommendations, smart assistants, and chatbot experiences.[18] More personalized marketing techniques will likely be developed and become more prevalent in consumer markets. The ultimate goal for marketers is that all types of marketing communications can be personalized, and with the technological developments in the digital age, it seems to become a reality. This will have a substantial impact on consumers' position in the market and, therefore, also on consumer policy. To make consumer policy future-proof, there is good reason to delve into the other personalization practices.

---

[18] Galli (2022).

7.2.2 A Comparative Consumer Policy Approach

The analysis of the EU legal framework in this study has been conducted from a generalist perspective. The common core of the EU *acquis* has been discussed in relation to personalized marketing. Nevertheless, EU consumer policy has not been maximally harmonized among Member States,[19] which means that differences in the level of consumer protection and enforcement of the Member States exist.[20] For example, the Netherlands and France have scored high on the legal protection index, demonstrating strong consumer protection levels. In contrast, Croatia, Romania, and Sweden scored low on the index, showing the opposite. Therefore, it is valuable to conduct future comparative analyses that devote special attention to the specificities of the national regimes. For the sake of completeness, special attention can be dedicated to consumer policy's social, enforcement, and associational dimensions.[21]

7.2.3 Sector-Specific Analysis

As with all marketing techniques, the applications and effects differ per industry. An extension of the present study could be to zoom in on specific industries and see if the identified effects are mitigated or exacerbated in particular contexts. As can be deduced from the developments in digital regulation, there seems to be a specific focus on (very large) online platforms and intermediaries. Accordingly, it could be the case that personalized marketing in these contexts will have more significant impacts than in industries in which there are fewer power asymmetries between sellers/service providers and consumers (e.g., the retail industry and the food and beverage industry). If it can be determined that specific industries are more likely to engage in consumer exploitation, the attention of consumer authorities can be directed in that direction. This would lead to better-targeted enforcement and potentially lead to more effective consumer protection. The present study can provide a valuable starting point for these sector-specific analyses.

---

[19] It must be noted that some directives, such as the UCPD, have been maximally harmonized, but others, such as the UCTD, have not. Therefore, one cannot speak of an overall maximal harmonization of all directives.

[20] Weber (2016); Nessel (2019).

[21] Cfr. Nessel (2019).

7.2.4 *Structural Reassessments*

The field of marketing is rapidly changing and continuously being developed. Consumer policy is always lagging behind the developments in marketing.[22] This study aimed to make consumer policy more future-proof in dealing with personalized marketing. Considering the nature of marketing, it is imaginable that the personalization mechanisms will become significantly more sophisticated and impactful over time. Personalization will take over online marketing in all its facets. Accordingly, these developments can pose new challenges to consumer protection in the digital age. The EU has made considerable efforts to regulate the technological developments that, among other things, give rise to personalized marketing. This is evident in the rapid adoption of new digital regulations, particularly the AI Act, whose effects will soon become apparent. More digital regulations will likely follow to address emerging technologies and make Europe fit for the digital age.[23] Consequently, it is highly recommended to have structural reassessments of personalized marketing, whereby the practice and the applicable legal framework are revisited.

It is paramount to revise consumer policies as they can strongly benefit from further research that draws insights from the state of the art in law and economics. In the words of Van den Bergh (2007): "Consumer protection is never complete. Law and economics offers legislators and judges guidelines to monitor and continuously improve the quality of this branch of law."[24]

References

De Geest G (2018) Rents: How marketing causes inequality. Beccaria Books, Leuven

European Commission (2020) A Europe fit for the digital age: New online rules for users. European Commission. https://commission.europa.eu/strategy-and-policy/priorities-2019-2024/europe-fit-digital-age

European Parliament (2021) Report on the proposal for a regulation of the European Parliament and of the Council on a Single Market For Digital Services (Digital Services Act) and amending Directive 2000/31/EC (Report No. A9-0356/2021). European Parliament https://www.europarl.europa.eu/doceo/document/A-9-2021-0356_EN.html

Galli F (2022) Algorithmic marketing and EU law on unfair commercial practices. Springer Nature, Cham

Nessel S (2019) Consumer policy in 28 EU Member States: An empirical assessment in four dimensions. J Consum Policy 42(4):455–482

[22] De Geest (2018).

[23] European Commission (2020).

[24] Van den Bergh (2007), p. 140. The original text in Dutch states: "Consumentenbescherming is dus nooit af. De rechtseconomie biedt aan wetgevers en rechters richtsnoeren om de kwaliteit van deze rechtstak te bewaken en voortdurend te verbeteren."

Van den Bergh RJ (2007) Economische analyse van het consumentenrecht. In: Weterings WTC (ed) De economische analyse van het recht. Boom Juridische Uitgevers, Den Haag, pp 119–140
Weber F (2016) The law and economics of enforcing European consumer law: a comparative analysis of package travel and misleading advertising. Routledge, London

Index

A. J. Van Heusden, *The Law and Economics of Personalization*, Economic Analysis of Law in European Legal Scholarship 20,
https://doi.org/10.1007/978-3-032-01468-9

The manufacturer's authorised representative in the EU is Springer Nature Customer Service Centre GmbH, Europaplatz 3, 69115 Heidelberg, Germany. If you have any concerns regarding our products, please contact ProductSafety@springernature.com

Printed and bound by CPI Group (UK) Ltd, Croydon, CR0 4YY
08/10/2026
02229867-0004